# PIDGINS AND CREOLES

Volume 15

Jacques Arends, Pieter Muysken and Norval Smith (eds)

*Pidgins and Creoles*
*An Introduction*

# PIDGINS AND CREOLES

## AN INTRODUCTION

Edited by

JACQUES ARENDS
PIETER MUYSKEN
NORVAL SMITH

JOHN BENJAMINS PUBLISHING COMPANY
AMSTERDAM / PHILADELPHIA

The paper used in this publication meets the minimum requirements of American National Standard for Information Sciences – Permanence of Paper for Printed Library Materials, ANSI z39.48-1984.

**Library of Congress Cataloging-in-Publication Data**

Pidgins and Creoles : an introduction / edited by Jacques Arends, Pieter Muysken, Norval Smith.
    p.   cm. – (Creole language library ; v. 15)
    "An annotated list of creoles, pidgins, and mixed languages :    p.
    Includes bibliographical references and index.
    Partial contents: pt. 1. General aspects – pt. 2 Theories of genesis – pt. 3 Sketches of individual languages: Eskimo pidgin, Haitian, Saramaccan, Shaba Swahili, Fa d'Ambu, Papiamento, Sranan, Berbice Dutch – pt. 4. Grammatical features – pt. 5. Conclusions and annotated language list.
    1. Pidgin languages. 2. Creole dialects. I. Arends, Jacques. II. Muysken, Pieter. III. Smith, Norval. IV. Series.
PM7802.P54     1994
417'.22 – dc20                                    94-24286
ISBN 90 272 5236 x (Eur.) / 1-55619-169-3 (US) (Hb; alk. paper)           CIP
ISBN 90 272 5237 8 (Eur.) / 1-55619-170-7 (US) (Pb; alk. paper)

John Benjamins Publishing Co. • P.O. Box 36224 • 1020 ME Amsterdam • The Netherlands
John Benjamins North America • P.O. Box 27519 • Philadelphia, PA 19118 • USA

# Contents

# Part III   Sketches of individual languages

# Part IV   Grammatical features

# Preface and acknowledgements

This is a new introduction to the linguistic study of pidgin and creole languages, written jointly by the creolists at the Department of Linguistics of the University of Amsterdam (with Ludo Verhoeven from Tilburg as a guest co-author). The contributing authors played an important role in the planning stage, when decisions were made about the themes to be emphasized.

The motivation for the book lies both in research and in teaching. From the perspective of research, we felt that enough new material is being uncovered and new insights are emerging to warrant a new book (realising full well that a few years from now some of the material presented here will be outdated). From the perspective of teaching we felt that the several excellent and very interesting books presently available either are insufficiently focused on the Atlantic creoles (Mühlhäusler 1986, Romaine 1988), which are emphasized in the present work, or are not designed as text books for a course (Holm 1988, 1989). The justification for a book on pidgins and creoles per se is clear of course. These languages are spoken by more than one hundred million people all over the world, and so cannot be ignored.

In addition to the Atlantic focus, the book has several other features worthy of note. First, pidgins are not treated as necessarily an intermediate step on the way to creoles, but as linguistic entities in their own right, with their own proper characteristics. In addition to pidgins, mixed languages are discussed in a separate chapter. Second, diversity rather than unity is taken to be the central theme. While every creolist will acknowledge the continuous excitement of little shocks of *déjà vu* when exploring the grammatical patterns of other creoles, careful analysis reveals as many differences as similarities. Third, the book does not demand a high level of previous linguistic knowledge, although theoretical concepts (particularly from the generative tradition) will often be introduced. We have taken care, however, to explain these concepts as they come up.

The book is structured in such a way that the eleven chapters in parts I and II, **General Aspects** and **Theories of Genesis**, constitute the core for presentation and discussion in the classroom, while the thirteen chapters in parts III and IV, **Sketches of individual languages** and **Grammatical features**, can form the basis for further exploration, student presentations, research for term papers, etc. They presuppose parts I and II, but the separate chapters can be read independently of each other. A concluding chapter attempts to draw together the different strands of argumentation, and the final chapter comprises an annotated language list with background information on several hundred pidgins, creoles, and mixed languages. There are language, author, and subject indices. Two maps, locating the languages most frequently cited, are included.

Our major problem in this book was selection: of languages, topics, theories, constructions to be discussed. While trying to maintain some overall representativeness and topicality, we were guided most by the areas of expertise of the various specialists involved. Thus, a number of chapters are based on original fieldwork or archival data collected by the authors. We can only apologize for the topics and languages left out of consideration.

The research in this book was made possible by generous grants and support from various institutions in the Netherlands:

–   The Tropical Research Foundation (WOTRO) of NWO (Netherlands Research Foundation) for Arends, Kouwenberg, Post, Veenstra, and De Rooij;
–   The Foundation for Language, Speech and Logic of NWO (Netherlands Research Foundation) for Arends, van Rossem, van der Voort, Bakker;
–   The Royal Academy of Sciences (KNAW) for Arends and Bakker;
–   The Faculty of Letters, University of Amsterdam, for Adamson, Appel, den Besten, Bruyn, Muysken, Post, Veenstra, and Smith;
–   the Institute for the Functional Study of Language and Language Use (IFOTT) in Amsterdam for de Rooij;
–   the Holland Institute of Generative Linguistics (HIL) in Leiden for den Besten, Muysken, and Smith;
–   The Research Group on Language and Minorities of Tilburg University for Verhoeven;
–   The P.J. Meertens Institute for Dialectology, Folklore and Onomastics for van der Voort and van Rossem.
–   The Department of Linguistics, University of Amsterdam.

The material presented here was tried out in various courses at the University of Amsterdam. We are grateful for comments and suggestions from numerous students over the years.

In addition, we have greatly profited from the comments of Salikoko Mufwene and Philip Baker on individual chapters, and from Philip Baker, Frans Hinskens, Anthony Grant, Maarten Mous, and Thilo Schadeberg on the language list. Needless to say all remaining errors are our own.

A number of chapters are based on fieldwork. We want to mention the
– the Berbice River community, in particular the speakers of Berbice Dutch Creole
– the inhabitants of Annobon, Equatorial Guinea
– Swahili speakers in Lubumbashi, Zaire
– Saramaccans both in Paramaribo and in Amsterdam
– Papiamento speakers from Aruba and Curaçao

Sranan literature in chapters 7 and 18 is quoted from Voorhoeve & Lichtveld (1975). An earlier and more detailed version of chapter 22 appeared in Adone & Plag (eds.) 1994. The Saramaccan passage in chapter 14 is from Rountree & Glock (1977). The English translation is adapted.

We are grateful, finally, for the encouragement and general comments by John Singler, co-editor of the Series. Peter Kahrel prepared the book for publication.

# List of abbreviations used in glosses

| | | | |
|---|---|---|---|
| 1SG etc. | first person singular etc | FN | future nominalization |
| 1PL etc. | first person plural etc | FOC | focus particle |
| 3SGM etc. | third person singular masculine | FUT | future tense |
| 3PLF etc. | third person plural feminine | GEN | genitive case |
| A | adjective | H | high tone |
| ABL | ablative case | HAB | habitual aspect |
| ABS | absolutive case | I | first person singular |
| AC | accusative case | IDEO | ideophone |
| ADV | adverb | IDNT | identifier |
| AG | agent | IMP | imperative mood |
| AN | animate | INAN | inanimate |
| ANT | anterior tense | INC | inclusive |
| AOR | aorist aspect | INF | infinitive |
| AP | adjective phrase | INT | intensive |
| APPL | applicative | INV | inverse |
| ART | article | IO | indirect object |
| ASP | aspect | IPF | imperfective aspect |
| BN | benefactive | IRR | irrealis mood |
| CI | cislocative | L | low tone |
| CL1 etc. | noun class 1 etc. | LOC | locative |
| CL1C etc. | noun class 1 etc. concord | N | noun |
| CLASS | classifier | NC | noun class |
| CM | class marker | NEG | negation |
| COMP | complementizer | NOM | nominalizer |
| COMPL | completive | NONP | nonpunctual |
| CON | concord | NP | noun phrase |
| COND | conditional | O | object |
| CONJ | conjunction | OBV | obviative |
| CONN | connective | OC | object concord |
| COP | copula | PA, PAST | past tense |
| CPE | Chinese Pidgin English | PART | particle |
| D | directional | PASS | passive |
| DEF | definite | PF | perfective |
| DEL | delimitative | PL | plural |
| DEM | demonstrative | PM | predicate marker |
| DET | determiner | POSS | possessive |
| DO | direct object | PP | prepositional phrase |
| EME | Early Modern English | PR | progressive aspect |
| EMP | emphatic | PREP | preposition |
| ERG | ergative case | PRES | present |
| ESS | essive case | PRO | null pronoun |
| FEM | feminine | PRON | pronoun |
| FIN | final vowel of verbal complex | Q | question marker |

| | | | |
|---|---|---|---|
| RC | relative concord | SD | sudden discovery |
| REL | relative marker | STAT | stative |
| RES | resultative | SUB | subordinator |
| RP | resumptive pronoun | SUBJAGR | subject agreement |
| S | subject | TMA | tense / mood / aspect |
| SC | subject concord | VP | verb phrase |

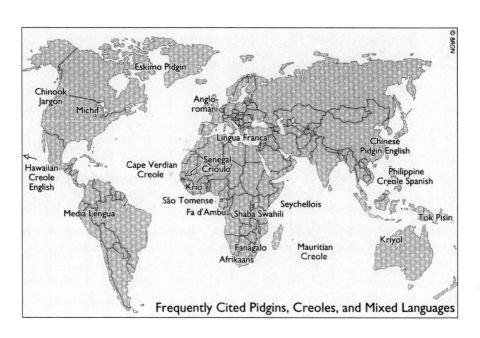

Frequently Cited Pidgins, Creoles, and Mixed Languages

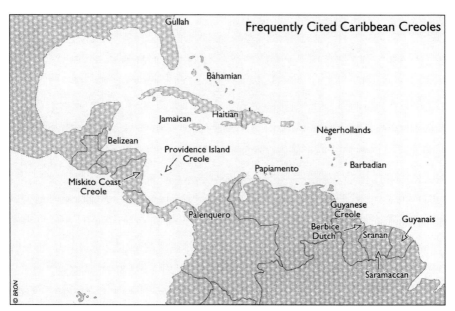

Frequently Cited Caribbean Creoles

Part 1
**General Aspects**

# 1 The study of pidgin and creole languages

Pieter Muysken and Norval Smith

## 1.1 Introduction

This book is concerned with pidgin and creole languages. This statement might well give the impression that we know precisely what is meant by these terms. In fact they are the subject of much debate. Creolists agree neither about the precise definition of the terms **pidgin** and **creole**, nor about the status of a number of languages that have been claimed to be pidgins or creoles. Mixed languages, introduced in chapter 4, have generally not been mentioned at all.

To turn first to **pidgin languages**, it is generally agreed that in essence these represent speech-forms which do not have native speakers, and are therefore primarily used as a means of communication among people who do not share a common language. The degree of development and sophistication attained by such a pidgin depends on the type and intensity of communicative interaction among its users. Mühlhäusler (1986) makes three basic distinctions amongst speech-forms that creolists have referred to as pidgins – (rather unstable) **jargons, stable pidgins**, and **expanded pidgins** (see further chapter 3).

To turn to **creole languages** (or just **creoles**), one vital difference from pidgins is that pidgins do not have native speakers, while creoles do. This is not always an easy distinction to make, as one aspect of the worldwide increase in linguistic conformity, and the concomitant reduction in linguistic diversity, is that extended pidgins are beginning to acquire native speakers. This has happened for instance with Tok Pisin, Nigerian Pidgin English, and Sango (Central African Republic), to name but three cases. In particular this has tended to occur in urban environments, where speakers from different ethnic groups have daily contact with each other. The pidgin then becomes the town language. The children of mixed marriages frequently grow up speaking the home language – the pidgin – as their native language.

## 1.2 Historical linguistics and the definition of a creole

A creole language can be defined as a language that has come into existence at a point in time that can be established fairly precisely. Non-creole languages are assumed (often in the absence of detailed knowledge of their precise development) to have emerged gradually.

So Archaic Latin developed into Classical Latin, the popular variety of which in turn developed into Vulgar Latin, which among other things developed into Old French, which developed into Middle French, which in turn developed into Modern French. While some stages of this development involved more radical changes in the language than others, we can claim with some justification to be able to trace the line of development from Modern French back to Archaic Latin – the earliest recorded stage of Latin, with on the whole little difficulty. Before that we have to rely on linguistic reconstruction, but once again it is fairly obvious that Latin is a typical Indo-European language, and can thus be safely assumed to have developed from Proto-Indo-European, through the intermediate stages of possibly Proto-Italo-Celtic and certainly Proto-Italic. Proto-Indo-European itself may have been spoken somewhere in Southern Russia (an anachronistic term, of course) around 5000 B.C.

This kind of statement we can definitely not make when talking about creole languages. These exhibit an abrupt break in the course of their historical development. So we cannot say that Sranan (the major English-lexifier creole of Surinam; see chapter 18) derives in any gradual fashion from Early Modern English – its most obvious immediate historical precursor. Even a cursory comparison of Early Modern English with the earliest forms of Sranan (first recorded in 1718) will make it abundantly obvious that we are dealing with two completely different forms of speech. There is no conceivable way that Early Modern English could have developed into the very different Sranan in the available 70 or so years. Even the phonological developments required would be extreme, not to speak of the wholesale changes that would have had to have taken place in the syntax.

So creole languages are different from ordinary languages in that we can say that they came into existence at some point in time. Applying the techniques of historical linguistics to creoles is therefore not simple, and in addition presupposes answering the question of which languages the creole should be compared with: the language which provided the lexicon, or the language(s) which were responsible for most aspects of grammatical structure – inasmuch as it is possible to identify these.

It is clear in fact that creole languages develop as the result of 'linguistic violence' (and, as we shall see, frequently social violence too). In other words, we have to reckon with a break in the natural development of the language, the natural transmission of a language from generation to generation. The parents of the first speakers of Sranan were not English speakers at all, but speakers of various African languages, and what is more important, they did not grow up in an environment where English was the norm. How **creolization**, the development of a creole language, takes place, or at least what the various theories are concerning how it takes place, we cannot really go into at this juncture – this is a controversial matter that will be dealt with in chapters 8 through 11, and briefly below.

What is clear is that creole languages are not in the slightest qualitatively distinguishable from other spoken languages. Many of them tend to have certain features in common, but creolists are divided as to the interpretation of this fact, and a language like Chinese resembles many creole languages in its grammar. This means that before we can claim a language to be a creole, we need to know something about its history, either linguistic or social, and preferably both. As we know comparatively little about the detailed development of most languages in the world, and virtually nothing of the history of most ethnic groups, this inevitably means that there may be many unrecognized creole languages around the world.

One problem in the identification of particular languages as creoles is caused by the not unusual circumstance that creoles tend to be spoken in the same geographical regions as the languages that provide the greater portion of their lexica (their donor languages, or **lexifier** languages). In some cases we find a **continuum** of speech-forms varying from the creole at one end of the spectrum (the **basilect**), through intermediate forms (**mesolectal** varieties), to the lexifier language (the **acrolect**). Sometimes speech-forms exist which apparently represent cases where the original mesolect has survived, while the basilectal creole, and sometimes also the original lexifier language have not. Such cases may be referred to as **post-creoles**. Other cases seem rather to involve partial creolization, or influence from a creolized form of the same language. These languages may be termed **semi-creoles** or **creoloids**. Afrikaans seems likely to have been the result of some such process. While linguists would not in general wish to recognize this language as being a full creole, many aspects of Afrikaans are reminiscent of the things that happen during creolization. Other cases of putative creoloids are American Black English, and at least some forms of Brazilian Portuguese.

A quite different situation involving an 'intermediate' status is the case of the **mixed languages**. This type which has until now been the object of comparatively little study, involves cases where two languages clearly make a significant contribution to language – frequently one language provides the content words, and another the grammar. Here there is not necessarily any question of simplification. A well-known case of this type to be studied – Media Lengua (lit. 'middle language') (Muysken 1981b) – is spoken in Ecuador, and involves Spanish lexical items, combined with basically Quechua syntax, morphology, and phonology. Bakker (1992) has referred to this kind of situation as **language intertwining**. We refer the reader to chapter 4. This whole subject has just started to be studied in any detail. Sometimes a creole involves substantial mixture at all levels of language structure. A case in point is Berbice Dutch Creole, described in chapter 19.

Other cases where languages have become simplified to some extent are **lingua francas** (not the Lingua Franca of the Mediterranean) and **koines**. These come into existence under similar circumstances – one speech-form becomes widely used by non-native speakers, undergoing a degree of simplification. Here, the process seems to be gradual – in other words, no linguistic or social violence is involved. We speak of a lingua franca when speakers of various different languages are involved, and of a koine when the dialects of a single language are involved.

In chapter 26 there is an annotated list of languages where these distinctions and some further ones are used to classify about 350 languages and dialects. To complicate matters speech forms may change in status over time. Various scenarios or **life-cycles** (cf. Hall 1966, who used the term somewhat differently) have been proposed for the development of creoles. Mühlhäusler (1986) presents three such scenarios:

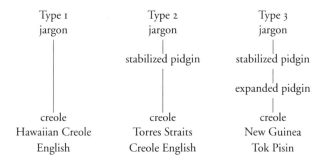

| Type 1 | Type 2 | Type 3 |
|--------|--------|--------|
| jargon | jargon | jargon |
| | stabilized pidgin | stabilized pidgin |
| | | expanded pidgin |
| creole | creole | creole |
| Hawaiian Creole English | Torres Straits Creole English | New Guinea Tok Pisin |

As will be argued in chapter 3, however, not all jargons or pidgins are part of such a life-cycle, and neither can we show that all creoles had a jargon or pidgin stage. It is in this respect that mixed languages display an important difference from creoles. On the one hand, mixed languages did come into existence at a particular moment in time, on the other hand they were formed from ordinary languages with native speakers – there was no jargon or pidgin phase.

## 1.3  Distribution of pidgins and creoles

The question of the distribution of pidgin and creole languages is one of the growth areas in linguistics. Because of their mixed character these speech varieties have frequently not been accorded the status of language. The frequent prejudice against their recognition as proper linguistic systems has meant that lists of the world's languages, produced up till fairly recently, tended to ignore these speech varieties. While many linguists, and sometimes educationalists, recognize the fact of their existence, this is by no means universally the case. The effect of this is that new creoles and pidgins are continually being added to the lists of such languages.

Recognition has come quickest for those creoles and pidgins (partially) based on European colonial languages, although even here we may be certain that some languages remain undiscovered. In the case of creoles and pidgins not involving a European base linguists have been faced with the above-mentioned problem that the history of very many languages is very poorly known. And as we will discover time and time again in the course of this book, a knowledge of the history of a language is often essential for determining its creole or pidgin status, or the lack of this. This means that creoles that came into existence hundreds of years ago may only be recognized as such in modern times.

The small size of many creole-speaking communities also militates against their recognition. A small linguistic community will more easily be assumed to represent a (deviant) dialect of a larger language than a large one will. Small communities also get overlooked more easily. So the Wutun 'dialect' of Qinghai province, China has been recognized as involving a problem in classification by Chinese scholars for quite some time. This mixed Amdo Tibetan-Kansu Mongol-Chinese language has certainly been in existence for several hundred years. It had been variously claimed to be Chinese, Monguor and Tibetan. Its essentially mixed status was first recognized by Chen (1982). The fact, however, that the language has only 2500 speakers in five villages has not helped it to appear in any list or classification of the world's languages. For instance, it does not appear in the 11th edition of Ethnologue (Grimes 1988).

We have cited the question of prejudice above. This is especially relevant in the case of pidgins. Pidgins, by their very nature, tend towards instability, both in terms of linguistic system, and in terms of their function. If they do not belong to the small group of pidgins that become standardized, or nativized, or both, they may well disappear completely when the social need that caused them to come into existence passes. An event so trivial as the disruption of a market may make a particular pidgin redundant. Population movements may have the same effect. So the raison d'être of the Pidgin Russian spoken in Harbin, Manchuria, between Russians and Chinese, disappeared when most of the Russians left in the fifties.

## 1.4 History of pidgin and creole studies

Why should there be a field of pidgin and creole language studies? Since the group of languages as a whole are not genetically related, nor spoken in the same area, the languages must be considered to have something else in common, in order to be meaningfully studied as a group. In the field there is an implicit assumption that the creole languages share some property that calls for an explanatory theory.

The earliest written sources for many creoles date from the 18th century, when missionaries started writing dictionaries, and translating religious texts into the languages of the slaves.

The first time the term 'creole' was applied to a language was 1739, in the Virgin Islands, when the very youthful Dutch-lexifier creole Negerhollands was referred to as *carriolssche* by a Moravian missionary (Stein 1987). The first grammar of a creole was written in the Virgin Islands by J.M. Magens, a scion of a local planter family (1770). In addition to missionaries, travellers or other laymen occasionally wrote brief dialogues etc. in the local creoles, at that time generally referred to as Negro-English, Negro-Dutch, etc. There are reasonable historical records for a number of creole languages, including Negerhollands, Sranan and Saramaccan (Surinam), Mauritian Creole, and Jamaican. These allow us to study the historical development of the creole languages (see chapter 10).

Creole studies originated as a systematic field of research over a century ago, with Schuchardt's (1842-1927) important series of articles. These started as an attempt to account for a more complex set of developments in the history of the Romance languages than was possible in the Neogrammarian preoccupation with the regularity of sound change. Hesseling's (1880-1941) work originally started out from an explanation of the developments in Greek, from the early dialects through **koine** Greek under the Roman Empire, to Byzantine and modern Greek. Both scholars found it necessary to allow for more complex types of linguistic change: mixture, simplification, reanalysis, and the complexity of their analyses characterizes modern creole studies as well.

Until 1965 the field remained, however, rather marginal. Creole languages were studied by a few enthusiastic historical linguists – usually Anglicists or Romanists, fieldworkers with an adventurous bent, or folklorists ahead of their time. Now the study of creole languages has moved to the center of linguistic research, a research program with universalist theoretical pretensions, half-way between theoretical linguistics and sociolinguistics. Reasons for this development are manifold, but include the political and cultural emancipation of certain parts of the Caribbean (most notably Jamaica), an interest in Afro-American culture, particularly in the U.S., and a partial reorientation of linguistic research.

## 1.5  Theories of origin in creole studies and theoretical linguistics

The main research effort in pidgin and creole studies has been to find a principled explanation for the genesis of the languages involved. There is an implicit assumption that the creole languages share some property that calls for an explanatory theory. What property this is depends on the theory concerned. Any of four properties are assumed to play a role:

(1) Creole languages are often assumed to be more **alike** than other languages. As we will see, creoles share many structural features, and many researchers believe that these resemblances cannot be simply due to the similarity between the languages of western Europe, or accidental.

(2) Creole languages are often assumed to be more **simple** than other languages. There is a wide-spread belief that creole languages are not just morphologically, but also syntactically and phonologically simpler than other languages.

(3) Creole languages are often assumed to have more **mixed** grammars than other languages. Many people have drawn parallels between language and biology, when thinking of creoles. It is assumed that just as many speakers of creole languages have 'mixed' African, European, Asian and in some cases Amerindian ancestry, the languages they speak are likewise simply a combination of a bit of European vocabulary with some African or Asian syntax and semantics.

(4) Pidgin and creole languages are often assumed to exhibit much more **internal variability** than other languages. They are assumed to be highly dynamic language systems and often coexist with their lexifier languages in the same speech community.

These assumptions play a role in the various theories of creole origin that have been proposed. The theories of origin have been developed in part to explain the assumed similarity, simplicity, mixing, and variability of the creole languages. We have chosen to group these theories into four categories, in chapters 8-11. Here we will briefly summarize the principal hypotheses put forward. References will be provided in the relevant chapters.

### 1.5.1 The European input

Some models attempt to trace the properties of the pidgins and creoles back to specific antecedents in Europe (see further chapter 8). The **Portuguese monogenesis** model has undergone several modifications. Crucial to all of these is the existence of a trade language with a predominantly Portuguese lexicon, used in the 15th to 18th centuries by traders, slave raiders, and merchants from throughout the then incipient colonial societies. The monogenetic theory holds that the slaves learned the Portuguese Pidgin in the slave camps, trading forts, and slave ships of their early captivity, and then took this language, really no more than a jargon, with them to the plantations. The different creole languages as we know them are based on this jargon, but have replaced the Portuguese words with words from other European languages. The supposed similarity of the creole languages is due of course to the underlying Portuguese jargon, and their simplicity to the simplicity of this jargon.

The **restricted monogenesis** hypothesis is less ambitious. It is mostly limited to the English and French-lexifier creole languages of the Atlantic and Indian Ocean, and proceeds from the idea that there was a jargon or pidgin spoken along the coast of West Africa that later formed the primary source for a wide range of creoles. The common features of these creoles are then assumed to be due to these early pidgins.

The **European dialect origin** hypothesis holds that creoles essentially developed from non-standard dialects of the colonial languages in an ordinary way, and are the result of migration by dialect speakers to the newly founded colonies, compounded with the existence of a strongly dialectal **nautical language**. In this theory, similarities between creoles hold only for those derived from a single colonial language; creoles may be simple because the non-standard varieties were simpler than the written national standard.

In other approaches, processes involving the transformation of the European languages play a central role, through imperfect second language learning or the reduction of speech directed at foreigners. The **baby talk** or **foreigner talk** theory is similar to the imperfect second language learning theory in postulating that creoles are frozen (i.e. fossilized) stages in the second language learning sequence. The difference lies in the fact that in the baby talk theory the responsibility for the simplification is shifted from the learners to the speakers of European languages, who provide a simplified model. The similarity between creoles would be due, in this view, to universal properties of the simplified input. The type of evidence adherents of the baby talk hypothesis are looking for thus includes simplifications made by native speakers, not by learners, in pidgins, such as the use of infinitives.

In the **imperfect second language learning** theory creoles are the crystallization of some stage in the developmental sequence of second language acquisition. The speakers of the proto-creole simply did not have sufficient access to the model, and had to make up an approximative system. In this view the fact that creoles are simple is due to the simplification inherent in the second language learning process. For some adherents of this view the possible similarities among the creole languages are due to universal properties of the learning process.

### 1.5.2  The Non-European input

The **Afro-genesis** model (in the sense of 'restricted monogenesis') really deals mostly with the creole languages spoken in the Atlantic region: West Africa and the Caribbean, and postulates that these languages have emerged through the relexification by the slaves of the West African languages, the so-called **substrate** languages, under influence of the European colonial languages (see chapter 9). An alternative explanation is in terms of the transfer of African language structures in the process of learning the colonial lexifier languages. The similarity of the languages involved is due, in this model, to the fact that they share the same African linguistic features, mixed together with the lexicon of the European languages. The main problems with the Afro-genesis model in its strict version are the large number of structural differences between West African languages and creoles on the one hand, and the linguistic differences among the various West African languages themselves on the other. What has been claimed to save the hypothesis is that in the process of relexification certain syntactic and semantic properties of European lexical items were incorporated as well.

### 1.5.3  Developmental approaches

Many researchers study pidgins and creoles from a developmental perspective, as **gradually** evolving and continuously changing systems rather than as stable systems that emerged rapidly. Within this approach, expansion of pidgins through their continued use and growth in functional domains is stressed above strictly grammatical or cognitive aspects. In chapter 10 we return to various developmental approaches.

The **common social context** theory adopts a such strictly functional perspective: the slave plantations imposed similar communicative requirements on the slaves, newly arrived, and lacking a common language in many cases. The commonality of the communicative requirements led to the formation of a series of fairly similar makeshift communicative systems, which then stabilized and became creoles.

### 1.5.4  Universalist approaches

**Universalist** models stress the intervention of a specific general process during the transmission of language from generation to generation and from speaker to speaker (see chapter 11). The process invoked varies: a general tendency towards semantic transparency, first language learning driven by universal processes, or general processes of discourse organization.

The **semantic transparency** theory is not a full-blown genesis theory, but simply claims that the structure of creole languages directly reflects universal semantic structures. The fact that they are alike, in this view, is due to the fact that the semantic structures are universal. They are simple because the semantic structures involved are fairly directly mapped onto surface structures, eschewing any very complex transformational derivation. An example of this may be the fact that creole languages have separate tense/mood/aspect particles, which reflect separate logical operators, rather than incorporating tense, etc. into the inflection of the verb.

The **bioprogram** theory claims that creoles are inventions of the children growing up on the newly founded plantations. Around them they only heard pidgins spoken, without enough structure to function as natural languages, and they used their own innate linguistic capacities to transform the pidgin input from their parents into a full-fledged language. Creole languages are similar because the innate linguistic capacity utilized is universal, and they are simple because they reflect the most basic language structures. One feature shared by all creoles that would derive from the innate capacity is the system of pre-verbal tense/mood/aspect particles. Not only do they seem limited in the creole languages to a particular set of meanings, but they also seem always to occur in a particular order. The system of tense/mood/aspect particles, its interpretation and its ordering would directly reflect universal aspects of the human language capacity.

### 1.5.5  Theoretical implications

In all these models or theories notions such as **alike, simple, mixed**, and **variable** play a role. They are in fact taken for granted, assumed to be what requires to be explained, and therefore not called into question. The contribution that the study of creole languages can make, in our view, to grammatical theory is that it can help to elucidate these four concepts 'alike', 'simple', 'mixed', and 'variable'. All four turn out to be relevant to the central concerns of modern grammatical theory. In order to help us understand this, let us examine the concepts involved more closely.

When we say that languages $x$ and $y$ are more alike than $y$ and $z$, we are claiming in fact that in the total (abstract) **variation space** allowed for by the human language capacity $x$ and $y$ are closer than $y$ and $z$. Consequently, the claim that the creole languages are more alike than other languages implies a clustering in the variation space. If we think of the variation space as defined by **parameter theory** (as in recent work by Chomsky and others), trying to develop a notion of 'alike' really boils down to developing a theory of parameters, parameters along which similarities and differences between natural languages can be defined.

Consider now the concept of simplicity. The idea that creole languages are simple has been taken to mean two things. On one level it has meant that creole languages do not have a rich morphology, on another that the overall grammar of creole languages is less complex than that of other languages. Both interpretations are relevant to grammatical theory. The idea that **absence of morphology** is related to grammatical simplicity needs to be evaluated in the context of contemporary research into morphology/syntax interactions, and the grammatical status of **inflection** or INFL (Chomsky 1982; Rizzi 1982, and others) and of case marking (Stowell, 1981). Even more importantly, the idea that the creole languages are not grammatically complex in general only makes sense if one has a theory of grammatical complexity to fall back on, and this brings in **markedness theory**.

Consider next the notion of mixing. Mixing implies that elements from one language are combined with elements from another, and this in turn calls into question the cohesion of the grammatical systems involved. The tighter a particular subsystem (e.g. the vowel system, or the system of referential expressions) is organized, the less amenable it will be to restructuring under borrowing. Tightness of organization in modern grammatical theory is conceptualized in terms of **modularity theory**: the grammar is organized into a set of internally structured but externally independent modules, the interaction of which leads to the final grammatical output. For this reason, the notion of mixing is important: it forces us to think about which parts of the grammar are tightly organized, and hence about the notion of modularity.

Tightness of organization or cohesion may have either a paradigmatic dimension, in terms of the hierarchical organization of **feature systems**, or a syntagmatic dimension, in terms perhaps of the notion of **government** (Chomsky 1981) as a central principle of syntactic organization.

An important group of creole researchers has focused on the dynamic and variable aspects of language (Sankoff 1982; Bickerton 1975; Rickford 1987). While linguists working in terms of the paradigm of generative grammar tend to abstract away from variation and change, focusing on the universal and invariable aspects of linguistic competence, many creolists have tended to put **variation and change** at the center of attention: only by studying the changes that languages undergo and the ways in which these changes are manifested in the speech community can we find out about the phenomenon of language. Pidgin and creole languages form a natural field of study for these researchers, precisely because they present so much internal variation and because they tend to change so rapidly. The extent of variation present (and this is particularly relevant for pidgins) again raises the questions mentioned above with respect to the internal cohesion of a grammatical system and how parameters determine the way languages vary.

Keeping this in mind, then, the contribution of pidgin and creole studies to linguistic theory is clear. We have to come to grips with one or more of the core notions of grammatical theory:

| | |
|---|---|
| alike: | parameter theory |
| simple: | morphology/syntax interactions |
| | markedness theory |
| mixed: | modularity |
| variable: | parameter theory, modularity |

Studying creole languages implies a constant confrontation with these notions, and helps one to develop a vocabulary capable of dealing with them.

### Further reading
The primary source for documentation on the different pidgins and creoles is still Reinecke's monumental bibliography (1975). There are a number of introductions to pidgin and creole studies on the market, including Hall (1966), Todd (1974; 1990), Mühlhäusler (1986), with much information about the Pacific, Holm (1988), strong on the history of the field, and Romaine (1988), strong on links with psycholinguistic research. In French we have Valdman (1978). In addition there is a large number of collections of articles, of which Hymes (1971), Valdman (1977), and Valdman and Highfield (1981) are the most general in scope.

Useful monographs by single authors are: Bickerton (1981), which contains a highly readable exposition of the bioprogram hypothesis; Alleyne (1980), which documents the Afro-genesis hypothesis with a wealth of detail (but cf. 'Afro-genesis in the sense of 'restricted monogenesis'); and Sankoff (1980), which presents the view that the structure of creole languages is finely attuned to their functional requirements with a number of insightful articles. There are two specialized journals, *Journal of Pidgin and Creole Languages* and *Études Créoles*. In addition there is a newsletter, *The Carrier Pidgin*.

# 2 The socio-historical background of creoles

Jacques Arends

## 2.1 Three types of creole

It has been argued by some creolists that creoles cannot be defined as a distinct group of languages on typological, intra-linguistic, grounds (e.g. Muysken 1988a). If this is true, the question arises whether there are any external, extra-linguistic, criteria according to which they can be grouped together in one category. The criterion that comes to mind most readily is that of the social history of these languages. Are creoles characterized by a particular social history, a social history that is common to all of these languages and that is not shared by any other group of languages? This question cannot be satisfactorily answered at the moment, simply because the external history of many creoles still has to be written, but there are strong indications that indeed in many cases there are a number of striking similarities among the historical processes through which these languages came into being. One of these concerns the fact that many creoles arose in the context of the European colonial expansion from the sixteenth century onwards. In many cases this expansion was accompanied by a specific type of economy, which had as its most characteristic feature the exploitation of relatively large agricultural units, plantations, for the production of largely new products such as sugar, coffee, and tobacco, for the European markets. Plantations, however, were not the only situations that gave rise to creolization. Therefore, before we go on to explore the commonalities in the external histories of creoles in general, we will first briefly discuss three different types of creoles that can be distinguished according to differences in their external histories.

According to their external history the following three types of creole have been distinguished: **plantation creoles**, **fort creoles**, and **maroon creoles** (Bickerton 1988). In addition, a fourth type may be distinguished: creolized versions of pidgins have emerged, e.g. in New Guinea and northern Australia. In the Atlantic area, plantations were worked by large numbers of African slaves, who were purchased along the western coast of Africa from Senegal to Angola. In the initial stage of colonization Amerindian slaves were also used, as well as indentured laborers – poor Europeans who were contracted for a specified number of years. In the case of the Pacific and the Indian Ocean, slavery was usually not the primary means of acquiring a labor force. Indentured workers from India, China, Japan, the Philippines and the South-West Pacific, were recruited to work on the plantations in Mauritius, Queensland (Australia), and Hawaii.

It is not only on the plantations, however, that creole languages arose. Apart from the plantation creoles, which emerged in the Caribbean (e.g. in Jamaica, Haiti, Guyana, Surinam), in West Africa (e.g. on the islands of Annobon and São Tomé off the West African coast), and perhaps in the southern parts of North America as well, a number of creoles developed at the so-called **forts**, the fortified posts along the West African coast, from which the Europeans deployed their commercial activities. In the forts some medium of communication must have been used, both among Africans from different linguistic backgrounds and between Africans and Europeans. More importantly, however, interethnic communication extended to the forts' surroundings where European men (so-called **lança-dos**) were living in mixed households with African women, with whom they spoke some kind of contact language. In the course of time these contact languages were expanded into creoles, in particular by the children that were born into these households. One of these is the alleged 'Guinea Coast Creole English', which, according to Hancock (1986), arose out of the interaction between English and African speakers in the settlements in Upper Guinea (Sierra Leone and surrounding areas) and which may have formed the basis of the Caribbean English-lexifier creoles.

A third type of socio-historical context that has given rise to the genesis of creoles is **marronage**, which refers to the fact that slaves escaped from the plantations and subsequently formed their own communities in the interior in relative isolation from the rest of the colony. Maroon communities developed in several parts of the New World (Jamaica, Colombia, Surinam) and in Africa as well (São Tomé). While most of these communities have been absorbed by the mainstream culture of the societies within which they existed, the Surinam maroons, who are distributed over several tribes, have preserved their own traditions and their languages up to the present day. But since these languages probably developed out of plantation creoles, we should not expect to find important structural differences between the two. What may have caused some divergence, however, is the fact that the maroon creoles developed in relative isolation from the metropolitan, European, language. This issue has as yet not been explored in any detail.

In Surinam, two maroon creole languages can be distinguished. One, consisting of the dialects spoken by the Saramaccan and Matawai tribes, is a 'mixed' creole, with two European lexifier languages, English and Portuguese (see chapter 14). In this respect it is clearly different from the coastal creole, Sranan, whose basic lexicon is English-lexifier, just like that of the other maroon creole language, spoken by the Ndjuka, Aluku, Paramaccan, and Kwinti tribes. While some of the dialects (e.g. Matawai and Paramaccan) have hardly been studied at all, Saramaccan has attracted the special attention of many creolists, who regard this language as the most pure or **radical** creole language extant today. According to these scholars Saramaccan, due to its supposedly rapid formation and its subsequent isolation from other languages, has preserved its original creole character in a purer state than other known creoles (but cf. Alleyne 1980 for a different view). Other maroon creoles, outside Surinam, include Palenquero (Colombia) and Angolar (São Tomé), which are still spoken today. Finally, remnants of another maroon creole have been found in the 'Maroon Spirit Possession Language' of Jamaica (Bilby 1983). This is not employed in ordinary situations, but it is used by people when they are possessed during religious ceremonies, to talk to the spirits of those of their ancestors who were born in Jamaica.

The three-way division made here at least to some extent cuts across the distinction between **endogenous** and **exogenous** creoles. This distinction was made by Chaudenson (1977) in order to distinguish between creoles that arose in areas where the native languages of the creolizing population were spoken (e.g. some African creoles, such as Kituba) and those that did not, since they involved the massive relocation of the creolizing population (e.g. the creoles that arose in the New World). The distinction is especially important with respect to the potential role of the substrate in creole genesis: a creole that arose in an area where its substrate speakers had ample opportunity to continue speaking their native language(s) next to the emerging creole is bound to show more substrate influence than one that did not (cf. Singler 1988).

## 2.2  Colonial expansion and the slave trade

The history of European expansion and the concomitant slave trade cannot be adequately described here, but it cannot be excluded entirely either since it constitutes the socio-historical matrix in which creolization took place. Therefore, in what follows a brief outline will be given of this history as far as it concerns the Atlantic area. The main European nations involved in the colonial expansion were Spain, Portugal, France, Britain and the Netherlands. While the Spaniards and the Portuguese were the first to actually found settlements in the New World during the sixteenth century, they were followed by the others a century later.

During the entire slave trade period some ten million Africans were captured and deported to the Americas (Curtin 1969). Many of these did not survive: some died during captivity in one of the forts along the African coast, before they had even embarked on their **middle passage**, the journey to the New World. Others perished during transport as a result of disease or other causes related to the poor conditions on the slave ships. Of those who did arrive in the New World, many died after a relatively short period in the colony: in 18th-century Surinam the life expectancy upon arrival was somewhere between five and ten years.

As far as the geographical origins and demographic behavior of these Africans is concerned, much remains to be discovered by historical research. In the case of Surinam extremely detailed information has been made available by the historian Postma (1990), whose findings are based on archival documents concerning the Dutch Atlantic slave trade. These findings relate to such variables as port of embarkation, dates of departure from Africa and arrival in the New World, age and sex distribution, and the numbers of slaves that were embarked and disembarked. While we cannot go into this in any detail, let us summarize Postma's main findings, as an example of what historical research can contribute to the study of creole genesis. Between 1650 and 1815 the Dutch shipped some 200,000 Africans to Surinam. At Emancipation, in 1863 – more than 200 years after importation began – the black population still numbered no more than some 36,000. This shows that during the entire period of slavery there was a very substantial population reduction, due to an exceptionally high death rate and an exceptionally low birth rate, while at the same time the rate of immigration was very high. As a result of this, the normal situation whereby a language is acquired natively through transmission from one generation to the next, with second language learning being only marginal, was completely disturbed. Although the precise linguistic consequences of this for creole genesis are not entirely clear, it seems evident that the role of demography should be taken into account.

As far as the geographical background of the Surinam slaves is concerned, Postma provides a wealth of interesting information. From his figures it can be inferred (Arends to appear b) that during the slave trade period there have been substantial variations in the areas from which the Dutch purchased their slaves. The general picture that emerges from these figures is that over the entire period (1650-1815) the **Windward Coast** (the area stretching from Sierra Leone to Ivory Coast) served as the main supplier of Surinam slaves. However, this area started to play this role only from 1740 onwards. During the first 70 years of slave importation (1650-1720, the formative period of Sranan and Saramaccan) the **Slave Coast** (Togo, Benin) and the **Loango** area (Gabon, Congo, Zaire, Angola) supplied more than 90% of all slaves imported into Surinam. In the intervening period (1720-1740), the **Gold Coast** (Ghana) served as the main supplier of slaves. Obviously, such a finding has important consequences for the investigation of African survivals in the Surinam creoles. Thus, it seems safe to assume that in the formation of these creoles, Windward Coast languages, such as Mande and Wolof, despite their ultimate overall numerical dominance can only have played a minor role, whereas languages spoken along the Slave Coast, such as Gbe, and in the Loango area, such as Kikongo, are much more relevant in this respect. This shows that detailed historical-demographic research may drastically reduce the set of relevant substrate languages for any given creole (see further chapter 9). Other colonies for which similar work has been done include Mauritius (Baker 1982), Cayenne (Jennings to appear), and Martinique and Guadeloupe (Singler 1992b).

## 2.3 The plantation system

Having discussed some relevant socio-historical factors at the macro-level, it may be useful to go in some detail into a social aspect of creolization at the micro-level, i.e. the social structure of the plantation. After all, the plantation must have been the main locus of creolization. While most of what follows refers to Surinam (largely based on Van Stipriaan 1993), it has some relevance for other creole societies too. The stereotypical image of a plantation colony as a severely dichotomized society, with a small number of whites holding power over large numbers of African slaves, needs some adjustment on the basis of what is known about how plantation life was socially structured. Although there certainly was a wide social, cultural and economic gap between the small white section of a plantation's population and the numerically dominant slave force (with ratios reaching 50:1 and more), the actual situation may have been a bit more complex than it might appear at first sight. The figure below charts the social stratification according to the division of labor on a typical Surinam plantation.

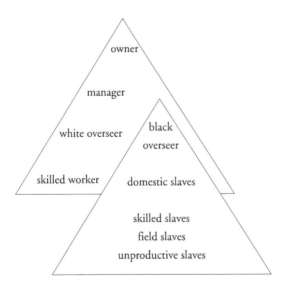

Within the black population there was a division of labor between field slaves (who on average formed no more than around 50% of a plantation's black work force), house slaves, slave craftsmen, and slaves performing various other tasks, such as hunting and fishing. These differences in function correlated not only with differences in status and power within the black community, but also with the amount of linguistic interaction with whites. A special function was that of the so-called **creole mama**, a black woman – usually elderly – who took care of the younger children. She is assumed to have provided an important model for the acquisition of language by these children, beside their parents and other relatives.

Apart from these, every slave community had one or more black overseers, who occupied an intermediary position in the power structure, between the white master and the black workforce. To him was delegated the execution of punishment and allocation of tasks, as also the decision on when sick slaves were fit to work. In addition to this, there is some evidence that he was also a religious leader in the black community. In many cases, quite surprisingly, the black overseer even seems to have been in a more powerful position than the white overseer. Probably these differences in power and status between different groups of slaves were reflected in their language use, just like in any other society, but, unfortunately, this cannot be empirically verified, due to the absence of documentary evidence.

Apart from this, there must also have been considerable differences in the quality and quantity of contacts between different groups of blacks on the one hand and whites on the other. Thus, among the blacks the overseer probably had, if not the most regular, the most elaborate verbal interactions with the whites, due to the necessity of discussing the technical details of plantation management. In descending order of frequency and intensity of contact with whites, the black overseer was probably followed first by the domestic slaves, then by the slaves who had special tasks and, finally, by the field slaves and the unproductive slaves. Although it is impossible to reconstruct the linguistic consequences this may have had, it still seems useful to be aware of the fact that the stereotypical image of plantation society as a strictly dichotomous one is an idealization, and that the actual situation was much more complex.

In the course of time, a group intermediate between the black and white populations of the plantations developed, consisting of mulattoes (coloreds), who were the results of sexual relationships between white men and black women. This was a privileged group, whose members were often sent to town in order to serve as house slaves, or, when they were recognized by their fathers, bought free. Together with manumitted black slaves, these mulattoes formed a growing intermediate group, between the small group of whites and the large mass of slaves. This adds to a further refinement of the image of slave society as multi-stratal rather than bi-stratal.

One other linguistically relevant feature of slave society is the fact that the black population consisted of two groups, the **bozals** or **salt water slaves**, those who had been born in Africa, and the **creoles**, those who had been born in the colony. Linguistically speaking, this difference is reflected in the fact that the former arrived in the colony speaking one or more African language(s), whereas the latter acquired their first language(s) (a creole, an African language, some version of the metropolitan language) in the colony. Although very little is known about differences in L1 versus L2 use of emergent creoles, it seems safe to assume, on the basis of what is known about L1 and L2 acquisition in general, that such differences were present. As to the L2 acquisition by newly arrived slaves, it is known that, as part of a general **seasoning** process, they were assigned to an experienced slave, whose tasks included introducing new slaves to the local language, i.e. the creole. This means that the model for language acquisition was largely provided by blacks, not whites. In colonies where, due to the demographic factors referred to in section 2.2, the number of creole slaves increased quite slowly, the task of seasoning must often have been performed by African-born rather than locally-born slaves. In other words, in these cases the model for the acquisition of the creole as a second language by the African-born slaves would be a second, not a first language version of that creole. But again, it is extremely difficult to estimate the influence this may have had on the emerging creole.

Finally, two points have to be mentioned. First, the slave population was not always as powerless as is often assumed. Because of their sheer numbers, the blacks were a constant threat to the whites, who could only control them by the use of force. The most important forms of resistance used by the slaves were rebellions, strikes and marronnage. Second, despite their lack of freedom, slaves were much more mobile than has often been assumed. Sexual relationships, funerals, festivities, trade and other activities provided opportunities for contacts outside the plantation (Muyrers 1993). The linguistic impact of these factors, however, can as yet not be established.

## 2.4 Demography

Although some demographic issues have been briefly touched upon in section 2.2 above, these issues deserve a more detailed discussion in relation to creolization. This is so for at least two reasons. First, certain demographic factors constitute preconditions for the process of creolization to be able to happen in the first place. For instance, models which assume that creoles are the result of L1 acquisition (or rather creation) by the first generation(s) of locally-born children, such as Bickerton's Language Bioprogram Hypothesis (1981, 1984), presuppose the presence of a sufficient number of these children during the formative period of the creole, say the first twenty-five or fifty years after initial colonization. Demographic data on some colonies, such as Jamaica and Surinam (Singler 1986), seem to show that this condition was not fulfilled there during this period. Thus, demographic findings may provide extralinguistic counter-evidence for some hypotheses about creolization.

Second, there are some demographic factors which, although they do not constitute preconditions for creolization, are nevertheless important because they may determine the nature of the creolization process. After all, our view of creolization is still largely based on

20th-century evidence, even though creolization is essentially a historical phenomenon. That is to say, while creolization is an event of the past for all creoles except those that are in the process of being formed today, almost anything that has been hypothesized about it has been based on knowledge of the outcome of that process (the present day creole language), not on knowledge about the process itself. One of the demographic factors that may contribute to our understanding of creolization concerns the development of the quantitative proportion between the black and white parts of the population, especially during the initial period of colonization. This is a relevant factor because the presence of models speaking the dominant language is a necessary condition for the transmission of that language to L2 learners. And although L2-speaking models were certainly present in all creolization situations that we know of, the availability of these models for L2-learning Africans may have differed widely, both among different locations, and over time in a single location.

It is for this reason that Baker (1982), who was the first to draw attention to the importance of demographic factors for creolization, introduced the term **Event 1**, referring to the point in time when numerical parity between the black and white parts of the population is reached. It is hypothesized that in the period between the beginning of colonization (which might be termed **Event 0**) and Event 1, there are sufficient L2 speakers present for every L2 learner to have adequate access to the language, i.e. to actually learn it, as opposed to having to revert to speaking a pidgin. After Event 1, when increasing numbers of slaves are imported while the number of whites does not grow in proportion to these, it becomes increasingly difficult for L2 learners to gain access to native speakers to learn the language from. Obviously, the issue of access to L2 models is not just a quantitative matter; as was noted in section 2.3, also the quality of the interaction between whites and blacks may have differed widely. Although differential access must undoubtedly have had a linguistic impact, at the moment not enough is known about it to specify this in any detail.

Another important demographic event, distinguished by Baker, is **Event 2**, which refers to the point in time when the number of locally born blacks, or creoles, reaches numerical parity with the total number of whites. (The third of Baker's Events, **Event 3**, which is not relevant for the present discussion, refers to the point in time when the immigration of substrate speakers stops.) Event 2 may be interpreted as the point in time at which the black population has creolized or nativized to such an extent that creolization of language may occur. In other words, at Event 2 the native black population has acquired the 'critical mass' necessary for creolization to take place. This does not mean, of course, that creolization necessarily has to take place, only that a condition for it is fulfilled. Whether creolization will actually occur, depends, among other things, on other demographic factors, such as the rate of post-Event-2 slave imports and demographic developments within the white population.

It should be borne in mind that, although Events 1 and 2 are historical occasions that can in principle be established empirically, the reason for their introduction is a heuristic, not an empirical one. In other words, it is not an established fact that precisely these historical events correlate with specific linguistic events such as the onset of the creolization process. Rather, the identification of Events 1 and 2 provides a means of getting at the relationship between demographic development and linguistic process more precisely. Much more research, however, is needed to gain a better insight into the significance of demographic factors for creole genesis.

The first, and up to now, only creolist who has attempted to formalize the importance of certain demographic factors for the processes of pidginization and creolization, is Bickerton (1984), who developed a **Pidginization Index** (PI), a demographic measure for the degree of pidginization. The degree of pidginization is defined by Bickerton in terms of structural distance from the lexifier language: the higher the PI, the smaller the distance. The PI takes into account three demographic factors: Y, P, and R. Y is the number of years between Event 0 and Event 1; P is the number of substrate speakers at Event 1; and R is the average annual import of substrate speakers after Event 1. The formula thus reads:

$$PI = Y \times P / R$$

Of course, this formula should not be construed as, nor is it intended as, in any way an absolute quantitative measure of pidginization. What it does attempt, is to relate the degree of pidginization to the demographic development of a particular colony. Thus, a black population that grows slowly until Event 1 (i.e. where Y is high) will yield a language with a relatively high PI. Similarly, a high rate of post-Event 1 importation of slaves (i.e. where R is high) will yield a relatively low PI. In the former case a colonial version of the metropolitan language will probably emerge, while in the latter the genesis of a pidgin is more likely. Although the PI has been severely criticized (Singler 1990), it may still serve a useful function, namely as a first heuristic in trying to come to grips with a number of complex and elusive extra-linguistic factors, which most creolists agree are of crucial importance for creolization but which are seldom dealt with in any systematic manner.

Another factor to be reckoned with is the degree of linguistic homogeneity of both the black and white populations. While in some colonies the bulk of the white population all spoke the same European language, there were others (Surinam, Virgin Islands) where a variety of European languages was spoken. More importantly, perhaps, the degree of the homogeneity of the substrate also differed widely. An extreme case is represented by Berbice, where a single African language, Eastern Ijọ, is assumed to have been spoken by most of the blacks. In other cases, the African substrate was far more heterogeneous. As shown by

Singler (1988), the homogeneity of the substrate is an important factor in determining the degree of substrate influence in creole genesis.

A concept, borrowed from population genetics, which has been introduced recently into the historical demographics of creole genesis (Mufwene 1993a), is that of the **founder principle**. This principle is supposed to account for the disproportionately strong influence the founder population of a settlement may have on the genetic make-up of the population at later stages. The idea is that, similarly, the language(s) of a colony's founder population, both European and non-European, may have had a disproportionately strong influence on the creole language(s) of that colony. Although the idea itself is interesting, its value cannot be established until more exact and more reliable data about the founder populations of a number of creole societies have become available. Summarizing, it is clear that much more research is needed before the exact impact of demographic factors on creolization can be established in a systematic way.

### Further reading
Rens (1953) is a social history of the Surinam creoles. Mintz & Price (1992) is a concise but excellent introduction to the social history of African-American culture, while Van Stipriaan (1993) provides a detailed study of the development of Surinam's plantation system. Chaudenson (1992) is an interesting and wide-ranging survey of linguistic and cultural creolization processes, with particular reference to the French-lexifier creoles. The history of the Saramaccan maroons is told in Price (1983). The classic work on the Atlantic slave trade is Curtin (1969), while Postma (1990) is a quantitative assessment of the Dutch participation in that trade.

# 3  Pidgins

Peter Bakker

## 3.1  Introduction

Pidgins are languages lexically derived from other languages, but which are structurally simplified, especially in their morphology. They come into being where people need to communicate but do not have a language in common. Pidgins have no (or few) first language speakers, they are the subject of language learning, they have structural norms, they are used by two or more groups, and they are usually unintelligible for speakers of the language from which the lexicon derives.

In most studies of pidgin and creole languages, pidgins fare rather poorly. Too often, they are assumed to be simple versions of creoles, or it is stated that creoles are just pidgins which suddenly acquire typical creole-like structural properties upon becoming mother tongues. Furthermore, forms of Pidgin English of the Pacific, especially New Guinea, are often given as examples, but these are not unambiguous examples of pidgins, as they may be both first and second languages and have been spoken for many generations. Hence, they share both pidgin and creole language properties. Pidgins undergo structural expansion when their use is extended to many domains. In this chapter, we want to discuss as wide a variety of pidgins as possible, focusing on pidgins which never became native languages, and never extended pidgins. These extended pidgins resemble creoles. Hence, Pacific and West African Pidgin English will not be the focus of our concern. We will argue that (a) pidgins are structurally strikingly different from creoles, (b) pidgins may have considerably complex morphology and (c) pidgins are very often based on the local language rather than on the colonial one.

The etymology of the word 'pidgin' was a subject of debate, but this has been settled recently. In Hancock (1979) several etymologies were discussed, but more recent research establishes the Chinese Pidgin English pronunciation of the English word *business* as its source (see Baker & Mühlhäusler 1990: 93), particularly because of its use in a popular Chinese Pidgin English phrase-book in Chinese characters in the early 1900's (Shi 1992). The word, spelled 'pigeon', was already used in 1807 for Chinese Pidgin English, and it was only many decades later that it became used as a generic term for all pidgins. Until then, the term **jargon** was commonly used for pidgins in some areas, as is still clear from all the North American pidgins which are called 'Jargons'. Europeans also used the term **lingua**

**franca** as a generic term for pidgins, after the Mediterranean pidgin of that name. Terms which were originally used for very similar phenomena, are now used to denote different types of language: a 'jargon' is now often a rudimentary pidgin and a 'lingua franca' is a language used for wider communication, but which may or may not be pidginized.

In this chapter we follow the usage in creole studies as regards nomenclature in mentioning first the main ethnic group speaking the pidgin, the type of language, and then the lexical base of the pidgin. For example, Hottentot Pidgin English refers to an English-lexifier pidgin spoken by (among others) Khoikhoin (Hottentots).

## 3.2 Definition

In this section we will try to delimit the concept of **pidgin** with respect to related notions. Pidgins are always simplified compared to the lexifier language, as is apparent in their loss of morphology and their more analytic structure. But not all **simplified languages** are pidgins.

The term 'pidgin' should not be confused with **broken language**. Not everybody who speaks a language imperfectly speaks a pidgin. A definition of a pidgin should include that it has to be learnt, that it has structural norms and therefore that people can speak a pidgin more or less well. This means that immigrant workers in e.g. Western Europe who speak broken versions of French, Dutch, German, etc., are not speaking pidgins. The target language of these immigrants (the language they attempt to speak) is not the broken version of the language, but French, Dutch or German – even if they decide not to try to learn these languages beyond a certain level. There may be exceptions, such as certain neighborhoods of Stockholm where second generation immigrants who are fluent in Swedish also use a form of broken Swedish in certain situations (Kotsinas 1988a, 1988b), and they even have a special name for this language. Cases like these may be called a pidgin, if they form targets for second language learning.

Also, there have to be two or more language groups who use the pidgin. If a form of broken language is used only by group A in their contacts with B, and not by B in their contacts with A, it is probably not a pidgin but either a form of foreigner talk (see chapters 8 and 12), or an imperfectly learned second language. An example of the first is Eskimo foreigner talk, where Eskimos in some cases deliberately simplify the highly complex morphology of their native tongue in dealing with foreigners (see chapter 8). An example of the latter is Trader Navaho, a simplified form of Navaho used only by European traders and not by the Navaho Indians themselves (Voegelin *et al.* 1967). Neither of these speech forms, though simplified, can be called pidgins. The use of pidgins is often limited to certain situations, e.g. trade, or communication among multilingual communities without a common language.

A number of pidgins are not limited in use as they have become the most widespread languages in their area. These extended pidgins are used in so many situations that they have become stabilized and structurally quite complex, especially when also spoken as first languages, i.e. **nativized**. It appears that in such cases it is often hard to decide on the status of these languages; this cannot be decided on the basis of the structure alone, which is often creole-like. This may be because the pidgin was already fairly elaborated when it became a first language. In these cases, nativization as such will have had little effect on the structure of the language, although stabilization and nativization generally do have structural consequences for pidgins (Hancock 1980). Apparently, the criterion whether or not a language is learned as a mother tongue is not sufficient to allow us to distinguish pidgins and creoles structurally.

A pidgin may be spoken alongside the language from which it is lexically derived. For instance, quite a few speakers of the **extended pidgin** called West African Pidgin English also speak English, and speakers of Chinook Jargon included native speakers of Chinook. In most cases, pidgins are rather variable. They usually have low prestige.

## 3.3 Types of pidgins

Pidgins may be classified according to the social situation in which they are used most often.

### 3.3.1 Maritime or nautical pidgins

Maritime or nautical pidgins came into being as the result of sailors communicating with people from other nations, either aboard ships, or with people living on coasts. Some examples are (a) the Lingua Franca, the Romance-based pidgin used all over the Mediterranean in interethnic contacts, at least from the Middle Ages onward (Schuchardt 1909); it became extinct only in this century; (b) the Basque-lexifier pidgin of Iceland and the Basque-Algonquian pidgins in contacts between Europeans and Indians of eastern North America of the 16th and 17th century (Bakker 1989); (c) the Russenorsk of Russian and Norwegian sailors around the North Cape in the 19th and 20th century (Broch & Jahr 1984).

### 3.3.2 Trade pidgins

It is not always easy to draw the line between a maritime pidgin and a trade pidgin, since maritime pidgins are often used for trading. Pidgin Eskimo of the Arctic Ocean, for instance, was used mainly in and around the American whaling ships in the 19th and early 20th century, and it was often used for trade between the Inuit (Eskimos) and the ships' crews. Chinese Pidgin English, spoken from 1715 (the first text is from 1743) until recently on the China coast in contacts between Chinese and Europeans, is more of a trade pidgin than a maritime pidgin, though spoken exclusively in sea ports. Some pidgins were used for trading also in the interior, such as Pidgin Ojibwe (an Amerindian language) used among Indians, and later also by Europeans around 1800 in the Western Great Lakes area in North America.

### 3.3.3  Interethnic contact languages

Other pidgins were used not just for trade, but also in a wide variety of other domains, such as the spread of religion, political negotiations, or ceremonies involving people with no common language. One could mention here the Amerindian-lexifier pidgins such as Chinook Jargon of the American Northwest (19th and 20th century), Delaware Jargon (17th century) and Mobilian Jargon (late 17th to 20th century). In Africa we have interethnic contact languages like Pidgin A-70, based on the African language Ewondo used in and around southern Cameroon.

### 3.3.4  Work force pidgins

Two kinds of pidgins came into being in work situations. First, there are pidgins which owe their existence to the contacts between colonial people and local workers in their household, such as Butler English and Bamboo English in India (Hosali & Aitchison 1985). Another example may be Fanagalo, a still widely used pidgin based on Zulu, which is used between white South Africans and their black personnel. It is also used in the mines of South Africa, Zimbabwe, and Zambia. Other pidgins developed in multilingual work forces, often for western colonial or industrial enterprises outside Europe (cf. Samarin 1987b), including slavery, of course. Examples are the Hawaiian-lexifier and English-lexifier pidgins of Hawaii, used in the harbor, and later on the plantations in the 19th and early 20th century, or the Japanese-Malay pidgin of the pearlers in Australia.

### 3.3.5  Further functions

Apart from those mentioned above, there are other functions of pidgins. There are songs in Chinook Jargon, for instance. Fishermen in British Columbia have used Chinook Jargon occasionally in ship-to-ship radio communication to hide information from Japanese fishermen. Some pidgins may have been purposely developed and used to keep trading partners from understanding the non-pidginized language, e.g. by the Delaware Indians (Thomason 1980).

## 3.4  Genesis and status

Under what social circumstances does a pidgin come into being? Typically, pidgins arise in situations of language contact, as we have stated above, when people who require to communicate do not speak each other's languages. These may be colonization, exploration, trade, or multilingual work-force situations. The different circumstances may produce different linguistic outcomes.

The most obvious way of solving the communication gap in situations lacking a shared language is the use of gestures and signs, as well as sound imitations. This strategy has been used by traders and explorers all over the world (Hewes 1974), especially in the early contact phase. It is possible that such gestures develop into a full fledged sign language, comparable to the sign languages used in deaf communities, which are complete communication systems. This happened in the Central Plains in North America, where a sophisticated sign language developed for intertribal communication (Samarin 1987a).

It is possible that people adopt words they have picked up from the other groups they are in contact with. In this way a **trade jargon** can develop. This may be rudimentary, with a very limited vocabulary, restricted to messages like 'give me this', 'what do you want?' 'a little bit'. If contact continues, this jargon develops into a more structured language, which we could call a pidgin. Jargons and pidgins usually do not have stable vocabularies or stable grammatical systems. A jargon or pidgin is often characterized by the attrition of morphological markers such as verb inflection or case endings. Often a series of word stems is just strung together. In a jargon, often only a limited number of subjects can be discussed, such as trading and bartering and the goods involved. This is of course highly dependent on the function of the contact language. If the pidgin has a restricted function, the vocabulary will be more limited. But it can easily be expanded. There is no strict delimitation between a jargon and a pidgin; both are part of a continuum.

Whinnom (1971) claimed that at least three different languages must be in contact in order for a pidgin or creole to emerge (a process he called **tertiary hybridization**). For pidgins, this has been proven to be untrue. In many cases there were just two groups involved, such as the Micmacs and the Basques, the Yimas and the Arafundi, the Vietnamese and the French, etc. In Russenorsk the two main groups were Russians and Norwegians, although there was also influence from other language groups, such as Saami, Dutch and English (Broch & Jahr 1984).

Social circumstances leave their mark on the form of the resulting pidgins. Most pidgins, just like the vast majority of creoles, have a lexicon derived almost exclusively from one language, so that we can justifiably speak of, for instance, Vietnamese Pidgin French, or Hottentot Pidgin Dutch. However, when two groups of equal status come into contact, the lexicon will be derived from both languages in roughly equal proportions. The most obvious examples are Russenorsk and Trio-Ndjuka Pidgin (De Goeje 1908, Huttar 1982). One could term these '50-50 pidgins' or 'mixed pidgins' (see chapter 26), to distinguish them. Their lexicons are mixed in an arbitrary fashion. In a list of pidgin words for tools in Trio-Ndjuka Pidgin of Surinam eight words are from Ndjuka (fishhook, cudgel, scissors, pin, needle, fan, pot, basket, plate) and nine from Trio (bow, arrow, arrowhead, cartridge, axe, machete, knife and again scissors) (Huttar 1982: 9). Often one entity can be expressed by words from both languages (like *scissors* in Trio-Ndjuka Pidgin).

Pidgins can exist for extended periods, in some cases even several centuries. Pidgins will naturally disappear when contacts cease to exist, often without leaving a trace. Pidgins can but need not disappear when there is sufficient bilingualism. With a growing intensification of the contacts, some people (for instance those who usually do the talking, or the offspring of mixed marriages) will often become bilingual. These people may act as interpreters. If a pidgin exists for a long period the structure will tend to become more fixed, and new grammatical categories may develop. Stable pidgins no longer have the communicative limitations that non-extended pidgins have.

Many existing pidgins have become stable or extended pidgins, such as Pacific Pidgin English and West African Pidgin English. There are also contact situations in which pidgins are still used, such as the Sino-Russian Pidgin which is still used on the Chinese-Russian border, and Fanagalo and Fly-taal (related to Afrikaans) in South Africa. Pidgin Malay is still widely spoken in Irian Jaya (West Papua).

The number of speakers of a pidgin can range from a handful (e.g. the male members of one trading family among the Yimas who have the monopoly of trade with a certain neighboring tribe), or less than one hundred (such as Eskimo Pidgin French in Labrador, East Canada in the 18th century), up to more than 100.000 people, like Fanagalo in South Africa, and early this century perhaps also Chinook Jargon. Pidgin Assamese is spoken by almost half a million people in Nagaland, India. West African Pidgin English in Nigeria has more than 20 million speakers.

Some pidgins are used in print. Bible translations have appeared in West African Pidgin English. Pidgin Assamese or Naga Pidgin (Sreedhar 1974) is the official language of Nagaland, and educational material in the language exists. There is still a quarterly magazine in Chinook Jargon (and much more material in this language from early this century), weeklies in Tok Pisin, and more.

Not all pidgins are transmitted only orally. Many Chinese learned Chinese Pidgin English through Chinese character phrase books. The writing even influenced the form of the pidgin: the use of *my* as a personal pronoun became widespread after it was used as such in one phrase book (Baker & Mühlhäusler 1990).

## 3.5 Linguistic features of pidgins

Despite the diversity of pidgins, a number of structural generalizations can be made. Their morphology is simplified, but nevertheless present, any word order is possible, while the phonology may or may not be simplified and the lexicon is reduced but rarely mixed.

### 3.5.1 Morphology

Pidgins have **reduced inflectional and derivational morphology** as compared to the source languages. This is about the only thing pidgins and creoles have in common (but see Muysken 1994). In cases of the pidginization of languages with little inflectional marking (like most European colonial languages), inflection will be totally absent, as in Chinese Pidgin English:

(1)　Boy!　makee　pay　my　that　two　piecee　book.　(Chinese Pidgin English)
　　　boy　make　give　1SG　that　two　CLASS　book
　　　'Give me those two books, boy!'
　　　(1860; cited in Baker & Mühlhäusler 1990: 99)

If there is productive inflection in the lexifier language, two patterns can be used in pidgins based on such languages. Either one inflected verb form is used for all persons, tenses, etc., or the bare stem is used for all forms. In both cases independent pronouns will indicate the grammatical roles of the participants. Chileno, Amerindian pidgin Spanish of California (Bartelt 1992), is an example of the first. Where Spanish has (2a), Chileno has (2b):

(2)　a.　Tene-mos　hambre.　(Spanish)
　　　　　have-1PL　hunger
　　　b.　Nosóotros　tiyéene　ʔáamre　(Chileno; Amerindian Pidgin Spanish)
　　　　　1PL　　　have-3SG　hunger
　　　　　'We are hungry.'

An example of a pidgin with inflectional morphology is the pidginized form of Ojibwe (an Algonquian language), which was used in the early 19th century by several Indian tribes in Wisconsin in their dealings with Europeans (Nichols 1993). The full Ojibwe form for 'he is afraid of me' would be:

(3)　a.　Ni-gos-ig　(Ojibwe)
　　　　　1SG-fear-INV.3SG.SUBJ
　　　　　'He fears me.'

In Ojibwe, the so-called 'inverse marker' *-ig* is suffixed to the animate stem *gos-* or *kos-* 'fear (an animate entity)', and a first person prefix precedes this. This inverse marker is used when a third person subject acts on a non-third object. In the pidgin, however, the **inanimate** verb stem is used and the object is expressed by an independent pronoun instead of an affix. Inanimate verbs and independent pronouns are always used in this pidgin, even for animate actors. So the pidgin form is:

(3)    b.    O-kot-aan                niin.                                          (Broken Oghibbeway)
              3SG.AN-fear-3.INAN       ISG
              'He fears me.'

In this pidgin example the verb 'fear' is indeed morphologically complex, since it has the regular Ojibwe third person prefix *o-* as well as the inanimate object suffix *-aan*. The stem *kot-* is the inanimate form ('fear an inanimate entity') of the animate stem *kos-*.

All pidgins known to date have at least some derivational morphology. Pidgin morphology is however always simplified compared to the morphological system(s) of the lexifier language(s). Chinese Pidgin English has the bound morphemes *-said* (< side), *-taim* (< time); Russenorsk has the suffix *-man* to denote nationality or social group (e.g. *filman* 'Lapp'), and this list could easily be expanded. Some of the same morphemes are also attested as morphological elements in creoles (see for example the suffix *-ma(n)* in Sranan and Saramaccan in chapters 14 and 18).

Other pidgins have affixes which distinguish nouns from verbs. In the Basque-lexifier pidgins of Iceland and Canada of the 17th century, all nouns and adjectives are marked with the suffixed Basque definite article *-a*, even when this would be ungrammatical in Basque, e.g.

(4)    Presenta  for    mi    berrua   usnia eta    berria bura       (Icelandic Pidgin Basque)
       give      to     me    warm     milk  and    new    butter

       eman    ieza-da-zu        esne   bero-a       eta     gurin    berri-a       (Basque)
       give    IMPER-ISG-2SG     milk   warm-DET     and     butter   new-DET
       'Give me the warm milk and new butter.'

Notice also that the orders of noun and adjective differ in Basque and the pidgin.

Further examples would be that in Icelandic Pidgin French all verbs end in *-er*, in Russenorsk most verbs end in *-um*, in Hottentot Pidgin Dutch in *um/om* and in American Indian Pidgin English and in post-1830 Chinese Pidgin English verbs end in *-im* or *-əm*. In Russenorsk, many nouns end in *-a*. Similarly, in Vietnamese Pidgin French the verbs end in *-er*, derived from the French infinitive marker *-er*. This ending is also used with French-derived verbs which do not have this ending. Thus, *savoir* becomes *saver* and *vendre* becomes *vender* in this pidgin.

An example of a pidgin which does have inflectional bound morphemes is Fanagalo of southern Africa, which has a past tense suffix, a passive suffix, a causative suffix on the verb and class prefixes on the noun, all apparently derived from the southern African languages (Nguni) Xhosa or Zulu. Nevertheless, its morphology is clearly much less complex than that of the lexifier language. Another example is the Trio-Ndjuka Pidgin, which has taken the inflectional suffix *-mee* (translative/essive, roughly a copula) and the negative suffix *-wa* from Trio. Compare example (5) (where the italicized elements are from Trio):

(5)  *Panakiri* so kong,  *pai,*  mooi-*mee*  kong,  krasji-*wa,*  *oli* wanni-*wa.*
     white    so come,  friend,  good-ESS  come,  fight-NEG,  child want-NEG
     'The white people are coming, friend, they are coming in peace, they will not fight, they will not take the children.'

The morphological process of reduplication is common (but not universal) in creole languages, but, strangely enough, rare in pidgins as a productive process, even where one of the contributing languages is rich in reduplication. Only in Fanagalo and Naga Pidgin does it seem to be productive, and both are extended pidgins. In Vietnamese Pidgin French and Chinese Pidgin English reduplication is very rare, although in Vietnamese reduplication is about the only derivational/inflectional process.

Most pidgins show a **reduced number of grammatical markers** compared to the lexifier language. The reduced number of grammatical words is closely connected with the absence of morphology, since bound morphemes generally express grammatical meanings. An example is Nauru Pidgin English, spoken on the tiny Pacific island of Nauru (Siegel 1990:168).

(6)  Mí hásıbən fl̃ɛn   nó   wáɪfu.  fínıši dáɪ  tín  yía  (Nauru Pidgin English)
     1SG husband friend  no   wife.   finish die  ten  year
     'My husband's friend has no wife. (She) died ten years ago.'

As a consequence of the above reduction processes, pidgin languages are more **analytic** than their lexifier languages. Pidgins typically have short words and these words are typically morphologically simple.

### 3.5.2 Word order

Whereas virtually all creole languages have strict SVO order, there is more **variation in basic**

**word order** among pidgins. This is the major difference between pidgins and creoles. In some pidgins, SVO order is the only one used, but there are also quite a few strict SOV pidgins such as Trio-Ndjuka Pidgin, Hottentot Pidgin Dutch and English (formerly in South Africa), Hiri Motu (a pidgin based on a Papuan language from Papua New Guinea) and Yokohama Pidgin Japanese. Even then, the possibilities are not exhausted. Mobilian Jargon (a pidgin based on the Muskogean Amerindian languages Choctaw and Chickasaw, formerly spoken in the American Southwest) has OSV order and Micmac Pidgin English (Amerindian in Canada) has OVS order. Some alternate between SOV and SVO, such as Russenorsk, Fiji Pidgin Hindustani and Eskimo Pidgin (for the latter, see chapter 12). Some examples:

Fanagalo, Zulu-lexifier pidgin spoken in southern Africa; (Mesthrie 1989: 235)

(7)    Mina  chena  ena   first,  mina  ai    az    khuluma  gagle  lo    English.    (SVO)
       1SG   tell   them  first,  1SG   not   can   speak    well   the   English
       'I told them first that I couldn't speak English well.'

Micmac Indian Pidgin English, East Canada (Webster 1894, Bakker 1991a)

(8)    'Long time ago, when Indian first makum God.'    (OVS)

Mobilian Jargon (Crawford 1978)

(9)    Tamaha   olčifo   inu   hakalo   banna.    (OSV)
       town     name     1SG   hear     want
       'I want to hear the name of the town.'

Sino-Russian Pidgin (Nichols 1980: 402)

(10)   Ryba   lovi   ponimaj   toče   netu.    (SOV)
       fish   catch  know-how  also   not
       '(I) don't know how to fish either.'

Delaware Jargon, Unami Delaware-lexifier Pidgin (Northeastern United States, 17th century) (Thomason 1980) has variable order:

(11)   a.  Kee    squa     og     enychan  hatah?    (SOV)
           2SG    woman    and    child    have
           'Hast thou wife and children?'

       b.  Nee    hata     orit        poonk    og...    (SVO)
           1SG    have     it-is-good  powder   and
           'I have good powder and...'

It is also sometimes the case that the order of adjectives and nouns, for instance, is different in the pidgin and the lexifier language. This could be seen in example (4), from Icelandic Pidgin Basque. In all these cases, the word order of the pidgin is identical to that of at least one of the languages involved in the contact.

### 3.5.3 Phonology

As a rule, the phonological system of pidgins is simplified as compared to the source language. For example, Fijian fricatives /ß/ and /ð/ become stops /b/ and /d/ in Pidgin Fijian, and the Zulu and Xhosa clicks become pulmonic stops in Fanagalo. Further, consonant clusters may be simplified, or adjusted to the phonotactics of the mother tongue of the speaker.

The fact that speakers generally adjust words to the phonological system of their first language, means that in some cases, different groups may pronounce pidgin words in different ways. The voiceless lateral fricative /ɬ/ of Chinook Jargon, for instance, was more often pronounced as [l] or [tl] by European speakers.

Also, tones are usually not present in pidgins, even when the lexifiers or other languages involved have tones. Vietnamese and Chinese are tone languages, but neither Vietnamese Pidgin French nor Chinese Pidgin Russian or Chinese Pidgin English have tones. Even pidginized Sango (Central Africa), spoken almost exclusively by people who speak tone languages as their first language, does not make phonemic use of tones. The lexifier language (also called Sango) is even a tone language.

Although the phonology is often simplified, pidgin sound systems are not always simpler than the lexifier phonological systems. The phonology of Chileno (example 2), for example, is influenced by the Amerindian language Bodega Miwok, in that it has glottal stops and long vowels not inherited from Spanish. Vietnamese Pidgin French is an example of a pidgin where the phonetics cannot be claimed to be simplified French, as is shown in the following example (from Reinecke 1971:53):

| (12) | [kʊu-beɪ | dɣɯ | sɣɯ | gˈatoʊ] | (Pidgin phonetic) |
|------|----------|-----|-----|---------|-------------------|
| | [kupe | dø | sə | gato] | (French phonetic) |
| | couper | deux | ce | gateau | (French words) |
| | cut | two | this | cake | |
| | 'Divide these two cakes equally.' | | | | |

This probably reflects the phonology of Vietnamese. It may sound differently when spoken by Europeans.

### 3.5.4 Lexicon

Pidgins rarely display a mixture of different languages in their vocabularies. Generally, the lexicon has one basic source. There may be some words from other languages as well, but this is usually similar to borrowing in other languages. Only very few pidgins (and creoles) show abnormal mixture of vocabulary. One pidgin word may have several equivalents in non-pidgin languages. In Chinook Jargon, for instance, the word *muckamuck* means 'eat, drink, bite' and more. Often fewer words are used, as many function words are omitted. Compare the following sentences in Pidgin Hawaiian and Hawaiian proper (Bickerton & Wilson 1987: 63):

(13)　a.　Iapana,　makana　dala　oe　hiamoe　ma　keia　hale　wau　(Pidgin Hawaiian)
　　　　　　Japan,　gift　　dollar　2SG　sleep　　at　this　house　1SG

(14)　b.　E　ke　　Kepanī,　inā　hāʻawi　mai　ʻoe　i　　kālā,　(Hawaiian)
　　　　　　Oh　the　Japanese,　if　give　　hither　2SG　CM　money,

　　　　　　e　　hiki　iā　ʻoe　hiamoe　ma　kēia　hale　o-ʻu
　　　　　　IMP　can　CM　2SG　INF　　sleep　at　this　house　of-1SG

　　　　　　'Japanese, if you give me money you can sleep at my house.'

It is often said that pidgins use the lexicon of the language of the dominant group in the contacts. Upon scrutiny, this appears rarely to be the case, so this constitutes another important difference between pidgins and creoles. Creole languages indeed often use the lexicon of the language of the dominant group, whether it be Arabic, Dutch, English, French, Portuguese or Spanish. Pidgins, however, often show the opposite. This is clear when looking at the list of pidgins in the appendix: pidgins based on colonial languages are rare. Fanagalo, the pidgin originating with Zulu miners in South Africa, is based on Zulu/Xhosa, not on Afrikaans or English, the language of the overseers. Pidgin Fijian is not based on English, Hawaiian Pidgin was (at least in the early stages) based on Hawaiian and not English.

A number of pidgins turn out to have mixed lexicons, such as Trio-Ndjuka Pidgin (see section 3.4) and Russenorsk. These pidgins seem to have such mixed lexicons because the two groups in contact have an equal interest in the interaction, and neither of the two is dominant. The following example from Russenorsk shows the mixed nature of the Russenorsk lexicon. Russian words are bold and Norwegian words are italicized.

(15)　**Kak**　ju　wil　*skaffom*　ja　*drikke*　te,　(Russenorsk)
　　　　what　2SG　want　eat　　　and　drink　　tea

**davaj** på  *sjib*  **tvoja**   *ligge  ne*  jes  på  slipom.
please on  ship  2SG=POSS  lie  down and  on  sleep
'If you want to eat and drink tea, then come on board and lie down to sleep.'
(*ju, jes* and *slipom* are English, *skaffom* is international nautical jargon – perhaps from Dutch
*schaften* – and *på* is both Russian and Norwegian)

It has also been documented, although not as fully yet as one would wish, that pidgins can
change their lexical affiliation. Pidgin Hawaiian seems to have been absorbed into Hawaiian
Pidgin English, and the lexicon of Chinook Jargon became largely English in the early part
of this century.

### 3.5.5 TMA marking

The marking of tense, mood and aspect (TMA) by means of pre-verbal 'particles' is one of
the most conspicuous features of creole languages (see chapter 20). In pidgins, however,
we encounter nothing of this kind. These features are marked in a different way from both
the contributing languages and from creoles, with the exception of some of the extended
pidgins as West African Pidgin English and Pacific Pidgin English. There are no preverbal
TMA particles in pidgins, except some marginal cases in Chinese Pidgin English.

In many pidgins, such as Chinese Pidgin English and Hottentot Pidgin Dutch, the
context has to show whether an utterance is referring to the past, present or future. Explicit
references can be made by adding **temporal adverbs**, like *today, before, later, tomorrow, soon,
already* etc. (cf. Den Besten 1987: 19):

(16)  Before my  sell-um  for  ten  dollar.          (Chinese Pidgin English)
  PAST  1SG  sell  for  ten  dollar
  'I sold it for ten dollars.'

(17)  Ons  soek  kost  hier,  ons al  gedaen  wegloopen.  (Hottentot Pidgin Dutch)
  1PL  seek  food  here  1PL already  done  run-away
  'We are looking for food here, we ran away.'

Remote past is indicated in CPE by a phrase like 'beefo tim wun moon' or 'before time one
moon'. Another example is Vietnamese Pidgin French (Reinecke 1971), where time can be
indicated by time adverbs rather than by the form of the verb:

(18)  Moi  bouver  thé  jour  avant.          (Vietnamese Pidgin French)
  1SG  drink  tea  day  before
  'I was drinking tea yesterday.'

(19)    Demain      moi   bouver   thé   avec   ami.                          (Vietnamese Pidgin French)
        tomorrow    1SG   drink    tea   with   friend
        'Tomorrow I shall drink tea with my friend(s).'

The marking of **aspect** is often lost in pidgins, even if the lexifier language has an elaborate aspect system. Neither is a new aspect system developed, as in creoles. For example Russenorsk and Chinese Pidgin Russian have no aspect marking, although aspect is an important grammatical category in Russian. Not enough research has been done on the lexical expression of aspect in pidgins, but if present at all, it does not appear to be as conspicuous as in creoles. Extended pidgins often do have elaborate aspect systems. In example (6), for instance, the element 'finish' seems to denote perfective aspect.

## 3.6  Some structural differences between pidgins and creoles

It is often said that creoles derive from pidgins: pidgins become creole languages (having different properties) once learnt by children, or used in the full range of speech situations. It may well be reasonable to hypothesize a pidgin origin for creole languages. The problem is that we do not have any historical evidence for any Caribbean creole language or Indian Ocean creole being preceded by a pidgin. It is true that early sources of Jamaican, Guyanese or Sranan show pidgin-like traits such as the absence of TMA marking (Arends 1989), but whether this is a reflection of an earlier pidgin stage, or just a case of poor observation is not clear. Further it is possible that creoles only gradually acquired their typological traits (cf. Jourdan 1991, Arends 1989, chapter 10 of this volume). In the Pacific there is documentation of both stages, but there appears to be hardly any structural difference between the varieties spoken as first languages by children and those spoken as second languages by adults. For example, Tok Pisin as a first language is not radically different from extended Tok Pisin spoken as a second language. It changed much more radically during its expansion process than during its nativization (Sankoff and Laberge 1974).

The only language where there is documentation of both a pidgin and a creole stage may be Hawaii English (Bickerton 1981 and elsewhere), if indeed the English speech of elderly people in the 1970s can be taken as representative of their speech early this century, when they were working on the plantations.

It appears that pidgins and creoles (as far as we can identify these as representing distinct types of languages) have few structural traits in common. Some of the most important structural differences were discussed above and are summarized here.

–   Whereas all creole languages have SVO word order, pidgins can have any conceivable word order, including variable order.

–  Time is expressed by adverbs, if at all, in pidgins but mostly by preverbal elements in creoles.
–  Reduplication is a common, almost universal process in creole languages, but it is rare in pidgins, though common in extended pidgins.

## 3.7  Conclusion

In this chapter we have seen that pidgins are a heterogeneous type of language, much more so than creole languages. Pidgins have very few of the typical structural properties of creole languages (although extended pidgins share more features with creole languages). The social circumstances under which they come into being play a major role, both in the shaping of the structure and in the source(s) of the pidgin lexicon. Pidgins are more often based on local languages than on colonial languages. The number of attested pidgins based on English, Dutch, French and Portuguese in the world is strikingly small. We cannot be certain whether such pidgins simply were not documented, or whether they did not exist.

### Further reading
There is no book devoted to pidgins in general, just one devoted to pidgins in the Arctic: Broch & Jahr (1994) and one dealing with Bantu contact languages (Heine 1973). There is a large number of articles on different pidgins, but few comparative studies. There are, however, a few monographs on pidgins (such as Crawford 1978 and Drechsel 1997 on Mobilian Jargon) and the extended pidgins of the Pacific and West Africa, such as Barbag-Stoll (1983), Mühlhäusler (1979), Todd (1982) and Keesing (1988). Samarin (1987b) and Foley (1988) are articles on pidgin genesis. Holm (1988) contains short sketches of the best known pidgins, and useful further references.

# 4 Mixed languages and language intertwining

Peter Bakker and Pieter Muysken

## 4.1 Introduction

This chapter is about languages in which the morpho-syntax of one language is matched with the vocabulary of another language. They are not creoles or pidgins in the strict sense, but they may shed light on the genesis of these languages as well. We will begin with a few examples.

Angloromani is the language of tens of thousands of Gypsies in Britain, the Unites States and Australia. The grammar (phonology, morphology, syntax) is English, but the words are overwhelmingly of Gypsy or Romani (Indic) origin. The following example, with Romani elements italicized, is from Smart & Crofton (1875: 218-221). In this example, and in the following, we will give the examples in the mixed language as well as in the two source languages.

(1)  *Palla  bish  besh*-es  *apopli* the  *Beng wel'*d  and  *pen'*d:  (Angloromani)
    after  20  year-s  again  the  Devil  came  and  said
    *Av*  with  *man-di*.
    come  with  me-DAT
    Palla  bish  besh-aw  apopli  o  Beng  vi-as.  Yov  pen-das:
    after  20  year-PL  again  the  Devil  come-3.PA  He  say-3.PA
    Av  man-tsa.  (British, inflected Romani)
    come  me-with
    'After twenty years the Devil came back and said: come with me.'

When Angloromani was first discussed by language contact specialists, it was related to creole languages (Hancock 1970), which are also said to have a different origin of lexicon and grammatical system.

Media Lengua (Ecuador) is another example. Virtually all the lexemes (italicized) are of Spanish origin, whereas the grammar is almost identical to that of the local Quechua.

(2)  *Yo*-ga  *awa*-bi  *kay*-mu-ni.  (Media Lengua)
    I-TO  water-LO  fall-CI-1

Ñuka-ga  yaku-bi  urma-mu-ni.                                              (Quechua)
I-TO      water-LO  fall-CI-I
Vengo despues de caer en el agua.                                         (Spanish)
'I come after falling into the water.'

Muysken (1981b) claimed that the lexical shapes of Quechua content words have been replaced by Spanish ones.

Ma'a or Mbugu (Tanzania) posed some problems for language classification, as it was sometimes classified as Bantu and sometimes as Cushitic (Goodman 1971). The grammatical system is virtually identical to the neighboring Bantu languages, but the lexicon of content words is overwhelmingly of Cushitic origin (Thomason 1983). In the following example, Bantu elements are italicized (Mous 1994a):

(3)    *hé-lo*       *mw-a*-giru     *é-se-we*       Kimweri,    *dilaó  w-a*
       16NC-have    INC-CON-big    INC-call-PA=PF  Kimweri    king  INC-CON

       *yá*    *idí*    *lá*    Lusótó.
       this   5NC-land  5NC-CON  Lushoto
       'There was an elder called Kimweri, king of this land of Lushoto.'

Thomason (1983) and Thomason & Kaufman (1988) took this language as being the result of massive grammatical replacement: the original Cushitic grammar had been replaced by Bantu grammar.

We have now looked at three cases of languages with a lexicon originating from a language different from that of the grammatical system. We propose one single general process as being responsible for the genesis of these three languages and the others like them. We call this **language intertwining**, which should be taken to be a type of language genesis different from cases like creolization or pidginization, and also from lexical borrowing and language shift. Language intertwining is a process which creates new languages which have roughly the following characteristics:

(4)    An intertwined language has lexical morphemes from one language and grammatical mor-
       phemes from another.

Media Lengua is spoken by people whose parents are Indians who spoke only Quechua, therefore the Spanish **lexical** elements must have been introduced into Quechua. In the case of Angloromani, the speakers are Gypsies who formerly spoke Romani; therefore the English (**grammatical**) elements seem to be the intruding element. The same holds for the Ma'a speakers, who are ethnohistorically Cushitic, and here as well the grammatical elements are what appears to have been added. While historically there would seem to be two different processes, they still lead to similar results. We claim that on a more abstract level, they are one and the same: intertwining a grammar and a lexicon from different sources. There is no reason to suppose that two entirely different processes would lead to the same type of mixed language, viz. massive grammatical replacement in the case of AngloRomani and Ma'a (as Thomason & Kaufman argue) and relexification in the case of Media Lengua.

Before we can explore the process of intertwining, we will need to look at several intertwined languages in more detail.

## 4.2. Media Lengua (Quechua grammar, Spanish lexicon)

The variety of Media Lengua (ML, lit. 'half language' or 'halfway language') described here is spoken natively by up to a thousand people in Central Ecuador (Muysken 1979, 1981b, 1988b, in press a.). Further examples of Media Lengua utterances are given in (5) and (6), with the (b) examples giving the regional Quechua equivalent, and the (c) examples the regional Spanish equivalent. A first example is:

(5)  a.  *Unu  fabur*-ta  *pidi*-nga-bu  *bini*-xu-ni.                (Media Lengua)
         one   favor-AC  ask-FN-BN    come-PR-I

     b.  Shuk fabur-da  maña-nga-bu   shamu-xu-ni.                  (Quechua)
         one   favor-AC  ask-FN-BN     come-PR-I

     c.  Veng-o      para  ped-ir   un   favor.                    (Spanish)
         come-1SG    to    ask-INF  a    favor

         'I come to ask a favor.'

It is clear that (5a) has resulted from combining the phonological shapes of the stems in (5c) with the grammar and lexical entries in (5b). Thus *shuk* is replaced by *unu*, *maña*- by *pidi*-, etc. Several things should be noted. First, we get an emphatic form of the indefinite article in Media Lengua, *unu*, rather than Spanish unemphatic *un*. Second, the Spanish irregular verb form *vengo* appears in a regularized stem form *bini*. Third, the Quechua rule voicing the accusative case marker -*ta* to -*da* after *fabur* has not applied in Media Lengua; Quechua dialectological evidence suggests that this is a recent rule. Fourth, the Spanish forms have been adapted phonologically to Quechua; mid vowels have been replaced by high vowels. Quechua word order and morphology have been retained.

(6)   a.   Kuyi-buk   *yirba*   *nuwabi*-shka.                                          (Media Lengua)
            cavia-BN   grass   there.is.not-SD

      b.   Kuyi-buk   k'iwa illa-shka.                                                 (Quechua)
            cavia-BN   grass   there.is.not-SD

      c.   No   hay   hierba   para   los   cuy-es.                                     (Spanish)
            NEG   there-s   grass   for   the-PL   cavia-PL

      'There turns out to be no grass for the guinea pigs.'

Note that the Quechua word *kuyi* 'guinea pig' appears in the local Spanish as well. The Media Lengua verb maintains the Quechua-specific 'sudden discovery tense' marking *-shka*. The Quechua negative existential verb stem *illa-* has been replaced by a newly formed 'frozen' stem *nuwabi-*, derived from Spanish *no* and *haber* 'have'. The Spanish verb 'have' has an impersonal form *hay* which also has existential meaning.

To summarize, Media Lengua is essentially the product of replacing the phonological shapes of Quechua stems with Spanish forms, maintaining the rest of the Quechua structure. The Spanish forms chosen have undergone regularization and adaptation to Quechua morphophonology. Media Lengua is conservative in sometimes reflecting earlier stages in Quechua pronunciation. It is not made up on the spot every time it is spoken. The occurrence of Spanish strong alternants (cf. Spanish *unu*), frozen composites (cf. *nuwabi-*), etc. is an indication that we do not have a simple process of vocabulary replacement here.

What is peculiar about Media Lengua is not so much that it contains Spanish words, but that almost *all* Quechua words, including all core vocabulary, have been replaced. All Quechua dialects borrowed heavily from Spanish, up to roughly 40%, but there are no dialects which borrowed more than 40%. Thus there is an enormous gap between the 40% of hispanicized Quechua dialects and the over 90% of Media Lengua.

Muysken (1981b) proposed that Media Lengua had come into being via a process of **relexification**: the replacement of the phonological shape of a root of one language (Quechua) by a root with roughly the same meaning from another language (Spanish). There were several reasons for supposing a process of borrowing of Spanish vocabulary into Quechua rather than the borrowing of Quechua affixes and grammar into Spanish. In the first place, borrowing of roots is much more common than borrowing of affixes – the latter is hardly possible without preceding massive lexical borrowing. Second, the Spanish roots sometimes have semantic properties identical to the replaced Quechua root. Thus Media Lengua *sinta-* 'live, exist, be in a certain place, sit' has the whole range of meanings of Quechua *tiya-* rather than that of Spanish *sentar(se)* 'to sit, sit down'.

Media Lengua is not the product of an interlanguage frozen and fixed, resulting from communicative needs; it is not used with outsiders, but it isn't a secret language either.

Rather it is an ordinary, day to day, community-level form of communication.

The Media Lengua-speaking communities studied here are located on the fringe of a Quechua-speaking area, to which the community historically belonged. Due to its geographical situation, and due to the necessity and opportunities for its inhabitants to make frequent trips to the capital to look for work, the community has come to be culturally differentiated from neighboring areas to the extent that its people find it necessary to set themselves apart from the neighbors. Between 1900 and 1920, the capital of Quito expanded enormously, and many Indian construction workers from the relevant area were employed there. It is possibly this group of migrant construction workers who started the process of relexification. Now, however, many people who never worked in construction speak Media Lengua as well.

## 4.3  Michif (Cree grammar, French lexicon)

Michif is a mixture of Cree and French which is spoken by fewer than 1000 people of Cree and French ancestry in Western Canada and in North Dakota and Montana, United States. Cree is the name of an Amerindian nation and their language, which belongs to the Algonquian language family. The Michif have considered themselves to be members of the Métis or Michif ('Mestizo') Nation since around 1800. The word *Michif* is an anglicized spelling of the Métis pronunciation of the French word *Métif.*

The Michif language differs in a way from the cases discussed here: it is often described as having Cree verbs and French nouns (cf. Thomason and Kaufman 1988, Rhodes 1977). Bakker (1992) calculates that between 83 and 94% French nouns and between 88 and 99% Cree verbs are used, depending on the community. It has been argued, however, that the real dichotomy between the two language components in Michif is that the grammatical system is Cree and the lexicon French (Bakker 1990, 1992). The verbs are claimed there to consist of only bound morphemes and are therefore always in Cree (cf. Goddard 1990). It is therefore a case of language intertwining, be it deviant because of the polysynthetic structure of Cree. Some examples of Michif from Bakker's field notes can be found in the sentences:

(7)  Kî-nipi-yi-wa     *son*     *frère*     aspin kâ-*la-petite-fille*-iwi-t.
     ST-die-OBV-3SG   his/her   brother   since  COMP-the-little-girl-be-3SG
     'Her brother died when she was a young girl.'

(8)  *John*   kî-wêyisim-êw   *Irene*-a     *dans*   *sa*     *maison*   kâ-pihtikwê-yi-t.
     John    PA-lure-3S.3O   Irene-OBV    in      3SG     house     COMP-enter-OB-3SG
     'John lured Irene into his house.'

In these examples we see that all the verbs are Cree. All the nouns (and nominal modifiers such as possessives) are French, and the proper noun 'Irene' in (8) has a Cree nominal marker for obviation (a third person noun phrase that is not a topic).

In Michif, nouns, numerals, definite and indefinite articles, possessive pronoun, some adverbs and adjectives are from French, but demonstratives, question words, verbs and some adverbs and (verb-like) adjectives are from Cree. Whereas French words can appear with Cree morphology, the opposite is not the case. Both languages retain their own phonological systems.

## 4.4  Ma'a (Bantu grammar, Cushitic lexicon)

Ma'a is spoken by approximately 12,000 people in the Usumbara district in north-eastern Tanzania, close to the Kenya border (Goodman 1971). It has been little studied so far in any detail. Mous (1994, to appear) is doing systematic fieldwork on the language. While there is still some disagreement about the specific provenance of certain elements, the structure of Ma'a is clear in general. Most of the basic lexicon is Cushitic but the noun class and verbal inflection system is Bantu, as is the word order.

Ma'a has been looked at from the perspective of language contact studies by several researchers, notably Goodman (1971) and Thomason (1983). Goodman hypothesizes that it came about through gradual convergence of the Bantu and Cushitic languages spoken in a bilingual community, and that there may have been simplification as well. He does not exclude imperfect second language learning of both component languages by yet a third group (1971:252). Thomason (1983) claims that a scenario by which there was massive interference from a Bantu language in a Cushitic language is the most plausible one. The circumstances were such that speakers attempted to maintain their Cushitic language while being under intense cultural pressure from a Bantu language. Thomason rejects a scenario by which there was massive interference from a Cushitic language B into a Bantu language A (1983:220-1), since then 'we would again expect Ma'a basic vocabulary to be primarily of Bantu origin.' Both analyses are quite different from what we claim.

## 4.5  Krōjo or Javindo (Low Javanese grammar, Dutch lexicon)

Krōjo is the language spoken by the descendants of European (mainly Dutch) fathers and Javanese mothers (formerly?) spoken in Semarang, Java. The discussion in this section is based on De Gruiter's monograph (1990) on the language, of which the author was a speaker in his youth. *Krōjo* is a derogatory term in Javanese for a person of mixed European – Indonesian ancestry (De Gruiter 1990: 17) and this is also used for this mixed language by the people who spoke it. De Gruiter prefers his coined term 'Javindo'. In addition to Javanese-related Javindo, there are other intertwined languages in Indonesia as well, which have Malay as their base.

An example of this language (from De Gruiter 1990) is (9); Dutch elements are italicized.

(9)  *Als ken-niet,* ja di-*ken-ken*-a,          wong *so*    *muulek*  kok  *sommen*-nja.
     if   can-not,  IM PAS-can=RED-IR, (EM) for   (so)   difficult  those sum-(PL)-DEM
     Nak ora isa, ya di-isa-isa-a, na wong angèl temen kok suwal an-é ekkok m-en-nja.
                                                                              (Javanese)

     Als het niet gaat, stel dan alles in het werk opdat je wel kunt, want die sommen zijn zo
     moeilijk.                                                                      (Dutch)
     'If it is not possible, try to get them done, for the sums are hard.' (-*nja* is a Malay demonstra-
     tive, -*ém* its Javanese equivalent.)

De Gruiter considers it 'a language which was structurally Javanese with as many Dutch words as possible.' (1990: 23).

## 4.6  Intertwined Romani languages

In Europe there are a number of examples of intertwined languages, mostly spoken by nomadic peoples such as (certain) Gypsies and Irish Travellers. Hancock first suggested a contact origin for Angloromani (1970, 1984a,b) and Shelta (Hancock 1974, 1984c), and Boretzky was the first who compared three languages with Romani (Gypsy) lexicon and grammars from other languages (Boretzky 1985). Bakker & Cortiade (1991) contains several studies on Romani mixed languages (Basque, Greek and Armenian) as well as a general article. Boretzky and Igla (1994) is another overview.

Romani is a language of Indic origin, most closely related to the languages of northwest India such as Punjabi. The ancestors of the Gypsies left India around the year 1000 and they arrived in Europe in the 14th century, where the language split into dialects with varying degrees of influences from Balkan languages, especially Greek, Slavonic and (in some varieties) Rumanian. Some of the Romani dialects, however, have lost the Indic and Balkan grammatical features and now have only the Romani lexicon but a different grammatical system. The cases of these Romani intertwined languages identified thus far involve Greek, English, Danish, Swedish, Norwegian, Occitan, French, Spanish, Brazilian Portuguese, Catalan, Basque, Turkish, and Western Armenian. Not all of these are well documented, however. In this section we will briefly deal with a number of the better documented Romani varieties, discussing in some more detail Basque Romani, Swedish Romani and

Spanish Romani, since these three languages are typologically rather different. Basque is a language with complex morphology, partly agglutinative and partly fusional, both in the noun and the verb. Swedish is a language with very little morphology and Spanish is an intermediate case, having fusional morphology in verbs and nouns.

Below are examples from Swedish Romani (Hancock 1992), Spanish Romani or Caló (Bright 1818), and Basque Romani (Ibarguti 1989).

(10)  Vi *trad*-ar     to      *fåron* en *vaver*    *divus*.              (Swedish Romani)
      Vi åk-er       till     stan  en annan    dag.                  (Swedish)
      we go-PRES to        town on other    day
      Dž-as ka o          foros vaver dives.                          (Romani)
      go-IPL to the       town other day
      'We('ll) go to town another day.'

(11)  Se    ha    *endiñ*-ado    el     *parné*   a la    *chai*.        (Spanish Romani)
      Se    ha    da-do       el     dinero   a la    muchacha.        (Spanish)
      one   has   give-PP      the    money    to the  girl
      E    ćha-ke   dend-ile o     love.                                (Romani)
      the girl-DAT give-PRT the    money
      'The girl was given the money.' (*parné* is R. for 'white (things)', here a metaphor for bank notes.)

(12)  *Bokalu*-ak    iya      *mau*-tu-a-n      ga-bil-tza.             (Basque Romani)
      Gose-ak      iya      hil-e-a-n       ga-bil-tza.              (Basque)
      hungry-ERG   almost   die-PERF-DET-LOC  IPL-walk-PL
      (Romani: *bokhalo* 'hungry', *merav* 'I die')
      'We are almost dying from hunger.'

For no variety is it known when the mixed Romani languages came into being. Traditional, inflected Romani was still recorded in England in the 19th century, sometimes from the same people who spoke Angloromani (Smart & Crofton 1875). In the Iberian peninsula no inflected Romani was ever recorded outside Catalonia, and the earliest sources of Caló go back to the 18th, perhaps the 17th century. A Spanish author, Martin Delrío, claimed in 1608 'that there was a language invented by [the Gypsies] to replace their native language, which they had forgotten' (cited in Pabanó 1915: 179, our translation). This suggests that Caló was already spoken in 1608, and that Indic inflected Romani was already lost by then, though memories of it were still extant.

The amount of Romani non-lexical elements varies from source to source. In Bright (1818) virtually all non-lexical elements are Spanish, whereas in Sales Mayo (1870) and De Luna (1951) many of these elements are Romani-derived. There seems to be a continuum between more and less Hispanicized versions, perhaps depending on the geographical area. This merits a much more detailed investigation than is possible within the scope of this chapter.

There is some debate as to the origin of the mixed Romani languages. Kenrick (1979) thinks that Indic inflection of Romani was gradually replaced by more and more English inflection. Hancock (1984a claims that it was a conscious creation in the 16th century, when Gypsies mixed with English speaking beggars, and he cites some early sources to substantiate this claim. Bakker & Van der Voort (1991) also claim a conscious and deliberate creation by adults, but they do not say when this could have happened. Boretzky & Igla (1994) claim that it is a consequence of partial language shift: there was a shift toward the language of the host country, and since there were still speakers of Romani, speakers could take over these Romani words which could then help create a language that could function as a secret code. Further research will be needed to choose between these equally plausible options.

## 4.7 Discussion

So far we have shown that there are mixed languages in all parts of the world and that they share a number of structural characteristics. They combine the grammatical system of one language with the lexicon from another language.

Any type of language can be involved in language intertwining. There apparently are no structural constraints that prevent the intertwining of any two languages – although the result may differ according to the typological properties of the languages involved.

The name 'intertwining' is chosen for the following reasons. It suggests an intricate mixture of two systems which are not necessarily of the same order, in this case lexicon and grammar. These two halves form an organic whole, and therefore one cannot remove one of the components without damaging the other component. None of the components can survive without the other. Furthermore, the term does not suggest a particular direction for the process, unlike 'relexification' and 'regrammaticalization' or 'massive grammatical replacement' which suggest the replacement of either the lexicon or of the grammatical system. Also, neither of the components (lexical or grammatical) in intertwining can be taken as being more important than the other. The term language intertwining is also ambiguous as to the **psycholinguistic** process and the **historical and sociolinguistic** events. These must be kept apart. Although the socio-historical facts may lead one to say that speakers of some language substituted a different grammatical system from their original one, the process of intertwining a lexicon and a grammar from two different sources can be defined independently from the historical directionality involved. For instance, the speakers of Ma'a are ethnically and historically Cushitic. Speaking from the perspective of their origin, they took over the Bantu grammatical system. Linguistically, however, there are arguments to claim that the Cushitic lexicon was adopted into a Bantu grammatical framework (M. Mous, in prep.). The term 'language intertwining' avoids confusion between the linguistic process and the sociohistorical facts.

The way in which intertwined languages are formed appears to be highly uniform. It is also possible to predict on the basis of the social background which languages will supply the lexicon and which one the grammar. The grammatical system (syntax, morphology, phonology) of the intertwined language is often derived from the language known best by the first generation of speakers, and from the language which it resembles most in its pronunciation (see below).

If an intertwined language is spoken by children of mothers speaking language X and fathers speaking language Y, the grammatical system will be the one from language X, the language of the mothers. This is the one mastered better, not only because of closer contacts with the mothers, but also because that language is spoken by the surrounding people – migrants tend to be men. This is true for all the cases where people of mixed ancestry speak an intertwined language. This also explains why there are regularly signs of simplification in the lexicon, in the sense that a number of fairly basic words are compounds or analytic constructions. In those cases the original term may have been unknown.

If a group creates an in-group language as a secret language, it will always use the grammatical system of the language of the immediate surroundings. This explains why all the intertwined languages spoken by Gypsies have a Romani lexicon and the grammatical system of the language spoken in the surrounding community, and never the other way around. For some cases it is certain that the language came into being at a time when the inflected Romani language was in serious decline (e.g. Britain, Basque Country, Greece) and only used in formulas, songs and the like. Furthermore, a lexicon is remembered longer than a more intricate grammatical system, and for this reason too the decaying language is a more likely candidate for supplying the lexicon.

The phenomenon of intertwining is hardly ever reported in the literature. Nevertheless language intertwining is not as rare as it seems. As these languages are without exception in-group languages, spoken by people who also know another language, outsiders hardly get to find out about their existence. Michif, for instance, had been spoken for at least 150 years before it was first cited in a publication. And it was only after three months of field-work on Quechua, when Muysken accidentally discovered that his hosts spoke a different language among each other when they thought he could not overhear them: Media Lengua.

Many secret languages, argots and other in-group languages of bilingual groups in all parts of the world have a large number of lexical items taken from other languages, so that these languages in extreme cases may have a grammar and lexicon from different sources. The grammar is identical to that of the environment, but the lexicon is not.

## 4.8 Social conditions

Language intertwining happens under specific historical circumstances. In the first place, the group must be bilingual when language intertwining starts. Fluent knowledge of the language that provides the lexicon is not necessary, but it has to be spoken to a reasonable degree.

Second, the resulting languages are intended as in-group languages. They are not contact languages in the sense that they are intended to bridge a communication gap between speakers of different languages.

Third, the members of the group do not identify themselves as belonging to either of the groups whose languages they speak. The Ma'a have no ties at all with Cushitic groups and no special ties with the neighboring Bantu groups. The speakers of Michif identify themselves as Métis or Michif, neither as French or French Canadian nor as Cree or Indian. The speakers of the mixed languages Krôjo/Javindo and Pecoh in Indonesia identify themselves as 'Indo-Europeanen' (from Indonesian + European), not as Dutch or Indonesian.

Not in every case does the intertwined language come into being as an expression of a new identity. In most of the Gypsy cases, a new, mixed identity played only a secondary role, if at all. Although it is an aspect of Gypsy culture to avoid intensive socializing with non-Gypsies, it can be questioned whether there were other Gypsy groups around to dissociate from. In these cases a different factor was responsible for the genesis of the intertwined language: the need to be unintelligible to outsiders. The Gypsies mostly had business contacts with non-Gypsies, and that is the situation where the intertwined language would be used (Kenrick 1979). In all cases the lexicon is Romani, and the grammatical system is the language or dialect of the non-Gypsies living in the immediate surroundings. This is not chance: by making one's in-group language sound like the language of the surrounding people, one can more easily hide the fact that one has a secret language.

The major factor, however, is that an intertwined language is an in-group language. We can actually expect similar languages to emerge between soldiers in armies protractedly residing in foreign territory, between pupils of foreign boarding schools (Smout 1988), between bilingual traders, etc., but it is unlikely that these people would consider their speech a separate language. Neither does it seem possible that they lose their ability to speak the two source languages. In short, language intertwining creates mixed languages. Intertwined languages differ from pidgins and creoles. It may well be a commoner type of language than people realize, even though few cases have been acknowledged and described.

**Further reading**

There are a few monographs relating to mixed languages: Rafferty (1982) on a Malay-Javanese mixed language, and Bakker (1997) on Michif. There are also a few comparative studies. One example is Bakker & Mous (1994). Thomason (1995) contains more detailed descriptions of these languages.

## 5.1. Introduction

For the student of pidgin and creole languages, there is no escape from addressing the problem of variation. This is due to the specific historical and social conditions that have shaped and are still shaping these languages. Of course, all languages show variation, but in the case of creole languages this variation is more visible and therefore harder to ignore for the linguist. Several factors characteristic of societies where creole languages are spoken contribute to this.

In these societies, one often finds that levels of literacy are low and that a firmly established standard language does not exist. Thus, unlike what we find in industrialized or industrializing societies where dialectal differences may be leveled under the pressure of a strong standardized national language, dialects in creole societies, especially the rural ones, show few signs of convergence.

Another characteristic feature of creole societies contributing to a distinctive kind of synchronic variation is the incidence of widespread bilingualism. Most creole languages co-exist with their lexifier languages giving rise to what is generally known as a **creole continuum** (see chapter 1). At the opposite ends of the continuum we find the variety that is closest to the local version of the lexifier language (**acrolect**) and the variety that is most divergent from the lexifier language (**basilect**/basilectal creole); in between we find transitional varieties (**mesolect**).

In this chapter it will become clear that synchronic variation, despite the serious problems it poses, can provide vital insights into (a) the development and change of creole languages; and (b) the interrelation between language variation and social identity.

## 5.2. The creole continuum

### 5.2.1. Non-discreteness and unidimensionality

To get an impression of the kind of phenomenon or situation referred to by the term **creole continuum**, consider the following series of sentences from Guyanese Creole (GC) given by Romaine (1988:158-9), who derived it from O'Donnell and Todd (1980) (figure 1, next page).

This series of sentences brings out two essential characteristics of a creole continuum: **non-discreteness** and **unidimensionality** (cf. Rickford 1987:16-30). The two extremes *mi gii am* and *I gave him* clearly belong to two different linguistic systems: GC, the basilect, and English, the acrolect, respectively. Somewhat unconventionally, the acrolect (lit. top-lect) is placed at the bottom instead of at the top. It is not clear, however, where GC stops and English begins or vice versa. Forms such as *did* belong to the mesolect as part of the meso-lect. The only thing you can say is that some sentences are closer to English than to GC, while others are closer to GC than to English. Together with the intermediate varieties, mesolects, the acrolect and basilect form a gradient scale that shade into one another. This property of a creole continuum may be referred to as non-discreteness, since discrete boundaries between the varieties do not exist. Unidimensionality, the second property of a creole continuum refers to the fact that varieties making up a continuum only differ from one another in being more or less creole or lexifier-like, and can therefore be ordered along a single, creole-lexifier, dimension.

Figure 1. The Guyanese Creole Continuum

|  |  |  |  | basilect |
|---|---|---|---|---|
| mi |  | gii | am | ↑ |
| mi | bin | gii | am |  |
| mi | bin | gii | ii |  |
| mi | bin | gi | ii |  |
| mi | di | gi | ii |  |
| mi | di | gi | hii |  |
| a | di | gi | ii |  |
| a | di | gi | ii |  |
| a | did | gi | ii |  |
| a | did | giv | ii |  |
| a | did | give | hii |  |
| a |  | giv | ii |  |
| a |  | giv | im |  |
| a |  | giv | him |  |
| a |  | geev | ii |  |
| a |  | geev | im |  |
| a |  | geev | him |  |
| I |  | gave | him | ↓ |
|  |  |  |  | acrolect |

Underlying the notion of a creole continuum are several assumptions which have all been criticized at one time or another. An account of these criticisms is to be found in Rickford (1987:15-39). According to Rickford, non-discreteness and unidimensionality are the only properties that are fundamental to the concept of a continuum. The main criticisms levelled against assumptions underlying the concept of a continuum involve the role of the concept in talking about decreolization and diachronic development of creole languages; these will be dealt with in section 5.2.4. These issues may be relatively extraneous (Rickford 1987:16). We will see, however, that without these additional assumptions the concept of a creole continuum loses some of its content and attractiveness as a theoretical model. Before dealing with the issues of decreolization and the diachronic development of creole languages in general, we will first have a look at the structure of creole continua, and more specifically the way in which individual speech varieties are patterned implicationally.

### 5.2.2 Implicational patterns in creole continua

In the proto-typical continuum situation exemplified by Jamaican Creole and Guyanese Creole, we find a number of mesolectal varieties in between the acrolect and basilect which shade into each other. In his oft-cited study of Jamaican Creole, DeCamp (1971) found that features belonging to different lects in the language use of different speakers could be arranged implicationally. For a concise history of the use of the concept predating De-Camp's classic 1971 article, see Holm (1988:52-55). In one of DeCamp's examples, he lists seven speakers according to their use of six linguistic variables each having two variants. The [–] variants are basilectal variants while the [+] ones are acrolectal variants, as shown in Table 1:

Table 1.

| Features | | Speakers |
|---|---|---|
| +A child | -A pikni | 1. +A +B +C -D +E +F |
| +B eat | -B nyam | 2. -A +B -C -D +E +F |
| +C /θ~t/ | -C /t/ | 3. -A +B -C -D -E -F |
| +D /ð~d/ | -D /d/ | 4. -A -B -C -D -E -F |
| +E granny | -E nana | 5. +A +B +C +D +E +F |
| +F didn't | -F no ben | 6. +A +B -C -D +E +F |
| | | 7. -A +B -C -D +E -F |

The next step taken by DeCamp involves the ordering of the speakers according to their usage of these variants. The use of one variant implies the use of certain others. Consider the use of [-A]: all speakers using [-A] (speakers 2, 3, 4, 7) also use [-C] and [-D]. Speakers using [-E] (3, 4) also use [-F], [-A], [-C] and [-D]. This implicational patterning is grasped more easily when tabulated as in Table 2.

Table 2.

| Speaker | Feature | | | | | |
|---|---|---|---|---|---|---|
| | B | E | F | A | C | D |
| 5. | + | + | + | + | + | + |
| 1. | + | + | + | + | + | − |
| 6. | + | + | + | + | − | − |
| 2. | + | + | + | − | − | − |
| 7. | + | + | − | − | − | − |
| 3. | + | − | − | − | − | − |
| 4. | − | − | − | − | − | − |

Looking at Table 2, we see that if a speaker uses a [-] variant, then all variants to the right of it are also [-] variants. If a speaker uses a [+] variant, then all variants to the left of it are also [+] variants. It is evident that the implicational strength of certain variants is stronger than that of others. The use of [-F] implies the use of [-A], [-C] and [-D], whereas the use of [-B] implies the use of [-E], [-F], [-A], [-C] and [-D]. The same goes for the implicational strength of [+D] which is greater than that of the other [+] variants.

Table 3. Implicationally arranged isolects in a poly-lectal grid

| Isolects | Environments | | |
|---|---|---|---|
| | III | II | I |
| 1. | 1 | 1 | 1 |
| 2. | 1 | 1 | 2 |
| 3. | 1 | 2 | 2 |
| 4. | 2 | 2 | 2 |

This technique of arranging data reflecting variation is called implicational scaling and was developed by Guttman (1944). Introduced in creole linguistics by DeCamp (ibid.), this technique became a core theoretical device in the study of decreolization by C.-J. Bailey (1973) and Bickerton (1973, 1975). Underlying their work is the assumption that the competence of each individual speaker is **poly-lectal**: that is, it consists of a number of separate **lects** or isolects. Lects are varieties of a language that differ from each other in a minimal way and can be arranged in a poly-lectal grid as in Table 3. In this table four isolects are arranged implicationally on the basis of the choice between two variants in different environments, that is, grammatical contexts.

Now consider Table 4, displaying the distribution of the *fu/tu* markers, which introduce verbal complement clauses in GC illustrated in (1) (Bickerton 1971):

(1)     a.   after **modal** and **inceptive** verbs (Environment I);
             Jan staat fu mek moni.
             'John started to make money.'
        b.   after **desiderative** and other 'psychological' verbs (Environment II);
             Op tu reeza bleed dem a trai fu tek yu.
             'They would even try to take razor-blades from you.'
        c.   after all other verbs (Environment III).
             I son-dem kom fu ker am wee.
             'Her sons came to take her away.'

The table is adapted from Bickerton (1973: 647) and only lists a subset of the speakers in Bickerton's original table. Data were gathered in a small community of mostly basilectal speakers of GC (Bickerton 1971:464). *fu* is the basilectal variant and *tu* the acrolectal variant.

Table 4: Speakers of GC ordered implicationally according to their use of *fu/tu* (adapted from Bickerton 1973:647; Bickerton's original table contains 26 speakers). 1 = *fu*; 2 = *tu*; 12 = variable use.

| Speakers | Environments | | |
|---|---|---|---|
|  | III | II | I |
| 9 | 1 | 1 | 1 |
| 13 | 1 | 1 | 2 |
| 26 | 1 | 1 | 2 |
| 11 | 1 | 12 | 2 |
| 25 | 1 | 12 | 2 |
| 8 | 1 | 2 | 2 |
| 14 | 12 | 2 | 2 |
| 1 | 2 | 2 | 2 |
| 19 | 2 | 2 | 2 |

As can be seen from the table, the distribution of *fu/tu* is patterned implicationally. Speakers using *tu* after Class III verbs also use *tu* after Class II and I verbs, and speakers using *tu* after Class II verbs also use it after Class I verbs. It is also evident that the change from *fu* to *tu* starts in environment I. According to Bickerton (1973), what we see here is a change in progress by the step-wise incorporation of an acrolectal element. In the process of decreolization, basilect speakers do not randomly adopt rules from the acrolect, but instead start applying a rule in one specific environment, generalize the rule in this environment before proceeding to apply the rule in the next environment. The rows in Table 4 are not isolects: they simply represent speakers' outputs in differing isolects. Constructing a table like Table 4 enables one to locate individual speakers' outputs in a poly-lectal grid as presented in Table 3. The data from speakers 1 and 19, for instance, may be considered as the output of the same most acrolectal isolect. The variable use of *fu/tu* by speakers 11 and 25 in environment II and by speaker 14 in environment III must be due to the application of two rules belonging to two different isolects: they are in the process of making the transition from one isolect to another.

The use of implicational scales has produced some interesting and important findings. On the basis of synchronic data it may reveal the ways in which ongoing changes spread through time and space. The technique of implicational scaling as used by e.g. Bickerton (1975) has been heavily criticized as being unreliable and methodologically unsound (e.g. Romaine 1982:177-182). Recent developments in variable rule analysis, however, have made it possible to uncover implicational patterns in variation, and to test the reliability of implicational scales(see Dittmar & Schlobinski 1988 and D. Sankoff 1988).

### 5.2.3 The applicability of the model of a unidimensional continuum

The language varieties in a creole-speaking community form a continuum only if they can be ordered along a single dimension: [+/-creoleness]. Consider Figure 2.

Figure 2. Graphic representation of a creole continuum

As long as varieties can be shown to differ only in creoleness, such a unidimensional continuum is an appropriate model. However, as soon as one or more other dimensions are needed to distinguish different varieties from one another, a multidimensional model is called for. A hypothetical example of a multi-dimensional (in this case two-dimensional) model is presented in Figure 3, where the varieties v3 and v4 all have the same creole features and can only be differentiated on the basis of features that are typical of urban versus rural varieties.

Figure 3. Language varieties located in a two-dimensional space (adapted from Rickford 1987:23)

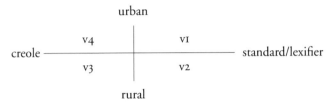

In order to invoke such a multidimensional model the dimensions involved should be (relatively) independent. You may find a rural-urban continuum, but if at the same time you find that urban varieties tend to be lexifier-like and rural varieties creole-like, it should be clear that the rural-urban dimension is in some way subordinate or parallel to the creole-lexifier dimension. A multi-dimensional model would then be inappropriate (Rickford 1987:23, 25-26). Rickford seems to suggest that in most, if not all, continua variants or varieties can be ordered along a single basilect-acrolect dimension in some way. This observation may hold true for creole speaking communities where there are only two easily available, vital language varieties, acrolect and basilect, which speakers may use as opposite points of orientation in giving social meaning to established and newly created ways of speaking. In such communities, differences may exist between urban and rural varieties, careful and casual speech, or between ways of speaking characteristic of the old and the young. These differences, however, will tend to be characterized by being more or less basilectal or acrolectal. This is more or less the case in Jamaica and (maybe to a somewhat lesser extent) in Guyana.

It is important to note that a creole-lexifier contact situation is not in itself a guarantee for a set of non-discrete varieties to emerge. In Haiti, for instance, creole and lexifier are rather separate. Here the situation resembles one of **diglossia**, functional specialization of the languages involved, although the 'high' variety, French, is little spoken in this highly stratified society. The same was argued for Martinique in Lefebvre (1974). Social and political conditions may prevent a continuum from emerging. DeCamp claims that for a continuum to come into being '... there must be sufficient social mobility to motivate large numbers of creole speakers to modify their speech in the direction of the standard, and there must be a sufficient program of education and other acculturative activities to exert effective pressures from the standard language on the creole (DeCamp 1971b: 351).'

So far, we have only talked about creole-lexifier contact situations. According to De-Camp these are the only situations in which a continuum can arise. However, there are some cases that suggest otherwise. The case of Sranan is particularly interesting. Here, we find that the lexifier, English, was replaced in an early stage by a genetically related superstrate language, Dutch. In Surinam itself, no true Sranan-Dutch continuum developed, but the use of varieties which are the product of convergence of both languages have been documented (Eersel 1971). Sranan speakers who migrated to the Netherlands during the 1970's have created additional intermediate varieties, while also displaying great skills in Sranan/Dutch **code-mixing**. It is not clear whether this particular situation may be characterized in terms of a continuum but it surely points to the possibility of a creole/non-lexifier language continuum. Robertson (1982) who argues for a Berbice Dutch-English continuum, linking the emergence of a continuum to **language death**.

Yet another kind of contact situation in which a creole language is involved has been studied extensively by a team of researchers led by Le Page (see Le Page & Tabouret-Keller 1985). Their studies of the multilingual communities of Belize and St. Lucia involve complex contact situations. In Belize, Belizean Creole is in contact with Spanish, Maya, English, Carib and (to a lesser extent) with Waika and Lebanese Arabic. In St. Lucia the French based creole, Kwéyòl, is in contact with English (used as the medium of instruction), and it is under the influence of Barbadian English Creole, and the French Creole of Martinique, and the English Creole of St. Vincent. It should come as no surprise that in this situation the unidimensional continuum model proved to be of little use. Le Page and Tabouret-Keller therefore propose a multidimensional model.

They subjected their data to cluster analysis, a statistical technique. Speakers were grouped together in different clusters on the basis of their language behavior in different contexts. The patterns of variation characteristic of these clusters were mixed: they were not simply charactarizable in terms of only +/-Spanishness, or only +/-Creoleness, or +/-Caribness. After cluster analysis, the correlation between clusters and non-linguistic attributes of the speakers (area of residence, occupation of the father etc.) was calculated. In this way, it was possible to get a picture of how the speakers use linguistic resources to locate themselves at a particular point in a multidimensional social space.

Rickford's (1987:26-30) critique of Le Page and Tabouret-Keller is quite interesting because it makes clear that his research goals are different from those of Le Page and Tabouret-Keller. Rickford argues that even in the Belizean case the concept of a unidimensional continuum can be applied. One might dissect the multidimensional continuum discovered into three separate unidimensional continua, thus making it possible to detect 'how many and what kinds of variables lie along each of the unidimensional continua' (Rickford 1987: 29). Another way of applying separate unidimensional continua would be to use them as vectors to locate outputs of idiolects in the multidimensional space. Some of the theoretically possible points are not realized in practice, which may suggest that the different continua are not independent.

What Rickford proposes is, of course, possible and may reveal how the multidimensional space is structured sociolinguistically. The problem is that the separate continua remain meaningful only in the case of an unevenly filled multidimensional space, because if the space is evenly filled the location of an output along one continuum does not say anything about the location of that output along the other continua.

Rickford's concern in saving the concept of a unidimensional continuum seems to be rooted in his pre-occupation with finding implicational variation patterns, whereas for Le Page and Tabouret-Keller it is not the structure of variation that is of primary importance: to them patterns of variation are first of all the product of socio-psychological processes underlying language use.

In conclusion, we might say that the concept of a continuum is definitely not universally applicable in communities where the creole is in contact with its lexifier. On the other hand, one should not exclude the possibility of a creole/non-lexifier superstrate language continuum. Depending on the specific social, political and historical conditions a continuum may or may not arise. We have also seen that in the case of a multidimensional continuum consisting of truly independent continua, the concept of a unidimensional continuum loses its significance, because implicational patterns dissolve.

### 5.2.4 The role of the creole continuum in development and change

DeCamp (1971) considered a creole continuum as one possible final stage in the life-cycle of a creole: the merger of the creole with its lexifier language. This merger takes place in what he calls a post-creole speech continuum. Underlying this view is the first assumption concerning creole development to be discussed here: the continuum is seen as a **recent phenomenon**. As we have seen in the previous section, DeCamp linked its emergence with the breakdown of slave labor based economy and the rigid social stratification that went with it. For Caribean creole speaking communities this amounted to saying that the continua found there could only have started to emerge in the late 19th century.

Furthermore, under this scenario, the emergence of a continuum is seen as the starting point of a process leading to the disappearance of the creole. DeCamp clearly implied this by talking about a merger of the creole with its lexifier, but also left some doubt as to what extent this would imply the actual disappearance of the basilect. It was Bickerton (1973, 1975, 1980) who argued much more forcefully in favor of viewing synchronic variation in the form of a continuum as reflecting a unidirectional process of **decreolization**. He defines decreolization as a process 'in which speakers progressively change the basilectal grammar so that its output comes to resemble the output of an acrolectal grammar' (Bickerton 1980:109).

Viewing a creole continuum as a recent, post-creole phenomenon is very much in line with the life-cycle theory of creole genesis (see chapters 1 and 10). This theory holds that creole genesis and development should be seen as the succession of different stages. After the pidgin phase, a creole may evolve. The continuum can then be seen as simply a further, and final stage in the life cycle. In view of what we know of the social history of creoles (see chapter 2), this scenario is clearly too simplistic and even patently misleading.

In early creole societies the creole language did not exist in isolation from the lexifier. On plantations, at least a small group of slaves, including the black overseers (see chapter 2), had access to the superstrate language to a significant degree. Thus, we may assume that the 'creole was in fact everywhere only a major segment of a continuum of variation' (Alleyne 1971:182). Nowadays, many researchers assume that such a continuum of variation must have existed from the start (see e.g. Rickford 1987, chapter 3). However, since social factors determining access to the superstrate in early creole society differed from present conditions, we may not automatically assume that present-day continua are comparable or related to early continua. In arguing that a present-day continuum is in essence a continuation of an early one, two dangers are present. First, the early continua may have been less smooth than the present day continua like those in Guyana and Jamaica. Secondly, one should keep in mind that the number of mesolect speakers has probably increased dramatically in comparison to the early period. It is more likely that the starting point of a process of decreolization in the Bickertonian sense of the word should be located somewhere during this later stage.

This brings us to the oft-assumed link between a continuum and decreolization. Bickerton elaborated Bailey's idea that continuum-like synchronic variation reflects diachronic change, taking the form of decreolization. This claim is too strong in several respects. When a speaker starts acquiring mesolectal varieties that are closer to the lexifier, this does not necessarily entail the loss of his more basilectal varieties. A basilectal speaker acquiring intermediate varieties may just as well simply expand his poly-lectal competence. An example of this is reported by Escure (1981:32) for (black) Belizean Creole speakers most of whom control a complex linguistic repertoire, including basilectal, mesolectal, as well as acrolectal varieties, and develop the ability to switch between codes and variants when appropriate without abandoning their native creole variety.

Progressive loss of the more basilectal varieties is most likely to occur in communities where the superstrate language is by far the most attractive target to aim at for socio-economic reasons. Still, such a unidirectional change towards the lexifier language is definitely not a natural concomitant of a continuum situation (cf. Mufwene 1991 on Gullah). One should not forget that in most creole speaking communities, the basilect is the preferred norm in more intimate contacts with peers and family members. It may also be the norm to aim at for youths who identify themselves with a sub-culture opposed to mainstream societal norms. An extreme and intriguing example of this is to be found in Britain among children of West Indian migrants (Romaine 1988:188-203; Sebba 1993). Many children who speak no creole in their early years start to 'talk Black' around the ages of 14-15. It is important to note that these youths have not simply adopted the language of their parents. Jamaican Creole is the norm at which they all aim, whether their parents are Jamaican or not. The result may be something which is indistinguishable from the original creole but normally it shows features not present in it.

A final cautionary remark is in order concerning the extent of decreolization. Decreolization need not be a process affecting the whole basilectal grammar. Labov (1971:469) observes that in Black English Vernacular (BEV) 'some elements in the grammar remain categorically different from those of other [non-Black English] dialects (such as the absence of the third person singular -s, attributive -s, or use of invariant *be*) so that it is not true that all elements of the grammar are being re-interpreted.' According to him it would be wrong to think that the grammar of present-day BEV is any more in flux than the eighteenth century varieties. The case of BEV, nowadays referred to as AAVE (African American Vernacular English), is interesting in another aspect as well: it has been noticed that during recent years AAVE speakers have been engaged in a process of refocusing away from Standard American English (Romaine 1988:172). The American contact situation is also a nice example of how the standard or lexifier language has changed under the influence of a vernacular. For African-isms in American English see e.g. Holloway & Vass (1993), and also Dillard (1973, 1992) who deals with possible influence of AAVE on Southern American English dialect. (The Black English influenced speech of the white characters in Mark Twain's *The Adventures of Huckleberry Finn* may give an impression of late 19th century Southern American English as spoken by whites, although Twain probably made heavy use of stereotypes.)

What conclusion do these criticisms lead us to? Should we simply give up the concept of a continuum because of underlying assumptions that may prove to be too strong or misleading? On the one hand, the application of the concept has furthered the study of variation in creole languages tremendously. On the other hand, we should be careful not to accept unquestioningly the assumptions discussed here. We may ask ourselves '(...) whether [the concept] has not shaped the space it seeks to describe, designing its own aptness, rather than mimicking the reality of the nature of that space (Carrington 1992:96).'

## 5.3 Conclusion

It is clear that the technique of implicational scaling, which is strongly associated with the concept of a creole continuum, has produced some important insights into the way creoles may develop in contact with their lexifier languages. A continuum that can be shown to consist of strictly implicationally ordered isolects shows where changes toward the lexifier start and how changes spread. The fact that rules of the lexifier are adopted in a step-by-step fashion before becoming categorical also provides us with clues as to how grammars of creole languages are organized internally. We have also noticed that not all creole-lexifier contact situations automatically result in a situation that can be characterized in terms of a unidimensional continuum. In the end, it is specific socio-historical factors (Thomason & Kaufman 1988) and socio-psychological processes underlying language use (Le Page & Tabouret-Keller 1985) that determine the course and direction of the structurally possible linguistic outcomes of creole-lexifier contact situations.

**Further reading**

Book-length studies of variation in creole speaking communities that also contain critical accounts of the techniques used in analyzing variation in creole languages are Bickerton (1975) and Rickford (1987) on GC, and Le Page & Tabouret-Keller (1985) on the creole speaking communities of Belize and St. Lucia. For Tok Pisin see G. Sankoff (1980). Bickerton (1980) is a highly readable article on decreolization. Critical studies of decreolization are Escure (1981), Mufwene (1991), and Washabaugh (1977) commented on by Bickerton (1977).

# 6 Decolonization, language planning and education

René Appel and Ludo Verhoeven

## 6.1 Introduction

Since World War II, a world wide process of decolonization has taken place. The processes of emancipation and liberalization of colonies reached their height in the fifties and sixties, but did not necessarily lead to self-government. In many cases a political affiliation with the former colonizer remained. The sudden transition from colonization to (partial) autonomy requires very careful planning. Planning for national development calls for an optimal appreciation of social and cultural resources and the possibility of their utilization. As such, national planning makes a heavy demand on public authorities. Within the agenda for national development, language planning usually plays a significant role. Not only is language obviously relevant as an instrument for communication, commercial relations and educational development, it is also considered to be a marker of identification, and a symbol of cultural distinctiveness.

In the present chapter the process of decolonization and language planning in the Caribbean will be dealt with. First of all, some relevant aspects of language planning in a post-colonial setting will be discussed. In addition, the issue of language planning in education will be highlighted. Special attention is given to the adoption of indigenous languages in the curriculum. Moreover, the adoption of Papiamento on the island of Curaçao is examined in detail as a case study.

## 6.2 Decolonization and language planning

Language planning has only been a research topic since the 1960s. It can be defined as an organizational device to solve current language problems in such a way that well-defined objectives can be attained in a reasonable period of time. It concerns a long sustained and conscious effort either to alter a language itself, or to change its functions in a society for the purpose of solving communication problems, educational problems etc. (cf. Weinstein 1983). This definition draws upon a distinction which is now widely recognized, i.e. the distinction between status planning, referring to the functional status of a language, and corpus planning, referring to language planning itself. A great variety of aims of language planning can be found in the literature. Hornberger (1990) makes a distinction between the following goals of status planning: officialization, nationalization, status standardization, vernacularization, revival, spread, maintenance, and interlingual communication. With respect to corpus planning she comes up with the following list of goals: plurification, reform, corpus standardization, lexical modernization, terminology unification, stylistic simplification, auxiliary code standardization, and graphization. Processes of language planning include not only the setting of goals, but also the implementation of these goals. The implementation of language goals refers to the allocation of resources in order to attain these goals. Moreover, the evaluation of both the attainment of the original goals and the methods of implementation can be seen as an integral part of the process of language planning. Such evaluation can lead to the formulation of new goals, which is a starting point for a new cycle of language planning activities.

Language problems in (post)colonial speech communities will vary according to the nature of the remaining colonial ties, the nature of linguistic diversity, the developmental state of the indigenous language(s), and the language attitudes among the speakers. Language planning in such communities, especially creole language communities, has hardly been examined. In most countries in transition from colonial to post-colonial government, the tension between the position of local mother tongues and the colonial language usually brings about an upgrading of the mother tongues and in some cases even a take-over of the position of the (post)colonial language (cf. Akinnaso 1991; Phillipson 1990). Decolonization not only implies the rejection of the domination of an alien language, but also the reduction of the influence of the small group of educated people who had set the rules for language planning thanks to political power. However, in the process of decolonization, societies often betray a dualism in their language attitudes. The desire to replace the colonial language tends to be weakened, usually resulting in a slowing down of the pace of enactment of new language laws. The call by the authorities for the wider use of indigenous languages does not result very often in the actual displacement of the colonial language in official institutions. Churchill (1986) makes a distinction between four increasing levels of aspiration regarding the use of the indigenous language. The first level is that of recognition of their existence in a speech community with special educational needs, the second level is termed the start up and extension phase, the third level is called the consolidation and adaptation phase, and the final level involves multilingual coexistence. In many cases only the first or the second level is attained.

Depending on the situation in a society, language planning may take different forms. In many cases the first task in a post-colonial state is to determine which language(s) should fulfil the role of national language. In many cases the colonial language is abandoned in favor of one of the indigenous languages. The adoption of Bahasa Indonesia in Indonesia forms a case in point. In addition to the processes of language selection, the position of minority languages may be dealt with. Moreover, decisions may be made as regards the developmental support of languages used in a society. A common procedure is that of codification, which can be seen as a prerequisite for the standardization of a language. Codification includes an explicit statement of the code by means of dictionaries, grammars, spelling, punctuation and pronunciation guides, etc. As Spolsky (1978) points out, any language variety is modifiable in such a way that orthographies can be developed and lexical elaboration provided. According to Valdman (1968) earlier failures to normalize the written representation of creole forms are ultimately due to the confusion between a form of transcription referring to surface representation, and an orthography based on underlying form. This is the universal debate between the phonemic principle (one sound, one symbol), and the morphemic principle (a fixed form for each morpheme).

Another conflict in the establishment of an orthography concerns the choice between an etymological and a phonetic spelling, especially in the cases of creole languages. Proposals for a phonetic spelling generally stress the 'independence' of the language, while etymological spelling underlines the historical dependence of the creole on its lexifier language. With respect to education both types of orthography have their benefits. In general a phonetic spelling makes it easier to learn to read and write. However, when the lexifier language is the prestige language in a creole-speaking community, reading and writing abilities can be transferred more easily from the creole to the lexifier language when an etymological orthography is employed. On the basis of specific characteristics of the Trinidad and Tobago situation, Winer (1990) presents guidelines for a standardized orthographic system following a continuum model, referring to the close relationship between the creole and the standard variety/lexifier language.

The codification of a language involves complex processes of language planning, incorporating implementation and evaluation. Dejean (1993) shows that, in spite of the official system of phonetic orthography for Haitian Creole adopted in 1980, nowadays 90 percent of the teachers in Haiti are still not familiar with it. Teacher training efforts during the past decade have mainly focused on techniques for teaching French as a foreign language.

It should be emphasized that the actual policies adopted by the authorities always take place in an existing legal framework. The number of levels of decision-making, the legitimate participants in this process, and the legitimate clients of the system are important variables in this process. Official or government language planning takes place via language agencies, academies or departments. Although governmental institutions may be powerful, the language behavior of individuals may conflict with the official policies. Personal attitudes turn out to be related to the social distribution of languages in the community, and the social meanings attached to these languages.

Language policy primarily manifests itself in two domains: mass media and education. As for the mass media, it is a matter of policy to what extent the (post)colonial language and the indigenous language will perform public functions in the community. Measures in this domain concern the use of written language in institutions, periodicals and libraries. With respect to education, the legal opportunities for the use of indigenous languages are generally defined by law.

One of the major problems with regard to language planning has to do with the fact that corpus planning and status planning ought to be dealt with together, but in practice they belong to different professional domains, corpus planning being part of the professional domain of linguists and status planning being part of the professional domain of politicians and/or authorities. However, linguists working on the codification and elaboration of languages have no political power, and politicians or authorities, deciding on the functions of language, generally have no (socio-)linguistic knowledge. Therefore, the necessary relation between status and corpus planning is often absent. This problem shows up in many developing countries. The result may be that the codification or elaboration of for instance a creole language is not performed, because the language only functions as a vernacular. When it is proposed to promote the language and to give it official status in the process of status planning, this aim cannot be realized because the language is not prepared for this function, i.e. it is not sufficiently elaborated and codified.

## 6.3  Language planning and education

With respect to children's cognitive and social development, it can be argued that school success will be facilitated if the instruction is linked up with his or her linguistic background (cf. Cummins 1984). Children who receive instruction in a foreign language will be faced with a double task: besides the content of school subjects, they will have to learn an unfamiliar language. It is evident that the essential topics in school subjects will be more easily taught when instruction is based on familiar exemplars from the mother tongue than in less familiar exemplars from the foreign language. Moreover, it is clear that the motivation of children to learn increases as the school and other societal institutions pay more attention to the language and cultural background of the learner. Spolsky (1978) argues that the major attitudinal argument in favor of home language instruction is that it enhances the pupils' self-respect to discover that the mother tongue in which they have invested so many years is respected by the school system.

According to Churchill (1986), educational initiatives are primarily dependent on the ways in which educational problems are defined. Problem definitions may range from learning deficits related to a limited knowledge of the colonial language to learning deficits as a result of mother tongue deprivation. For instance, Bolleé (1993) lists three reasons for language reform in public schools in the Seychelles: the apparent inadequacy of the existing school system, the inequality of educational opportunities for children of different social and linguistic backgrounds, and the need for promotion of the local culture.

Once educational problems have been defined, educational arrangements can be proposed in order to overcome these problems. A distinction can be made between different kinds of educational arrangements. First of all, different roles can be assigned to the indigenous language(s) and the (post)colonial language under consideration. These roles may vary from no encouragement to a short-term transitional medium, or a medium for language maintenance. It should be mentioned that in a post-colonial society, the granting of a formal status to one or more indigenous languages besides the colonial language may result in a dual system of language use which is associated with economic power. The use of the indigenous languages in education will result in a much higher level of school succes for the mass population. However, at the same time, a privileged group will often safeguard their educational opportunities by providing special forms of schooling. Their children will attain a high proficiency in the colonial language, have better access to higher education and thus achieve better positions on the labor market.

The facilities a school has at its disposal in order to set up educational programs play a significant role. Financial means are necessary to develop and implement new educational arrangements. First of all, there must be suitable curriculum materials available in the target languages. The development of appropriate materials in a post-colonial setting often poses a serious problem. When a bilingual program is planned, two sets of educational materials need to be made available. Materials in the colonial language which are used in schools in the country of the (former) colonizer are usually not totally suitable. The content of the materials often reflects the values of the colonizer's culture which will make it difficult for the child to relate it to his/her own social and cultural context. In order to arrive at a better connection between the child's background knowledge, and the content of the foreign language curriculum, materials should be produced which reflect an ethnically appropriate picture of society. As to the material of the indigenous language, the problems may be even greater. When the language is not standardized, work on language standardization must be carried out. In addition, new instructional materials must be developed for every school subject. Besides the development of curricula, literary books and reference works must be written and put on the reading lists. If bilingual instruction is planned, it will be a complex matter to integrate the two curricula in such a way that an optimum route to bilingual proficiency is guaranteed.

Another educational issue concerns the availability of qualified teachers. Teachers must be well trained and sufficiently literate to be able to offer a preplanned educational program. Therefore, there is an urgent need for an efficient framework incorporating local management, teaching units, and ancillary services, such as specialist advisory centers and teacher training. A final consideration concerns the attitudes held by school teachers and school boards. Schools may either respond favorably to new educational policies, or ignore them. A positive response to educational renewal can be stimulated through intense school and community involvement during the process of curriculum development and curriculum implementation.

## 6.4  Creole languages in education: the case of Curaçao

An important question in educational planning in Caribbean territories is how the vernacular language can be used as a medium of instruction. As Carrington (1976) points out the degree to which creoles have been recognized for educational purposes has varied over the years and from one territory to the next. Policy decisions turn out to be based on sociolinguistic factors, such as the linguistic relationship between the vernacular and the official language, the identifiability of a norm acceptable to the population, the level of national consciousness, and the geographical and age distribution of languages. According to Carrington, conditions are linguistically favorable for the use of the vernacular as a medium of instruction if it is unrelated to the official language. As other favorable conditions he considers the identification of a norm for the creole language which is acceptable to the population, the inner-centeredness of the societal value-system and the geographical concentration of its speakers.

In the remainder of this section the use of Papiamento in education on the island of Curaçao will be examined. Papiamento is in no way structurally related to the official Dutch language (see chapter 17). The only Dutch influence is to be seen in the numerous loanwords from Dutch. A norm for the language has widely been accepted. Recent societal developments suggest that the population on the island has gained sufficient confidence as a nation-state with a clearly defined and separate identity. Compared to other creole languages in the Caribbean, Papiamento is highly developed as a written language and has a high social prestige.

With respect to the following it should be born in mind that the political administrative situation in the Dutch Antilles is rather complex. On the one hand there is the central government of the Dutch Antilles, which is politically responsible for the educational system. On the other hand there are the five respective Island Boards ('Bestuurscolleges'), each having administrative responsiblities with respect to the educational system. Sometimes conflicts of interest arise between the central and the island authorities.

### 6.4.1  Historical and sociolinguistic background
Curaçao forms part of the group of islands referred to as the Dutch Antilles. After the islands were captured by the Dutch in 1634, it was more than two centuries before any serious governmental attention was given to educational opportunities for children on the islands.

Before then, education (especially for children from lower classes) was run by the Roman Catholic mission for several decades. In their religious instruction Papiamento was used. However, a law banned Papiamento completely from all schools on the islands in 1936. It was the time of a renewed economic and hence political interest in the islands on the part of its colonizers. The use of Dutch was dictated and for decades Papiamento was felt to be an obstacle to learning and teaching the official Dutch language in a school-system which was – and still is – a copy of the Dutch system. The use of Papiamento in school was no longer allowed, despite the fact that it was the home language of almost 90 percent of the population on the islands.

In the past decades there has been much discussion about the frustration of the majority of the school children, their parents, and their teachers, about the economic waste in education and about the use of Dutch as language of instruction in schools. The limited usefulness of Dutch in the region and the low educational output has been discussed at length. Each year roughly one quarter to one third of the primary school population does not pass to the next grade, and the number of dropouts is alarming. But a final decision about the use of the mother tongue in education has still not been taken. One reason is the ambivalence about the structure of the schooling system, which is associated with higher education forms in Holland. Papiamento is now being taught as a subject in elementary school, and being illegally and unsystematically used on a large scale as a medium of instruction. One could expect the historical colonial contempt for Papiamento by the economically and politically more powerful group to be shared by the users of the language and consequently to affect its common use. Surprisingly, this is not the case. Although the vernacular language is not completely standardized and codified, it has gradually become the major medium for public communication in newspapers, television and radio broadcasts (Devonish 1986). The movement toward (more) independence has been accompanied by an upgrading of the creole language and a gradual shift in the attitude towards Dutch, for many Antillians a prominent feature of colonization. Proficiency in Dutch, still the official language, is no longer a guarantee for higher social prestige, although it does indicate a certain level of education and thus societal success. This still affects the attitude of many Antilleans towards Dutch. From an instrumental point of view they value Dutch, but from a social perspective they may reject it to a certain extent. The most common languages in business and industry at present are English and Spanish. The position of Dutch is strong only in those domains where the language is still legally required, such as in court, in official documents and in education.

### 6.4.2 Language proficiency and school success

Empirical data show that the submersion of Caribbean children in a foreign language curriculum at school is not very feasible. More than 70 percent of the children do not succeed in finishing primary school without repeating a class. At the same time, the proportion of children being referred to schools for special education is still growing.

In a study by Narain & Verhoeven (1994) the language development in Papiamento and Dutch of 80 four to six year olds, living on the island of Curaçao, was examined. Language data were collected at three points: the beginning of kindergarten, and after one, and after two years in kindergarten. In order to explore the relationship between language proficiency and background features socio-cultural background characteristics were also measured. The results showed that the development of Dutch is much slower than Papiamento and that notably the productive abilities develop much later. Another conclusion was that the linguistic and cultural orientation of the children and their parents substantially predicted the children's first and second language proficiency.

In a study by Severing & Verhoeven (1994) an attempt was made to assess the proficiency in Papiamento and Dutch of children on Curaçao, in grade 5 of primary school. In order to assess the children's bilingual proficiency, a distinction was made between language comprehension tasks, dealing with lexicon, syntax and semantics, on the one hand, and word decoding tasks on the other. The results make clear that the children's level of language comprehension is better in Papiamento, while their level of decoding is better in Dutch. The comprehension and decoding proficiency in the two languages turned out to be related to both sociolinguistic factors and background characteristics, such as repeating classes at school, length of residence, and family size.

From Kook & Vedder (1989) it has become clear that children from lower social class Papiamento-speaking homes have a substantial deficit with respect to lexical skills in Dutch, as compared with children from higher social class, who speak Papiamento, Dutch, or both languages at home. In general lexical skills in the school language correlate strongly with school achievements (cf. Anderson & Freebody 1981). This implies that the Papiamento speaking children from lower social class, who form the vast majority of the school population, will often not be very successful at school.

### 6.4.3 Educational planning

Since 1983 a group of researchers in the Instituto Lingwistiko Antiano, the Language Agency of the Dutch Antilles, has been working on the standardization and elaboration of Papiamento with respect to orthography, lexicon and syntax, one result of which was for example Dijkhoff (1990), establishing certain aspects of Papiamento grammar.

In 1983 Papiamento was introduced as a subject in all grades of primary school for half an hour a day. Instructional materials were developed by the Sede de Papiamento, the Language Agency for the island of Curaçao. Teachers received supplementary courses in Papiamento. However, the language of instruction for all subjects remains Dutch. Reading and writing are also being taught in Dutch. In 1990 the Minister of Education reopened the discussion on the introduction of Papiamento as the language of instruction in primary school.

In 1993 a new plan for primary education was issued (*De Nieuwe Curaçaose Basisschool* 'The New Curaçoan Primary School'). One of the main proposals in the plan concerns the proposed use of Papiamento, the mother tongue of about 90% of the children, as the language of instruction throughout the primary school. Dutch should be treated as a 'foreign language', because it is not a regular medium of communication in the Curaçon speech community.

This new plan is one in a series of status planning activities, and it remains to be seen whether the next planning stage, i.e. the implementation, will be attained. As is always the case there is political opposition, because many members of the higher social classes prefer to stick to Dutch as the main language of schooling. It is also argued that Papiamento is such a 'minor language' and that it is not elaborated and codified to such a level that its introduction in school is justified. Furthermore, the lack of sufficient human and financial resources might obstruct or at least seriously delay the implementation and effectuation of such a substantial and radical educational innovation.

## 6.6 Conclusions

From a sociolinguistic point of view, it is clear that the development of the indigenous language(s) in a (post)colonial society can have a great impact on the individual child and its community. It provides a major socialization channel into the community and a means to acquire a knowledge of one's culture. It can be seen as a prerequisite for the optimum attainment of both intragroup communication and ethnic continuity. In addition, the (ex)colonial language can fulfil a role in intergroup communication and in schooling in higher educational settings. It can be argued that functional bilingualism in (post)colonial settings will only be acquired when the language needs of speech communities are seriously taken into account by the responsible authorities. With respect to language and educational planning, policy makers are recommended to analyze the language needs of communities by means of ethnographic interviews with teachers, parents and students. Such an analysis of linguistic needs should yield guidelines for the determination of final objectives in education. If there is a need to use the indigenous language in education, not only must legal measures be taken, but also adequate sources of information and instructional materials in that language must be made available and qualified teachers trained.

The case of language planning on the island of Curaçao makes clear that the standardization of a creole and its implementation in education is feasible. However, a few words of caution are in order. First of all, the consequences of language planning are usually costly. The poor socio-economic background in (post)colonial states may hamper the execution of educational plans. The provision of new instructional materials in the vernacular, and in the official language, now being taught as a foreign or second language, as well as the training of teachers require ample funds.

In addition, the comparative study of language planning has shown that in many cases there has been a considerable accomplishment as regards the quantity of word lists, dictionaries, and teaching aids, while the quality of such materials often turns out to be much less impressive (cf. Das Gupta 1988). Moreover, little attention has been paid to the question of who will use the additional capacity of the vernacular language. All too often, implementation and evaluation have been neglected as necessary stages in language planning. In many cases too much emphasis has been laid on general plans, without paying attention to the effects of proposed legislation. In this light Roberts (1993) advocates an integrative approach to the use of creole in the classroom with sustainable development as its major objective, and affective rather than material and physical factors as the key to development. Because of its status and traditional educational role the national language, which is a second language for most people, should keep a strong position, according to Roberts. At the same time, negative attitudes towards the vernacular, related to its low status, should not be neglected.

Finally, it is important to note that the case of Curaçao refers to a linguistic situation in which the creole language and the colonial language are not related, except for borrowings. We should not forget that in other communities in the Caribbean, there is a great deal of variation in creole speech. In areas such as Jamaica, a continuum is supposed to exist between creole varieties on the one hand, and the standard language on the other (cf. DeCamp 1971; see chapter 5). In such cases the processes of language planning in the context of education may become rather complex. Decisions have to be made with regard to the creole variety which will be selected as the medium of instruction. Moreover, given the fact that the prestige of creole varieties is much lower than that of the standard language, the adoption of creole in educational settings may be troublesome. In such cases the processes of both corpus and status planning deserve special attention.

## Further reading

Fishman (1974) is a collection of articles on theoretical aspects of language planning and various case studies, especially on language planning in Africa and Asia. Cobarrubias & Fishman (1983) can be considered as an update of Fishman (1974). Eastman (1983) is an introductory handbook on language planning. Devonish (1986) deals with language planning in the Carribean from a social emancipatory point of view. Case studies and general papers on language planning can be found in the journal *Language Problems and Language Planning*.

# 7 Creole literature

Lilian Adamson and Cefas van Rossem

## 7.1 Introduction

In every society, and creole societies are no exception, literature is a central component of language and culture. Under literature we understand both written (7.4) and oral (7.3) literary traditions. Besides the written tradition, different oral genres are still operative in creole speaking societies. For this reason we must take the socio-historical background into account while studying the historical development of creole literature (7.2). Our discussion will not however give a complete overview of the creole literary tradition. Using the metaphors of the following Sranan poem, the aim of this chapter is to introduce you to the *yeye* 'living spirit' of creole literature by looking in the *eygi* 'own' creole literary *spikri* 'mirror'.

| | | |
|---|---|---|
| *Duman* | *Man of action* | (Sranan) |
| Mi no wani / wan ati | I will no heart | |
| di n'abi kra, | without a soul, | |
| mi wani / wan yeye d'e libi. | I want a living spirit. | |
| | | |
| Mi n'e wer / susu | I wear no shoes | |
| di n'e fit mi, | which do not fit, | |
| m'e wer / mi eygi krompu. | I wear my very own clogs. | |
| | | |
| Mi n'e sdon / luku | I do not look | |
| a fesi fu sma, | at another's face, | |
| m'e luku ini / mi eygi spikri. | but in my very own mirror. | |

(J. Schouten-Elsenhout 1910-1992, cited in Voorhoeve and Lichtveld (1975), translated by Vernie February)

## 7.2 Socio-cultural background

The cultural expressions of a society: religion, music, dance, sculpture, literature and theater are constantly being reinterpreted and redefined. This may lead to new phases of cultural life, or more drastically, may create new cultural expressive forms, styles or genres. In the earlier days of creole societies, particularly during slavery, this process was even more complex and profound, given the cultural conditions (no racial or cultural assimilation allowed) and the socioeconomic matrix (the plantation economy) under which it evolved. It involved all levels of life for millions of culturally heterogeneous Africans, several Amerindian nations, and various European nationalities (see chapters 8 and 9). For Surinam these three main cultural groups were represented by Amerindian cultures, primarily Arawak and Carib, African cultures, e.g. Akan, Kikongo and Dahomean, and the European cultures, in particular English, Portuguese and Dutch. In this environment a completely new culture was forged through the interaction of cultural values and norms.

This new culture was one with its own characteristics, in particular, its own literary characteristics. The oral literary tradition of this period could have been easily converted into a written tradition through the missionary activities of the churches. For example in Surinam and in the Danish Antilles, the Moravian Brethren translated biblical and liturgical texts into the local creole languages (Oldendorp 1777). The underlying reasons for the translation activities seem to reinforce one another: firstly, the policy of the Moravian Brethren was to approach people in their own languages, and secondly, colonial policy did not provide the African immigrants the opportunity to speak their masters' language. Although, the immigrants were confronted with a religion different from their own, this was one of the opportunities which could have led to an early literary written tradition. The reasons why this did not happen had to do with the socioeconomic structure and the cultural policy of the colonial society, the most important one being the low social status enjoyed by the creole language and its speakers. This fact is also reflected in the lack of (printed) texts concerning cultural life, the 'white observers were apparently not sufficiently interested to give accurate descriptions...' (Voorhoeve and Lichtveld 1975:16). Despite this lacuna, the post-slavery sources and the present-day cultural heritage point to the existence of a flourishing cultural life during the period of slavery. This rich oral literary culture still has its influences on oral and written literature, e.g. the use of song techniques found in poetry.

## 7.3  Oral literature

In this section we deal with the legacy of cultural life in the period of slavery. Although not freed from social pressure, these forms of oral literature continued functioning in society after emancipation. The creole societies now had to adapt themselves to European cultural norms and values, by means of education and religion. This was in sharp contrast with the former period, and the thread of a flourishing cultural life was broken. Song, dance, theater and folktales are mentioned, besides fixed and movable festivals in Surinam. For instance, we might mention New Year's Day, the 1st of July and the harvest festival (Brathwaite 1974; Voorhoeve and Lichtveld 1975). We still find songs from this period, as well as other reflections of the oral culture in the modern creole societies.

In the Caribbean five oral literary genres can be distinguished which are also to be found in Nigeria (Dalphinis 1985:174). These are: the **riddle**, the **proverb**, **tongue twisters**, **prose narratives** and **song**. Helman (1977) distinguishes eight genres in Surinam, **myths**, **legends and sagas**, **tales**, **stories**, **riddles**, **gnomic literature** (philosophic proverbs), **mantic literature** (the formulae of exorcism, blessings, traditional prayers and hymns, and curses) and **popular lyrics** (religious lyrics, ballads, love songs and lullabies, work songs and dance songs). Several of the categories Helman mentions fall within Dalphinis' genre of prose narratives. For example, myths, legends and sagas, tales (often didactic), and stories. The characteristics of oral literature can be recognized in the regular structures in rhyme, rhythm and dialogue, and in audience participation. This kind of interaction is also present in songs, with a lead voice and chorus, and in folktales where the story-teller may be interrupted by the audience. Now we will present some examples from the various genres.

*Song, dance and theater.* The songs, dances and plays mentioned in Voorhoeve and Lichtveld (1975) for Surinam include the **Banya** (a special type of song and dance); Banya evenings were held until this century (De Drie 1984). The **Du** (a dramatized, mostly satirical form of the Banya with set characters acting out different roles) was performed by companies organized along the lines of literary societies in Europe. The companies had names like *Boenhatti gi ondrofenni* ('mercy leads to experience') or *Lavender* ('lavender'), names which would have not been out of place in European literary societies. Their productions were spectacular. Later, the Europeans used the Du (in a commercial form) to ridicule their opponents (Lichtveld and Voorhoeve 1980). We also have the **Laku**, with more elaborate drama than the Banya, and the **Lobisingi** ('love song' often dealing with jealousy in lesbian or heterosexual relations, and performed on the street, in the presence of the rival or in front of his/her house). This last genre is believed to have originated after the time of slavery.

All these forms were executed by large groups of costumed actors, both men and women, in special societies also called *Du*. Every plantation, where these plays were also performed, had its own performing group. Their public performances consisted of two parts: the preparation, a ceremony at one of the participants' homes which in turn consisted of two parts: the **komparsi**, a musical rehearsal, and the **opo dron** 'to start drumming', a religious preparation. The second part is the stage performance which was introduced by the **krioro dron** 'creole drum'. The characters were for instance: Afrankeri, the defender of the high morals, Abenitanta or Momoi, the criticizers of persons or events, and Temeku, the narrator of the hidden allusions in the songs. The songs vary according to the genre of the play. This in turn determined the content, functions and setting, and the way the songs were performed, i.e. accompanied or unaccompanied. For example, in the first part of the public performance, the songs were not accompanied by drums. There were greeting songs, satirical songs including those referring to the conditions of slavery, and dramatic songs setting out the theme of the play. Many of these songs are still sung, including the lobisingi, sometimes used with their original intensions e.g. to scoff.

To illustrate one aspect of such a performance we give an example here of an **opo dron**:

| | | |
|---|---|---|
| Mama Aysa fu goron, | Mama Aysa of the earth | (Sranan) |
| die u kon, u no kon | in coming here we come | |
| a yu tapu nanga tranga. | not unannounced to you. | |
| Un bun mama, | Oh good mother, | |
| di u kon, un no kon | in coming here we come | |
| a yu tapu nanga tranga. | not unannounced to you. | |
| Un seti begi na oso, | We've been in prayer at home, | |
| bifo un kon dya. | before we came to you. | |

(cited in Voorhoeve and Lichtveld 1975; song nr 1:22, translated by Vernie February)

*Riddle.* The riddle is one of the short oral narratives used by speakers to test and amuse each other. These questions or short descriptions - formulated in a cryptic way - often reflect conventional wisdom. Riddles may have different lengths, but tend to be extremely short. The subject of the riddle-story may refer to an everyday experience or to family matters. This, however, does not usually lead to the solution of the riddle, as we may judge from the answers. The riddles show similarities in form and content with West African sources. The examples are from Haitian (Hall 1953:201-209):

> Zepeng dò leve rwa lan-dòmi: leve pise.                    (Haitian)
> 'A needle of gold which wakes the king from sleep: getting up to urinate'.
> Dlo kouche: melon.
> 'Water lying down: melon'.

*Proverbs.* Proverbs are used in daily life, in poetry, in songs, and in folktales. They express not only conventional wisdom, but they are also used to scoff, to correct, or to communicate in secret. The first two proverbs are taken from Negerhollands (Pontoppidan 1891), followed by two Jamaican proverbs.

> As ju goi en steen na himmel, di sa faal bo ju koop.       (Negerhollands)
> 'If you throw a stone in the air, it will fall on top of you'.

Makakku weet wa fo een boom fo klemm, am no klemm stakkelboom.
'Makakku (monkey) knows what kind of tree to climb, he does not climb a thorn tree'.

In Jamaica the proverbs are put into Anancy's mouth.

Anancy says: When cockroach gib party, 'im no ax fowl.                    (Jamaican)
'When Cockroach throws a party, he does not invite Chicken.'
Anancy says: Pot say a kettle, 'tan 'way, you smudge me.
'The pot calls the kettle black'.

*Folktales.* The tradition of storytelling in creole societies originated under slavery. This in turn is derived from the storytelling tradition of Africa. Many Caribbean folktale themes and genres can be traced back to African sources. These are stories in which an animal, the hare/rabbit or the spider, is the chief protagonist who outwits his adversaries by cunning. The Jamaican Creole Anancy, the Papiamento Nanzi and the Surinamese Anansi spider stories are also common to many West African ethnic groups in which the spider outwits his enemies, e.g. Hausa Gizo the spider and his wife K'ok'i, and the Akan Anansi. The St. Lucian Patwa Kompè Lapèn 'Brer Rabbit' stories are related to the Wolof tales about Leuk, and the Hausa tales about Zomo, a hare who outwits his often physically superior adversaries (Dalphinis 1985). Voorhoeve & Lichtveld mentioned the appearance of the hare as trickster instead of the spider in one of their stories told by an old man. They consider this as exceptional for Surinam because, according to Lichtveld (1930:31,34) in North and Central America the trickster is a hare or a rabbit, but in the Windward Islands and on the mainland of South America it is a spider.

For Surinam, the occasions when stories are told can be divided roughly into two types. The informal occasion, such as when a spontaneous story telling session starts among the guests at a birthday party, purely meant for entertainment, or when bed time stories are told. The second type of occasion can be characterized as formal not only because of the character of the occasion but also because of its content and its highly formalized structure. One of the special occasions on which these formalized folktales are told is during wakes on the **ayti dey** - the eighth night after death - but also at a later stage during mourning ceremonies. The formalized folktale in Surinam has three main forms, one of which we have already seen, i.e. **laytori** 'riddles'. The two other types are **Anansitori** 'spider tales', and **Ondrofenitori** 'experience stories'. The Anansitori are partly or wholly educational stories. The Ondrofenitori can be divided into two types. The first type consists of tales in which the subjects are diverse as are their origins. The second type is the **Srafutentori** 'tales of the slavery period' or **Fositentori** 'tales from the past' with themes derived from oral literature, and with their setting in the historical past. According to Voorhoeve and Lichtveld (1975) these stories are not cases of informal historical tradition, but highly formalized folktales. As they go on to say, the historical truth behind them is uncertain, although the names of plantations and plantation owners are frequently mentioned (see Price 1983 for a different view). The formalized stories follow a fixed pattern of rules and formulas, which the story-teller and the audience have to adhere to. These special procedures are neccessary, because these forms of literature are unwritten and have to be learned by heart. The structure of the narratives, the rhythm of the texts, and the participation of the audience can be seen as having a mnemonic function.

One of the characteristics of oral literature is the active participation of the audience varying from handclapping to actually interrupting the story-teller. The interruption may be in the form of a song, a proverb or a story. In the last case the new story will be embedded in the first. There can be many embedded stories. After each interruption the first storyteller gets to continue his story first.

*The different functions of oral literature.* The functions of oral literature are diverse and seem to support the idea that people will always need some 'belief' to hold on to in life. This is also valid for written literature, at least to some extent. One may call this 'belief' a philosophy of life. It emphasizes or illuminates aspects of life: the way one functions or disfunctions, or one's position within a particular community. As mentioned previously, we are still confronted with oral narratives which may carry the label 'philosophy of life' since they tend to tell a moral, give advice, or propagate norms and values. These aspects of life can be found also in the five functions of oral tradition distinguished by Dalphinis (1985). The **archival** function (storage of items of historical value), the use of **praise and abuse** (praise is used to reinforce conformity to the particular society's values), the **political** function, the **social** function (transmission or analysis of social events, norms and values), and **audience participation** (without an audience the story-teller cannot function properly). All these functions are present in West African oral literature, and can be found in creole societies in the Caribbean.

Some of these functions are still operative in the creole speaking maroon communities of Surinam who have preserved a rich oral culture. These communities are organized according to the conditions set down in their oral traditions (Pakosi 1989). The oral mode of these communities consists of a total of six categories, and the functions related to them: 1. **Baka-koni** (all the specific knowledge every person has concerning him/herself and other members of the tribe. This knowledge is used only when necessary), 2. **Gaanmama-sani** (the material and immaterial inheritance of the ancestors), 3. **Fositen-toli** or **gaansama-toli** (the history of the sons of the tribe), 4. **Mato** or **Anainsi-toli** or **Kontu** (fairy tales and spider tales by means of which a lifestyle is transferred to the next generation. At the end of these tales an answer is given to the question why something must or must not be done. Part of the upbringing of the youngsters of the tribe is done by means of **Anainsi** tales ), 5. **Kiya** (rules concerning upbringing and education) and 6. **Leli** (what and how one learns about life).

If we compare the five functions given by Dalphinis with these six categories, it is obvious that the archival function and the social function are strongly represented in the way the maroon society is organized. In those creole societies which are not organized according to an oral tradition remnants of all these functions can still be recognized in written literature, poetry and prose, and plays and songs. For example, the archival function can be found in epic poetry, in historic novels, in plays and songs telling of heroic events, especially about freedom fighters from the time of slavery.

## 7.4  Written literature

The written literary tradition can only be said to have begun after emancipation, as an extension of the European literary tradition, and through education. Although the literary movements within the creole societies cannot be considered as identical to their European counterparts, some Caribbean writers can be classified within these movements on the basis of features common to the European and creole cultures (Debrot 1977). Typical aspects encountered in creole literature might include the vivid style of story telling, the long dialogues reflecting oral techniques, the incorporation of proverbial wisdom in prose and poetry, and the above mentioned use of song techniques (Brathwaite 1974, 1984; Dalphinis 1985; Voorhoeve & Lichtveld 1975). Education also determined to a large extent the language in which the literary product was to be written, since there was no education provided in the creole language. It is true that as a result of education in one of the European languages (English, Dutch, French, Spanish) the writer could reach a larger public, but the disadvantage was that, until recently, there were very few literary products composed in the creole languages, and therefore little opportunity of developing a literary vocabulary. Given that no language has such a vocabulary to start with, this can be seen as a great loss for many creole communities. Brathwaite (1984) discusses the frequent inability of creole writers to convey emotions due to the lack of a creole literary vocabulary. He illustrates this with a poem by the Barbadian writer Anthony Hinkson which describes the experience of a hurricane. This writer catches the essence of the imminent hurricane in a unique way. He says, 'but when the hurricane itself comes, when "leaves collapse" and "ever man turn owl/ever jack/ eye wide/mout twist in surprise", not even Hinkson can catch all the right syllables' (Brathwaite 1984:11). The pentameter, supplied as a verse form by Eurocentric education expresses an experience which is not that of a hurricane. Hurricanes do not roar in pentameters. In this first period then the literary enterprise of the creole societies was strongly associated with and fed by European literary traditions. The critique of and reaction to this fact was also one of the reasons leading to literary movements focused on the creole speaking communities itself.

*Literary movements.* We may classify the written literary traditions of the creole societies into roughly four main strands. In the first strand we observe a considerable influence from European literature in content, form and style. We refer here both to literature written in a non-creole language, and translations of texts and plays into a creole language. With respect to the European influence, Broek (1988) remarks that some Caribbean writers use European texts, taken, for instance, from the Bible, Robinson Crusoe, Gulliver's travels, Jane Eyre and Shakespeare's dramas, as a vehicle for discussing certain phenomena of creole society. The interpretations given to the themes of these literary pieces are Caribbean. He mentions the Jamaican writer Roger Mais who presents his own version of the Bible story of Samson and Delilah, in order to criticize the phenomenon of 'alienation' within Caribbean society.

The second literary strand can be characterized by its strong emphasis on and the re-evaluation of the African cultural heritage. This strand can be dated to 1898 and formed a response to the American occupation of the Greater Antilles (Brathwaite 1974). It was also meant as a protest against the rejection by the creole elite of creole culture and against Western cultural influences in general. This strand corresponds to the movements known as: **Indígenismo, Poesía Afro-Antilliana** (as represented by the Cuban writer Nicolás Guillén), **Négritude** (as represented by the Martiniquian writer Aimé Césaire), and **Indigé-nisme** (as represented by the Haïtian ethnologist Jean Price-Mars). Their literary products reflect the characteristics of the oral literary tradition. In poetry we may encounter melodies and rhythms imitative of African music.

The third main literary strand can be characterized by its orientation towards creole society and culture, i.e. without emphasizing the African heritage. Writers such as Maryse Condé, and other young Caribbean writers who may be regarded as representatives of this third strand, dissociate themselves from the preceding, Afro-centric, view of creole literature. In terms of the content of these literary products, we witness a focus on creole cultural events, and severe criticism of some aspects of creole societies. An example is the *barrack-yard* (Trinidad) or *bakadyari* (Surinam): the back yard-theme which describes the existing socio-economic conditions and their consequences for the people involved.

The fourth strand is represented by the four types of 'African influenced-writing' Brathwaite (1974) distinguishes. The first is **Rhetoric Africa** where Africa is used as a 'mask, signal or nomen'. In these literary manifestations the writer expresses a deep desire of connection with Africa. The second is the literature of African **survival** in which African survivals in the Caribbean society are dealt with quite consciously. Here the writer does not necessarily try to interpret or reconnect these survivals with the traditions of Africa. The third is the literature of African **expression** with its root in folk material. An attempt is made here to adapt or to transform folk material into literary experiment. The fourth is called the literature of **reconnection**. Writers belonging to this fourth category try to relate experiences garnered in visits to Africa, to their New World existence. We also find writers who are reaching out to bridge the gap with their spiritual heartland. This strand differs from the second strand in that the African factor plays the largest role.

However, it is obvious from the literary movements discussed above that for a large group of writers the spiritual heartland is the creole society they are a member of. This is most strongly expressed in Louise Bennett's poem, written in reaction to the Back-to-Africa movement with its advocates in Jamaica among the Ras Tafari, who believe in the divinity of Haile Selassie, Emperor of Ethiopia, and in the pre-destined repatriation of the 'black Israelites' (Jamaican blacks) to the Promised land (Africa, in particular Ethiopia). In this poem the aspirations of this movement are seen as a rejection of common sense, and of the realities of the historical situation of the Jamaican people. The seventh verse alludes to the confusion which would indeed be the result,

> Ef de whole worl' start fe go back
> Weh dem great granpa come from!                    (L. Bennett 1972:214-215)

This poem was written in 1947, but belongs in spirit to the Jamaica of the sixties (Nettleford 1989). Although the sixties are long gone, the spirit of this poem is still relevant, in a broader sense. This Back-to-Africa movement has no advocates in Surinam. For the majority of writers, Surinam was and is the spiritual heartland.

## 7.5 Conclusion

In prose and poetry various themes are dealt with, for instance, those relating to socio-economic, political, environmental, historical, racial and socio-cultural issues. Writers living abroad also influence creole societies by virtue of their exposure to a different cultural and political life.

One barrier to the development of creole literary language is that, in many domains of style and subject matter, European languages are preferred. The choice of theme still seems to determine to a great extent the language in which the writer communicates with his/her readers. Some of the poems and novels are completely written in a creole language, but sometimes only the dialogues. Another group of writers write solely in one of the European languages regardless of the theme. An important reason for this situation is economic. The choice not to write in a creole language has its advantages and ensures one a larger readership and the possibility of international recognition. All or most Caribbean writers who have won prizes, such as the Nobel Prize for literature for Derek Walcott in 1992, write in a European language.

**Further reading**

A good anthology of Surinamese literature is Voorhoeve and Lichtveld (1975). For the cultural background of Surinam, the reader should consult Helman (1977), for the Dutch Antilles, Römer (1977), for the English-speaking Caribbean, Brathwaite (1984) and for the Caribbean in general Broek (1988). Brathwaite's book contains a useful bibliography.

# Part II.
# Theories of Genesis

# 8  Theories focusing on the European input

Hans den Besten, Pieter Muysken and Norval Smith

## 8.1  Introduction

In this chapter we will discuss a number of theories concerning the development of creole languages which lay the prime responsibility for this at the door of the languages of the European colonial powers. These theories are of various types.

First there are those theories that look to **specific European or European-derived language forms** to explain creole origins. We have first the monogenetic theory which claims in its most radical form that all the creole languages of the world derive ultimately from a Portuguese-based pidgin spoken on the coast of West Africa. Then we have the approaches that claim that creole languages are (partially) derived from mixtures of European dialects of European languages. Another type of explanation is claimed to be provided by accounts of influence from European languages in the various locations connected with the slave trade: in Africa, during the 'Middle Passage', and in the Americas. Lastly, we will examine various accounts of the development of mixed European-source creoles.

Second, we have theories that lay stress on the **transformation of European language structures**. The first of these theories – the foreigner talk/baby talk hypothesis – proceeds from the assumption that Europeans deliberately simplified their languages when talking to Africans, so that the Africans did not have a proper chance to learn English, French, etc. The next hypothesis is the imperfect second language learning hypothesis which claims that creoles are basically European languages which the slaves simply failed to learn properly.

## 8.2  Monogenetic theories

So-called monogenetic theories are theories hypothesizing a single origin for (pidgin and) creole languages. There are basically two primary versions of this. The first would derive all creoles from a West African Pidgin Portuguese. The second version incorporates the first and assumes additionally that this pidgin in turn was derived from the Lingua Franca of the Mediterranean.

Variations on this theme concern the various donor-language groups: Portuguese, English or French, in particular, hypothesizing a single origin for the Portuguese-based, English-based, or French-based creoles alone. We could refer to this type of theory as involving a restricted monogenetic approach.

### 8.2.1  Monogenesis and West African Pidgin Portuguese

In the 60's and early 70's the monogenesis theory was much in vogue. This theory, articulated first in Taylor (1961) and Thompson (1961), assumed that a West African Pidgin Portuguese (WAPP) was spoken from the 15th century to the 18th century in and around the numerous forts and trading settlements founded by the Portuguese along the West African coast. This was the direct precursor of the various Portuguese-based creoles spoken there. In an attempt to provide an explanation for the deep-seated similarities between these and creoles with different lexical bases, it was hypothesized that the French, English and other creoles were also derived from the WAPP by **relexification**, or the word-for-word replacement of Portuguese lexical items with French or English items.

As such the concept of relexification was sound enough. Clear cases of relexification have come to light – most notably the case of Media Lengua in Ecuador (Muysken 1981b), where several originally Quechua-speaking communities have basically kept the Quechua grammatical structure of their language, but replaced the Quechua lexical stems with Spanish ones (see chapter 4).

As proof for the relexification of Portuguese words in Atlantic creoles by other lexifier languages, linguists used to cite the case of Saramaccan – one of the so-called Bush-Negro languages of Surinam. This language has roughly about 400 lexical items of Portuguese origin, as compared with around 600 of English origin. This is a fairly unusual situation among creole languages. The Saramaccan case is however no longer regarded as proof for the monogenetic position. A closer examination of the Saramaccan facts makes this clear (see Smith 1987).

### 8.2.2  Monogenesis and the Lingua Franca

An outgrowth of the hypothesis that all Atlantic creoles were to be derived by relexification from a West African Pidgin Portuguese was the further hypothesis that the WAPP was derived by relexification from the Lingua Franca spoken in the Mediterranean. This primarily Italian-based pidgin is assumed to have come into existence around the year 1000, although the first records of it date from the 14th century. The possibility of a role for Lingua Franca in the formation of WAPP cannot of course be denied, but cannot be proved either. In any case, since it must be regarded as clear that the English-based and French-based creoles of the Atlantic area did not arise by relexification from WAPP, it is equally clear that the Lingua Franca cannot have had any role in their formation either.

It must be stated that the monogenetic hypothesis, or any weaker version of it, is fundamentally flawed in any case. The idea that all pidgins and creoles, or even all creoles, or even all creoles in the Atlantic area, require to be derived from a single case of pidginization is completely irrational. A **unique** example of any **type** of phenomenon connected with human conceptual and cultural activity is just inconceivable – anything that can happen once can also happen more frequently.

### 8.2.3 Restricted monogenesis

A more restricted approach to explaining the occurrence of English and French-based creoles is to assume that these derive respectively from a West African Pidgin English (WAPE) and West African Pidgin French (WAPF). Each of these two 'families' of creoles display significant parallels, which are not all shared between the two groups. Without going into details, the main question raised in this debate is whether the two main groups of English-based creoles – the Atlantic and the Pacific groups – have a common origin, and similarly whether the two main groups of French-based creoles – the Atlantic and the Indian Ocean groups – have a common origin.

## 8.3 European dialect (partial) origin hypotheses

We frequently find, in connection with creoles and pidgins based on the European colonial languages, attempts to relate them, in whole or in part, to particular local or regional dialects of these languages. This has been especially noticeable among students of English and French creoles (cf. Chaudenson 1992).

For instance, Faine (1937) makes the claim that Haitian is three-quarters derived from Norman French, a claim he later abandoned. Among the early representatives of this group such explanations of the 'derivations' of creole languages from non-standard European dialects usually go hand-in-hand with attempts to deny more than trivial influence from 'substrate' languages on the development of the creoles. So Faine wishes to deny any significant influence from African languages on any of the French-based creoles of the Americas, barring certain aspects of pronunciation such as the unrounding of French front rounded vowels, and the occurrence of a number of African lexical items.

Turner (1949) cites a number of workers on Gullah (the creole of the Carolina/Georgia coast), writing in the first forty years of this century, who claim that the 'peculiarities' of Gullah are to be explained as a combination of dialectal forms of English, and the influence of other factors usually concerned with language acquisition, such as the effects of the baby talk theory discussed in section 8.6.

The identification of regional and dialectal lexical elements, and occasionally of syntactic influence, has not always proceeded according to a strict methodology. Holm & Shilling's 1982 dictionary of Bahamian is criticized in this respect by Smith (1983), and these criticisms could fairly be applied to many such studies examining the regional provenance of the English creole vocabulary. The basic problem is that dialect lexicographical studies of the various types of European languages are extremely uneven in their geographical coverage.

### 8.3.1  English dialects

While in no sense wishing to deny the undoubted contribution of Scotsmen to the development of the various seventeenth century English colonies, the relatively high proportion
of lexical items with a specifically Scottish distribution claimed to be found in several
lexicographical studies of English-based creoles cannot but be connected with the fact that
the coverage of Scots lexicography is better than that of the various English dialects of
England, not to speak of those of Ireland or Wales.

It cannot be denied that non-standard lexical items occur with some frequency in both
French and English creoles. However it is also notable that **phonological** dialectalisms are
conspicuous by their absence, especially in English creoles. For instance, among the Bahamian words claimed to have a Scottish origin by Holm & Shilling, there is not a single
instance of an incontrovertible Scots dialectal pronunciation. In this respect the creoles do
not differ from non-creole colonial English. With respect to American English we can point
to a similar general lack of dialectal phonetics and phonology, although dialect words are
common enough. Smith (1987) demonstrates that virtually all cases of superficially non-
standard pronunciations occurring in the English-derived vocabulary of the Surinam creoles
are amenable to explanation in terms of the various sociolects of 17th century London
English. One (!) very early form may be interpretable as deriving from the local dialect of
Bristol, the second-largest important port of England.

### 8.3.2  French dialects

Goodman (1964) argues that many of the claimed cases of Norman and Picard phonological
influence in the French creoles are explicable from earlier standard forms, or forms from
dialects very close to the standard language of Paris. Hull (1979), on the other hand, does
find some evidence of regional French. Apart from Maritime French (on which see below),
the influence of the dialects of La Rochelle in the Aunis-Saintonge region of France appears
sporadically in creoles.

### 8.3.3  Dutch dialects

As an illustration for the varying influence of Dutch dialects on the creation of creoles, we
can compare the Dutch-derived vocabulary in Sranan with that in Berbice Dutch. Lexical
items in Berbice Dutch differ from those in the Surinam creoles particularly in that *ij* – now
[ɛi] – is fairly regularly represented by undiphthongized /i/ in Berbice whereas this reflex
is rarer in Surinam, with /ei/ occurring much more frequently. This is perhaps to be explained not so much in terms of the 50-year time gap between the settlement of Berbice

by the Dutch, and the beginning of Dutch control of Surinam, as due to the fact that the first colony was founded from Middelburg (Zealand), while the second was run from Amsterdam (North Holland), and that these two maritime provinces, separately responsible for 17th century Dutch colonialism, possessed fairly divergent dialects.

Note that the greater amount of dialect influence observable in Dutch-based and Dutch-influenced creoles is presumably due to the fact that the Netherlands was a much less centralized country than England or France at that time, with a consequent reduction of linguistic standardization.

## 8.4 Theories concerning the influence of the Atlantic slave trade

The possibilities for the influence of European languages on the development of the various European language-based creoles which came to be spoken in the Atlantic area – of whatever type this influence may be – may be logically divided up into three types. We will discuss this largely from the point of view of English. The three types are:

a) in Africa
b) at sea (nautical language)
c) in America

### 8.4.1 Influence from English in Africa (Hancock's Domestic Origin Hypothesis)
The most persuasive scenario for the early development of a local form of English in West Africa is provided by Hancock (1986). Towards the end of the 16th century English-speaking traders, etc. began to settle in the Gambia and Sierra Leone rivers, and neighbouring areas such as the Bullom and Sherbro coasts. These intermarried with the local population leading to a mixed population. A Krio-like Pidgin English is spoken at various places southwards along the coast of West Africa, and this was taken, according to Hancock, to the West Indies with African slaves who had learned it in the slave depots of West Africa, forming one component of the emergent creole languages.

Note that as far as Surinam is concerned any influence from early West African Pidgin English (WAPE) would have to date from the third quarter of the 17th century, and be located in the Slave Coast area – i.e. from Eastern Ghana through Togo (and Benin) to Western Nigeria. So, it is of some considerable importance to attempt to establish if this represents a possible scenario. We have in fact little in the way of direct evidence bearing on this, although Hancock (1969) quotes Barbot (1732) as finding 'good English' spoken by canoemen he met at sea near Elmina on the Gold Coast in 1679.

An indication of the necessity of assuming a connection between forms of West African

English (and Krio) and the English-based creoles of the Americas is provided by the existence of what Smith (1987) has called Ingredient x. This consists of a number of items derived from African coastal languages ranging from Wolof (Sierra Leone) to Kimbundu (Angola). Largely the same group of lexical items is found evidenced in most English-based creoles/pidgins on both sides of the Atlantic. Cf. Wolof *njam* 'eat', found in Sranan, Saramaccan, Ndjuka, Krio, Gullah, Jamaican, Guyanese, Miskito Coast Creole, and Bahamian, among others. In general this group only occurs as such in English-based creoles. Thus we find the word *bakra* 'European' of Efik origin in the English group. In French creoles 'European' is usually *beke* of Ijọ derivation, for instance.

We would assume these elements to have been present in a pidginized form of English, closely related to the precursor of WAPE, spoken along the West African coast in the 17th century. Krio-like phonological effects are most widely evidenced in the transatlantic creoles spoken in Surinam, as well as in the Jamaican Maroon Spirit Language (MSL) only surviving as a ritual language among the Eastern Maroons of Jamaica (Bilby 1983), but undoubtedly representing a survival of an earlier creole language.

### 8.4.2 Influence from nautical language

There is a nautical element in the vocabulary of a number of English, French and Dutch-based, creoles and pidgins. Krio has for instance the following elements (Hancock 1969; 1976):

| (1) | gjali | 'kitchen' | <galley | (Krio) |
|-----|-------|-----------|---------|--------|
| | kjapsaj | 'overturn' | <capsize | |
| | bambotgjal | 'prostitute' | <bumboat-girl | |

In Surinam this element is less prominent but still present:

| (2) | drifi | 'edge up' | <drift | (Sranan) |
|-----|-------|-----------|--------|----------|
| | ari | 'pull, draw' | <haul | |

In French creoles there is a similar nautical influence, sometimes involving related items.

| (3) | *Fr. creole* | | | *distribution* |
|-----|--------------|---|---|----------------|
| | hale/rale | 'pull, drag' | <haler | LA,HA,ANT,FG,IO |
| | mare | 'tie' | <amarrer | LA,HA,ANT,FG,IO |
| | hele/rele | 'call' | <héler | LA,HA,ANT |

(LA = Louisiana; HA = Haiti; ANT = Lesser Antilles; FG = French Guiana; IO = Indian Ocean (Goodman 1964))

In the case of Dutch creoles we find items derived from the Dutch nautical term *kombuis* 'galley' used in Berbice Dutch, Skepi Dutch, Negerhollands and, very significantly, the creoloid Afrikaans.

The precise means of transference of this nautical vocabulary to the various creoles is unclear. A number of possibilities suggest themselves (see also Hancock (1986).

1) they were acquired by the mixed population of the Gambia-Sierra Leone coast.
2) they were acquired by slaves during coastwise sea journeys in Africa.
3) they were acquired by slaves during their imprisonment in slave depots in Africa.
4) they were acquired by slaves during the Middle Passage (from Africa to America).
5) they formed part of the vocabulary of the colonial whites, having been picked up by them during the week/month-long voyages from Europe to the colonies.

Note that very likely a combination of these factors played a role, rather than that any single factor was responsible.

### 8.4.3 Influence from English in the Americas

Our examples of English input are taken from the creole languages of Surinam. This is because the English items in these languages have been fairly closely examined, and because the influence of English itself has been negligible in modern times.

The area of English influence is virtually restricted to the lexical. Although there are only about 700 English lexical items represented in the languages of Surinam, different strands of English influence may be recognized. Most striking is the fact that two types of English at least may be distinguished. There are clear indications of the presence of an **r-less** and an **r-ful** form of English. These two types are both frequent in the English-speaking world. Notable is the fact that both are represented in the colonial English of North America. In the Caribbean, however, most forms of English are r-less, except for the English of Barbados. As the major colonial effort in Surinam came from Barbados, the presence in Surinam of an r-ful strand may be connected with that island. Examples of the developments reflecting the r-less type are as follows:

| (4) | EME | *via* | *Surinam* | *examples* |
|---|---|---|---|---|
| | εɪr | eɪə | ei | ei (Sr: hare), séséj (Nd: shear) |
| | ɛ:r | ɛə | e/ɛ (Sar) | dé (Sar: there), ke (Sr: care), hé (Nd: hare) |
| | air | aɪ-ə | aja | fája (Sr,Sar,Nd,Al: fire) |
| | ɔ:r | ɔə | o/ɔ (Sar) | fɔ (Sar: four) fo (Sr,Nd,Al: four) |

The r-ful type is on the other hand reflected by developments such as:

(5)    EME    *via*    *Surinam*         *examples*
       ɛːr    ɛːr    er(i)             Sr. kwéri 'square'
       ar  =  ar    ar(a)             Sr. fára 'far'
       ɔːr    ɔːr    or(o), (ɔɔ) (Sar) Sr. móro 'more'

The r-less forms of English are very close to what we find in Krio and WAPE, so that we may hypothesize that the source of these items in Surinam is similar to that we suggested for Ingredient above. The scenario would then be that in Surinam/Barbados two strands of English became united in a pidgin/creole – the local (r-ful) colonial English and an (r-less) pidgin English brought from Africa by the slaves. This would be supported by the nautical evidence in most creoles.

## 8.5  Mixed European-source creoles

We have seen above that the European evidence itself is often complex. For some creoles the full story is even more complicated. These are creoles that appear to have not one but two European lexifier languages. For instance Smith (1987) proposes the following historical descent for (components of) Saramaccan. Saramaccan is the descendant of a mixed language – a mixed pidgin or creole in fact – known as Dju-tongo (Jews' language). This resulted from the marriage of a putative Surinam Pidgin English of Barbadian provenance, and what has been described by Smith as Surinam Portuguese Creole – from which a couple of sentences have been preserved. This marriage took place on the middle Suriname River where Portuguese Jews from Brazil owned many plantations. Both the English and Portuguese strands in Saramaccan have been claimed to derive ultimately from Africa (see above for the English strand).

(6)    West African Pidgin Portuguese

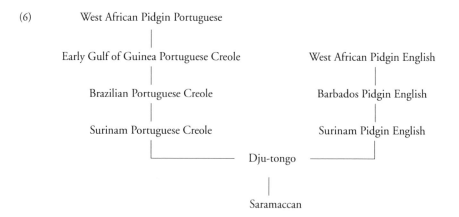

It is of interest to examine the evidence for this claimed Surinam Portuguese Creole:

(7) Praga beroegoe no mata caballo. (Wullschlägel 1856)
/praga burugu no mata kabalo/ (phonological interpretation (Smith))
curse ass NEG kill horse (glosses)
'The curse of an ass will not kill a horse.' (literal meaning)

This proverb, or something similar, is known from numerous languages, including Portuguese creoles like Senegal Crioulo, and the mixed Spanish-Portuguese Papiamento. New evidence for the Brazilian connection is provided in Holm (1992), which gives a Brazilian Portuguese parallel for the proverb.

(8) Surinam: Praga beroegoe no mata caballo Brazil: Praga de burrico não mata cavalo

Other evidence of a lexical and phonological nature is available which would tend to confirm the Brazilian connections of Saramaccan.

## 8.6 Foreigner talk and baby talk

It is commonly known that people will simplify their speech when talking to foreigners. The result has been called Foreigner Talk in the sociolinguistic literature, and some authors claim that this could have formed the basis for the formation of pidgins and ultimately creoles. We will first briefly look at the characteristics of foreigner talk and then consider the possible consequences for pidgin genesis. Foreigner talk is in fact the result of at least four separate processes: accommodation, imitation, telegraphic condensation, and adoption of conventions, often derived from holiday experiences or colonial usage.

**Accommodation** to the non-native competence of the other results in slower speech, shorter and less complex sentences, the introduction of pauses between constituents, the use of general and semantically unspecific terms, and repetitions. An example would be:

(9) NS: Could you please repeat the problem that your wife was mentioning?
FS: What you say?
NS: You wife has a problem, a difficulty. ... Please say it again, please repeat the problem. ...
Please say it again.
(NS = native speaker; FS = foreign speaker)

**Imitation** of the speech of the non-native interlocutor can take various forms, depending on the nature and level of the interlocutor's second language competence. An example:

(10)    FS:  I no hear vot you say.
        NS:  You no hear?

**Telegraphic condensation** leads to deletion of function words such as articles, auxiliaries, and copulas.

(11)    NS:  Did you get the package that was sent from Hongkong?
        FS:  What you say?
        NS:  Package arrive Hongkong. You get?

The adoption of **conventions** again can take various forms, of course: often it involves traditional pidgin-like features such as epinthetic vowels, the use of strong pronouns, specific foreign vocabulary, etc. Here a colonial tradition in the community of the native language may provide certain elements. In literature such forms are often perpetuated in the way low-status foreigners' speech is portrayed. An example from the way a non-European sailor is presented in Herman Melville's Moby Dick:

(12)    kill-e ... ah! him bery small-e fish-e; Queequeg no kill-e so small fish-e; Queequeg kill-e big
        whale.

In addition to these four processes, often speakers will adopt strategies used with the hard of hearing such as very loud speech, gestures, etc. Sometimes people will fall back on conventional aspects of ways of speaking with children, such as diminutive use. Hence the term Baby Talk, which is often used as an equivalent term for Foreigner Talk. An important point, stressed by Valdman (1981), is that the social status of the non-native speaker is a crucial factor. Speech addressed to low-status foreigners will often draw on conventions such as those mentioned above, while speech addressed to foreigners accorded a high-status often relies on accommodation strategies.

After this introduction, let us now turn to the role that Foreigner Talk may have played in the genesis of pidgins. Schuchardt (1909) drew attention to the fact that verbs in the Lingua Franca of the Mediterranean often have a form derived from the Romance infinitive. Now, infinitives, Schuchardt claims, are not the most frequent verb forms in ordinary spoken language. Hence we must assume that simplification of Romance languages (Italian, French, Spanish) must have been the basis for the Lingua Franca, i.e. a kind of Foreigner

Talk. The most vocal supporter of this line of thinking in the recent literature is Naro (1978), who formulated the Factorization Principle: 'express each meaning-bearing element with a separate stress-bearing form', as a way of accounting for the genesis of West African Portuguese Pidgin. Naro also tries to show, on the basis of historical documents, that the Portuguese pidgin must have emerged in Portugal itself as a **reconnaissance language** (i.e. a simplified form of Portuguese deliberately taught to African interpreters), rather than in Africa.

Whatever the merits in the Foreigner Talk theory, it is fairly clear that it (a) risks being circular; (b) that it makes certain specific predictions that are not borne out. The risk of circularity lies in the fact that forms of Foreigner Talk are often modeled on pidgins, so that the latter may erroneously be thought to have emerged out of the former. It is particularly the 'conventionalized', non-accommodative type of Foreigner Talk that resembles pidgins.

Those cases where we know that Foreigner Talk-type simplification and the type of simplification resulting from second language (L2) learning (see below) differ (rather than surmise it, as Schuchardt did), the pidgins and creoles resemble the result of L2 learning rather than of Foreigner Talk. A case in point is word order in Negerhollands and Berbice Dutch Creole. Dutch Foreigner Talk, particularly the type directed at low-status foreigners, is highly OV in its nature, consisting mostly of commands that take the infinitive form:

(13)    Tafels   schoonmaken!
        tables   clean
        'Clean [the] tables'.

However, it is well-known that the Dutch creoles show very consistent SVO order. Since this cannot be attributed completely to substrate influence (notice that the African source language of Berbice Dutch Creole is the SOV language Ijǫ; see Chapter 19), and fixed SVO patterns are highly characterisic of the L2 learning of Dutch, this fact speaks against the Foreigner Talk hypothesis as a general solution in the Dutch case.

## 8.7  Imperfect L2 learning

This brings us to the imperfect L2 learning hypothesis, which claims that pidgins are primarily the result of the imperfect L2 learning of the dominant lexifier language by the slaves. This was first proposed by Coelho (1880) (see also chapter 11 on universalist approaches). The large research literature on naturalistic L2 processes that has appeared since around 1970 has revealed a number of features of 'interlanguage systems' that we also see in many pidgins and creoles:

(14)　a.　invariant verb forms, derived either from the infinitive, or from the least marked finite form of the verb;

　　　b.　either no determiners, or else the use of demonstratives as determiners;

　　　c.　the invariable placement of the negator in preverbal position;

　　　d.　the use of adverbs to express modality;

　　　e.　a fixed single word order, no inversion in questions;

　　　f.　reduced or absent nominal plural marking.

While certainly not all features of creoles can be explained by appealing to imperfect L2 learning, it must have played an important role. In chapter 9 we look at the role of interference or transfer in L2 learning, when discussing the role of African substrate languages.

**Further reading**
For an up to date view on a number of different types of European influence on creole languages the reader should consult Goodman (1986), Hancock (1987) and Smith (1987).

# 9 Theories focusing on the non-European input

Jacques Arends, Silvia Kouwenberg and Norval Smith

## 9.1 Substrate, superstrate, adstrate

A superficial look at European-lexifier creoles is enough to show that these languages are not solely composed of European elements. The Atlantic creoles, for instance, display a clear African element that cannot be overlooked. This element is commonly referred to as the *substrate* or *substratum*. This term is not restricted to the African element in the Atlantic creoles, but is used more generally to refer to the presence of linguistic influence from the language(s) of the lower prestige group in a pidgin or creole. As for the Atlantic creoles, the presence of West African substrate influence is extensively discussed in Alleyne (1980), Boretzky (1983), Holm (1988), and Mufwene (1993a).

One group of West African languages in particular, the Kwa branch of the Niger-Congo family, mainly represented in Ghana, Togo, and Benin, has frequently been adduced as a source of substrate influence. The languages mentioned in this connection are Twi, a language cluster including Asante and Fante, spoken mainly in Ghana, and Gbe, a cluster including Vhe (Ewe) and Fon, spoken mainly in Togo and Benin. (Often the term Fongbe is used as well.) This, however, by no means implies that Kwa languages are the only West African languages that have left traces in the Atlantic creoles. Depending on where the slaves that were imported into a particular colony came from, other branches within Niger-Congo, such as Bantu and Mande, have left their stamp on the creoles that have developed in these colonies.

The term substrate has its origin in 19th-century historical linguistics and dialect geography. It refers to the language or dialect of the non-prestige group(s) in language contact situations. Gaulish, the former Celtic language of France for instance, was assumed to be the substrate for the Latin that developed there during Roman rule. Similarly, the language of the group with highest prestige is termed *superstrate* or *superstratum*. Finally, when two languages of roughly equal prestige are in contact, they are referred to as *adstrate* languages. In creole studies, however, the term adstrate is often used to refer to languages that were involved in the genesis of a creole without belonging either to the substrate or the superstrate. Apart from referring to particular languages involved in language contact situations, the terms substrate, superstrate and adstrate are also used to refer to the effects caused by these languages in the languages resulting from such contact.

Although at first sight it would seem quite logical to expect a greater or lesser substrate element in languages that have arisen out of the contacts of speakers of European languages with speakers of African languages, this is not accepted by all creolists. During the past two decades there has been a lot of controversy between the *substratists* on the one hand, and the *universalists* on the other. (For a representative collection of papers on this controversy, see Muysken & Smith 1986a; see also Mufwene 1993a). The universalist position, which holds that the extensive similarities between creoles of diverse historical and linguistic background are the result of the universal aspects of the human language faculty, rather than of transfer from some common substrate, is most prominently represented by Derek Bickerton (1974, 1981, 1984, 1988) (see chapter 11).

## 9.2  Substrate in creole genesis

In this section some of the more relevant issues in the substratist approach to creole genesis will be discussed. The first of these concerns a methodological problem which is known as (the problem of) the **Cafeteria Principle**, a term coined by Dillard (1970) to refer to the practice of arbitrarily attributing features of Atlantic English-based creoles to superstrate influence from assorted English dialects. With regard to substratal influence, the term Cafeteria Principle refers to a similar procedure, which is sometimes followed in order to 'demonstrate' influence from particular West African languages in particular Atlantic creoles. In its extreme form the method consists simply of picking some element present in the creole at hand, and then going through as many dictionaries or grammars of West African languages as necessary until some more or less plausible correspondence is found. As was argued most perseveringly and most cogently by Bickerton (1981), such a procedure is methodologically unsound. Because of the huge numbers of different languages in West Africa it is simply a matter of chance that sooner or later some apparent correspondences will be found.

Another methodological problem is that, in order to establish with some degree of certainty the substrate as the origin of a particular creole feature, we have to exclude the possibility that it may be due to universals of language. In other words, the phenomenon to be ascribed to a substrate origin will have to be a marked feature in the languages of the world, since otherwise its emergence in a creole may simply be a matter of universal grammar (Muysken & Smith 1986b).

In addition to these methodological problems, substrate research is confronted with an empirical problem, and this is how to know which substrate languages were represented when and where and with how many speakers. Although it has often been said that this problem is too complex to be solved, much progress has in fact been made in recent years in this area (see chapter 2). Thus it has been established that in the formative period of the

Surinam creoles the majority of Africans spoke languages belonging to either the Gbe or the Kikongo language clusters (Arends, to appear b). No doubt future research will reveal similar findings for other creole regions.

The above finding is related to an issue which is important for substrate research more generally, and that is the question of the homogeneity versus heterogeneity of the substrate. Did the substrate consist of many, partly unrelated or only remotely related languages, or was only a small number of more or less closely related languages involved? Obviously, the more homogeneous the substrate, the better the chance of it having an impact on the creole (see Singler 1988 for an especially illuminating study of this issue).

Although significant substrate influence has been demonstrated for at least some creoles, some creolists, such as Bickerton, have argued, mainly on theoretical grounds, that, apart from phonology, the substrate can only have played a marginal role at best. In earlier versions of Bickerton's theory (1981, 1984), the only stages at which substratal influence could occur was during pidginization (through transfer or calques) or during later stages in the development of a creole (through borrowing). In the former case, however, substrate influence is supposed to be temporary since it will be erased by the bioprogram during nativization. Bickerton's more recent adoption of the lexical-learning hypothesis of language acquisition (1988, 1989) has forced him to allow for more significant substrate influence. If a function word or morpheme is adopted from a substrate language, then a number of the associated morphosyntactic characteristics may be adopted along with it.

Apart from this weak version of the substrate hypothesis, claiming that some creole features should be attributed to one or the other out of a number of African languages, during the last decade a stronger version has been put forward under the name of relexification by Lefebvre and her associates with respect to Haitian Creole (e.g. Lefebvre 1986). Put simply, the relexification hypothesis (not to be confused with the monogenesis-relexification hypothesis discussed in chapter 8) claims that Haitian is a relexified version of Gbe. In other words, one particular substrate language is singled out as the origin of many structural properties of Haitian Creole. It should be noted that this hypothesis is couched in the framework of modern generative theory, which means that the investigation of parallels between Haitian and Gbe is performed at a deep syntactic level rather than in terms of surface structures. Although at first sight the selection of only one particular substrate language may seem implausible, the evidence from Berbice Dutch, where one particular West African language (Eastern Ijọ) is responsible for the majority of African elements (see chapter 19), shows that it can certainly not be excluded in principle.

Finally we must mention one case where the Cafeteria Principle does seem to be justified after all. Most of the English-based creoles of the Atlantic area, but not those that are French- or Portuguese-based, share a number of words from geographically diverse African languages, termed Ingredient x by Smith (1987). It consists of lexical items from languages like Igbo, Kikongo, Wolof, Twi, Kimbundu, Efik, Gbe and Yoruba. Some of these languages – Gbe, Kikongo and Twi – are definitely substrate languages for certain creoles. Others, such as Efik, Igbo and Wolof are definitely not. The most likely explanation for the occurrence of this African ingredient in these creoles is that these words were not taken directly from the substrate, but from the Pidgin English claimed by Hancock (1986) to be in existence along the 17th-century West African coast. During trade contacts these words were adopted by this pidgin, from which they were later transferred to the different Atlantic creoles.

## 9.3 West African substrate languages

In the remainder of this chapter attention will be focused on Surinam and Berbice. Daeleman (1972) was the first to point out that there was a considerable Kikongo lexical element present in Saramaccan. This is the case in the other Surinam creoles too, although to a lesser extent in Sranan. Other African languages that have left their stamp in Surinam are Gbe and, to a lesser extent, Twi. These three languages are the only ones that have been identified as contributing more than a handful of words to the Surinam creoles.

In all these cases of African lexical influence, the main contribution is to the more 'cultural' parts of the lexicon. Typical lexical domains for African words to be found in creoles are those connected with religion, family relationships, customs, traditional implements, cooking, fishing and hunting, etc. In addition the natural world – flora and fauna – is another place where such words appear, although to a lesser extent. Here lexical items from Amerindian languages play an important role as well (see section 9.5).

Quite different is the situation in Berbice Dutch, where uniquely, a significant proportion of African lexical items also appears in the basic vocabulary. The widespread lexical influence from Eastern Ijǫ is unparalleled among the Atlantic creole languages. Although Berbice Dutch may not be the only creole language to exhibit the influence of African languages in its morphology, it is the only case where derivational morphemes appear in their African phonological form. What is even more unusual is that inflectional morphemes and syntactic particles are retained from Eastern Ijǫ. In fact this case is the only one so far where not only the language, but the dialect that forms the major substrate element has been securely identified.

In a number of former plantation societies ritual or cult languages are or have been employed, such as the English-based Maroon Spirit Possession Language of Jamaica (see chapter 2). In general, however, these languages are based on African languages. In Brazil and Cuba, for instance, Yoruba and other African languages are used by the Candomblé religious societies. In Surinam ritual languages based on Kikongo, Gbe, and Twi are used during religious sessions among the various creole groups.

The identification of African languages that have had an influence on the Surinam creoles and that have formed the basis for the cult languages is fully confirmed by Postma's (1990) findings concerning the regional origins of the slaves brought to Surinam (see chapter 2). Although much less is known about the origin of the Berbice slaves, it is certain that Dutch traders were active in the Niger Delta region, where Eastern Ịjọ is spoken, around the time of the foundation of Berbice as a Dutch colony.

## 9.4  Evidence for substrate influence

In this section some examples of direct substrate influence will be given for all levels of grammar, i.e. phonology, morphology/lexicon, syntax and semantics. In doing so we will concentrate on the Surinam creoles and on Berbice Dutch. Although as yet not very much is known about substrate influence on the pragmatic level, it seems certain that at least in one type of speech event, story telling, African modes of behavior have left their traces in the Atlantic creoles (see chapter 7). We will not discuss that issue here.

### 9.4.1  Phonology

In this section phonological substrate influence will be illustrated for the Surinam creoles.

The **syllable structure** of the most important substrate languages in respect of the Surinam creoles – Gbe and Kikongo – is very different from that of the lexifier language English. Gbe only allows open syllables. These are of two types – with oral vowels, and with nasal vowels. Kikongo has only (oral-voweled) open syllables, except that word-internally syllables may be closed with a nasal homorganic to a following obstruent.

| (1) | Gbe types | Kikongo types |
|-----|-----------|---------------|
|     | CV, CṼ    | CV, CVV, CVVN |

A comparison of the Surinam languages suggests that at an earlier stage all the languages were basically of an open-syllable structure, as all the Maroon languages are now at the phonetic level, and Sranan is at the phonological level. European-derived items with final consonants were in general supplied with supportive (epithetic) final vowels. Phonetically, however, Sranan allows closed syllables, due to the extensive syncope of unstressed vowels. In addition, Sranan allows complex onset clusters, as does the Ndjuka-Paramaccan-Aluku-Kwinti (NAPK) language optionally with /sc/-clusters. All the languages allow medial nasal clusters, with Saramaccan and NAPK also allowing these initially.

(2)　　lob(i)　　'rub　　　　　　　　　　　　　　　　　　　　　　　(Sranan)

　　　　wak(a)　　'walk, go

　　　　pot(i)　　'put'


(3)　　**Saramaccan　Ndjuka　Sranan**

　　　　sindeki　　s(i)neki　snek(i)　　'snake'

In certain styles of Sranan the epenthetic vowel between the /s/ and /n/ may reappear.

All the Surinam creoles except for Sranan as well as both Gbe and Kikongo possess distinctive **lexical tone**. Sranan does have a morphological process involving tone (Smith and Adamson, to appear).

(4)　　agama　　LLL　　'chameleon'　　　　　　　　　　　　　　　(Saramaccan)

　　　　alatu　　-H-　　'rat'

　　　　alibi　　LLH　　'kidney'

　　　　katjaa　　HHH　　'flat on the back'

　　　　mutjama　LHL　　'rainbow'

Note that Saramaccan words of European origin represent the original main stressed vowel with a high tone, and the other vowels with a tone varying according to rules of tone-sandhi (- in the above table). The default value for such vowels is L. In words of African origin the L tones (L in the above table) are immutable.

The Bush Negro languages possess **complex stop** segments in their phonological inventories – /kp, gb/. These occur both in African-derived lexical items, and in certain words of European origin. As chance will have it, the only substrate language with such stops is Gbe.

(5)　　kpefa　　'baby hood' (< Portuguese *coifa*)　　　　　　　　　　(Saramaccan)

　　　　kpei　　'square off' (< English *square*)

　　　　agbadjá　'crab egg pouch' (< Gbe *àgbajá*)

In Sranan these complex stops are usually replaced by /p,b/ in African words.

### 9.4.2 Morphology

In this section we will discuss African influence in the morphology of Berbice Dutch. In spite of the abundant evidence for substantial Eastern Ijọ influence in BD morphology, a word of caution is in order: BD has inherited only a subset of EI morphology, and even this subset does not function in the same way as its etymological source. In the following we will pay some attention to the differences as well as the similarities, since we feel that lessons can be drawn that are relevant to other claimed cases of substrate morphological influence.

Clear evidence for continuity can be found in BD affixational morphology: the plural suffix -*apu*, the aspectual suffixes -*tɛ* and -*arɛ*, the bound nominalizer -*jɛ*, and frozen causative forms in -*ma*. In fact the only BD morphological types not represented here are compounding, conversion and reduplication (apart from verbal iterative reduplication), processes which are so common cross-linguistically that any attempt to argue for substrate influence in this area would be unconvincing in any case.

*Nominalization and plural formation.* The plural suffix -*apu* and the nominalizer -*jɛ* can be related to EI nominalizers, as the following table of Kalaḅarị (Eastern Ịjọ) nominal-izers shows (Jenewari 1977:229; examples from Owiye 1986/1987). EI distinguishes between human/non-human and singular/plural forms. The EI etyma evolved from full nouns, and still have nominal properties, as is shown by the fact that they may head relative clauses and appear as (generic) objects of verbs. In contrast, BD -*apu* and -*jɛ* are bound mor-phemes.

(6)  **nominalizer**                                   **Kalaḅarị**

    ḅọ́   person, one (human)      *kɛ́-ḅọ́* writer < write-BO

    ápú   persons, ones (human)    *sɛ́kịápú* dancers < dance-APU

    yé   thing, one (non-human)  *fịyé* food < eat-YE

    áị́   things, ones (non-human)  *mịẹaị* responsibilities < do-AI

BD does not replicate the EI distinction between human/non-human forms. Also, while the EI forms mark the contrasting values of a binary opposition between ±plural, BD -*apu* contrasts with the absence of any marking, and -*jɛ* participates in processes quite unrelated to the use of -*apu*. The plural suffix -*apu* is used (i) to mark plural number on nouns, (ii) to mark an associative plural with names or epithets, and (iii) to form emphatic plural pronouns.

(7)   (i)   kɛnapu < kɛne-apu   people < person-PL            (Berbice Dutch)

      (ii)  emjapu < emi-apu   Amy and her group < Amy-PL

      (iii)  enjapu < eni-apu   THEY/THEM (emphatic) < they-PL

The nominalizer (NOM) -*jɛ* is attached (a) to adjectives to form referential nouns, (b) to adjectives and nouns to form generic or type nouns, (c) to adjectives, pronouns and nouns to form possessive nouns, and (d) to pronouns – both singular and plural – to mark them as emphatic forms.

(8)     a.   di kalijɛ < di kali-jɛ 'the small one < the small-NOM'                    (Berbice Dutch)
        b.   di jɛrmajɛ < di jɛrma-jɛ 'the female kind < the woman-NOM'
        c.   ɛkɛjɛ < ɛkɛ-jɛ 'mine < 1sg-NOM'
        d.   ɛkɛjɛ < ɛkɛ-jɛ 'I/ME (emphatic) < 1sg-NOM'

*Aspectual affixes.* BD replicates fully the EI system of aspectual suffixes: *-arɛ* Imperfective, *-tɛ* Perfective, and the Iterative reduplicative morpheme, derive transparently from EI suffixes, both in form and in function. Kalaḅarị employs the following system of suffixes for the marking of tense, mood and aspect (Jenewari 1977).

(9)     -m      factitive: marks state on statives, past completed on non-statives          (Kalaḅarị)
        -tɛ́     completive: marks past, present and future completed
        -ḅa     future: marks future or likelihood
        -árị     general: marks progressive, habitual, and (on a limited class of verbs) present state
        -RED    reduplication marks iterative

In EI, iterative reduplication of verbs may cooccur with any of the suffixes, but no other combinations are possible. For instance, a past habitual is marked only as habitual. The only restriction in BD is on the occurrence of the imperfective and perfective suffixes which are incompatible. The BD preverbal past tense and irrealis mood markers – of non-EI derivation – may cooccur with suffixes and reduplicated verb forms. Examples of the use of these markers may be found in chapter 19. The continuity of the EI morphological subsystem of aspect marking has been ascribed to a superficial similarity between the EI suffix *-tɛ́* and the Dutch past imperfective suffix *-də/tə* (Kouwenberg 1994).

### 9.4.3 Lexicon

In this section we give examples of African lexical items in the Surinam creoles inherited from the two major substrate languages – Gbe and Kikongo.

*Fon(gbe).* Fon – the Gbe language of Benin – is the major source of Gbe lexical input in the Surinam languages. The total Gbe contribution of about 130 words is roughly equal to the Kikongo contribution. Some examples are:

(10)    **Fongbe**                    **Saramaccan**
        zoká    'charcoal'           zonka    'charcoal'
        àze     'magic'              azɛ      'magic'
        ah mɛ   'brains'             ahumɛ    'fontanelle'

*Kikongo.* Kikongo is the most important source of Bantu items in the vocabulary of the Surinam languages. In addition there are a couple of items from the neighbouring language, Kimbundu, spoken in northern Angola.

(11)    **Kikongo**                                **Saramaccan**

     tuutu    'horn'                      tutú     'horn'

     toonzo   'brains'                    tɔnzɔ   'brains'

     nsusu    'hen'                       súsu     'hen'

     ma-kuku 'hearthstone'                makúku 'hearthstone'

### 9.4.4 Syntax

The domain of language that has been investigated most thoroughly for substrate influence is syntax. Thus, in Boretzky (1983), the most elaborate study of substratal influence in a variety of Atlantic creoles to date, more than three quarter of the actual discussion is concerned with syntactic phenomena. In Alleyne's (1980) discussion of the African element in 'Afro-American' (i.e. New World creoles), again the bulk of attention is devoted to syntax. Similarly, Keesing's (1988) book on the Oceanic substrate in several Pacific pidgins is concerned almost exclusively with aspects of syntax. Some examples may serve to illustrate the kind of parallels that can be found between creoles and their substrates.

A syntactic area where examples of substrate influence have been claimed to abound is the **serial verb construction** (SVC), where a single subject is accompanied by two or more verbs in a single (surface) clause (see chapter 23). The combination of verbs is used to express functions which in non-serializing languages are performed by non-verbal categories such as adverbs, prepositions and conjunctions. Serial verbs are relatively rare among the world's languages: apart from creoles they have been reported for Sino-Tibetan languages, Papuan languages, and, significantly, for a number of relevant West African languages, such as Twi, Gbe, Gã, and Kru. They come in a variety of types, including instrumental, directional and benefactive SVC's. Some examples from creoles and West African languages are given below:

*Instrumental* SVC

(12)    A   tei    goni  suti  di      pingo.                (Saramaccan)

       he  take  gun   shoot the   pig

       'He shot the pig with a gun.'

(13)    Ode     adare   no    twaa     nkromata.           (Akan)

       he-take  machete the  cut-PAST branch

       'He cut the branch with a machete.'

*Directional* SVC

(14)    A   waka go na    wowoyo.                                        (Sranan)
        he  walk go PREP  market
        'He went to the market.'


(15)    Oguang      koo      ahabang mu.                                 (Akan)
        he-flee-PAST go-PAST  bush    in
        'He fled into the bush.'


Although the superficial similarities are quite striking, this does not mean, of course, that these structures were **necessarily** transferred from West Africa. A more thorough analysis, which takes into account not only the surface similarities but more abstract properties as well, is needed before such a conclusion can be drawn. Indeed, the fact that substratists' analyses of serialization have sometimes been limited to superficial parallels has given reason to others (e.g. Bickerton 1981) to question the West African origin of these structures, and to attribute them to Universal Grammar, even though they appear to be universally marked. For a more thorough analysis the reader is referred to chapter 23 of this book.

### 9.4.5  Semantics

In one of the very few studies on the role of the substratum in (lexical) semantics, Huttar (1975), in a comparative study of Ndjuka and 43 other languages, shows that the substrate is the most important factor in determining the lexical semantic structure of Ndjuka. Universalist explanations, such as reference to semantic universals or universals of borrowing and semantic change, do not seem to play a significant role.

Although, due to the relative underdevelopment of the area of investigation and the restricted availability of data, these conclusions should be interpreted carefully, the method of investigation is interesting enough to be discussed here in some detail. Twenty Ndjuka morphemes were selected, for which the 'area of meaning', i.e. the union of all the different senses of a particular morpheme, differs from that of the corresponding English morpheme, such as the word *mófu*, meaning both 'mouth' and 'pointed end of a pointed object'. For each sense of each morpheme an English sentence was constructed illustrating that particular sense. Correspondents for 43 languages, including both Caribbean, West African, and non-Atlantic pidgins/creoles, and West African, Caribbean, and miscellaneous non-pidgins/creoles were then asked to give the equivalent for each sense of each selected morpheme. Finally, by scoring the extent to which in each particular language one and the same morpheme was used to express different senses of each of the twenty morphemes, these languages could be arranged according to the degree to which their lexical semantic structure resembled that of Ndjuka.

The methodology employed made it possible to sort out the different factors that might have played a role in the formation of the Ndjuka lexical-semantic system. Unfortunately, this line of research has not been followed up, and the area of semantic substrate influence has remained largely unexplored.

## 9.5 Evidence for adstrate influence

Influence from the indigenous (i.e. Amerindian) languages is largely restricted to lexical borrowing. In the case of the Surinam creoles the main influence is from Carib. In fewer cases we find influence from Lokono (Arawak), the other major Amerindian language of Surinam. Most of these words refer to the native fauna and flora of the area.

(16) **Carib**

| *Saramaccan* | *Sranan* | *Carib* | |
|---|---|---|---|
| awala | awara | awará | 'sp.palm' |
| awalí | awarí | awarí | 'opossum' |
| aputú | aputú | aputu | 'club' |

(17) **Arawak**

| *Saramaccan* | *Sranan* | *Arawak* | |
|---|---|---|---|
| matúitui | matjiwitjiwi | | 'sp.bird' |
| jumáa | anjumára | ajomarha | 'sp.fish' |

In Berbice Dutch the major influence is from Arawak. Here too, the main emphasis is on the natural environment, although words in other domains, e.g. kinship terms, have been borrowed from Arawak too.

### Further reading

Alleyne (1980) is the first full-scale analysis of African patterns in the English-based Atlantic creole languages. Boretzky (1983) (written in German), while similar in its aims, includes creoles with other lexifiers than English. Mufwene (1993a) is a collection of papers discussing the issue of Africanisms in Atlantic creoles, while Muysken & Smith (1986a) is focused on the respective roles of universals and substrata in creole genesis.

# 10 Gradualist and developmental hypotheses

Jacques Arends & Adrienne Bruyn

## 10.1 Introduction

Until recently, most creolists (with the exception of Alleyne 1971, Chaudenson 1979, Hancock 1980, and a few others) have shared the assumption that creoles, by definition, emerge out of pidgin languages through a process of nativization. Creoles, in other words, were regarded as nativized pidgins. This position was explicitly taken by Hall (1966:xiv), who in this context developed the notion of the pidgin-creole life cycle introduced in chapter 1. This notion was adapted and further refined by Mühlhäusler (1986:11) under the name of developmental continuum. The equation 'creolization = nativization' was tacitly adopted by the majority of creolists during recent years, becoming the cornerstone of Bickerton's bioprogram theory, for which, by its very nature, this assumption is critical. The bioprogram hypothesis makes the additional assumption that the nativization process is completed within one or two generations (Bickerton 1988, 1991).

However, in contrast to the assumption of creolization as an 'instantaneous' or 'abrupt' process, during the last decade an alternative view was developed, which has variably been referred to as the **Gradualist Model** (Carden & Stewart 1988; Arends 1993) or the **Gradual Creolization Hypothesis** (McWhorter 1992). Although these are cover terms for ideas and proposals that were initially put forward independently by a number of different scholars, such as Carden and Stewart (1988), Singler (1986, 1990a), and Arends (1986, 1989), they contain enough similarities to discuss them together here. As its name implies, the gradualist model claims that creolization, at least in a number of cases, such as Sranan, Haitian, and Jamaican, is not an instantaneous, but rather a gradual process, extending over a number of generations of speakers.

The emergence of this view is related to the fact that it was not until the 1980s that creolists began to use historical documents, containing early linguistic material on creoles, as a source of information about the genesis and historical development of these languages. This formed the beginning of a new, historically oriented branch of creole studies, which was explored for several creoles, such as Mauritian (Baker 1982), Sranan (Arends 1989; Bruyn 1993a; Plag 1993; Smith 1987), Saramaccan (Smith 1987), Haitian (Carden & Stewart 1988), and Negerhollands (Muysken & Van der Voort 1991; Van der Voort & Muysken, to appear).

Not only linguistic, but also demographic evidence was adduced (Arends 1989, to appear b; Singler 1986, 1990a, 1992a, 1993) to show that the **demographic** development of some slave societies, such as Surinam and Jamaica, was such that the nativization of Sranan and Jamaican can only have been a rather slow process. The rate of nativization of these societies, i.e. the rate at which the proportion of locally-born blacks to African-born blacks changed in favor of the former, was so slow that it seems highly unlikely that creolization could have taken place instantaneously.

Apart from diachronic and demographic evidence on clear-cut creoles, additional evidence for the gradualist hypothesis can be derived from another area. A number of **pidgins**, such as Tok Pisin, have expanded and stabilized into full-blown languages before being nativized. This not only casts some doubt on the validity of the traditional distinction between 'pidgin' and 'creole', but it also supports the idea that the formation of language can take place over a number of generations, without nativization playing a major role. Rather than treating these cases as not being true creoles (Bickerton 1981), they may more profitably be viewed as modern replicas of what happened to some of the other 'true' creoles in the past. In the next section, one particular case, Sranan, will be discussed more fully. In 10.3 the implications of the gradualist view for the relation between creole genesis and language change are explored, while in 10.4 attention is focused on the role of grammaticalization in pidginization and creolization.

## 10.2  Sranan: a case of gradual creolization?

The evidence presented by Arends (1989) to support a gradualist view of the formation of Sranan falls into two categories. Apart from purely linguistic evidence, external (demographic) factors play a role in the argumentation as well. As to the former, this relates to diachronic changes in the syntax of Sranan between 1700 and 1950 which point to a gradual formative process. The most important demographic factor is the rate of nativization, i.e. the rate at which the African-born part of the black population is replaced by locally-born slaves. These two types of evidence will each be dealt with in turn.

The cases where the development points towards gradual formation are the copula system (in a broad sense, i.e. encompassing existential, locational, and possessive BE) and the comparative. Approximately half of the texts in the database were written by native speakers, whereas the other half derived from nonnative, European, authors. Due to limitations of space, only the copula system will be discussed here (for further information see Arends 1989).

Before that, however, a brief word of caution is in order regarding the problems related to working with older texts. First, the earliest texts written in any of the Surinam creoles go back no further than a post-initial stage of the language formation process. In other words, the very earliest stages of the creolization process remain undocumented. Second, the bulk of creole texts from the hundred year-period following the first text derive from nonnative speakers, such as European missionaries, travelers, and colonial administrators. Therefore it is necessary to determine as precisely as possible if and to what extent their representation of the language deviates from the creole as spoken by the native speakers. One possible way of doing that is by making use of metalinguistic information regarding linguistic variation in contemporary works, such as the Saramaccan and Sranan dictionaries by the Moravian missionary Schumann (1778, 1783).

The idea that the formation of Sranan was a gradual process is based, among other things, on the fact that in the first half of the 19th century (i.e. 150 years after the beginning of creolization) a major split occurs within the copula system. Whereas up to around 1800 there was a monolithic category of equation (including both **attribution** and **identification**, both expressed by *da*), this was differentiated after 1800 into two subcategories, each having its own copula form: *de* for attribution and *da* for identification. Compare the pre-1800 sentences (1) and (2), both of which have *da*, regardless whether attribution or identification is concerned, and the post-1800 sentences (3) and (4), where *de* is used for the former and *da* for the latter:

(1)  Hoe fassi joe    man    da    granman vo joe?         (attr.; Van Dyk c1765:69)
     what-way 2SG    man    COP    boss      of 2SG?
     'Your husband doesn't own you, does he?'

(2)  Mie    no    sabie o    sama    da    em.              (ident.; Weygandt 1798:91)
     1SG    NEG   know what person   COP   3SG
     'I don't know who he is.'

(3)  Mi wefi  de    wan   bejari soema    toe.             (attr.; Anon. 1829:8)
     1SG wife COP   an    aged   person   also
     'My wife is old too.'

(4)  Mi da    Gabriel, disi de  tanapoe na   Gado fesi  alatem.  (ident.; Anon. 1829:8)
     1SG COP  Gabriel  REL ASP stand    LOC  God  face  always
     'I am Gabriel, who is always standing before God.'

As to the comparative, the most important finding was that throughout its documented history Sranan had a wide variety of construction types, such as the serial and the particle comparative as well as others. Despite its proliferation of comparative types, new types were introduced into the language while others were lost. This suggests that, although the formation of a creole subsystem may be completed fairly rapidly, it may take a lot more time for that subsystem to become stabilized.

As observed by Bickerton (1991), the crucial question is whether such a change should be regarded as part of the creolization process or simply as a case of normal language change. The answer, of course, depends on one's definition of creolization. In a narrow sense, adopted by Bickerton and others, creolization is taken to relate only to the minimal requirements for language, whereas in a broad sense, adopted by Labov (1990) and others, other (e.g. stylistic) properties of language are included in the definition as well. Neither of these views is entirely unproblematic. At least one problem with the narrow definition is to decide what the minimal requirements for language are. On the other hand, those who adopt the broader definition have to decide where creolization stops and normal language change begins. At the moment, these problems have not yet been satisfactorily solved.

As far as demographic evidence for the gradualist position is concerned, it seems unlikely that nativization by children took place during the first one or two generations of slaves, simply because the children required to perform such a process were not present in sufficient numbers (see chapter 2). Although Price's (1976) claim that after four generations still less than 10% of the slave population was Surinam-born is an estimate rather than an exact calculation, there is reason to believe that it is not too far off the mark (cf. Arends 1994). Proceeding from Price's figures, there can only have been an average of just a few locally-born children per plantation. It was probably not until the balance between locally-born and African-born blacks had shifted further in favor of the former that the nativization of Sranan really started. It should be added, however, that there is no agreement about how many children are required in order to be able to carry the process of nativization.

## 10.3  Creolization as language change

In chapter 1 we briefly discussed the relation between creolization and language change. There are widely differing views on the relation between creoles and the languages that contributed to their formation, and, concomitantly, on the similarities or differences between creolization and general processes of linguistic change. Some researchers focus on the contribution of the substrate languages, with or without explicit reference to the mechanisms involved. Lefebvre (e.g. 1986) argues that Haitian is relexified Fon(gbe). Alleyne (e.g. 1971) regards the Caribbean creoles as continuations of the African languages spoken by the imported slaves and as the linguistic product of the more general process of acculturation. In other theories, the substrate languages do not constitute the starting point, but rather emphasis is laid on continuity in the development of the lexifier language (see chapter 8). Chaudenson (1992), for example, argues that many of the properties of the French creoles can be traced back to the French dialects spoken by the first colonists. The assumption of continuity is associated with the view that, apart from the speed with which they take place, the processes at work during creolization are not different from the processes of language change in general.

Drawing on the sharp break in transmission involved in creole genesis, others arrive at the opposite conclusion. For Bickerton (e.g. 1981), the discontinuity of the lexifier language resulting from imperfect acquisition is crucial to the emergence of the typical creole structures (see chapter 11). From a rather different view-point, Thomason and Kaufman (1988:165-66) take issue as well with the view that creolization is change at a high rate. With regard to 'abrupt creolization', the situation where a creole evolves from a pidgin that has not yet stabilized, they argue that the affinities of a newly created creole with its lexifier language are so weak that the whole concept of change is not applicable. With regard to pidgin genesis, they emphasize the aspects in which it contrasts with other contact situations likely to induce borrowing or substrate interference. These are the multilingual (as opposed to bilingual) settings, the fact that speakers do not shift to another language, and the absence of full bilingualism. These differences notwithstanding, they see substantial similarities between contact-induced change and the genesis of pidgins and creoles. In all cases, there is transfer from the mother tongues represented in the situation in which speakers of different languages try to communicate. Which features will ultimately survive depends, apart from the social context, on factors such as markedness, typological distance, and whether a feature is shared by the languages involved. Whereas in other contact situations the interference may result in changes in an existing target language, in certain sociolinguistic settings a mixed language emerges. According to this view, the processes involved in creolization and pidginization are similar to the processes at work in other contact situations, and they are subject to the same type of constraints, even if the concept of change is inappropriate because new, non-genetic languages are involved.

In the approach of Thomason & Kaufman the genesis of pidgins and creoles is compared with contact-induced, external, change. The same goes for theories in which relexification plays a role: more than one language is involved in relexification by its very nature. Alternatively, one might explore the similarities and differences between developments in pidgins and creoles on the one hand, and cases of internal change on the other. Be the comparison with external or with internal change, in both cases the question is whether pidginization and creolization are instances of change at a high rate, or whether they are qualitatively distinct from ordinary language change. Therefore, it is important to investigate the type and rate of developments in pidgins and creoles in order to be able to compare these developments with processes of change in less extreme situations. In the next section we will address this issue from the perspective of grammaticalization.

## 10.4 Grammaticalization in pidgins and creoles

In rudimentary pidgins some concepts and relations are expressed by circumlocution, or are not overtly expressed at all. Distinctions which are often not systematically coded include tense, mood, and aspect in the VP, number and definiteness in the NP, complementation, and subordination (see chapter 3). In the absence of the morphosyntactic marking of these and other features the interpretation of utterances depends heavily on factors such as intonation, linguistic context, extra-linguistic situation, and shared knowledge. Linguistic communication of this type can be regarded as belonging to what has been called the 'pragmatic mode' by Givón (1979). In the course of expansion and creolization, a shift to a more 'syntactic mode' occurs: more and more relationships and distinctions are expressed morphosyntactically and become part of the grammar. TMA- and number-marking, articles, complementizers, and subordinating conjunctions may emerge.

One possible source for the functional morphemes needed for the expression of grammatical concepts is the **grammaticalization** of content words. Consider the Tok Pisin form *baimbai*, a reflex of English *by-and-by*. In earlier stages, *baimbai* functioned as a sentential adverb, meaning 'afterwards', 'later'. Later, it became a preverbal particle, and eventually a verbal prefix expressing future (Sankoff & Laberge 1974). At the same time, it was reduced in form: *baimbai* > *bəmbai* > *bai* > *bə*. This is a typical example of grammaticalization: a lexical element becomes part of the grammar as a functional morpheme. Grammaticalization is a general process occurring in all languages (Hopper & Traugott 1993), whereby patterns that occur frequently in discourse may get reinterpreted. As a result lexical items acquire a grammatical function, or functional elements become more grammatical, e.g. when personal pronouns develop into agreement markers, or postpositions into case suffixes. Often, the change in categorial status goes hand in hand with a **phonological reduction** and a shift from more to less concrete on the semantic level, or, especially in later stages of the development, with semantic generalization or **bleaching**.

With Tok Pisin *baimbai*, phonological reduction has taken place indeed, and *bai/bə* has acquired grammatical meaning as a tense marker at the expense of the concrete lexical meaning. Preverbal *bai* (or *bə*) is also used when adverbs such as *klostu* 'soon', or other explicit indications of future time are present in the sentence. Semantically, *bai* is redundant in such cases, and the fact that it occurs nevertheless indicates that it has become a grammatical marker.

Because the paradigms of verbal inflection and auxiliary forms of the lexifier language are generally not transmitted into pidgins and creoles, TMA-marking is one of the domains where the creation of morphosyntactic markers through grammaticalization may occur. Such developments do not necessarily proceed along exactly the same route in different languages.

Whereas Tok Pisin *bai* has an adverbial source, the immediate future marker in Sranan is *(g)o*, related to the full verb *go* 'to go'. On the other hand, some patterns recur in languages of different lexical stock. As pointed out by Holm (1988:155ff), the progressive aspect marker is related to an expression of location in various creole languages. In some English-related creoles, for example, the progressive marker is *(d)e*, derived from *there*. Holm suggests substrate influence in some cases, but he also mentions the possibility of a universal relation. The development from a locational source to progressive aspect is attested indeed in many languages (Heine, Claudi, & Hünnemeyer 1991). It constitutes evidence for the **localist** approach, in which it is assumed that spatial relationships are the most basic ones and may provide the structural model for the expression of more abstract grammatical concepts.

Another phenomenon which can be accounted for in the localist perspective is the development from a preposition to a clause-introducing element. In many creoles, there is a complementizer which is homophonous with or related to a preposition which has among others a locative meaning, as *pu* (< *pour*) in French-, *pa* (< *para*) in Portuguese-, or *ful fo l fi* in English-derived creoles. In present-day Sranan, *fu* can be a preposition meaning 'for', 'of', or 'from' (5a), and it can introduce a clause, either without an overt subject (5b), or with a subject (5c):

(5)   a.   Ma   yu     na     obiaman       fu     foto.              (Sranan. De Drie 1985)
          but   2SG   COP   medicine-man   from   town
          'But you are a medicin-man from town.'

     b.   Omu Fresi opo     wan   neti   fu go gi     Adeykeku   nyan
          uncle Fresi get-up   one   night   to go give   Adeykeku   food
          'One night, uncle Fresi got up in order to bring Adeykeku food.'

     c.   Dan mi o     puru   tifi   f'en       fu     a          no   beti sma      moro
          then 1SG FUT   pull   tooth   of=3SG   so.that   3SGNOM NEG   bite people    more
          'Then I'll pull out his teeth, so that he won't bite people anymore.'

Although there is much debate on the categorial status of *fu* and similar items when occurring as in (5b) and (c), and on issues such as the finiteness of the complement clause, most researchers would not challenge the idea that the clause-introducing function has evolved from that of the preposition, as was first proposed by Washabaugh (1975) for a variety of creole languages. While Washabaugh arrived at his conclusions on the basis of 20th-century data, Plag (1993) concluded that in the case of Sranan *fu* a language-internal development has taken place.

Turning now to another area, derivational morphology is not abundant in pidgins and creoles, but if it is there, it is often the result of grammaticalization. In Sranan, there is a nominal suffix *-man*, as in *takiman* 'speaker', similar to the suffix *-ma* in Saramaccan (see chapters 14 and 18). The semantic specification [+male] of the original full noun *man* 'man' has disappeared, and the meaning is generalized to 'someone who does/is/has x'.

It will be clear by now that various kinds of functional elements in pidgins and creoles may have lexical origins, and that certain aspects of the elaboration of pidgin and creole grammars can be viewed as instances of grammaticalization. The question could be raised whether the ways in which grammatical morphemes originate and develop in pidgins and creoles exhibit particular characteristics, or that they are basically similar to processes of grammaticalization in languages with a longer history. Because many aspects of the early developments of pidgins and creoles are still unknown, the discussion of this issue must remain somewhat speculative. Nevertheless, we think some points should be mentioned.

One difference concerns the motivation for the developments. Whatever the impetus for grammaticalization in languages with an uninterrupted development, communicative need would not seem to be a major contributory factor (see e.g. Hopper & Traugott 1993:66-7). In cases of disrupted transmission, however, communicative need can be expected to be a major force behind the processes of grammaticalization, to compensate for the large-scale loss of morphosyntactic elements. This difference is reflected in the fact that in pidgins and creoles it is not exceptional for new categories to be created, for example TMA-markers or subordinators, whereas grammaticalization in languages with a longer history usually involves already existing categories. The emergence of new categories is especially relevant in the earlier stages of expansion. Later, when the most basic functional needs are fulfilled, the various factors behind grammaticalization resemble those in languages with a longer history: the tendency for speakers to be expressive and creative in their language use on the one hand, and regularization and routinization on the other.

The 'need for grammar' in the earlier stages has consequences for the time it takes for grammaticalization processes to evolve. Whereas in languages with a longer history this is usually a matter of several centuries, developments will often proceed much more rapidly in pidgins and creoles, especially in the case of abruptly nativized creoles. Although this difference could be considered to be merely quantitative, it bears upon the nature of the development as well, in so far as grammaticalization is intricately linked with gradualness. For the shifts and reinterpretations to be possible intermediate stages are necessary, in which the functional extension of forms may proceed step by step. Sudden developments in expanding languages, prompted by a paucity of morphosyntactic elements, need not follow the same routes as more gradual grammaticalization.

An important factor determining the route of development is the presence of other languages. Whereas grammaticalization is normally conceived of as a language-internal process, language contact and concomitant external influences may be crucial in the case of pidgins and creoles. On the basis of material or structures from lexifier or substrate languages, the developments in expanding pidgins or creoles can involve shortcuts. This is for example the case when grammatical morphemes are derived from elements which never functioned as content words in the creole language itself, although they might have had such a function in the source language. In many creoles with English as lexifier language, there is an anterior marker *ben* or *bin*, derived from the English participle *been*. The fact that, as far as we know, *ben/bin* did not function as a content word in the early stages of these languages, implies that there has not been a language-internal development of a lexical item into a functional one. Cases like this, where an item from the lexifier language is taken over to perform a new grammatical function in the expanding pidgin or creole, are relatively easy to establish. More problematic are cases where the influence from other languages involves not the form but the semantics or the function of a certain category or construction.

To the extent that the route of grammaticalization processes is determined by universal cognitive patterns, parallel developments can be expected to occur in all human languages, including the languages present in situations of creolization. This makes it difficult to establish the origins of a certain functional item. It may be the result of the grammaticalization of a lexical element in the creole language itself, but its presence may also be due to calquing from substrate or lexifier language.

There are also cases where internal development appears to be minimal. The ambiguous status of *gi* in modern Sranan as a verb 'to give' or a preposition 'for, to' could be analyzed as reflecting the grammaticalization of a serial verb into a preposition. However, *gi* occurs in contexts where the original meaning 'give' is already absent in the earliest existing sources. In the following example, no transfer is involved, and *gi* expresses a beneficiary rather than a recipient.

(6)  Dem   sa     hoppo   dorro gi     hem                (Sranan. Schumann 1781)
     3PL   FUT    open    door  give   3SG
     'They will open the door for him.'

The occurrence of non-verbal *gi* in the second half of the 18th century suggests that either the grammaticalization from the verb *gi* in the direction of a preposition proceeded very fast in the earliest stages, or that the prepositional function of *gi* is calqued on a pattern existing in substrate languages. This pattern might well be the result of grammaticalization in the substrate languages themselves. The point we want to stress is that there has not necessarily been a long-term change within Sranan.

Influence may also come from the lexifier language. The evolution of the Sranan verb *go* to a marker of immediate future, mentioned before as an example of grammaticalization, may be affected by the fact that English *be going to* can express future as well.

These examples show that what at first sight looks like internal grammaticalization may well be due to influence from other languages as well. To assess the external influence of the various languages it will not be sufficient to investigate present-day languages only. Diachronic investigation is needed to establish whether synchronic patterns suggesting grammaticalization do indeed reflect language-internal developments. Convergence of substrate and superstrate patterns together with universal developments is likely to have occurred in many areas of the grammar. By studying a variety of aspects, in a variety of languages, it will be possible to make a plausible reconstruction of grammatical expansion in pidgins and creoles. The way in which certain functions and categories emerge, and the time span in which this takes place, may provide insight into the question of where structural expansion and creolization ends, and normal development begins. The grammaticalization approach offers a useful framework for this type of research.

### Further reading
A number of papers that touch on the issue of gradualism in creole genesis are collected in Arends (to appear a). A general developmental approach of pidginization/creolization is taken by Mühlhäusler (1986 [1997²], esp. chapter 5). The few case studies of grammaticalization in pidgins and creoles that are available include Sankoff (1990), Keesing (1991), Plag (1993), and Bruyn (1993b).

# 11  Universalist approaches

Pieter Muysken and Tonjes Veenstra

## 11.1  Introduction

The general idea that universal aspects of the human linguistic capacity are somehow responsible for the specific features of pidgins and creoles goes back at least to the Portuguese creolist Coelho, who writes in 1881:

> 'The Romance-creole and Indo-Portuguese dialects and all similar formations owe their origin to the action of physiological or psychological laws [that are] the same everywhere and not to the influence of the preceding languages of the peoples where these dialects are found.' [translated from the Portuguese]

However, early authors are not very specific about the kinds of universals that may have played a role. In essence, Coelho's statement is primarily directed against the idea of substrate influence (see chapter 9).

The reason that universals are mentioned at all when we discuss pidgin and creole genesis, is that the newly formed languages are often assumed to be alike in ways that cannot be explained exclusively by reference to similarities among the contributing languages. Hence the appeal to universals. In this chapter we will outline the different approaches that have been brought to bear on this.

## 11.2  Types of universals

The two dominant conceptions of pidgin and creole universals may be termed **procedural** and **constitutive**. Procedural universals are universal properties of processes (such as second language learning, or grammaticalization), and constitutive universals are universal properties of the resulting pidgins and creoles (such as their TMA systems, or their word orders).

### 11.2.1  Procedural universals

Procedural universals generally have a (more or less precisely defined) psycholinguistic basis and are formulated as strategies a speaker may employ in the language contact situation.

For pidgin genesis universal properties are attributed either to the adaptation mechanisms of speakers of the dominated languages, as possibly in (1), or of the dominant colonial languages, as in (5) below.

(1)    Disregard pre-verbal unstressed elements in the target (Schuchardt 1883: 237)

(1) can account for the fact that the Romance pre-verbal clitics have disappeared in the creole languages. Thus Spanish (2a) has a Papiamento reflex (2b), and French (3a) a Haitian reflex (3b):

| (2) | a. | Él **me** mira. | 'He looks at me.' | (Spanish) |
| | b. | E ta mira **mi**. | '(S)he sees me.' | (Papiamento) |
| (3) | a. | Il **se** voit. | 'He sees himself.' | (French) |
| | b. | Li we **li**(-**mem**). | 'He sees himself.' | (Haitian) |

Since the strategy is one of reduction, it is assumed to characterize pidgin genesis. It is problematic in that it cannot correspond to a learning process in the form formulated: how do you disregard something you do not know about? If we assume it is part of one of Slobin's operating principles (e.g. 1978) governing language learning, as in (4), this problem disappears:

(4)    Pay attention to the end of the word.

Since the clitic elements in the Romance languages occur at the beginning of the word and are unstressed, or may even form part of the phonological word, they escape notice and disappear in the pidginization process.

Anthony Naro (1973 and later work) has formulated principle (5) to describe the way speakers of the dominant languages may have adapted their speech in the language contact situation (see chapter 8):

(5)    Express each separately intuited element of meaning by a phonologically separate invariant stress-bearing form.

Such a principle would explain the amount of semantic transparency characteristic of some aspects of pidgin and creole systems.

For creole genesis we must think of the kind of developmental universals suggested (but never formulated clearly) in the work of Mühlhäusler (1986), governing the gradual expansion and development of systems of signifiers. The theory of grammaticalization (see chapter 10) will put this approach on a firmer basis, once it has reached a more definitive form. We have no quarrel as such with procedural universals. Undoubtedly there are general mechanisms of language learning. They are, however, rather vague in many cases.

## 11.2.2 Constitutive universals

Constitutive universals belong to the domain of the theory of grammar. A first example might be (6):

(6)    Every natural language must conform to Universal Grammar.

This principle, which has its basis clearly within the generative research tradition, is interesting in two respects. First of all, it undercuts the basis for the commonly held assumption that creoles are in some sense special languages. Second, it potentially allows us to make a principled grammatical distinction between pidgins – which need not conform to UG – and creoles – which must conform to UG. This in turn could lead to research into the development from pidgin to creole where we could see UG in action, as it were. The trouble is that strong versions of the Interlanguage Hypothesis, which holds that even intermediary products of second language learning are natural languages, would imply that pidgins, inasmuch as they are like interlanguages, fall under (6). Thus (6) offers not much of particular interest, however true. A principle such as (7) is more promising:

(7)    Creole languages present the unmarked option in each domain of Universal Grammar.

This proposal was made concretely by Bickerton (1984), building on his well-known *Roots of Language* (1981), but the idea behind it appears in much work from early on in the field of creole studies. If it were plausible, it would lead to a fruitful set of research questions: we would have an independent check on markedness theory, the theory that specifies what is marked and what is unmarked. We return to Bickerton's theory below.

To get some idea of what features creoles have in common, consider (8) and (9):

(8)    Wanpela man  i    bin   skulim   mi    long Tok  Pisin.              (Tok Pisin)
       one      man PM   ANT   teach    me    in   Tok  Pisin
       'A man was teaching me Tok Pisin.'

(9)    Só    mõ   ka    ta    tóka palmu.                                (Senegal Crioulo)
       one   hand NEG   HAB   touch palm
       'One hand can't touch its palm.'

Generally we find a subject-verb-object (SVO) word order, and various particles can occur between the subject and the verb. In the Tok Pisin example (8) a predicate marker *i* and an anterior tense marker *bin* (see chapter 20). In the Senegal Crioulo example (9) these are a negation marker *ka* and a habitual or generic marker *ta*. In addition to word order and pre-verbal particles, a number of other features have been claimed to be fairly general across creoles. These include:

(10)  a.  the use of serial verbs
      b.  transparent question word systems
      c.  morphologically complex reflexives
      d.  plural marking involving the third person plural pronoun
      e.  a generalized locative prepostion, often *na*
      f.  fronting rules: focus and predicate cleft
      g.  the presence of double object constructions

However, the extent to which these features are general and what the explanation is for the similarities is highly controversial. Various authors have tried to explain the universal characteristics of creoles from very different perspectives.

## 11.3  Semantic perspectives: transparency

The issue of universals in pidgins and creoles came to be addressed seriously in the seventies, in the work of Traugott, and Givón, and later in work of Seuren & Wekker (1986). The **semantic transparency** theory claims that the structure of creole languages directly reflects universal semantic structures. The semantic structures of creoles are fairly directly mapped onto surface structures, without very complex intermediary relationships. An example of this, to return to the examples above, may be the fact that creole languages have separate tense/mood/aspect particles, which reflect separate logical operators, rather than incorporating tense, etc. in the inflection of the verb.

We can illustrate the semantic transparency approach with reference to question word systems. As is well known, the majority of known creole languages have adopted their vocabulary to a large extent from colonial languages. For this reason we often speak of French, English, Portuguese, Dutch, etc. creoles. For function words, such as question words, there is a much more indirect correspondence. The most striking characteristic of question words in a number of creole languages is their analytical character. In (11) we give some examples:

(11)  a.  wa tit (Q-time)    'when'                                (Negerhollands)
          (compare Dutch *wanneer*)
      b.  o ten (Q-time)    'when'                                (Sranan)
          (compare English *when*)

c.  ki gen (Q-genre)   'how'                                     (Haitian)

(compare French *comment*)

In all these examples we find a form that can be represented abstractly as QUESTION PARTI-
CLE (Q) + QUESTIONED SEMANTIC UNIT (QSU).

We will analyze question words from the perspective of semantic transparency: do the
question words perhaps reflect universal tendencies towards semantic transparency in the
creole languages (Seuren & Wekker 1986; Bickerton 1988)? Next to forms such as (11),
presented above, we also find other types, such as those in (12):

(12)   a.   wen taym    'when'                                   (Jamaican)
       b.   ken         'who'                                    (Papiamento)
       c.   andí        'what'                                   (Saramaccan)

These forms deviate in various ways from the analytical model in (11). They may be a direct
reflex of a form from the colonial language, as in (12b), or consist of a mixture of the full
colonial language form and a questioned element as in (12a). Finally there is the possibility
that they reflect neither the colonial language nor the analytical model in (11), as in (12c). Not
all systems are transparent, some are opaque. In (13) we present the transparent system of
Chinese Pidgin English, and in (14) the opaque system of KiNubi, a form of creolized Arabic
spoken in Southern Sudan. A transparent system can also become opaque through time.

(13)              *forms*            *analysis*          Chinese Pidgin English (Bisang 1985)
       WHO        who (-man)         who (-man)
       WHAT       wat ting           Q-thing
       WHEN       wat-time           Q-time
       WHERE      wat-side           Q-side
       WHY        wat-for            Q-for
       HOW        how (-fashion)     how (-fashion)
                  wat-fashion        Q-fashion

(14)              *forms*            *analysis*                   (KiNubi; Heine 1982)
       WHO        munu               who
       WHAT       s(h)unu            what
       WHICH      yatuu              which
       WHEN       miteen             when
       WHERE      wen                where

| | | |
|---|---|---|
| WHY | lee/malu | why |
| HOW | keef/kefin | how |

A mixed transparent system is to be found in a number of English-based creoles, where the Q-element varies according to the QSU-element. Here we typically find the forms in (15a) as opposed to the purely transparent forms of (15b):

(15)   a.   *mixed transparent*   b.   *(pure) transparent*

| | |
|---|---|
| who-man | Q-man |
| what-thing | Q-thing |
| which-one | Q |
| when-time | Q-time |
| where-part | Q-part |
| why-reason | Q-reason |
| how-fashion | Q-fashion |

A system which is to a large extent mixed transparent is Jamaican Creole (Bailey 1966; Cassidy & LePage 1980), some of whose question words are presented in (20):

(16) | | *forms* | *analysis* | (Jamaican) |
|---|---|---|---|
| WHO | huu(-dat) | who (-that) | |
| WHAT | wa(t)/we/wara | what | |
| WHICH | wich | which | |
| WHEN | wen-taym/wen | when-time/when | |
| WHERE | we-paat/we | where-part/where | |
| WHY | wa-mek | what-make | |
| HOW | ou | how | |

A final type of question word is derived from the transparent type, but results from the dropping of the Q-particle, so that only the questioned element remains. This type we will call **atrophied**. Sranan is an example:

(17) | | *forms* | *analysis* | (Sranan) |
|---|---|---|---|
| WHO | (o)s(u)ma | (Q-) person/(Q-) *sma* > who | |
| WHAT | (o)san | *san* > what | |
| WHICH | o-disi / (o)sortu | Q-this / (Q-) sort | |
| WHEN | o-ten | Q-time | |

| WHERE | (o)pe | (Q-) *pe* > where |
|---|---|---|
| WHY | (fu)san-ede | for-*san*-head |
| HOW | o-fasi/fa | Q-fashion/ *fa* > how |

In nearly all the cases where the Q-particle is dropped the reason why this is possible is obvious. In a number of these cases the QSU-element has undergone a change such that it is no longer homophonous with the corresponding free morpheme. The two forms that have lost the Q-particle altogether, *fa* and *san*, are distinct from their etymological antecedents *fasi* and *sani*. When the full forms are used the Q-particle is compulsory. All the compulsory cases of the Q-particle, moreover, involve such full forms. There are three forms not covered by these statements. *(o) suma* does not contain the usual free form, for which *sma* is now more normal. *(o) pe* contains an element which also occurs marginally in compounds such as *beri-pe* 'graveyard' (i.e. 'bury-place') and as such might be felt to be more meaningful. *(o) sortu* lacks an obvious explanation.

The existence of partially atrophied systems brings to mind the fact that we must be careful in taking contemporary descriptions as representative of the early forms of creoles (see chapter 10). Whenever we have good documentation for earlier stages of a creole, we can see that question words have undergone a number of changes.

Many of the systems of question words in creoles show a greater or lesser degree of semantic transparency. This may well represent a basic strategy of creolization. The application of the theory of Seuren & Wekker (1986) to question word systems would appeal to three basic principles:

– uniformity, i.e. the maximum uniformity in the treatment of semantic categories;
– universality, i.e. the minimum of reliance on language particular rules;
– simplicity, i.e. the minimum possible of processing necessary in proceeding from semantic analyses to surface structures, and vice versa.

This would result in a question word system of a uniform type, involving separate adjacent Q-elements and questioned elements in a consistent order.

With the exception of the Saramaccan items for 'who' and 'what', *ambɛ* and *andí* respectively, the question word systems for this language, and also late 18th century Sranan would seem to be totally transparent. Outside the traditional Q-word system the Q-particle is productively used with nouns and adjectives. We give some examples from Saramaccan (De Groot 1977):

(18)  a.  Un-ne   fi-i?                                    (Saramaccan)
         Q-name   for 2SG
         'What is your name?'

b. Un-dégi mi    músu san   di    paánga?
   Q-thick ISG   must saw   the   board
   'How thick must I saw the board?'

In Muysken & Smith (1990), from which most of the information presented here is drawn, a number of other factors are explored as well, particularly the role of substrate languages and of the colonial superstrates. It is clear that substrate influence is undeniable, but with limited structural effect. Superstrate influence concerns both the lexical choice of the Q element (e.g. for English creoles based on *which* in the Atlantic and on *what* in the Pacific), and subsequent transformations of originally constituted creole question word systems.

The common social context theory adopts a strictly functional perspective: the slave plantations imposed similar communicative requirements on the slaves, newly arrived and without a common language, in many cases. The commonality of the communicative requirements led to the formation of a series of fairly similar makeshift communicative systems, which then stabilized and became creoles. To give an example of what this may imply, consider the following Tok Pisin relative clause, from an article by Sankoff & Brown (in Sankoff 1980):

(19)   Boi    **ia** (i    gat   fiftin   yias   **ia**) em   i    tokim   ologeta    (Tok Pisin)
       boy          PM   have  fifteen  years  he   PM   tell    all
       liklik   boi   ol i    kam.
       little   boy   PL PM   come
       'This boy, who was fifteen years old, he told all the little boys to come.'

Sankoff & Brown show that the marker *ia* 'here' has developed out of a conversational focus marker into a grammatical element setting a relative clause apart from the matrix clause.

## 11.4 Universals of second language learning

In the imperfect second language learning theory (see also chapter 8) creoles are the crystallization of some stage in the developmental sequence. The speakers of the proto-creole simply did not have sufficient access to the model, and had to make up an approximative system. In this view the fact that creoles are simple is due to the simplification inherent in the second language learning process. Thus we find in the intermediate stages of the acquisition of several European languages (e.g. English and German) a phase in which there is an invariant negative element in preverbal position:

(20)  a.  He **no** eat        'He doesn't/won't eat.'                (L2 English)

      b.  Ich **nix** arbeite    'I don't/didn't work.'               (L2 German)

         (compare standard German: *ich arbeite nicht*)

This same feature was mentioned before as characteristic of many creoles. For some adherents of this view the creole languages are also similar, and this similarity is due to universal properties of the learning process. A quite well-developed view holds that creoles are really the result of gradual stabilization and expansion of jargons by second-language learners (see chapter 10). Here commonalities with patterns of second-language development become the object of interest. The issue of what crucially distinguishes first- from second-language acquisition has not been settled yet at this point.

## 11.5 Universals of first language learning I: the bio-program

The clearest exponent of the view that universals of first language development are responsible for many of the parallel features of creoles is Bickerton, in a number of publications, starting in 1975. Although his theory has undergone slight changes, we will refer to the total set of his ideas as the **bio-program** theory.

This theory claims that creoles are inventions of the children growing up on the newly formed plantations. Around them they only heard pidgins spoken, without enough structure to function as natural languages, and they used their own innate linguistic capacities to transform the pidgin input from their parents into a full-fledged language. Creole languages are similar because the innate linguistic capacity applied is universal, and they are simple because they reflect the most basic language structures. One feature shared by all creoles that would derive from the innate capacity is the system of pre-verbal tense/mood/aspect particles. As is shown in chapter 20, this proposal has not met with universal acceptance among creolists. In spite of its shortcomings, the seriousness of which is judged quite differently by different researchers, the orientation of Bickerton's research has been highly inspiring and has led to an enormous amount of subsequent fruitful research.

## 11.6 Universals of first language learning II: parameter theory

In the early eighties, the notion of parameter was introduced to account for grammatical variation (e.g. Chomsky 1981). The basic idea was that:

(a) A single abstract grammatical difference (a so-called parameter setting) can be manifested in a number of very different constructions;

(b) The child developing the grammar can learn the setting of the parameter from a simple, frequently occurring, and locally processable manifestation of this setting. Schematically:

(21)

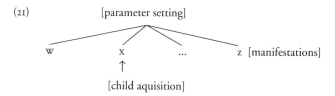

This intuitively rather attractive idea has given an impetus for integrating the results of comparative grammatical research with those of the study of language acquisition.

A good example of this general approach is *pro*-drop (Rizzi 1982), which we will illustrate with examples from Spanish rather than Italian, the language for which it was originally proposed. Consider the contrasts in (22) through (25). In each case the Spanish (a) example is grammatical, the corresponding English (b) example ungrammatical. In Spanish the subject pronoun may be absent, but not in English.

(22)    a.   Come.          b. *eats

Similarly, there is no semantically empty pronoun in the Spanish example (23a), while it is obligatory in (23b).

(23)    a.   Parece que ...    b. *seems that

In several cases, the subject may be in post-verbal position in Spanish, but not in English. Consider first the case of so-called stylistic inversion:

(24)    a.   Ha venido Juan.   b. *has come John

A second case involves passive, where movement of the underlying object is obligatory in English, but not in Spanish:

(25)    a.   Ha sido devorada la oveja por el lobo.
        b.   *has been devoured the sheep by the wolf

Finally, the contrast in (26) indicates that in English, it is possible to extract arguments from object position, but not from subject position. This holds in English, but not in Spanish.

(26)  a.  Quien$_i$ dijiste que ha venido [e$_i$]?
      b.  *who$_i$ did you say that [e$_i$] came

Notice that (27), corresponding to (26b), is judged fully grammatical:

(27)  Who$_i$ did you say that John had met [e$_i$] at the bar?

All these contrasts were explained by Rizzi (1982) by the assumption that in languages like Spanish, but not in English, it is possible to have a null pronoun in subject position (so-called *pro*-drop). In (24a), (25a), and (26a) this null subject pronoun is coindexed with a post-verbal subject: a lexically realized noun phrase in (24a) and (25a), an empty position from which the question word has moved in (26a).

The appeal and success of this analysis derives from two things: (a) a single underlying difference between Spanish and English explains four more superficial differences; (b) the underlying difference is learnable from a frequently occurring construction, exemplified in (22) above. Thus *pro*-drop is a classical instance of the schema in (21).

We should mention an additional attraction of the null pronoun analysis for Spanish. Notice that the morphology marking verbal agreement in this language is much richer than its English counterpart:

(28)  a.  yo vengo              b.  I come
          tu vienes                 you come
          ella/él viene             she/he comes
          nosotros venimos          we come
          vosotros veneis           you come
          ellas/ellos vienen        they come

It is easy to imagine that the person and number features of the null pronoun can be recovered from the verb morphology in Spanish, but not in English.

Here we want to illustrate research on the pro-drop parameter in Papiamento. In this language, we find the following pattern:

(29)  a.  E ta kome.(compare (22a))   b. *ta kome                    (Papiamento)
          '(S)he is eating.'

With respect to ordinary pronominal subjects carrying person features, Papiamento patterns like English. Null-subjects are ungrammatical. With semantically empty subjects, however, it patterns like Spanish, as can be seen in (30):

(30)     Parse ku Maria ta kanta. (compare (23a))
         'It seems that Mary sings.'

We also find, in specific circumstances, cases of inversion, as seen in (31):

(31)     Riba e isla aki ta biba un million hende. (compare (24a))
         'On this island a million people live.'

With respect to passive, Papiamento is like English:

(32)     a.  *ta wordu komí e karne (compare (25a))          b.  E karne ta wordu komí.
                                                                  'The meat is being eaten.'

In the case of movement of the subject, Papiamento is like Spanish once again:

(33)     Ken$_i$ b'a bisa k(u)' [e$_i$] a bai fiesta? (compare (26a))
         'Who did you say that ___ went to the party?'

It may come as a surprise, however, that the language shows no morphological person marking whatsoever, anywhere in the verbal paradigm:

(34)     mi ta kome              'I am eating.'
         bo ta kome
         e ta kome
         nos ta kome
         boso(nan) ta kome
         nan ta kome

Therefore we need to explore the relation between the possibility for the subject to remain empty and parameter theory in more detail. It is clear that more research is needed here. A number of questions come to the fore. First of all, if creole grammars share certain features with child grammars due to genetically programmed design features, then how does creole language development proceed? To what extent is acquisition input-driven, and to what extent is it programmed by innate mechanisms? Derek Bickerton systematically examined the input available to Hawaiian creole learning children, arguing that its unsystematic and impoverished nature is a challenge for any current assumption about language acquisition.

Apart from a group of researchers who studied the development of Tok Pisin as a first language – research often involving older children and adolescents –, there is only a handful of scholars working on the acquisition of creoles, however. Adone (1994) presents evidence from Mauritian Creole that the inflection phrase in that language is acquired only gradually.

So far most of the work is theoretical. DeGraff (1992) cites assumptions from first-language acquisition research that *pro*-drop is the unmarked option, and argues that Haitian is a *pro*-drop language. It would be worthwhile to compare his analysis of Haitian more systematically with the Papiamento data analyzed here.

Veenstra (1994) also argues for the *pro*-drop status of at least some creole languages. The assumption that Saramaccan is a pro-drop language makes it possible to give a unified account of a number of unrelated grammatical properties. The discussion centers on semantically empty subjects and on subjects of complements of perception verbs, and can serve to illustrate the approach taken within the Government and Binding literature on creoles.

The argument runs as follows: the subject of a complement of a perception verb behaves syntactically like the object of the matrix verb, although an apparently nominative pronoun appears in that position:

(35)  Mi sí     a/*en            go.                    (Saramaccan)
      1SG see   3SG(nom)/3sg(ACC) go
      'I saw him leave.'

The subject (and hence nominative) pronoun *a* is possible here, but accusative *en* is not, unlike English *him*. Nominative Case is assigned by finite Tense. One piece of evidence for the object-like behavior of embedded subjects comes from binding possibilities of pronouns. The presence of Tense (finiteness) makes a binding domain referentially opaque (cf. Lasnik & Uriagereka 1988), a separate referential island:

(36)  A$_i$ jéi  a$_{*i}$   ta fán.
      3SG hear  3SG    PR talk
      'He heard him talking.'

The obligatory disjoint reference of pronouns in (36) (the two *a*s cannot refer to the same person) shows that there is no Tense in the embedded complement and, therefore, no nominative Case assigned to its subject. The conclusion is that accusative Case is assigned to the subject. Furthermore, the so-called nominative pronoun exhibits properties of being a clitic syntactically. It cannot be coordinated, cannot be used in isolation and it cannot bear focus (Kayne 1975). This observation, combined with the object-like behavior of embedded subjects, leads to the conclusion that there is a hidden element, a null subject, which is Case-marked by the verb of perception and is identified by the clitic *a*. The corollary is that in Saramaccan clitics and overt NPs are in complementary distribution. If a clitic is present, the subject is null and if a clitic is absent, the subject is overt (lexically realized):

(37)    a.  pro$_i$  *(a$_i$)  wáka.           b.  Di    wómi$_i$  (*a$_i$)  wáka.
            3SG            walk                     the   man       (3SG)    walk
            'He walked.'                            'The man walked.'

Support for this conclusion comes from expletive constructions. In typical null subject languages expletives are non-overt. A similar situation we find in Saramaccan. Only clitics are possible in subject position of expletive constructions, full NPs are not:

(38)    a.  A/*en kéndi a    dóo.              b.  A/*en de    fanódu   fu-u     fán.
            3SG   warm  LOC  door                  3sg   COP   need     for-IPL  talk
            'It is hot outside.'                    'It is important that we talk.'

The question, now, is how Saramaccan acquired null subjects. Veenstra (1994) dismisses the possiblities of substrate transfer and inheritance from a pidgin. The relevant substrate languages for Saramaccan do not have null subjects. Studies of Arctic pidgins point towards the same conclusion for pidgins. In contrast, he argues that principles operative in language acquisition are ultimately responsible for the emergence of null subjects in Saramaccan.

## 11.7 Conclusion

The universalist approaches constitute a good occasion for child developement specialists, sociolinguistics, syntacticians and historical linguists, to refine the questions needed to be asked and the way they should be investigated.

### Further reading

The main source for the universalist approach is still Bickerton's work (e.g. 1981 1984). A book contrasting universal and substrate explanations is Muysken & Smith (1986a). A general work on the generative perspective on universals is Lightfoot (1982).

Part III.
**Sketches of Individual Languages**

# 12  Eskimo pidgin

Hein van der Voort

## 12.1  Introduction

In this chapter, we will deal with pidginized forms of the Eskimo language. By 'Eskimo' we refer to Eskimo languages in general. We use the English equivalent of a local name when dealing specifically with a particular variety, and the name Inuit to refer to Eskimo-speaking indigenous people in general, even in cases where this name is not used for self-reference. The term Eskimo Pidgin refers to contact-induced varieties of Eskimo.

Because of the orientation of this book, which mainly concerns pidgins and creoles in the Circumatlantic Hemisphere, our main consideration here will be Eskimo-lexifier pidgins from Greenland. However, Eskimo-lexifier pidgins have been attested elsewhere, and furthermore, all Eskimo pidgins share specific typological traits, and they may also be historically connected. Therefore we will on certain occasions divert our attention to other parts of the Arctic. We lack clear data from Canada's Atlantic coast.

One of the things that make the Eskimo-lexifier pidgins particularly interesting for the study of language contact is the fact that they are contact-induced forms of a polysynthetic language. Few pidginized, mixed and creolized forms of polysynthetic and agglutinating languages are to be found in the Atlantic. Consequently, they have not been studied as thoroughly as contact-induced forms of other types of languages. The typological background of adstrate languages (here mainly Eskimo, Germanic and Romance languages) has as such not been the subject of much systematic research. Eskimo-lexifier pidgins can tell us something more about the relation between language type and contact-induced processes of linguistic accomodation. This again, further refines our picture of what really may be universal consequences of language contact.

Another interesting aspect of research on Eskimo pidgins is the history and the nature of the contact between the Inuit and other groups and their cultures, like the very different 'Qallunaat' (white non-Inuit).

## 12.2  The Inuit, their language and its dialects

Originally, the Inuit were a nomadic people, with a culture and a societal structure well adapted to the Arctic environment, living by seasonal gathering and hunting. Due to the sparse vegetation of the land, most of the Inuit lived by the sea and were almost totally dependent upon the hunting of sea mammals. Some Inuit groups in Canada's Great North, however, lived almost exclusively off the wild caribou herds until the 1930's.

It is thought that the Inuit originally come from Asia, and that their ancestors crossed the Bering Strait some 8.000 years ago. Nowadays, they are spread over the Arctic from Northeast Siberia to East Greenland. This area is intersected by four political borders, established by people from basically four different linguistic backgrounds (Danish, English, French and Russian). In spite of the vastness of this area, and its division, the Eskimo language is spoken in adjacent varieties that form a continuum with a rough total of 100.000 speakers today. It must be added that there are some 'cracks' in the continuum, i.e. it consists of some mutually rather unintelligible subareas.

Genetically (i.e. in the sense of historical linguistics), the Eskimo language is only distantly related to Aleut.

## 12.3  Inuit - Qallunaat contacts in the Atlantic

### 12.3.1  The Greenlandic Inuit

The Inuit of Greenland, or the Kalaallit, 'Greenlanders', as opposed to the Qallunaat, 'the Danes and originally all other whites', only live in coastal areas. The present Greenlanders are descendants from the Neo-Eskimo (Thule) culture that migrated from Canada around the year 1000 AD.

The West Greenlanders (±45.000) live on the west coast and in the south. Here the climate is best because of the warm current coming up to the Davis Strait. Their dialect, West Greenlandic (henceforth **Greenlandic**), is spoken as a native language by the vast majority.

The East Greenlanders (±3000) have lived in near-total isolation and under severe climatic conditions for the last few centuries. Their first recorded contact with Europeans was in 1884. Their dialect is related to West Greenlandic, but displays strong phonological differences, as well as lexical differences because of local death-related taboos on names.

The Polar Eskimos (±770) of the Northwest Greenlandic Thule district are the northern-most indigenous people in the world. They were first contacted by whites in 1818. Their dialect shows similarities to archaic dialects in Canada and Alaska.

### 12.3.2  European contacts in the Northwest Atlantic

The history of international and interethnic contacts in the northern regions of the Atlantic is long and complex. The following subsections form a short and simplified schematized presentation of relevant facts. Important dates are given, and the linguistic implications are summarized.

## The Norse

900    The Norse (i.c. Icelandic and Norwegian Vikings) encountered indigenous people in Labrador, whom they called 'Skrælingar'.

1000   The Norse established permanent settlements in Greenland. They only found traces of other people.

1200   The Norse encountered 'Skrælingar' in Greenland. These were Inuit of the Thule culture expanding southward.

1450   The Norse became extinct, most probably because of climatic deterioration and increased isolation from Europe.

*Linguistic implications:* From this period, only a few Norse lexical items survive in later Eskimo pidgins, e.g. *kona* 'woman/wife'. Remarks in travelers' accounts from the 18th century indicate that there was a special register for communication between the Norse and the Inuit. The origin of the modern Greenlandic word *Kalaaleq* (pl. *Kalaallit*) 'Greenlander' is generally supposed to be the aforementioned Skræling. In early missionary times, the Inuit explained to Paul Egede that *Kalalæ* was how they were referred to by the Norse (Egede 1750:68), and that they still used this word for themselves when communicating with foreigners. Normally, they call themselves *Inuit* (sg. *Inuk*) 'humans'.

## Other early European contacts

1450   The Basques started whaling expeditions to the Arctic. Nothing is known about possible contacts with Greenlanders.

1500   Portuguese cod fishers frequented Northwestern Atlantic waters.

+1500  The beginning of extensive Basque whaling in Labrador, also trade with Inuit.

+1700  The French started to frequent the Canadian east coast for commercial reasons.

*Linguistic implications:* There is one Greenlandic word that may have a Portuguese origin: *paliaarpoq* 'takes part in singing and dancing' from Portuguese *bailar* 'to dance'. In the late 1600's Labrador Inuit Pidgin French emerged in contacts between Breton and Basque fishermen, French and Inuit, and was used until ±1760. The sparse linguistic evidence, which also contains some Basque items, is supplemented by metalinguistic evidence (Dorais 1979, 1980; Bakker 1991a, to appear).

## Later European explorations

1576   The British explorer Martin Frobisher who sailed North in search of the Northwest Passage to China, met and traded with Inuit in Baffin Island, and listed 17 Eskimo words.

1586    The British explorer John Davis met and traded with Inuit in West Greenland and listed 40 Eskimo words.

+1600   A short-lived period of Danish interest in Greenland, part of the Danish empire. It is considered possible that the Norse still lived there.

1600    Dutch expeditions to the eastern Arctic, and trade contacts with Greenlandic Inuit.

1700-1777   Dutch and Frisian whaling and trading in Davis Strait, especially in Greenland (Gulløv 1987).

1721    The period of Danish colonization of Greenland officially begins with the establishment of missionary Hans Egede's colony.

+1777   Whaling in Davis Strait dominated by the English and Danes.

*Linguistic implications:* During this period, a Greenlandic Pidgin emerged (Van der Voort forthcoming a). Inuit were often kidnapped and taken to Europe where they usually soon died. Resen's (1687) long word list containing pidginized forms, was based on information from three kidnapped women. With the beginning of Christianization of the Inuit by Lutheran missionaries, and soon thereafter in 1733 by Moravians (Herrnhut), the serious study of Greenlandic was taken up by Europeans.

### 12.3.3  Contact varieties of West Greenlandic

Since the late 17th century, the Greenlandic language has been documented by Europeans. Since that time, written sources sometimes contain data and information on contact-induced varieties of Greenlandic as well. Not everyone was aware of the difference. However scarce the data, they exhibit some traits that clearly remind us of other Eskimo pidgins of which we have more data. We have a number of reasons for positing the existence of one or more Greenlandic pidgins. There are some purely linguistic indications such as word lists containing simplified and strange forms, and sentences that contain Greenlandic words but not Greenlandic morpho-syntax. This Greenlandic data shares specific traits with Eskimo pidgins from other places, such as the well known Herschel Island Trade Jargon (Stefánsson 1909) of western Canada. There are also remarks about a contact language in the literature. Finally, the circumstances, such as the tradition of frequent short contacts on a seasonal basis over centuries, and the near total absence of bilingualism among the two groups in contact, who spoke mutually unintelligible languages, make the emergence of a pidgin highly likely.

Today, probably no Eskimo pidgin is in use anymore, while no Eskimo-lexifier creole has emerged. The rise of bilingualism among the Inuit has enabled them to communicate with foreigners in many more contact situations than those for which a non-native contact-induced language variety is sufficient (see chapter 3), while maintaining their original native tongue. It is for this reason that research into Eskimo pidgin mainly has to be historical in nature. Before we discuss the Eskimo pidgin data, we will give a brief outline of Greenlandic 'proper'.

## 12.4 A short characterization of the West Greenlandic dialect

Here, we will deal only with the West Greenlandic dialect explicitly, but because of its close ties with other dialects, what is said here can be taken to apply to them as well. Typologically, Greenlandic is a **polysynthetic** language, i.e. a language in which complex semantic contents are expressed through morphology.

As to the **lexicon**, it is estimated (Bergsland 1955) that the West Greenlandic lexicon contains just about 1.800 synchronically determinable roots. Greenlandic has only three lexical categories: nouns, verbs and so called uninflectible particles. There are no adjectives, articles or prepositions.

West Greenlandic **phonology** has undergone little change since the 18th century. In this paper, we will touch upon phonology only occasionally. The phonological system:

(1)    a.   vowels: /a/, /i/, and /u/ (allophones: [e] [o] before /q/ or /r/)

        b.   consonants: /f, g, j, k, l, m, n, ŋ, p, q, r, s, t, v/. (The old distinction alveolar /s/ vs. post-alveolar /š/ is disappearing. The /q/ is a voiceless dorso-uvular plosive.)

There are two phonologically distinctive quantities: long and short. A geminate (long) /l/ is voiceless and fricative: [ɬ:].

Verbs **agree in person and number** with both subject and object, and personal pronouns are only used for emphasis. Verbs are also inflected for different 'moods'. Nouns are inflected for case, among which two grammatical cases, the absolutive and the ergative. This means that the subject of an intransitive verb has the same case marking as the object of a transitive verb, in Eskimo absolutive, whereas the subject of a transitive verb is marked differently, here ergative. Transitive:

(2)    Anguti-p   arnaq      taku-aa.                 (West Greenlandic)

        man-ERG  woman.ABS  see-3SG.3SG

        'The man saw the woman.'

Intransitive:

(3)    Angut     pisup-poq.                        (West Greenlandic)

        man.ABS  walk-3SG

        'The man walked.'

Subordinate mood and absence of lexical pronoun:

(4)      taku-gakkit                                                                (West Greenlandic)
         see-1SG.2SG
         'because I saw you'

In **possessive constructions**, the possessor is marked with the ergative case suffix. The possessed element agrees in number and person with the possessor. In principle, the possessor can be omitted.

(5)      (anguti-p)    illu-a                                                       (West Greenlandic)
         man-ERG       house-3SG.ABS
         '(the man's) his house'

An Eskimo word has a lexical stem to which by **recursive derivation** an in principle endless string of suffixes (±400 different ones) can be attached. Compounding, is in principle not possible because the basic Eskimo word contains only one lexical stem. An example with the stem *iminnger-* 'to be inclined to drinking':

(6)      iminnger-          naveersaar-tu-       nngor-    tussaa-    vunga
         [stem-             derivation-derivation-derivation-derivation-inflection]
         be.inclined.to.drinking-try.not.to- one.who-  become-   should-   1SG
         'I should become a teetotaller.'

Many morphophonological processes modify the derived forms, but they are quite regular.

In spite of the little ambiguity that the morphology leaves to be resolved by the syntax, Greenlandic has a fairly **rigid SOV word order** for pragmatically unmarked sentences (Fortescue to appear). The basic structure of the NP is Head - Modifier, and of possessive constructions Possessor - Possessed.

As will be clear morphology is a very important component of Eskimo grammar, and although regular and productive, it is far more elaborate than that of any Indo-European language. Both historically and typologically, Eskimo and the European languages are far apart.

## 12.5 Greenlandic Pidgin: a sketch

Now we will discuss aspects of the different linguistic components of Greenlandic Pidgin. There are three essential sources from the 17th to 19th century: Resen (1687), Meyer (1767) and O'Reilly (1818). These sources are word lists containing a few unanalyzed forms and short sentences. They were recorded by newcomers in the Arctic, who spoke no Eskimo and were not aware of the pidgin character of their data. For a comprehensive overview and analysis of all hitherto attested data of Greenlandic Pidgin see van der Voort (forthcoming a).

### 12.5.1 Lexicon

The main lexifier language of Greenlandic Pidgin appears to be West Greenlandic. Some Greenlandic words are clearly pidginized. Yet, several sources also contain words of European origin. Highly intriguing are specific entries shared by other Eskimo pidgins.

In the table below we listed some Greenlandic Pidgin words of non-Eskimo origin. We know *picaninnee* 'child' belonged to an international nautical pidgin. Other words, especially those present in other pidgin lists, may have also belonged to such a language. As some of the etymologies are controversial, this list is only illustrative:

| | | | |
|---|---|---|---|
| abysie (M) | 'gun' | <DU bus(se), DK bøsse | 'gun' |
| bliktemik (M) | 'tin' | <DU blik | 'tin/white iron' |
| bogaklek (M) | 'whiting' | <PO bacalhau | 'cod' |
| canu (O) | 'boat' | <AR canoa | 'canoe' |
| cuná (M, S, O) | 'woman, wife' | <ON kona | 'woman, wife' |
| dennemik (M) | 'sword' | <DK degen | 'sword' |
| hageltimek (M) | 'shotgun charge' | <DU or GE hagel | 'shotgun charge, shot' |
| handlabasche (M) | 'to trade' | <GE handlen, DK handle | 'trade' |
| hœkemik (M, T) | 'stockfish' | <DU heek WG uu(g)aq | 'cod for stockfish' |
| kralit (M, O) | 'aboriginal' | <ON skræling | 'savage' |
| musaq (S) | 'carrot' | <ON mura | 'carrot' |
| niisa (S) | 'Porpoise' | <ON hnísa | 'porpoise' |
| picaninnee (O) | 'child' | <PO pequeninho | 'little child' |
| promek (M, O) | 'bread' | <DU brood, GE Brot | 'bread' |

Sources: M = Meyer (1767), O = O'Reilly (1818), S = several other sources, T = Thevet (1558). Language abbreviations: AL = Algonquian, AR = Arawakan, DK = Danish, DU = Dutch, GE = German, MO = Montaignais, ON = Old Norse/Old Icelandic, PO = Portuguese.

Most words, however, stem from the lexifier language, and they are almost fully equivalent to their contemporary Eskimo forms (and may provide information on the pronunciation of older Greenlandic):

| ajongelak | <ajunngilaq | 'it is all right' |
| aleksemik | <alersaq | 'spoon' (Instr. alersamik) |
| baussamek | <paassat | 'gunpowder' (Instr. paassanik) |
| bœse, pusee | <puisi | 'seal' |
| engeltimek | <inngilik | 'knife' (Instr. inngilimmik) |
| immik | <imeq | 'water' |
| kyak, kaiak | <qajaq | 'kayak' |
| sovitch | <savik | 'iron, knife' |
| tœwak | <tuugaq | 'narwhal tooth' |

The following pidgin words are derived from the lexifier language, but either their shape or their meaning is markedly different from the original, which points to innovative expansion:

| bœmek (M), pumà (B,O) | 'whale' | <puisi | 'seal' |
| kakkamia (M) | 'fox-skin' | <kakap amia | 'fox-skin' |
| kynoka (M) | 'commander' | <qinigaq | 'elected / chosen one' |

Sources: B = Brown (1868), M = Meyer (1767), O = O'Reilly (1818)

The word *kona* is attested widely (Van der Voort to appear b). The word *\*kone* <Danish *kone*, Old Icelandic *kona* 'wife' has two equivalents in Greenlandic: *arnaq* 'woman', *nuliaq* 'wife'.

| Greenland Pidgin | 1656 | konâ | 'wife, woman' |
| | 1687 | kona | 'woman' |
| | 1722 | kóna | 'woman' |
| | 1746 | kona | 'woman' |
| | 1764 | kœne | 'the son's wife' |
| | 1817 | cunà | 'woman' |
| Hudson Bay Pidgin | 1897 | koo-nee | 'woman' |
| Arctic Alaska Pidgin | 1885 | ku-ní-ä | 'woman' |
| | 1890 | koo ne'a | 'wife' |
| | 1892 | kunia | 'woman' |
| | 1909 | ku'-ni | 'wife, woman' |

## 12.5.2 Phonology

As to phonology, the orthography used in our sources does not provide a clear picture. Certain sounds strange to the European ear, such as the [q] and the voiceless [ɬ:] are systematically written as variants of a [k] or [k + r] and a [sibilant + l] or [plosive + l] combination respectively. The latter may point to an earlier stage, or to a foreigner's interpretation of the /ł:/, which can be observed with second language learners of Greenlandic today. Eskimo pidgin examples of the uvular quality of the /q/ (and /r/):

(7)  oksok 'bacon'     < WG orsoq 'blubber' (whale or seal fat)
     kyak 'ship'       < WG qajaq 'kayak'
     kralit 'run'      < WG qaagit! 'come.here-2SG'

and the geminated voiceless /ł:/:

(8)  altlemeck 'something else, other' < WG allamik < alla '(an)other' + Instr.: 'something else', older WG spelling avdla

Phonological quantity seems to be absent in Greenlandic Pidgin.
The above-mentioned features are also found in other Eskimo pidgins.

## 12.5.3 Morphology

Specific grammatical traits that this pidgin displays are also encountered elsewhere in the Arctic among Eskimo pidgins of various periods. Some of these are traits commonly observed in pidgins in general. Especially the relative scarcity of productive morphology, which contrasts sharply with the polysynthetic character of the Eskimo language.

In Eskimo, inflection is obligatory. Here it is absent, and recognizable morphemes are really unanalyzable parts of the words, to be considered as fossils at the most. Much Eskimo inflection has a pronominal function. Proof of the absence of this function in Eskimo pidgin is found when independent pronouns are used next to fossilized inflection, without having an emphatic function as they do in Eskimo proper (see 12.3.3). Consider the following Greenlandic Pidgin expression from 1687:

(9)  Uvanga   ocaluctung   maccua   invin.                              (Pidgin)
     I        speak        much     Greenlandic
     'I speak a lot of Greenlandic.'

Petersen and Rischel (1987) give the following possible Greenlandic transcription, which would not make much sense:

(10)    Uanga oqalut-tunga    makkua    inu-it.
        1SG    speak-1SG      these     person-PL
        '(it is) I, (who) I speak these persons.'

In (9), the pronominal reference function of the last syllable of the verb *ocaluctung* 'speak' is absent. In (Old) West Greenlandic, this would be an inflected form, meaning 'I speak'. For pronominal reference in (9), a separate lexical pronoun *uvanga*, also from the lexifier language, is used. A modern Greenlandic semantic equivalent of (9) might be:

(11)    Inut-tut       oqallorip-punga.                            (West Greenlandic)
        person-like    speak.well-1SG
        'I speak Greenlandic well/fluently.'

Put differently, pidgin words are morphologically simple. We have seen that this means that the apparent morphological structure is no longer productive, and does not have the morphosyntactic functions it has in Eskimo. Sentence (12) from Hudson Bay (Hanbury 1904) shows this too. This sentence is contrasted with a literal (but ungrammatical!) equivalent in modern Greenlandic (13), and a Greenlandic rendering of the contents (14).

(12)    Awonga  igbik  ukaktūk                                    (Pidgin)
        1SG     2SG    talk.3SG
        'I told you.'

(13)    *uanga illit   oqar-poq                             (West Greenlandic)
        1SG    2SG     talk-3SG
        'I you he talked.'

(14)    Oqaluttuup-pakkit.                                  (West Greenlandic)
        tell-1SG.2SG
        'I told you.'

In example (15) from 1687 we see that the main verb, *tiva-sar-* 'dance-habitually', has no inflection at all, something that is impossible in genuine Eskimo:

(15)    Ibling tovarsan pinialugo.                             (Pidgin, 1687)
        'You    dance    beautifully.'

Petersen & Rischel's (1987:121) Greenlandic interpretation is as follows:

(16)   Illit   tiva-sar-tutit   pinna-ra-lugu                                   (West Greenlandic)
       2SG    dance-HAB-you   nice-consider.as-(1SG).3SG
       'I like (that) your dancing.'

The same phenomenon is found in possessive noun phrases. The following pidgin example from 1687 in West Greenland (17), shows an **analytic** (see chapter 3) possessive construction where the possessor is an independent pronoun, instead of a **synthetic** expression as in the Greenlandic semantic equivalent:

(17)   *Pidgin*                          *West Greenlandic*
       Uvanga Nulia        ⟷          nulia-ra
       1SG wife/3SG.wife               wife-1SG
       'my wife'                       'my wife'

If *Nulia* is a rendition of Greenlandic *nuliaq* 'wife', it contains no inflection at all, unless it is derived from the zero marked third person possessive form *nulia* 'his wife'. Because of the incompatibility of this form with the actual first person possessor it must be regarded as fossilized. In both analyses, (17) exemplifies the analytic nature of the pidgin. The following example (18) from 1885 from Point Barrow, Northern Alaska may be rather an indication of foreigner talk (see chapters 3 and 8):

(18)   *Pidgin*                          *West Greenlandic*
       wû'ñä adigátka      ⟷          assak-ka
       1SG hands(.1SG)                 hand-1SG
       'my hands'                      'my hands'

The possessive inflection *-ka* is maintained here, together with the corresponding pronoun, however without the emphatic function which it would have in Eskimo.

There are no productive derivational suffixes in the pidgin. However, compounding, a morphological process non-existent in Eskimo, appears to be possible. The left part of (19) from the western Hudson Bay area (Hanbury 1904) shows juxtaposition of two bare nouns without Eskimo morphology like in the right part:

(19)  *Pidgin*                        *West Greenlandic*
      ummingmuknekki ⟷              umimma-ap        neqa-a
      musk.ox.meat                   musk.ox-ERG      meat-3SG
      'meat of musk-ox'              'meat of musk-ox'
                        *umimmak neqi
                        musk-ox meat

Something similar is found in 18th century Greenlandic Pidgin (Meyer 1767):

(20)  *Pidgin*                        *West Greenlandic*
      bosamia           ⟷           puisi-p     ami-a
      seal.skin                      seal-REL    skin-3SG
      'sealskin'                     'seal's skin'
                        *puisi ami-a
                        seal skin-3SG

### 12.5.4 Syntax

In chapter 3 variable word order, corresponding to the different orders of the languages in contact, is mentioned as a typical pidgin trait, contrasted with the characteristic creole feature of rigid SVO order. The syntax reflected in Eskimo pidgins is variable. Germanic SVO word order is encountered in (9) above, and SVO is the most common order in Eskimo pidgins. The following examples, as well as (12), show an OV order, however:

(21)  Una      pile.                                  (Pidgin. Resen 1687)
      3SG      let.3SG (OV)
      'let him/her (get/have (?) it)'

(22)  Awonga    pihuk.tuk    shiku   tekuli.          (Pidgin. Hanbury 1904)
      1SG       walk.3SG     ice     see (SVOV)
      'I will take a walk to look at the ice.'

(23)  Awoña     cavik    aitcū.                       (Pidgin. Stefánsson 1909)
      1SG       knife    give (SOV)
      'I gave him a knife.'

When contrasted with Greenlandic, (24) (Hanbury 1904) shows adjective-noun order which is unlike the canonical Eskimo noun-modifier order and is the same as the English order:

(24)  *Pidgin*                              *West Greenlandic*

      aupuluktuk  hauik ⟷            savik  aappalut-toq

      be.red.N    iron                 iron   be.red-N

      'Copper'                          'red iron'


## 12.6  Further issues

### 12.6.1 Classification as a pidgin

We have shown above how the language variety presented in this chapter differs from Greenlandic Eskimo. It agrees with the criteria for pidginhood set out in chapter 3. It is not a creole language, as it does not have typical creole features like TMA markers, strict SVO word order, etc. (see chapter 2), nor did it ever function as a first language.

Still, as there was hardly any bilingualism, some vehicle of communication was badly needed. The Inuit may then have simplified their language by means of foreigner talk strategies, something which is suggested by our sources. In fact, possible foreigner talk universals may help to explain the similarities among the Eskimo pidgins mentioned here.

Yet, there are some grounds against identifying this body of data as ad-hoc foreigner talk, instead of as a pidgin. First, there was a long tradition of intensive seasonal trade contact, and mention is made in the literature of a tradition of communication with foreigners dating back to Viking times. The length of this period, and the continuity of traditions of contact, make the emergence of a pidgin highly likely. Secondly, as foreigner talk is by definition created by speakers from their own language, our material should contain no elements from languages unknown to the Inuit, such as European lexemes and word order, which it in fact does.

Whether certain material reflects a pidgin, a jargon, imperfect second language learning or foreigner talk is a matter of definition (cf. Bakker to appear). The difference between these results of language contact is not absolute, and the former may feed on the latter, e.g. a pidgin may evolve out of a jargon, and may use foreigner talk strategies. Typical jargon characteristics like instability and inconsistent application of grammatical rules can be found as well. However, a jargon is by definition not a goal of language acquisition, and should be intelligible for all participants in the contact. The presented material reflects a language form that is unintelligible without prior experience, even for the Inuit.

### 12.6.2  Typological shift in the pidginization of Eskimo

In section 5, we have seen that Greenlandic Pidgin is based mainly on West Greenlandic. When compared to this Eskimo language, the Greenlandic Pidgin turns out to be greatly reduced in morphological complexity. Greenlandic Pidgin confirms the statement in chapter

3.5.1, that morphologically complex languages, when pidginized, may still contain words with fossilized inflections (e.g. example 12 of the present chapter), but also words that are not inflected at all (e.g. 15). The functions these inflections have in Greenlandic are fulfilled by different means in Greenlandic Pidgin, viz. by pronouns.

The pidgin then, is clearly of a different typological nature (i.c. analytic). The result of pidginization seems to be a language which is morphologically less complex than any of the languages involved in the contact situations that led to the emergence of the pidgin. Furthermore, it may have characteristic traits absent in the main adstrate language, like productive compounding in Greenlandic Pidgin.

### 12.6.3  Why was Eskimo the lexifier language?

One of the reasons for the many similarities between Eskimo pidgins everywhere is that their input language always was an Eskimo dialect. A likely explanation for this is the fact that the whaling crews were often multi-ethnic. Especially in the 19th century western Arctic, crews were often mixed, with such varied nationalities as Americans, Cape Verdians, English, Germans, Hawaiians, Portuguese, Scandinavians and Spanish. Furthermore, whereas crews of earlier whaling ships to the eastern Arctic were often homogeneously Basque, Danish, Dutch, English or German they all landed at the same places, and consequently, the Inuit met a variety of nations in a short time. So the Inuit were the main invariant factor everywhere in the interethnic contact.

Second, the Inuit were also the dominant group in another way. Without the Inuit, the crews that wintered in northern Alaska, near Herschel Island, in order to ensure a bigger catch on the return journey the following summer, or crews that had been shipwrecked and had to wait for rescuing vessels, could never have survived had they not been helped by local Inuit. Certainly in earlier days, the Inuit were relatively independent vis-à-vis the foreigners, whereas the whalers were rather dependent on the Inuit for food, shelter, clothing and other goods, etc.

A third explanation might be that the Inuit did not want to learn any single foreign language (which one would they choose anyway?), or any sailors' pidgin because they wanted to preserve a certain distance in respect of the foreigners (see Bakker 1993, and Drechsel to appear). There are many reports even at the present of Inuit mocking their countrymen for 'starting to resemble a Qallunaaq'. Confirmation of this wish to keep themselves apart comes from Stefánsson (1909), who writes that attempts by the whites to speak Eskimo 'proper' were considered laughable. Furthermore, the fact that the whites often asserted that they had learnt Eskimo in the space of a few months, indicates that the Inuit were not much inclined to teach them their native language. The development of an Eskimo-lexifier pidgin was the ideal compromise.

**Further reading**

The Inuit are one of the most studied Native peoples of the American continent, and more than thousand publications have appeared on their languages alone, for which see Krauss (1973). Eskimo-Aleut dialectology is treated in Woodbury (1984). West Greenlandic in Fortescue (1984). On Eskimo-lexifier pidgins, however, only very little work has been done. The seminal article is Stefánsson (1909), which contains much data on one specific pidgin. Pidginized Eskimo-Aleut is further to various extents touched upon in Bakker (1991, 1993, 1996), Drechsel (1981,1996), Drechsel and Makuakāne (1982), Golovko (1995), Golovko & Vakhtin (1990), Hancock (to appear), Holm (1989), Mühlhäusler (1986), De Reuse (1994,1996), Schumacher (1977), Van der Voort (1996, 1997) and Wurm (1992). The history of the westward expansion of the Norse is a fascinating one, described in several standard works (e.g. Gad 1970-1973, or more popularized, Mowat 1976).

# 13 Haitian

Pieter Muysken and Tonjes Veenstra

## 13.1 Introduction: origin, present status, relation with other creoles

Of all the Caribbean creoles, Haitian has the largest number of speakers, almost six million. These live in the western part of the island of Hispaniola (the eastern part is the Dominican Republic) as well as in many other parts of the Caribbean and North America. There has been a steady exodus of political refugees and emigrants throughout the eighties and early nineties, and hence a number of Haitian diaspora communities have developed. The Republic of Haiti is one of the poorest countries in the Americas and the country has suffered a great deal of political oppression and unrest since it became independent in 1804.

In 1697 the French took over control of Haiti from the earliest colonizers, the Spanish. It is not clear precisely when Haitian Creole emerged, but by 1728 there was a slave population of 50,000. At the time of independence slavery was abolished. Since then, Haitian has been the main language of the country, with French retaining the status of official language, though spoken only by a minority. In recent years, Haitian has gained prestige as a language of literacy, and it now has an official orthography.

## 13.2 The study of Haitian

Haitian is one of the best-studied creole languages, as one might expect from its historical and demographic importance. Nonetheless, there is also considerable controversy surrounding it. This controversy was first clearly articulated in two works from the thirties: S. Sylvain (1936) and J. Faine (1937). In Sylvain's book, the claim is voiced that many features of Haitian are African in nature. Faine, on the other hand, acribes most features of the creole to French dialects, notably those of Normandy. The section on further readings mentions more recent work.

## 13.3 Phonology and lexicon

Haitian has a symmetrical seven vowel system:

(1)  |  i  |  u  |
     |  e  |  o  |
     |  è  |  ò  |
     |     a     |

The consonants are equally unremarkable:

(2)
| | | |
|---|---|---|
| p | t | k |
| b | d | g |
| f | s | š |
| v | z | ž |
| m | n | ñ |
| | l, r | |

A prominent feature of Haitian phonology is nasal assimilation, as described in Tinelli (1981).

## 13.4  Grammar

We will illustrate a number of the grammatical features of Haitian with the aid of proverbs and riddles, pointing out aspects of the grammar and the lexicon, and mentioning a few of the studies that have been carried out on Haitian.

### 13.4.1  Tense/mood/aspect
Consider first a riddle:

(3)  Gran-papa-m      t-ap-kondi        you    lame,
    grandfather-1SG  PAST-PR-lead   one    army
    you    lapli  bare-l,        li      rale  sab-li,
    one    rain   overtake-3SG,   3SG   draw  saber-3SG
    you    solda      pa-mouye;
    one    soldier   NEG-wet
    poul      ki    kouvri   pitit li    ak-zèl li.
    chicken   REL   cover    little 3SG   with  wing 3SG
    'My grandfather was leading an army, a rainfall overtook him, he pulled out his saber, not one soldier got wet: a hen covering her chickens with her wings.' [Hall 203]

In this example there is the sequence of preverbal particles *t-ap* /te ap/ 'past tense progressive'. These are among the most frequent tense/aspect elements in Haitian.

    Notice further that in (3) the form *lame* 'army' etymologically contains the French article, as in French *l'armée*. This is a typical feature of many French creoles. The 3SG object pronoun *l* is phonologically enclitic upon the verb. Notice finally that the possessive pronoun *li* occurs after the noun.

Lumsden (1993), basing himself on seminal work by Damoiseau (1988), shows that the interpretation of TMA markers depends on the aspectual verb class they combine with. There are three classes to be distinguished: dynamic verbs, resultative verbs, stative verbs. For instance, aspect marker *ap* is interpreted as future or present progressive if it is combined with a dynamic verb. The combination with a resultative or a stative verb results in a future interpretation only. The tense marker *te* also allows for different interpretations. Dynamic verbs yield a past perfect interpretation, resultative verbs allow either a past or a past perfect interpretation, while stative verbs only have a past interpretation.

Spears (1990) also notes the ambiguity in the interpretation of the aspect marker *ap*. He contrasts it with the mood marker *(a)va*, which also marks future. According to him, the semantic difference between *ap* and *va* corresponds to the dichotomy indicative-subjunctive.

In addition to the proto-typical TMA markers, we also find a group of markers that can be termed **auxiliaries**. The main insight of Magloire-Holly (1982) is that these markers interact differently with TMA-markers. The modal auxiliary verb *dwe* is ambiguous between a deontic and an epistemic reading. This ambiguity disappears when *dwe* is combined with tense markers. If it precedes the tense marker, it has an epistemic interpretation (*she must have come*. If it follows the tense marker, it has a deontic one (*she could come*).

Damoiseau (1988) observed that the tense interpretation of dynamic verbs depends on the specificity of their object. The contrast, termed the **factitive effect** by Africanists, is the following: when the object is specific, the bare verb is interpreted as past, but with a non-specific object, it is interpreted as non-past (habitual). This contrast is not found with stative verbs.

### 13.4.2 Noun phrase
Consider now the following:

(4)　Rat　kay　manje　pay　kay.
　　　rat　house eat　　straw house
　　　'The rats of the house eat the straw of the house.' [Hall 198]

In this example we notice that the genitive is formed with a simple postposed possessor noun. That this can be recursive is shown in the following example:

(5)　Kabrit gade je　mèt　　kay　avan　　l-antre.
　　　goat　look eye　master　house before　3SG-enter
　　　'The goat looks at the eye of the master of the house before he enters.' [Hall 198]

See Lumsden (1989) for a full exposition of the internal structure of noun phrases. In particular he focuses on cooccurrence restrictions involving determiners, genitive NPs and the plural marker. It also includes a discussion of the different realizations of genitive case in Haitian.

### 13.4.3  The marker *pou*

An important element in the grammar of Haitian is the marker *pou*. Consider first:

(6)    Li    pa-jam    tro    ta    pou    chen    anraje.
       3SG NEG-ever too    late    for    dog    go mad
       'It's never too late for a dog to go mad.' [Hall 192]

In this example *pou* is a subordinator, while in the next two examples we see *pou* as a modal verb, marking obligation.

(7)    Lè    rich    jete,    pou-pòv ranmase: tach    palmis.
       When rich    throw,    for-poor pick    up:    spathe palm
       'When the rich man throws it away, the poor man must pick it up: spathe of a palm tree.'
       [Hall 209]

(8)    Tèt    ki    abitie    pote chapo    pou-li    pote.
       head    REL    be-used    wear hat    for-3SG    wear
       'A head which is accustomed to wear a hat should wear it.' [Hall 195]

Notice *ki* as a relative clause marker when the subject is relativized. The same was already seen in (3). See Koopman & Lefebvre (1981) for an overview of the different uses of the morpheme *pou*.

### 13.4.4  The determiner

Much attention has been paid to the determiner in Haitian:

(9)    M-mande    fè    yon    kou    t-kouto    sou-yon    tab.
       1SG ask    do    one    cut    little-knife in-one    table
       Mwe    koupe    pen-a,    banan-la,    vian-la
       1SG    cut    bread-DET, banana-DET,    meat-DET
       men    gen    yon    bagay ki    di    mwen
       but    there be    one    thing REL    say 1SG

| m-pa | kapab | koupe | li | | |
|------|-------|-------|-----|---|---|
| 1SG-NEG | able | cut | 3SG | | |
| se-enpe | mwen | oblije pran | | la-dan: | diri |
| FOC-a | little | 1SG | obliged take | there-in: | rice |

'I asked to do the cutting at a table, I cut the bread, the banana, the meat, but there was a thing which told me I couldn't cut it, [and] it was only a little I was obliged to take thereof: rice.' [Hall 209]

In this example we see the use of *la* and *a* (the form is phonologically determined) as determiners with definite noun phrases. In (9) we can discern another part of the pattern of noun phrase marking. Generic noun phrases are unmarked, indefinites can be marked with *yon*.

Furthermore, (9) illustrates the use of *se* as a focus particle, and of *pa* as a preverbal negation marker. DeGraff (1993) is the first complete study on negation. He shows that there is negative concord. Different negative elements do not cancel each other's negative force. He compares the Haitian system with the French system and shows that despite the phonetic resemblance Haitian *pa* and French *pas* do not behave syntactically alike. Rather, *pa* has to be equated with French *ne* with respect to its syntactic characteristics.

An example in which *se* and *pa* are combined is (10):

(10)    Se    pa    pou-tèt    you    pen    ou    pèdi    tout    you    founo.
        FOC    NEG    for-head    one    bread 2SG    lose    all    one    oven
        'It's not for the sake of one loaf that you lose a whole ovenful.' [Hall 199]

The periphrastic expression *pou tet* is used for 'for the sake of'.

### 13.4.5 Predicate doubling

In many Haitian sentences, the verb is doubled:

(11)    Gran-papa-m    gen    youn    pitit,    li     mèt    ale    an-Frans,
        grandfather-1SG    have    one    child,    3SG    allow    go    LO-France
        toune li      toune li jwen    pitit-la     chita    mem    plas       dlo    riviè,    sous.
        turn    3SG     turn    he find    child-DET    sit    same    place      water    river,    source
        'My grandfather has a child, he can go to France, when he comes back he finds the child sitting in the same place: river water, spring (water).' [Hall 208]

Here *toune li toune* represents one of the forms of predicate doubling in Haitian. Notice further that *gen* is used here as the verb of possession, 'have', while elsewhere it functions as existential 'there is'.

(12)  Abiye kon li    abiye, kan midi      sone fòk  bourik  Sen-Domeng  rani
      dress how 3SG   dress, when midday  strike must donkey  S.D.        bray
      'However he may be dressed, when midday strikes the donkey from Santo Domingo has to bray.' [Hall 196]

In this example there is a different use of predicate doubling (also called predicate cleft), indicating contrast. Consider also:

(13)  Piti  kon  yo   fam      piti,  li   toujou  kapab  okipe   you  kay.
      little how  one  woman   little, 3SG  always  able   occupy  one  house
      'No matter how small a woman is, she can always take care of a house.' [Hall 189]

Here a structure with adjective doubling occurs, rather similar to the previous example.

Lefebvre (1994) distinguishes four types of predicate doubling. Two of them are used in adverbial clauses, either temporal or causative, respectively (14a) and (14b). The two other constructions are factive clauses (topic relativization in Sebba's (1987) terminology) in (14c) and predicate cleft (14d):

(14)  a.  Rive Jan   rive  Mari pati.
          arrive John arrive Mary leave
          'As soon as John arrived, Mary left.'
      b.  Rive Jan   rive  Mari pati.
          arrive John arrive Mary leave
          'Because John arrived, Mary left.'
      c.  Rive Jan   rive  a    fe    li   kontan.
          arrive John arrive DET  make  3SG  happy
          'The fact that John arrived made her happy.'
      d.  Se    rive Jan   rive.
          It-is arrive John arrive
          'It is arrive that John did (not e.g. leave).'

For a discussion of the analysis of such constructions, see the chapter on fronting.

### 13.4.6 Reflexives
Another subject of much interest is the forms the reflexive can take in Haitian:

(15)  Sèl pa   bezwen  vante tèt-li.
      salt NEG  need    boast head-3SG
      'Salt doesn't need to boast of itself.' [Hall 200]

This is an example where *tet li* is used as a reflexive. Reflexives have been studied in two recent articles by Carden & Stewart (1988) and Déchaine & Manfredi (1994). See further chapter 22.

### 13.4.7 Double objects, serial verbs, and prepositions
As in other creole languages, there is a complex relationship between the marking of double objects, and the use of serial verbs and prepositions. Consider first:

(16)  Kan  ou   jwe  ak-ti-chen,      la   ba    ou   pis.
      when 2SG  play with-little-dog, 3SG  give  2SG  flea
      'When you play with a puppy, it gives you fleas.' [Hall 200]

Here we notice the use of a double object construction with *ba* 'give'. The occurrence of this construction in Haitian is remarkable given that the lexifier language, French, does not allow this construction, at least not with noun phrases. The verb *ba* also occurs in serial constructions:

(17)  Men  li,   al pran-l    ba    mwen:  lombraj.
      here 3SG,  go take-3SG  give  me:    shade
      'There it is, go get it for me: shade.' [Hall 201]

This riddle contains an example of serially used *ba* 'give'; here it marks benefactive. While in this example the literal meaning of 'giving' is still there, this is not the case in the next riddle:

(18)  Gran-papa-m        rete     an-le,     li lage    you  asièt ba     mwen
      grandfather-1SG    stay     in-air,    he drop    one  plate give   me
      li  tonbe a-tè         pa-kase,   li   tonbe nan-dlo li    kase:    papie.
      3SG fall  LOC-earth    NEG-break, 3SG  fall  in-water 3SG  break:   paper
      'My grandfather stayed in the air, he dropped a plate on me, it fell on the earth and didn't break, it fell into the water and broke: paper.' [Hall 202]

Here the object of *ba*, *mwen*, is in no way the beneficiary.

Consider now (19):

(19)    Pa-koke    makout    pi    ro    pase    men    ou.
        NEG-hang   basket    more  high  pass    hand   2SG
        'Don't hang a basket higher than your hand.' [Hall 198]

In this example *pase* 'pass' is used in a serial verb construction to mark a comparative. Notice, however, that the adjective, perhaps redundantly, receives the degree marker *pi*.

Serial verb constructions are well-studied in Haitian. Wingerd (1977) is based on natural data and contains a frequency-analysis. Déchaine (1986) contains the most elaborated classification of the construction. She argues for a lexical analysis in which the two verbs are somehow semantically merged. Law & Veenstra (1992) and DeGraff (1993) opt for a syntactic analysis.

Dialect variation seems to exist with respect to the possible range of serial verb constructions. Déchaine (1986) reports that Haitian only allows for theme serials and not for instrumental serials (see chapter on serial verb constructions). In Lefebvre (1989) the occurrence of instrumental serials is limited to very specific contexts. It only occurs with verbs involving change of location (and not change of state). Furthermore, the action has to be accidental and involves only pragmatically inappropriate instruments:

(20)    a.    Kwafe         a      pran   sizo     koupe    zorey  mwen.
              hairdresser   the    take   scissor  cut      ear    1SG
              'The hairdresser cut my ear with a scissor.'
        b.    *Jan    pran   sizo      koupe    cheve-m.
              John    take   scissor   cut      hair-1SG
              'John cut my hair with a scissor.'

Law & Veenstra (1992), on the other hand, found that Instrumental-serials are possible across-the-board. Verbs involving change of location as well as change of state can participate in the construction.

Notice the extensive use of prepositions in many of the examples in this chapter. In contrast with creoles such as Saramaccan and Sranan, Haitian and other French creoles are quite rich in prepositions.

### 13.4.8 Passive
Notice the use of an unmarked passive in (21)-(22):

(21)   Mèt   kabrit   mande   kabrit,   plen   pa   plen   se-bay-li.
         master goat   ask   goat,   full   NEG   full   FOC-give 3SG
         'If the goat's master asks for the goat, pregnant or not pregnant she must be given [back] to
         him.' [Hall 194/5]

(22)   Rakata   fè   klwa,   nan-gine tande:   loraj.
         noise   make 'clwa',   in-Africa hear:   thunder
         'The noise goes "clwa", it is heard in Africa: thunder.' [Hall 201]

In (21) *bay* 'give' and in (22) *tande* 'hear' must be interpreted as passives. In contrast, the passive meaning in (23) is conveyed by using an indefinite third person plural pronoun *yo* in an active sentence:

(23)   Se   sou   chen mèg   yo   wè   pis.
         FOC   LOC   dog   thin   3PL   see   flea
         'It's on a thin dog that the fleas can be seen.' [Hall 193]

These examples also provide further illustration of the focus marker *se*.

### 13.4.9 Other general creole features
(24)   Kat   je   kontre,   manti   kaba.
         four   eye   meet,   lie   stop
         'When four eyes meet, lying stops.' [Hall 190]

Notice the Portuguese word (very general in creoles) *kaba* here, in its literal sense of 'stopping', rather than as an adverb indicating accomplishment or perfective. Another general creole feature illustrated in (24) is the use of a preposed conditional or adverbial clause without conjunction.

(25)   Mwen pase   you   kote;   mwen   wè   blan   k-ap-niche   dèyè   nèg:
         I   pass   one   place:   I   see   white   ASP-ASP-lick   behind   black
         chodie ki   sou-dife.
         kettle   REL   LOC-fire
         'I passed by a place [where] I saw a white man licking a Negro's behind: kettle on the fire.'
         [Hall 204]

In this example we see that the complement of the perception verb *wè* 'see' is marked by continuous aspect *k-ap*, similar to English *-ing*. This is quite common in the Caribbean creoles. Notice that the bare form *pase* 'pass' is interpreted as a simple past here. Consider finally a complex example:

(26)  Gran-pap-m      gen   you   ban     pitit, men  yo    te    radi,
      grandfather-1SG  have  one   group   little, but  they  TNS   isolent
      pou-li-te-sa          pini    yo,   li   dekouvri  kay   li    te-ba      yo
      for-3SG-TNS-know  punish  3PL,  3SG  uncover   house  3SG  TNS-give  3PL
      rete-a;       dan   yo    rete   grigne   nan-soley:  lè    you   riviè  chèch
      stay-DET   tooth  3PL   stay   grin     LOC-sun;    when  one   river  dry
      roch   yo    lan-soley.
      stone  3PL   LOC-sunz

      'My grandfather had a lot of children, but they were insolent; in order to be able to punish them, he uncovered the house he had given them to stay in; their teeth remained grinning in the sun: when a river bed dries the rocks in the sun.' [Hall 205]

This example reveals a number of the complexities of Haitian subordination. We see a purposive clause introduced by *pou* which at the same time has a (resumptive) lexical subject *li* and a past tense marker *te*; the latter makes the purposive clause somewhat hypothetical ('so that he might be able to'). Then there is a somewhat complex relative clause [*li te-ba yo rete-a*], marked by the determiner *a* (from *la*), but without an overt relative introducer; finally there is a serial construction *rete grigne* 'stay and grin'.

### 13.4.10  Relative clauses

Relative clauses not marked with an overt complementizer only occur with non-subjects. We saw above that with subjects, we find the relative marker *ki*. Consider also the following example:

(27)  Papa-m      gen   de    ti-nèg        k-ap-fan          bwa   tout  lajoune
      father-1SG  have  two   little-boy   REL-ASP-split     wood  all   day
      li   pa    jwen  bwa   yo    fan:   je.
      3SG  NEG   find   wood  3PL   split:  eye

      'My father has two little boys who are splitting wood all day long, [but] he never finds the wood they split: eyes.' [Hall 207]

In this example the difference between relative clauses where the subject has been relativized (with *k* or *ki* as in ... *ti-nèg k-ap-fan* ...) and those where the object has been relativized (without *k* or *ki*, as in ... *bwa yo fan* ...) is clearly indicated. This pattern has been interpreted by Koopman (1982) as indicating that the subject position is not licensed by the inflectional elements in a clause. *Ki*, therefore, is required as a licenser of that position. She posits it in the complementizer position. The subject/object asymmetry with respect to the presence of *ki* has been used in a number of analyses of Haitian syntax. Law (1994), for instance, has used it to show that there is a nominative/accusative distinction despite the fact that pronominals exhibit the same surface form in the different cases. Extraction from nominative case-marked positions requires *ki*, but extraction from accusative case-marked positions does not.

### 13.4.11  The relation between the verb and the position of the tense elements

In (28) the placement of *pa-janm* before *envité*, rather than after it as in the French *il n'invite jamais une poule*, suggests a profound difference between Haitian and French (DeGraff and Dejean 1994). In Haitian, the verb does not move to the auxiliary or inflection (INFL) position, and remains in the verb phrase, adjacent to the object.

(28)  Lè      ravèt       vlé    fè     dans,    li     pa-janm       envité     poul.
      hour    cockroach   want   make   dance,   3SG    NEG-never     invite     chicken
      'When a cockroach wants to have a dance, he never invites a chicken.' [Hall 197]

Thus *envité poul* in (28) remains a single constituent. In French, the root *invit-* is moved, in the analysis of DeGraff & Dejean (1994), which builds on much recent work in the generative tradition, to the auxiliary or inflection position, where it is fused with the tense and agreement morphemes. Since it has to cross *jamais* while being moved, the latter ends up between *invite* and *une poule*. In summary:

(29)  French:   [invit-]   jamais    [e]        une poule
      Haitian:   INFL      pa-janm   envité     poul

## 13.5  Variation

A major issue in the study of Haitian concerns variation. Valdman (1978:287-299) gives a useful overview. There are three main dialects: northern, including Cap-Haïtien, central, including the capital Port-au-Prince, and southern. In addition to numerous lexical differences, there is some phonetic and morpho-syntactic variation. The northern variety tends not to nasalize the determiner: instead of southern *baton-an* 'the stick' we have *baton-la*.

From the perspective of grammar, the most important feature of the northern variety is a postposed possessive marked with *a* (rather than null as in the rest of Haitian), as in *papa a i* 'his father' rather than *papa li*, the southern and central form. The southern variety is characterized by the form *pe* 'continuative' instead of *ap* or *ape*. There is evidence that the dialect of the Port-au-Prince area is the prestige form, and that some Haitians are bi-dialectal in their native dialect and the prestige variety. As noted by Valdman, a thorough study of syntactic dialect variation in Haitian still remains to be done. Carden & Stewart (1988) have used Haitian dialect evidence about the distribution of reflexive forms in Haitian dialects to argue for an early stage in Haitian without an overt pronoun/anaphor distinction.

Stylistic variation in Haitian manifests itself through vowel elision in the pronouns or vowel merger. Thus we have [l gō kaj] for *li gen un kaj* '(s)he has a house.', in casual style. A third dimension of variation concerns the amount of French influence. Thus rural Haitian will have [i] where urban Frenchified Haitian may have [y], as in [diri] versus [dyri] 'rice'

### Further reading
Robert A. Hall's valuable *Haitian Creole. Grammar, Texts, Vocabulary* (1953) places the study of Haitian within the framework of American structuralism. Albert Valdman has been enormously influential in stimulating the study of Haitian Creole in the United States, and his *Le créole: structure, statut, origine* (1978) is a comprehensive introduction to the language, although his book has the curious feature that it treats the various French-lexifier creoles as belonging to one system. Tinelli (1981) is one of the few book-length treatments of any creole phonological system. Yves Déjean, working in Port-au-Prince, has contributed a number of important studies about grammatical and educational aspects of Haitian.

The work of Claire Lefebvre and her research team at the Université du Québec à Montréal has been very influential in setting new standards for syntactic analysis, and in pushing the substrate hypothesis for Haitian to its logical conclusion. Recently, researchers such as Rosie-Marie Déchaine, Viviane Deprez, and Michel DeGraff have been presenting increasingly sophisticated studies of Haitian syntax within the framework of GB theory. Singler (1990a, 1992a,b) has carried out careful historical demographic studies that are possible now with fuller access to the archival materials.

# 14 Saramaccan

Peter Bakker, Norval Smith and Tonjes Veenstra

## 14.1 Introduction and text

Saramaccan is the language of the roughly 25,000 members of the Saramaccan (or Saramaka) tribe, and the roughly 2000 members of the Matawai tribe - two of the so-called Bush Negro tribes of Surinam, South America. There are three main Saramaccan dialects, the Upper and Lower Suriname River dialects, spoken by the Saramaccan tribe, and the Matawai dialect spoken on the Saramaka River. A large number of speakers are temporarily or permanently resident in Paramaribo, the capital of Surinam, or in other locations in Surinam, and a fair-sized expatriate population lives in the Netherlands.

A fair amount of work has been done on the two Saramaccan dialects, but very little indeed on Matawai. Outside the primary use of the language as the spoken vehicle for Saramaccan daily life, some teaching in primary schools in the Saramaccan area involves the reading and writing of Saramaccan. The main available literature is educational or religious in nature.

In creole studies Saramaccan has played an important role. It is claimed, for example, to be the **purest** creole, the **deepest** creole, the most **radical** creole, the most **African** creole, and the creole which is grammatically the most deviant from its lexifier language, of which it might be said to have two - English and Portuguese.

In fact, however, its purity must be relativized - it involves after all a mixture of two lexifier languages. Whether the supposed purity or deepness derives from the workings of universals, or from its African substrate(s), or both, is a matter of some controversy. It is also due, to be sure, to the relative isolation of Saramaccan as a maroon language in the forest.

To start off with, we will quote a fragment of a text in Saramaccan. It is part of a traditional story. In this story, water is hidden under a rock. All the birds are invited to try to break the rock, but nobody succeeds. Then the woodpecker shows up. This fragment is taken from SIL (1977).

(a) Hɛn totómbotí táa wɛ a o-du lúku tu
    Then woodpecker said well 3SG IRR-do look too
    'Then the woodpecker said that he would try too.'

(b)    'Gaamá,    mi    o-gó    náki  lúku.'
        Granman,  ISG  IRR-go  hit   look
        "Chief, I am going to try to hit it."

(c)    Hɛn  déé      ótowan  táki  táa:
        Then  the-PL  other   say   that
        'Then the others said:'

(d)    'Ku  ún-búka,  i    lánga bákahédi   ku  dí   gaán taku   fi-i  dέ?'
        With  which-beak, 2SG  long back-head  with  the  big   ugliness of-2SG there
        "With what beak, you long back-of-the-head, with your great ugliness?"

(e)    'Um-fá  a    dú   ufɔ   i    sa   boóko  ɛn?'
        How   3SG  do   before  2SG  can  break  3SG
        "How is he going to break it?"

(f)    'U túu  wɛ... lúku dí    bígi   dέ   ku   mi,  wokó.'
        IPL all  FOC  look  the   bigness there  with  ISG  woko
        "All of us [have tried] ... look how big I, woko, am."

(g)    Gbaniní táa:  'wɛ  lúku mi.   Ún      totómbotí?'
        Hawk   say   well  look  ISG.  Which  woodpecker
        'The hawk said: "Well, look at me [how big I am]. Which woodpecker [is going to try such
        a thing]?" '

(h)    Hɛn  totómbotí     wáka te    kó   dóu.
        Then  woodpecker walk  till    come  arrive
        'Then the woodpecker walked out there.'

(i)    Hɛn  a    tjɔkɔ dí    sitónu   kookookoo.
        Then  3SG  stab  the   rock    IDEO
        'Then he pecked at the rock. Peck! Peck! Peck!'

(j)    Hɛn  a    wáka gó seeka taámpu.
        Then  3SG  walk  go  arrange  stand
        'Then he walked to [another place] and got himself ready.'

[The woodpecker finally succeeds in breaking the rock, and thus provides water for all the birds. However, since that time the woodpecker has not been able to stop pecking at things.]

| (k) | Hɛn | a | táa | án | sa | disá | soní | u | náki | mɔɔn. |
|-----|-----|---|-----|-----|-----|------|------|-----|------|-------|
|     | Then | 3SG | say | 3SG-not | can | quit | thing | for | knock | more |

'After that, he said that he can't stop knocking any more.'

In this text, a number of things can be noticed which will be discussed in more detail below. It is striking that most words are extremely short. Although completely unintelligible to speakers of English, the bulk of the vocabulary is in fact derived from English, for instance in the first line *dú* 'do', *lúku* 'look', *tú* 'too'. There are also a number of Portuguese-derived words, but these are less numerous, such as *ku* 'with' (Port. *com*), *disá* 'quit' (Port. *deixar*) and *búka* 'mouth, beak' (Port. *boca*). There are also words from other sources, such as *totómbotí* 'woodpecker', *taku* 'ugly', and *kookookoo*, imitative of the pecking on a rock. These words are presumed to be mostly African in origin. The last word, *kookookoo*, is an example of an ideophone (see section 14.6.3).

The meanings of some words also deviate from the meanings of the corresponding items in the various lexical sources. The meaning of the Portuguese word *boca* 'mouth', for instance, is extended to cover also the meaning 'beak' in Saramaccan *búka*, for which Portuguese has a separate word (*bico*). Some words also have different grammatical functions from their source words. For instance *táa*, the short form of the verb *táki* 'talk, say', is used as a complementizer meaning 'that', as in (c). The verb *boóko* 'break' is derived from the English past tense or past participle form *broke(n)*.

Although the lexicon is mostly English, the sound structure is very un-English. Saramaccan is a tone-language, there are three degrees of distinctive vowel length in non-ideophonic words, the syllable structure is preferably CV (Consonant-Vowel), and there are phonemes like /kp, gb/, which are unknown in European languages, but quite common in West African languages.

There are hardly any morphologically complex words in the text. There are a few cases of compounding, such as *baka-hedi* 'back of head' and some preverbal markers, such as in *o-gó* and *o-dú*. The *o*-element is a preverbal marker indicating intention, irrealis, future, and the like. In some cases, two elements have merged into one phonologically, such as *fii* from *fu i* 'for/of you' and *án* from *a an* 'he/she/it not'.

Personal pronouns have just one form for subject, object and possessive in the 1st and 2nd persons, e.g. *i* 'you, your' in (d) and (e), and *mi* 'I, me, my, mine' in (h), (f) and (g). There are emphatic forms, such as *mí* for 1st singular, and *jú* for 2nd singular. The third singular does have distinct forms to express various syntactic relations - *a* subject, *ɛn* object/possessive, and *hén* emphatic subject/object/possessive.

The sentence structure differs significantly from English and Portuguese. In (j), for instance, we find four verbs in a row, an example of a so-called serial verb construction (see chapter 23). In Saramaccan, word order is basically SVO (subject - verb - object), but almost anything can be fronted for purposes of focus. Note that this kind of fronting does not affect the position of the subject, which stays in front of the verb phrase. Any fronted elements go in front of the subject.

## 14.2  Position within lexifier language creole group

Saramaccan is, as we have stated above, a mixed English and Portuguese-based creole. The English element is dominant in the language as compared to the Portuguese element, making it possible to regard Saramaccan as basically a member of the Atlantic group of English-based creole languages. Although the Portuguese words are so numerous that one could perhaps say that Saramaccan has two lexifier languages, it is clear that Saramaccan remains essentially an English-based creole, into which the Portuguese elements have intruded (Smith 1987), conceivably by relexification. Most function words are from English. A study of the phonology of words from both languages shows that the English words - or at least a part of these - have been longer in Saramaccan (or its precursors) than the Portuguese words.

Nearly all the English elements present in Saramaccan are also present in Sranan and Ndjuka, the unambiguously English-based creoles spoken in Surinam, although Saramaccan does have fewer English elements. The question of the provenance of these two portions of the lexicon is briefly dealt with in chapter 8.

Saramaccan - or at least the English elements of Saramaccan - belongs to a clearly defined Surinam subgroup within the English-based creoles. This subgroup can be identified in historical linguistic terms (with three languages: Sranan, Ndjuka-Aluku-Paramaccan-Kwinti, and Saramaccan(-Matawai)). Outside the Surinam subgroup it has a particular relationship with Krio, and other similar languages on the West African coast, as well as with the Maroon Spirit Language of Jamaica (Bilby 1983).

## 14.3  Origin of the Saramaccan tribe and language

The linguistic origins of Saramaccan are controversial. Not so the historical origins of the Saramaccan and Matawai tribes, for their history as Maroons has been fairly well established by the work of Price (1976, and especially 1983). It is virtually certain that the first mass-escape by slaves leading to the formation of what was to become the Matjáu clan of the Saramaka tribe took place in 1690, when slaves belonging to Imanuël Machado left their plantation en masse. The name Matjáu is derived from the Portuguese Machado.

Most of the groups of refugees from the plantations who were to form the Saramaccan tribe - the Matawais represent a later split-off from the Saramaccans - had escaped before about 1710. As a result of the periodic wars between the Saramaccans and the Dutch, it was dangerous for escaped slaves to attempt to join up with a Saramaccan group, because of the risk of being taken for spies of the Dutch. After the peace treaty the Dutch colonial authorities concluded with the Saramaccans in 1762, and the Matawai in 1767, the tribes were supposed to be closed to further escapees - under the terms of treaties they were required to hand over any who fell into their hands, although they certainly did not always do this.

A mixed form of speech - a mixture of English and Portuguese elements - appears to have arisen in the late 17th century in an area on the mid-Suriname River where many Jewish plantations were situated (see also above). According to a number of authors (Price 1976; Goodman 1987; Smith 1987) this mixed language is what was referred to by later writers as **Dju-tongo** [toŋ(g)o] ('Jew language'). Schumann (1783) lists a number of Dju-tongo items in his Sranan dictionary, and it can be seen that this list involves the same mix of English, Portuguese and African elements as Saramaccan. It is virtually identical - though not completely - to recorded 18th century Saramaccan. This Dju-tongo - presumably a mixed English-Portuguese pidgin rather than a creole - seems to have formed the precursor of Saramaccan.

## 14.4  Type of creole

Lexically, Saramaccan deviates in two main ways from other creoles, both inside and outside Surinam.

In the first place, it is one of the few known **creole** languages with a mixed lexicon, as distinct from normal mixed languages. Although it is basically an English-based creole, there is, as we have said, a significant proportion of Portuguese-derived vocabulary in the language. Smith (1987) shows that some 35 percent of the basic vocabulary is from Portuguese, as against 50 percent from English. Some of the most basic words are indeed from Portuguese, such as *wómi* 'man', *mujɛ́ɛ* 'woman'. In fact there is no way to predict whether a particular word will be Portuguese-derived or English derived. The word for 'foot', *fútu*, is from English, the word for 'hand', *máun*, from Portuguese. The word *wójo* 'eye' is from Portuguese, the word for 'nose' *núsu* is from English.

Second, Saramaccan has the highest proportion of identified words from African languages of any creole of the New World. Although only about five percent of the basic vocabulary is from African languages, hundreds of words have been identified so far, most of them in the more 'cultural' domains of the lexicon: food and cooking, religion, utensils and tools, as well as flora and fauna. More than 125 words are from Kikongo (Daeleman 1972, Price 1975) and a similar number are from Gbe (Ewe-Fon), as well as a smaller number of words from other African languages (in particular Twi). There are also many words from Amerindian languages, and an increasing number from Dutch.

## 14.5  Phonology and phonetics

The consonants are as follows:

| (1) | | labial | dtl/alv. | palatal | lab-velar | velar |
|---|---|---|---|---|---|---|
| | stops | p b | t d | tj dj | kp gb | k g |
| | fricatives | f v | s z | sj | | |
| | nasals | m | n | nj | | |
| | nasal stops | mb | nd | ndj | | ng |
| | liquids | | l | | | |
| | semivowels | w | | j | | |

The 'palatal' consonants /tj, dj, nj, ndj/ can be defined as dorso-postalveolar, while /sj/ is rather a dorso-palatal sibilant.

The vowels are:

| (2) | | front | back | | front-nasal | back-nasal |
|---|---|---|---|---|---|---|
| | high | i [i] | u [u] | | iN [ĩ] | uN [ũ] |
| | high-mid | e [e] | o [o] | | eN [ẽ] | oN [õ] |
| | low-mid | ɛ [ɛ] | ɔ [ɔ] | | ɛN [ɛ̃] | ɔN [ɔ̃] |
| | low | | a [a] | | | aN [ã] |

Three contrastive lengths of vowels, or vocalic elements are possible:

| (3) | fa | speak | bɛ | 'red' |
|---|---|---|---|---|
| | fáa | far | béɛ | 'belly' |
| | baáa | brother | bɛ́ɛ | 'bread' |

There are two surface tones - H(igh) and L(ow), and three underlying tones - H, L, and ø (unspecified) tones. Generally, in European-derived words the vocalic element corresponding to the primary-accented element in the European language will bear a H tone, while all other vocalic elements will be unspecified for tone. In the absence of tone-sandhi rules applying to such vocalic elements, these will appear as ʟ on the surface.

African-derived words will normally have a tone specified on each vocalic element.

(4)  pílá        ʜʜ   'still (ideophone)'

pína    ʜø   'pin'

kabá    øʜ   'finish'

pindi   ʟʟ   'idol'

zónka   ʟʜ   'charcoal'

Tones do not only have a lexical function, but also a grammatical function. For example, unspecified tones become high between high tones in adjoining words standing in certain syntactic relationships.

(5)   dí foló 'the flower'   >   dí fóló

## 14.6 Lexical categories and morphology

Although creole languages are noted for their lack of inflectional and derivational morphology, Saramaccan possesses both to a limited degree. Apart from the arguments one could raise in favour of the analysis of the preverbal 'particles' as prefixes, there are other clearer cases of morphological formations. We will illustrate two of these: deverbal adjectivalization by reduplication, and ᴍᴀ-nominalization.

### 14.6.1 Reduplicated adjectives

As in many other Atlantic creoles, it is not easy to distinguish between stative verbs and adjectives in Saramaccan. It is possible however, to change a verb into an adjective by reduplicating it. These reduplicated forms are real adjectives, for the following reasons.

(i) the reduplications can be used attributively:

(6)   dí fátufátu wómi 'the fat man' (**not** 'the very fat man')

(7)   dí wípiwípi wómi 'the whipped man'

as well as predicatively with the copula *dé*:

(8)   Dí wómi dé nákináki. 'The man has been beaten (is in a beaten state).'

(9)   Dí goónlíba dé lóntulóntu. 'The earth is round.'

In addition to the reduplicated forms, only *bun* 'good' may appear with *dé*, but not other items that would normally be translated as adjectives in English. For this reason such items used predicatively are assumed to be stative verbs too. In their **attributive** pronominal use we assume that they **are** adjectives - note that the reduplicated forms may also occur prenominally.

(ii) In contrast with the non-reduplicated 'adjectivoids', these reduplicated forms cannot receive tense or aspect marking:

(10)    a.   Dí mií tá-bígi.             'The child is getting big.'
        b.   *dí mií tá-bígibígi

(iii) The copula is compulsory with the reduplicated forms, while it is ungrammatical with the unreduplicated forms:

(11)    a.   Dí mií dé nákináki        'The child has been beaten (is in a beaten state).'
        b.   *dí mií nákináki
        c.   *dí mií dé náki
        d.   Dí mií náki.              'The child was/has been beaten.'

(iv) Verbs can be fronted for contrastive emphasis (focusing). A copy of the verb is obligatorily left in the original position. This is usually referred to as the **predicate cleft** construction (see chapter 24).

(12)    a.   Náki dí wómi náki dí mií.    'The man **beat** the child (i.e. did not caress him).'
        b.   *náki dí wómi dí mií

Reduplicated forms, however, cannot leave a copy of the verb behind.

(13)    a.   *lóntulóntu dí goónlíba dé lóntulóntu
        b.   Lóntulóntu dí goónlíba dé. 'The earth is **round**.'

This movement is more like the kind of fronting which is possible with NPs, PPs and adverbial phrases, but different from verb fronting.

To sum up, we might say that these reduplicated forms display a distribution typical of adjectives (predicative and attributive use, obligatoriness of copula), while they have few of the diagnostic features of verbs in Saramaccan (no copying, no tense marking, no objects).

We may conclude then that adjectives are derived from verbs by reduplication.

### 14.6.2 V(P)-nominalizations

Nominalizations can be formed from nouns, verbs, and verb phrases with the help of the suffix *-ma*. In this section we shall only deal with verbal formations. The element *-ma* is derived from English 'man', but cannot itself be a (phonological) word as it does not have a tone of its own, its tone being determined by the tone of the preceding syllable. If this is L then the suffix bears a H tone; if the preceding syllable has a H or **zero** tone the suffix is L. Other arguments can be adduced to support an affix status for *-ma*. Rather unusual is the possibility of suffixing *-ma* to verb phrases. What we find in the examples below goes much further than the object-incorporation that is possible in English in cases such as *tree-pruner* beside *pruner of trees* (see Veenstra & Smith, in prep.). Some examples derived from simple verbs:

(14)  V-**ma**

  a.  hondi-ma  hunt-AG  'hunter'
  b.  sabi-ma  know-AG  'expert'

Some examples with a verb plus object:

(15)  V-N-**ma**

  a.  bebe-daan-ma  drink-rum-AG  'drunkard'
  b.  tei-manu-ma  take-man-AG  'woman who frequently picks up (married) men'

Some examples consisting of a verb plus generic prepositional phrase.

(16)  V-P-N-**ma**

  a.  pali-ku-mujɛɛ-ma  give birth-with-woman-AG  'midwife'
  b.  siki-n'-en-edi-ma  sick-LOC-his-head-AG  'insane person'

Some examples of a serial verb construction with an object following the first verb, and prepositional complement following the second verb:

(17)  V-N-V-P-N-**ma**

  a.  tja-boto-go-a-wosu-ma  carry-boat-go-LOC-house-AG  'pilot'
  b.  subi-kununu-go-a-liba-ma  climb-mountain-go-LOC-TOP-AG  'mountain climber'

Examples where the first verb is followed by a complementizer introducing a second verb:

(18)    V-C-V-**ma**

    a.  seti-u-kanda-ma    start-to-sing-AG    'precentor'

    b.  bigi-u-wooko-ma    begin-to-work-AG   'first worker'

The possibility of incorporating VPs containing subordinate clauses as in the last two examples is particularly striking.

### 14.6.3 Ideophones

Ideophones are words used to modulate more closely the meanings of verbs and adjectives. They are partly onomatopoetic (sound-symbolic), and particular ideophones can only be used with particular words. They are also sometimes referred to as 'phonaesthetic words'. They can be most closely identified with adverbs as a category. A sample sentence with two ideophones:

(19)    A    bi-djombo    *viiin*    te    a    wáta    *djuubu.*

    3SG PAST-jump    QUICKLY    till    in    water    SPLASH

    'He jumped quickly, splash! in the water.'

Some parallel examples from Saramaccan and Yoruba, as one example of a West African language (where this category is equally common):

(20)    'it    is    snow-white'

    a    wéti    *fáán*                          (Saramaccan)

    o funfun **láúláú**               (Yoruba; Rowlands 1979: 146)

(21)    'it    is    crimson'

    a    bɛ    **njaa**                          (Saramaccan)

    ó pupa *fòò*                                  (Yoruba)

Not only are ideophones a rather typical African grammatical category, sometimes the phonological form is identical to the ideophone or the normal word for the same feature in the relevant African donor language. Saramaccan *fáán* (intensifier for 'white'), for example, may well be related to Gbe (Ewe) ɸ*áá,* also with a high tone.

    Ideophones, in languages which have them, form a separate grammatical class. They are never inflected, they are only used with specific lexical items, and, although they are somewhat adverb-like, they are formally and functionally distinct from that class. In their phonological shape, they may also deviate from the canonical syllable shape. In contrast to ordinary words, Saramaccan ideophones are either solely low-toned or high-toned. Furthermore, despite the fact that Saramaccan syllables are strictly CV, there are ideophones which end in consonants, like *temmmm* 'sound of breaking a rock' and *tjim* 'arrow hitting target'. Some are extreme reduplications such as *titititi*, and in some cases a vowel can be abnormally long, like in *voooo*, as:

(22)  Hɛn   mi   hai   ɛn  **voooo**                     so.
      then  1SG  haul  it  DRAGGING THROUGH WATER  thus
      'Then I drag it through the water.'

## 14.7 Function words and syntax

### 14.7.1 The order of the main constituents of the sentence

Saramaccan is a head-initial language. It has a strict word order. The subject always comes before the verb and the object follows the verb (SVO). In both cases there holds an adjacency requirement, i.e. no elements, like adverbs, can occur between the verb and its arguments, apart from TMA markers which appear in front of the verb:

(23)  A    bi   ta    mbei  tembe.
      3SG  ANT  CNT   make  wood
      'He was making wood-carvings.'

The main deviation from this order is caused by various fronting phenomena (see (36) and chapter 24), but in those cases the verb never moves to second position:

(24)  Andi  a    ta   sei   a    Saamaka    Sitaati?
      what  3SG  CNT  sell  LOC  Saramacca  Street
      'What is he selling at Saramacca Street?'

The most remarkable feature of Saramaccan word order is that the strict VO order is maintained in nominalizations. See (15) for a relevant example. In most VO languages we find the reverse order, e.g. English, Fon.

### 14.7.2 Copula System

Saramaccan has two forms of the copula BE: *dɛ* and *da*. It appears that *dɛ* has a verbal status, while *da* has a pronominal status. Two arguments for this distinction derive from the distribution of TMA-markers and subject pronouns in copular sentences (see below). The two forms are not mutually exclusive in their combinatory possibilities as both may occur with NP-complements. However, only *dɛ* may occur with PP and AP-complements:

(25)    Etnel  dɛ/dɛ  wan   malɛngɛ-ma.
        Etnel  COP   one   lazy-MA
        'Etnel is a lazy guy.'

(26)    Valerie  dɛ/*da  n'en     wosu.
        Valerie  COP    LOC-3SG  house
        'Valerie is in his house.'

(27)    Kone  dɛ/*da  siki-siki.
        Kone  COP    sick-sick
        'Kone is sick.'

TMA-marking is only possible with *de*, not with *da*. This suggests the non-verbal status of the latter copula, since TMA-markers only occur before verbal elements:

(28)    Etnel  bi/o      dɛ   wan   malɛngɛ-ma.
        Etnel  PAST/IRR  COP  one   lazy-MA
        'Etnel was/will be a lazy guy.'

(29)    *Etnel  bi/o      da   malenge-ma
        Etnel   PAST/IRR  COP  lazy-MA

Negation occurs before *de* as with regular verbs, but in the case of *da* a contracted form surfaces, i.c. *na*.

(30)    Me       de   siki-siki.
        1SG=NEG  COP  sick-sick
        'I am not sick.'

(31)    Mi  na       wan   malenge-ma.
        1SG  NEG=COP  one   lazy-MA
        'I am not a lazy guy.'

(32)　*me　　　da　　wan　malɛngɛ-ma
　　　1SG=NEG　COP　one　lazy-MA

With *da* the order of the two NPs can be reversed, unlike with *de*. If one of the NPs is pronominalized, the pronoun has to be the first NP.

(33)　Asondone　da/dɛ　Feledi　mujɛɛ.
　　　Asondone　COP　Freddy　woman
　　　'Asondone is Freddy's wife.'

(34)　Feledi　mujɛɛ　da/*de　Asondone.
　　　Freddy　woman　COP　Asondone
　　　'Freddy's wife is Asondone.'

(35)　Hen　da　Feledi　mujɛɛ.
　　　3SG COP　Freddy　woman
　　　'She is Freddy's wife.'

(36)　*Feledi　mujɛɛ　da　hen
　　　Freddy　woman　COP　3SG

The form of subject pronouns in copular sentences can also be used as evidence for the different status of the two copulas. With *da* the subject can only be the strong pronominal form. In case of *de* it can be either:

(37)　*A/Hɛn　da　wan　bunu sondi.
　　　3SG　　COP　one　good thing
　　　'That is a good thing.'

(38)　A/Hɛn　de　wan　bunu sondi.
　　　3SG　COP　one　good thing
　　　'It is a good thing.'

In sum, Saramaccan exhibits two copular constructions with quite striking differences that suggest both a different categorial status for the 'copula' and different developmental paths for the two constructions.

## 14.8  Conclusion

Saramaccan is both a typical and an atypical creole language. Structurally it is typical with its serial verbs, SVO order, verb-fronting, NP-fronting, etc. It is atypical in that its lexicon has significant portions from two European languages, as well as having an unusually large African component. Some of these features can be explained as the result of the fact that Saramaccan developed in isolation from other European languages. It is the heritage of people who were courageous enough to escape the barbarism of the plantations to live freely in the South American rain forest, where they could carry on their African culture in relative freedom.

### Further reading

A good idea of the shape of the language can be got from De Groot (1977), which is a dictionary where each entry is richly illustrated with sentences exemplifying usage. For the history of the two tribes Price (1983) is essential reading.

# 15 Shaba Swahili

Vincent de Rooij

## 15.1 Introduction

Shaba or Lubumbashi Swahili is the restructured variety of Swahili spoken on the copperbelt of Zaire's south-eastern Shaba province. The case of Shaba Swahili (henceforth ShS) as a contact-induced language is interesting for two reasons. First, as Kapanga (1993:441) observes, it is 'one of the very few non-western based languages classified as pidgin/creole (PC)'. Secondly, despite the fact that the language has resulted from contacts between speakers of genetically closely related Bantu languages, ShS has several structural features characteristic of creole languages as will be shown below. Before turning to these structural features (section 15.4), we will briefly sketch the sociolinguistic situation of the Copperbelt (section 15.2), and present some views on the genesis of ShS (section 15.3).

## 15.2 The sociolinguistic situation on the Zairean Copperbelt

ShS is spoken by an estimated number of 2 million people. It is acquired as a first language by almost all children born in the cities of the Copperbelt and spoken as a second language lingua franca by the rural population of southern Shaba.

In the urban centers of the Copperbelt multilingualism is a wide-spread phenomenon. Apart from ShS most people speak French, Zaire's official language, and some ethnic language (Kabamba 1979). Studies on language use and language choice dating back to the mid-fifties (LeBlanc 1955; Polomé 1971b; Kabamba 1979) all indicate that ethnic languages play a steadily diminishing role. These studies also show that ShS is by far the most important language in informal interactions, and probably has been since the 1930s (cf. Fabian 1990a:44-6). French is the language used in more formal situations (e.g. secondary and higher education, and higher levels of administration).

As a consequence of this multilingualism there is an enormous amount of variation in the way ShS is spoken. There is influence from French in the form of lexical loans (cf. Fabian 1982; Kalunga 1979; Nkulu 1986) and Swahili/French codeswitching (Gysels 1992; De Rooij, in prep.), but also from ethnic languages and KiSwahili Bora (literally: excellent Swahili), the high prestige variety of Swahili that closely resembles East Coast Swahili (ECS). Stylistic repertoires may vary considerably from speaker to speaker depending on levels of proficiency in French, some ethnic language, and KiSwahili Bora. Needless to say that speakers may use code-switching and style-shifting to (re)construct social meanings and identities.

## 15.3  Genesis and development of Shaba Swahili

The genesis and development of ShS is closely linked to the colonial history of Shaba. During the first decades of this century the Belgians began to exploit the cupriferous soils of Katanga (present-day Shaba). Workers in the copper mining industry were recruited, often by force and deceit, from all over Central Africa and spoke many different, yet related, Bantu languages. It was in this context of multilingualism that ShS arose.

For the genesis of ShS, two different scenarios have been proposed. Under the first, advocated by Polomé (1968, 1969, 1971a, 1971b, 1972, 1983, 1985, 1986), locally-born children played a crucial role in the formation of the language by creolizing a locally spoken Swahili pidgin in a process of nativization. This pidgin-into-creole scenario is contested by Fabian (1986) who claims that ShS developed in a short period of time, between around 1920 and 1940, and did not involve a pidgin phase. Until 1918, when the mining company imposed Swahili as the work language, it was not Swahili but some variant of Fanagolo that was used as the work language in the mining industry.

Given the fact that Swahili played no significant role in Katanga prior to 1920 but was well established by 1940 and given also that Swahili was not the native language of the population, one is led to the conclusion that the Swahili spoken by 1940 had resulted from a process of second language learning by adults. However, the children born during this formative period may have been partly responsible for the genesis of ShS by acquiring Swahili, presented to them in the form of an interlanguage variety spoken by their parents, as a first language and thereby creolizing it.

From this cursory treatment of the history of ShS it is clear that the factors involved in the genesis of ShS differ from those usually associated with creole genesis. First, ShS resulted from the contact of substrate languages and a lexifier language which are all closely related. Secondly, the main process involved in the formation of the language was adult second language learning instead of first language acquisition. These findings cast some doubt on the classification of ShS as a creole. In fact, structural analyses of ShS have taught us that it cannot unproblematically be classified as a creole language, as Polomé (1971a) has done (cf. Mufwene 1989; Kapanga 1993).

## 15.4  A structural sketch of Shaba Swahili

### 15.4.1  Introduction

Since ShS came into being as a result of contact between genetically related, Bantu, languages, it is interesting to see which structural features of ShS can be traced back to the lexifier language (ECS), which to Bemba or Luba-Kasai, two of the most important substrate languages, and finally, which features can be attributed to universals of language contact.

The aspects of ShS phonology and morpho-syntax dealt with here will be illustrated using examples taken from the text below and other field work data unless indicated otherwise. The text gives an impression of what the language looks like. It consists of an excerpt from a transcription of a recording made in Lubumbashi (the capital of Shaba) in September 1992. The speaker is a 26 year old woman from Kolwezi, some 250 kilometers west of Lubumbashi. She is a native speaker of ShS with a limited proficiency in French. At the time of recording she was visiting relatives in Lubumbashi. The excerpt given here is the conclusion of a story about a *ndumba* (*femme libre* in French) who is in search of traditional medicine or a charm (*dawa*) in order to be successful in life. By using witchcraft, however, she has caused the death of several of her relatives. This behavior is criticized as selfish and originating from lust, or a craving (*tamaa*) for material prosperity ultimately leading to the death (*lufu*) of others.

Immediately visible from this text is the rather prominent presence of inflectional morphology in ShS. This feature sets ShS apart from prototypical creoles such as Saramaccan or Jamaican Creole. However, a comparison of ShS with ECS will show that much of the inflectional morphology present in ECS has been lost in ShS where it has been replaced by periphrastic or analytic constructions.

*Tamaa inazalaka lufu*     'Greediness bears death'

[The speed of delivery of the story is very high causing deletion of certain sounds; these are given between brackets; derivational verbal affixes are not always glossed separately; French material is italicized. Given the oral style, interpunction and capitals are minimal.]

(a)  a-na-anza              tena  ku-tafuta    dawa.      paka  sasa      ku-tafuta
     CLISC-PRES-begin       next  INF-search   medicine   just  now       INF-search
     'then she started to look for medicine. the moment she found'

(b)  dawa,        a-na-shinda              sa(w)a  yee   ku-fanya
     medicine  CLISC-PRES-continue     like    3SG   INF-do
     'this medicine, she continued in the way she had done before (viz. performing witchcraft)'

(c)  juu          ni     mu-ntu        a-ri-t, ...       a-ri-zobelea
     because   COP   CLI-wo/man  CLISC-PAST-t<    CLISC-PAST-be used to
     'because she was someone who was, .. who was used to looking for'

(d)  dawa        ku-i-tafuta.         (n)a  yee   e-ko        paka
     medicine  INF-CL9OC-search   CONN  3SG   CLISC-COP  just
     'medicine (in performing witchcraft). and she has'

(e)    damu  ya   mu-ntu.     a-na-shindwa
blood  CONN  CLI-wo/man.   CLISC-PRES-continue
'the blood of a man (on her conscience).'

(f)    kwa  yee  ku-fany(a).  njo    sasa  a-na-*finir*,
PREP  3SG  INF-do       COP   now   CLISC-PRES-finish
'like she had done before. now at this moment she finished,'

(g)    a-na-isha         yo:te.
CLISC-PRES-finish    everything
'she used up everything (*money*)'

(h)    bwana   a-na-mu-fukuzana      mu   fukuza,
husband  CLISC-PRES-CLIOC-chase  LOC  chase
'(so) her husband and she were after one another,'

(i)    a-na-shinda        kwa  ku-ikala,   ba-nduku
CLISC-PRES-continue  PREP  INF-live/stay  CL2-kin
'she continued living (there),'

(j)    yake    ba-le      ba-na-sema    yee   sa(w)a
POSS.3SG  CL2C-DEM  CL2SC-PRES-say  3SG   like
'his relatives they were saying she is like'

(k)    vile   mu-ntu     ya     kamata-kamata,   a-ba-mu-*recevoir*
thus  CLI-wo/man CONN take-take         NEG-CL2SC-CLIOC-receive
'a person who just grabs and grabs, they would not receive her'

(l)    tena.  a-na-shinda       ku-rudi-ak-a
next   CLISC-PRES-continue  INF-return-INT-FIN
'any longer. (so) she returned'

(m)    kw-abo    Kolwezi, a-ri-kimbia    na   ku
LOC-POSS.3PL Kolwezi  CLISC-PAST-fly  CONN LOC
'to her native Kolwezi, she also ran off from'

(n)    bu-kweri,    a-ri-fany-ak-a         tena  paka  m-ambo
CLI4-marriage  CLISC-PAST-do-INT-FIN  next  just  CL6-business
'her marriage, (and) she again took to the business'

(o)    m-a        ma-dawa.   njo  pa-le  i-i        *histoire*
CL6C-CONN  CL6-medicine  COP  LOC-DEM CL9C-DEM  story
'of medicine. now this story'

(p)    i-na-ni-fundisha         ku-sema kama
CL9SC-PRES-CLIOC.ISG-teach  INF-say  if
'teaches me that if'

(q)     tu-ko         mu    vie,   paka   i-le        baati         mungu
         CLISC.1PL-COP    LOC   life   just   CL9C-DEM   good fortune   God
         'we are alive, only the good fortune God'

(r)     a-ri-ku-kubar-i-a                  njo   i-le         tuu
         CLISC-PAST-CLIOC.2SG-grant-APPL-FIN    COP   CL9C-DEM   just
         'has granted you, this good fortune only'

(s)     i-na-endelea            na-ye.         kama   mungu
         CL9SC-PRES-progress       PREP-CLIRC.3SG   if     God
         'will progress with him. if God'

(t)     a-ri-ku-andika                ase(ma)
         CLISC-PAST-CLIOC.2SG-arrange     COMP
         'has it planned for you to'

(u)     u-ta-ol-ew-a                ku    masikini,
         CLISC.2SG-FUT-marry-PASS-FIN   LOC    poor (man)
         'get married to a poor man,'

(v)     u-ta-ol-ew-a                ku    masikini.
         CLISC.2SG-FUT-marry-PASS-FIN   LOC    poor (man)
         'you will get married to a poor man.'

(w)     kama   tena    mungu   a-ri-ku-andika
         if       next    God      CLISC-PAST-CLIOC.2SG-arrange
         'if, on the other hand, God has it planned for you'

(x)     u-ta-ol-ew-a                ku    mu-tajir(i),
         CLISC.2SG-FUT-marry-PASS-FIN   LOC    CLI-rich (man)
         'to get married to a rich man'

(y)     u-ta-ol-ew-a                ku    mu-tajir(i).
         CLISC.2SG-FUT-marry-PASS-FIN   LOC    CLI-rich (man)
         'you will get married to a rich man.'

(z)     lakini   mungu    a-shi-andik-ak-a          mu-ntu
         but      God      CLISC-NEG-arrange-INT-FIN   CLI-wo/man
         'but (to be sure) God never plans it for a woman that'

(aa)    ase(ma)    oh   a-ta-kuy-ak-a        ndumba      apana.
         COMP      oh   CLISC-COP-INT-FIN   femme.libre   NEG
         'he says: oh she will be a *femme libre*, no way.'

(bb)    i-le          mungu    a-shi-andik-ak-e        mw-anamuke
         CL9C-DEM   God    CLISC-NEG-arrange-INT-FIN   CLI-woman
         'such a thing God doesn't plan for not even one woman'

| (cc) | ata | moya. | kama | mu-ntu | | a-na-kuwa |
|---|---|---|---|---|---|---|
| | even | one | if | CLI-woman | | CLISC-PRES-COP |

'if a woman is/becomes'

| (dd) | ndumba | ni | tamaa. | | na | tamaa |
|---|---|---|---|---|---|---|
| | femme.libre | COP | lust/greed | | CONN | lust/greed |

'a *femme libre* it is greed. and greed'

| (ee) | i-na-zal-ak-a | | | lu-fu. |
|---|---|---|---|---|
| | CL9SC-PRES-bear-INT-FIN | | | CL11-death |

'(always) bears death.'

| (ff) | njo | *histoire* | i-i. |
|---|---|---|---|
| | COP | story | CL9C-DEM |

'this is how the story is.'

## 15.4.2 Phonology

The vowel system of ShS (1) is the same classic five vowel system as encountered in ECS. This system is also found in the substrate languages. In a number of these, however, vowel lengthening is distinctive while they are all tone languages. In ShS, apart from very few exceptions (cf. Kapanga 1993), as well as in ECS, distinctive vowel lengthening and phonemic or grammatical tone do not occur.

(1)    Vowels

| | front | back |
|---|---|---|
| close | i | u |
| close-mid | e | o |
| open | | a |

In (2) the consonants are listed. The Swahili orthography is used here for the phonemes, rather than IPA. <c> indicates a consonant the phonemic status of which in ShS has weakened or changed vis-à-vis ECS, due to substrate influence from Bemba and/or Luba-Kasai, where they do not function as phonemes (Burssens 1939; Kashoki 1968). In the basilectal styles of ShS they are devoiced: /v/, /z/, /g/ change into [f], [s~sh], and [k], respectively) while others are often replaced by phonetically related sounds in a number of specific contexts (/r/ replaced by [l], /l/ by [r], /d/ by [l], and /j/ by [y]), or deleted (h→ø).

(2)    Consonants in ECS and ShS

|  | bi-lab | lab.-dent | alv. | post-alv | pal. | vel. | glott. |
|---|---|---|---|---|---|---|---|
| plosives |  |  |  |  |  |  |  |
| *unvoiced* | p |  | t |  |  | k |  |
| *voiced* | b |  | <d> |  |  | <g> |  |
| nasals | m |  | n |  | ny | ńg [ŋ] |  |
| prenasals | mb | mv | nd/nz |  | nj | ng |  |
| fricatives |  |  |  |  |  |  |  |
| *unvoiced* |  | f | s | sh |  |  | <h> |
| *voiced* |  | <v> | <z> |  |  |  |  |
| affricates |  |  |  |  |  |  |  |
| *unvoiced* |  |  |  | ch |  |  |  |
| *voiced* |  |  |  |  | <j> |  |  |
| vibrants |  |  | <r> |  |  |  |  |
| laterals |  |  | <l> |  |  |  |  |
| glides | w |  |  |  | y |  |  |

### 15.4.3 Noun class agreement

ShS has, in a reduced and simplified form, retained the typically Bantu noun class agreement system. In Bantu languages, nouns fall into different noun classes, each of which is characterized by its own, distinct, class prefix. All nominal modifiers show concordial agreement with the noun they modify. Noun class agreement is also marked on the verbal complex. Example (3) gives an idea of how the system works in ECS. This sentence is contrasted with its equivalent in ShS in (4) which is similar in structure and only differs in the morphophonemic shapes of the concord prefixes. The modifiers of the subject *mtu/muntu*, a class 1 noun, show concordial agreement. The subject marker *a-* also shows concordial agreement with *mtu/muntu*. The same goes for the object *mtoto/mutoto*, also a class 1 noun: its modifier *wake/yake* takes a class 1 concord and there is optional, pragmatically motivated, object agreement on the verb.

(3)    Yu-le    m-tu    m-refu                                      (ECS)
        CLIC-DEM CLI-man CLIC-tall
        a-li-(m)-piga            m-toto    wa-ke.
        CLISC-PAST-CLIOC-hit    CLI-child CLIC-POSS.3SG
        'That tall man hit his child.'

(4)    U-le            mu-ntu    mu-lefu                            (ShS)
        a-ri-(mu)-pika    mu-toto    {wa}{ya}-ke.

Table 1 lists the noun class prefixes in use in ShS. In the restructured system, one recognizes strong substrate influence: only one prefix, having a morphophonemic shape diverging from substrate forms, has survived from ECS (CL.5), viz. *ji-*, but in basilectal varieties we often find *ri-* derived from Luba-Kasai *di-*.

Not visible from this table is the re-allocation of class 5/6 and class 9/10 nouns with the feature [+human] to classes 1/2, typically denoting nouns with the feature [+human] in all

Table 1. Noun class prefixes in ECS, ShS, Bemba and Luba-Kasai. ShS prefixes and phonologically similar prefixes in other languages are given in italics. In Bemba prefixes can take two forms: VCV or CV. The distribution of these variants and corresponding meaning differences are discussed by Givón (1972:68-73). Infinitival (class 15) and locative classes (classes 16 through 18) are not listed.

|        | ECS        | ShS       | Luba-Kasai | Bemba      |
|--------|------------|-----------|------------|------------|
| 1.     | m-/mw-V    | *mu-*     | *mu-*      | (u-)*mu-*  |
| 2.     | wa-/w-V    | *ba-*     | *ba-*      | (a-)*ba-*  |
| 3.     | m-/mw-V    | *mu-*     | *mu-*      | (u-)*mu-*  |
| 4.     | *mi-*      | *mi-*     | *mi-*      | (i-)*mi-*  |
| 5.     | *ji-*      | *ji-/ri-* | *di-*      | (il)i-     |
|        | ø-         | ø-        |            |            |
| 6.     | *ma-*      | *ma-*     | *ma-*      | (a-)*ma-*  |
| 7.     | *ki-/chi-* | *ki-/chi-*| *chi-*     | (i-)*chi-* |
| 8.     | vi-/vy-    | *bi-*     | *bi-*      | (i-)fi-    |
| 9.     | *N-/ø-*    | *N-/ø*    | *N-*       | (i-)*N-*   |
| 10.    | N-/ø-      | N-        | (i-)N-     |            |
| 10.>6. |            | *ma-*     |            |            |
| 11.    | u-         | *lu-*     | *lu-*      | (u-)*lu-*  |
| 12.    |            | *ka-*     | *ka-*      | (a-)*ka-*  |
| 13.    |            | *tu-*     | *tu-*      | (u-)*tu-*  |
| 14.    | u-         | *bu-*     | *bu-*      | (u-)*bu-*  |

Bantu languages. An example in the text is *banduku* (line i) which takes the class 2 prefix *ba-* instead of class 10 zero prefix. This tendency of restructuring the system on the basis of an animacy distinction has been noted earlier by Mufwene (1989).

Another, apparently semantically motivated, change is the merging of class 10 nouns, denoting plurals of class 9, with class 6, denoting plurals of class 5: the change results in a transparantly morphophonemic marking of the feature [+plural] by the prefix *ma-*. Substrate pressure must have put a brake on this trend and has prevented total restructuring of the system, as in Kenya Pidgin Swahili (KPS). Heine (1973) notes that in KPS the whole noun class system has disappeared: gender distinctions have been lost completely and replaced by a singular-plural distinction.

In ShS, noun-adjective agreement has been simplified radically: most adjectives have only one (semi-)generalized form that is used with nouns from different classes. Reduction and simplification is also found in subject and object agreement on the verb. Noun class prefixes and their agreeing subject and object markers are listed in Table 2. In ShS object markers co-indexing non-human objects are very rarely used, except for cl. 7/8, and are therefore not listed.

Table 2. Noun class prefixes and s/O-agreement markers

| | prefix | | subject marker | | object marker | |
|---|---|---|---|---|---|---|
| | ECS | ShS | ECS | ShS | ECS | ShS |
| 1. | m- | mu- | a- | a- | -m- | -mu- |
| 2. | wa- | ba- | wa- | ba- | -wa- | -ba- |
| 3. | m- | mu- | u- | *i*- | -u- | |
| 4. | mi- | mi- | i- | *i*- | -i- | |
| 5. | ji- | ji-/ri- | li- | *i*-/ri- | -li- | |
| 6. | ma- | ma- | ya- | *i*- | -ya- | |
| 7. | ki-/ | ki-/ | ki-/ | ki-/*i*- | -ki-/ | -ki-/-*i*- |
| | ch-V | chi- | | | | |
| 8. | vi- | bi- | vi- | bi-/*i*- | -vi- | -bi-/-*i*- |
| 9. | N-/ø- | N-/ø- | i- | *i*- | -i- | |
| 10. | N-/ø- | ma- | zi- | *i*- | -zi- | |
| 11. | u- | lu- | u- | lu- | -u- | |
| 12. | | ka- | | ka- | | |
| 13. | | tu- | | tu- | | |
| 14. | | bu- | | bu- | | |

The generalized use of *i*- as subject marker of nouns belonging to classes 3 through 10 is striking. This restructuring cannot be explained by invoking substrate influence, because the substrate languages make use of the same agreement system as ECS, where markers have roughly the same morphophonemic shape as the prefixes of the nouns they refer to. The use of marker *i*- seems to correlate strongly with the feature [-animate]: it does not occur with nouns belonging to classes 1/2, denoting animate beings while its use is favored in all other classes except classes 7/8 and 11 through 14. Noun class prefixes 11 through 14 stand apart from the others in that they are used productively to derive nouns with specialized meanings (e.g. diminutives).

It is clear what has been achieved by this simplification. The semantic distinctions on which the noun class system was originally built have become opaque in modern Bantu languages. The only distinction that has remained wholly transparent is the one between classes 1/2 to which nouns denoting [+animate] beings belong on the one hand, and the remaining classes 3 through 10, consisting of nouns denoting [-animate] objects on the other. In ShS this distinction has been recoded morphologically in such a way as to maximize semantic transparency.

### 15.4.4 Tense, mood, aspect

Although ShS still has some of the typical Bantu preverbal TMA affixes instead of the typical creole preverbal TMA markers, its system is built on semantic distinctions characteristic of prototypical creoles. According to Schicho (1988, 1990) the ECS preverbal affixes that have survived in ShS have lost much of their meaning as realizations of TMA and may be regarded as a kind of dummy-elements that have to be realized for morphosyntactic reasons. Time reference need only be marked once by a tense affix, by sentence-initial adverbs, or may be left unexpressed if time reference can be inferred from contextual information (Schicho 1988:568). In the text for instance, the present tense affix -*na*- is used several times in the first few lines to refer to past events. This time reference was made clear earlier however by the speaker by explicitly mentioning that she was going to tell a story about something that happened in the past. Also note the use of *tena* (lines a,n,w) to express sequential action which in ECS is expressed by the tense affix -*ka*-. Time reference expressed by adverbials also occurs in lines (a) (*paka sasa*), (f) (*njo sasa*), and (o) (*njo pale*). Schicho claims that the following distinctions provide the basis for the system:

(5)     A. [+anterior]
             (including [perfect/resultative])
        B. [-anterior, -posterior]
        C. [+posterior/irrealis]
        D. [progressive]
             (including [habitual], [intensive], [durative], [iterative])

Here 'posterior' refers to events that have not yet taken place. TMA is often expressed by main verbs functioning as auxiliaries. [+anterior] (perfective/resultative aspect) can be expressed by -*toka* (leave), and -*isha* (finish), also shortened to -*sha*. [posterior/irrealis] can be expressed by -*tafuta* (look for) or by -*enda* (go) as in (6).

(6)     A-ba-ta-**enda**    ku-ra    nani,    ku-ra    nkuku.                     (ShS)
        NEG-3PL-FUT-go    INF-eat    FILLER,    INF-eat    chicken
        'They will not eat ehm, eat chicken.'

The category [progressive] (habitual, intensive, durative, or iterative aspects) can be expressed by the main verb -*anza* (start, begin) as in line (a) of the text or by the copulative element -*ko*- used as a preverbal affix as shown in (7).

(7)  Aba    bafilles  tu-ko-na-ona        ba-na-zunguluka   umu.              (ShS)
     these  girls     1PL-COP-PRES-see   3PL-PRES-walk     around here
     'These girls we see walking around here.'

The thorough restructuring of the TMA system has to be seen in the light of the significant differences in the semantics and the morpho-syntactic means of expressing TMA in the substrate languages. During the formative period of ShS promoting semantic transparency must have been the most effective way of communicating with other second language learners, resulting in a TMA system built on a few, clear semantic distinctions and favoring a transparent means of expressing aspectual meanings, viz. periphrastic constructions with main verbs functioning as auxiliaries.

### 15.4.5 Negation
In ECS and the substrate languages, negation is expressed by verbal affixes. In ShS this strategy is still used, but in most cases a sentence final second negation element has to be present (cf. Schicho 1992:84-88) as in (8) and line (aa) of the text. This also points to the decreasing importance of agglutinative morphology in ShS.

(8)  A-i-kuwa       fura(h)a   ya       famille   **apana.**          (ShS)
     NEG-it-COP    joy       CONN family  NEG
     'It was no joy for the family at all.'

### 15.4.6 Relative clauses
Relativization in ShS also shows loss of verbal morphology in favor of periphrastic constructions. In ECS the relativizer is infixed or suffixed to the verbal complex. In ECS, we also find an alternative, periphrastic construction which makes use of a relative pronoun with a relative concord suffixed to it. This construction alternates with the one in which the relative concord (in this case -*ye*-) is inserted between the tense marker -*li*- and object clitic -*mu*-. Both are exemplified in (9).

(9)  Mtu  {**amba-ye**}  a-li-{**ye**}-mw-ona         simba a-na-ogopa  sana.        (ECS)
     man  {Pron-RC}    3SGm-PAST-{RC}-it-see  lion   3SGm-PRES-fear  much
     'The man who saw the lion is very frightened.' (Vitale 1981:90)

In ShS we find a demonstrative, agreeing with the noun it modifies, which functions as a relativizer. It may be placed before -as in (10)- or after the noun. Another example can be found in the text in line (q) (*i-le baati*).

(10)    U-ko    d'accord na    **ii**    mambo e-ko-na-sema?                        (ShS)
        2SG-COP    agree    CONN DEM    things    3SGf-COP-PRES-say?
        'Do you agree with the things she's saying?'

In KPS, the same strategy is used (Heine 1973) while parallel constructions occur in the substrate languages Bemba (cf. Givón 1972) and Luba-Kasai (cf. Burssens 1939). As pointed out by Romaine (1988:250), the grammaticalization of deictic elements into relativizers is a widespread phenomenon in creoles. Strategies of relativization in ShS seem to have resulted from substrate pressure reinforced by this universal trend.

## 15.5  Conclusion

Despite the fact that it has resulted from adult second language learning by speakers of genetically closely related languages, ShS has some features which also occur in many creoles:
- loss of agglutinative morphology in favor of analytic constructions
- a TMA system built on semantic distinctions characteristic of creole languages
- a preference for double negation

In De Rooij (to appear) it was suggested that second language learning strategies optimizing semantic transparency and reducing redundancy may be responsible for this outcome. These strategies are applied most forcefully under circumstances that are adverse to second language learning. In the case of ShS, what has prevented the full application of these strategies leading to e.g. a total loss of agglutinative morphology exemplified by KPS, is the close genetic relatedness, and hence structural similarity, of ECS and the substrate languages. In view of this one might conclude that ShS is a partially creolized language.

### Further reading

Structural aspects of ShS are dealt with by Schicho (1982, 1988, 1990, 1992) and Kapanga (1993). Fabian (1986) gives an account of the historical and political factors involved in the genesis and development of ShS. A history of Elisabethville (present-day Lubumbashi), written in ShS, has been published and analyzed in Fabian (1990b).

# 16  Fa d'Ambu

Marike Post

## 16.1  Introduction

Fa d'Ambu is a West African Portuguese-lexifier creole, spoken on the island of Annobón (Equatorial Guinea). The language belongs to a family of four creoles, all spoken on an archipelago of three islands situated in the Gulf of Guinea, off the West African coast. Two of the creoles are found on the largest of the three islands, São Tomé. The one generally known as São Tomense, is the main language of the island and spoken by the majority of the inhabitants, the other, known as Angolar, is only spoken by a small section of the population, in the south of São Tomé. On the island of Principe, people speak a creole known as Principense. Finally on by far the smallest of the three islands, Fa d'Ambu is spoken, a language also known as Annobonese. The total number of Fa d'Ambu speakers may lie between 4500 and 5000.

## 16.2  History and current status

Fa d'Ambu, like the other languages of the the Gulf of Guinea family, probably developed from the creole of São Tomé as it was spoken at the beginning of the sixteenth century (Ferraz 1979). Although no written sources are available to confirm this hypothesis, the history of São Tomé and the large amount of shared lexical and grammatical features seem to leave no doubt.

All three islands were uninhabited at the moment of their discovery by the Portuguese in the second half of the fifteenth century. São Tomé was populated first. The sources mention that by the end of the fifteenth century, it was already populated by a number of Portuguese settlers, who were granted the privilege of keeping slaves. At the beginning of the sixteenth century our sources already mention São Tomé as being a port of transshipment for the slave trade. It is probable that it was at this period that the first inhabitants of Annobón and Principe were sent as slaves to their respective islands to work on the plantations. Through the centuries the inhabitants of Annobón have always lived in fairly complete isolation. The island was too small to function as a commercial center, and although every now and then ships called at it in order to take in fresh water or to barter, few whites stayed on the island for more than a short period.

After its introduction on the island, Fa d'Ambu developed more or less on its own, with little influence from outside. The fact that in 1771 the island was ceded by the Portuguese to Spain, apparently did not have a major impact on the language. Although all Annobonese nowadays are bilingual in Fa d'Ambu and Spanish, and words borrowed from Spanish are found in modern Fa d'Ambu, the language remains indubitably Portuguese-based.

On Annobón, Fa d'Ambu is still used in all situations of every day life. The Annobonese have a very strong sense of identity even if they live away from the island. Fa d'Ambu therefore is not only fluently spoken by Annobonese living on the island itself, but also by those born and brought up in the capital. However, one can observe a difference between the way Fa d'Ambu is spoken on Annobón and in Malabo. This difference lies in a neutralization of certain typical creole features that are still in full use in Annobón, in favour of more Spanish-like constructions in Malabo.

The explanation for this difference probably lies in the fact that the linguistic environment in Annobón is extremely simple in comparison to the one of Malabo. Until they go to school, children on Annobón are fully monolingual. Malabo is a melting-pot of languages and normally children are already bi-, tri- or even quadrilingual at a very young age. Besides their mother-tongue they all speak Pidgin English, an English-based creole, which is the vernacular language of Malabo, often Spanish and, depending on the ethnic origin of their friends, they may also speak Bubi, Fang or another Bantu language.

Fa d'Ambu is a spoken language only. Written literature does not exist. Although most of the Annobonese know how to read and write, they will never use Fa d'Ambu for this purpose.

## 16.3 Phonology and phonetics

The sound inventory of Fa d'Ambu contains the following consonants, vowels and diphthongs:

| (1) | Consonants | *labial* | *alveolar* | *palatal* | *velar* |
|---|---|---|---|---|---|
| | stops | p b | t d | | k g |
| | fricatives | f v | s z | š | x |
| | affricates | | | tš dž | |
| | nasals | m | n | ñ | ŋ |
| | liquids | | l | | |
| | semivowels | w | | j | |
| | prenasalized stops | mb | nt nd | | ng |

(2)  **Vowels**  *front*  *back*
    high  i i:  u (u:?)
    mid  e e:  o o:
    low  a a:

(3)  **Diphthongs**  *front*  *back*
    high  uj
    mid  ej
    low  aj

Some observations can be made about the above table.

Fa d'Ambu is a language which has undergone **lambdacism**. The liquid /r/ is absent and only its counterpart /l/ is found. Occasionally /r/ may appear in proper names borrowed from Spanish, or when a Spanish word is used within the conversation, but the moment a Spanish word is integrated into Fa d'Ambu, the phonological system of the language blocks the sound [r] replacing it by [l] or simply omitting it.

(4)  Malí < Port. Maria
    paatu < Port. prato 'plate'

The voiced affricate /dž/ (spelled as 'dy') and its unvoiced counterpart /tš/ (spelled as 'tsy') both occur and have a palatal-alveolar articulation. This is also true for the unvoiced fricative /š/ (spelled as 'sy'). The voiced palatal-alveolar fricative /ž/ only occurs as part of the affricate /dž/.

(5)  dyia  'day'
    tsyila  'throw'
    syiolo  'gentleman'

When situated in word final position, the nasals [n] and [ŋ], and in some words optionally also [m], cause nasalization and some lengthening of the preceding vowel, while they turn into a semi-suppressed velar [ᴺ] themselves.

(6)  lazan > [lazã̄ᴺ] 'news'
    ku amu > [kem] or [kẽŋ] 'that I ..'

Although the phonetic system contains four different prenasalized stops, these are far from being frequent. In certain words they tend to be neutralized with the result that they are normally heard without, but may be heard with prenasalization.

(7)    nge      'person'   but:   gatu/ngatu 'cat'
       ntela    'star'            tela/ntela 'land'
       mba      'to fold'         baga/mbaga 'to separate'

When a morpheme ending in a vowel precedes such a consonantal diphthong, the nasal part of the sound forms the rhyme of the preceding syllable.

(8)    nange < na=nge [naŋ+ge] 'the person(s)'
       ndanda < nda=nda [ndan+da] 'to stroll'

The vowel system is phonemically rather simple. It consists of the five standard vowels. Generally these vowels are short, but in some words long vowels occur. Syllables with long vowels are not obligatorily stressed, but they are always pronounced with a high rise tone while the following syllable, stressed or not, is pronounced with a high tone.

(9)    [pá:tu]     LH-H   'plate'
       [pátu]      H-H    'bird'
       [dé:ntši]   LH-H   'in front of'
       [déntši]    H-H    'tooth'
       [ke:sé]     LH-H   'to grow up'
       [kesé]      HH     'to forget'

Notice that only in a small number of cases is vowel length distinctive.

In conversation the phonemic structure of Fa d'Ambu words and sentences undergoes a number of modifications such as omission of phonological segments, contraction of segments across word boundaries, merger of vowels or vowel harmony. The following sentence illustrates these processes in terms of its phonetics:

(10)   [namenensy sātutelai]
       Namen=nensyi   sa san         úntulu   tela=ai,
       brother=DEM     be ground  in       land=ADV
       'Those who are on land (and not on the water) on the island'. (free transl. Those who stay on the island)

## 16.4 Lexicon and morphology

A certain number of productive (non-inflectional) morphological processes occur in Fa d'Ambu. These are affixation, zero-derivation, reduplication and compounding. Below follows a short overview of affixation, reduplication and compounding.

The amount of **affixes** is not very large. One finds prefixes with a diminutive or augmentative meaning and suffixes used for participle formation. There are two prefixes with a **diminutive** meaning: *fi*- and *mina*-, literally 'child'. The prefix *fi*- may be used in a concrete as well as in a figurative way:

| (11) | **fi**- | kumu | 'food' | fi-kumu | 'some food' |
|---|---|---|---|---|---|
| | | kuzu | 'thing' | fi-kuzu | 'something small' or 'something unimportant' |
| | **mina**- | kuzu | 'thing' | mina-kuzu | 'something small' |
| | | palma | 'palmtree' | mina-palma | 'small palmtree' |

Prefixes with an **augmentative** meaning include *taba*- (general augmentative meaning), *xatán* 'major, of a high rank (lit. captain)', *pe*- 'large', *vala*- 'long, tall' and *syiolo* 'very good (lit. gentleman)'.

| (12) | **taba**- | xá-syigadu | 'problem' | taba-xá-syigadu | 'big problem' |
|---|---|---|---|---|---|
| | | patsyi | 'part' | taba-patsyi | 'big piece' |
| | **xatán**- | dadalán | 'crook' | xatán-dadalán | 'a real crook' |
| | **pe**- | namina | 'child' | pe-namina | 'big child' |
| | **vala**- | moso | 'woman' | vala-moso | 'tall woman' |
| | | opá | 'stick' | vala-opá | 'long stick' |
| | **syiolo**- | palma | 'palm tree' | syiolo-palma | 'very good palm tree' |

Combinations of certain prefixes are possible, as is shown in the following example:

| (13) | pe-vala=vala-nge | 'a big and very tall person' |
|---|---|---|

The above prefixes are only added to nouns. At least some of them are etymologically nouns. The process of prefixation is not used much, however. Far more common is the process of adding an adjective with a diminutive or augmentative sense to the noun. Unlike prefixes, these are always placed after the noun.

A second type of affixation is the realization of the participal adjective through **suffixation** of -*du* to the verb. The derived form only appears as a predicative adjective. Its use is not (yet) generalized to all verbs. Some of them may undergo this process, others may not.

| (14) | xansa | 'to get/make tired' | xansadu | 'tired' |
|---|---|---|---|---|
| | xaba | 'to finish' | xabadu | 'finished' |
| | xomesa | 'to begin' | xomesadu | 'begun' |
| | xama | 'to burn' | xamadu | 'burned' |
| | baya | 'to dance' | *bayadu | 'danced' |
| | mindyi | 'to measure' | *mindyidu | 'measured' |

**Reduplication** consists of doubling (a part of) v, n or a. The resulting meanings can be intensive, iterative and distributive:

| (15) | **intensive** | kitsyi | 'small' | kitsyikitsyi | 'very small' |
|---|---|---|---|---|---|
| | | gavu | 'good' | gagavu | 'very good' |
| | **iterative** | nda | 'walk' | ndanda | 'to stroll' |
| | | fa(la) | 'speak' | fafal | 'to chat' |
| | **distributive** | dosy | 'two' | dodosy | 'both' |
| | | bodo | 'edge' | bódobodo | 'coast' |

**Compounding** is the most common process used in Fa d'Ambu to form new nouns or adjectives, from already existing nouns and adjectives or even from complex expressions. The words that form the compound may still be entirely intact or may have undergone readjustment.

| (16) | lensu-zubela | 'handkerchief (lit. rag-pocket)' |
|---|---|---|
| | xa-xole-san | 'car (lit. thing-run-ground)' |

## 16.5 Syntax

### 16.5.1 Word Order

As in most creole languages the basic word order is strictly svo in Fa d'Ambu. This is true for all sentence types: declaratives, interrogatives, main clauses and subordinate clauses. The indirect object (io) precedes the direct object (do), prepositional phrases follow the do and adverbials normally show up either at the beginning or at the end of the sentence.

Verbs are not specified for person or number. They do not bear any inflexion as such but preverbal particles may be used in order to specify tense, mood and aspect (tma): *bi* for perfective past, *sxa/ska* for progressive, *ske* for potential or irrealis, *xa* for continuative (see also chapter 20). Imperfective past is usually expressed by zero-marking (although zero-marking is not exclusively reserved for this tense). Schematically then, the sentence would be as follows:

(17)     ADV - S - TMA - V - IO - DO - PP - ADV

The following examples show a simple sentence with a combination of an IO and a DO (18), a sentence with a DO followed by a PP (19), and finally one with a subordinate clause (20).

(18)     Malía da     pe-d'eli      tabaku.
         Maria give   father-3SG   tobacco
         'Maria gives (the) tobacco to her father.'

(19)     No sxa    fe     wan   xadyi pa    non-tudu.
         IPL TMA   make   ART   house for   IPL-all
         'We are building a house for us all (our family).'

(20)     Poxodul-nensyi ku    fe    vadyi-ai sa    na-nge       gavu.
         person-DEM     CONJ  make  trip-ADV COP   ART-person   good
         'The people who traveled are good people.'

### 16.5.2 Negation
Fa d'Ambu has double negation which is expressed by the combination of the two elements *na* and *-f* (*-af* or *-fa*), *na* being preposed to the verb and the TMA particles (if present) and *-f* being attached to the last word of the sentence.

(21)     Odyai amu   **na**   be    mem=bo      xama-kumu=f.
         today ISG   NEG    see   mother=2SG   place-food=NEG
         'I did not see your mother at the market today.'

The rule is as stringent as formulated above. If a sentence contains a subordinate clause, the second part of the negation, *-f*, will still appear at the end of the sentence, even if the subordinate clause is not (fully) part of the scope of the negator, as in example (22):

(22)     Se     eli    **na**   ngo    pa    se    fa    eli    sa    nge       d'Ambu-f.
         CONJ   3SG    NEG    want   for   know  speak 3SG   COP   person   of Annobón-NEG
         'And he did not want them to know that he was an Annobonese.'

The location of the first negative particle, *na*, indicates the starting point of the negation within the sentence. This is not necessarily the first verb, even if that verb is a modal:

(23)    Amu    **na**    po    fe-**f**.
      1SG    NEG    can    make-NEG
      'I am not able to do it.'

(24)    Amu    po    **na**    fe-**f**.
      1SG    can    NEG    make-NEG
      'I am able not to do it.'

In imperatives negation is often reduced to the second particle only, but this does not always happen:

(25)    Li-**f**!           b. **Na**    fe-**f**!
      laugh-NEG         NEG    make-NEG
      'Don't laugh!'      'Don't do it!'

When negation applies to PPs *na* cannot occur:

(26)    ku    bo-**f**
      with    2SG-NEG
      'not with you'

A negation is not always to be interpreted as a negation of the content. It may also indicate an exclamative affirmative:

(27)    **Na**    sa    tabaya    odu-syi-**f**!
      NEG    COP    work    hard-DEM-NEG
      'It was a very hard job!'

### 16.5.3 Interrogative

Yes/no questions usually are formed the same way as declaratives. They do not undergo any shift in basic word order, regardless of whether they are main clauses or embedded interrogatives. When they are main clauses, interrogativity is expressed by just an intonation rise at the end of the sentence.

When the utterance contains a question word, this will be placed in first position, irrespective of its syntactic category:

(28)   Xa     bo     fala?        b. Xama Zwan    sa?
       thing  2SG    speak           place John   be
       'What do you say?'            'Where is John?'

The question words in Fa d'Ambu are:

(29)   *xa*     'what'      *kenge* 'who'     *xáma* 'how'
       *xamá*   'where'     *ke ola* 'when'   *xafe* 'why'

All question words are (originally) either complex expressions or simple (pro)nouns, e.g. *xa* derives from *xa* '(some)thing', and *kenge* derives from *ke/ku* 'what' + *nge* 'person'.

### 16.5.4 Passive

Authentic passive constructions do exist but are hardly used at all. There is a strong preference for active or semi-passive constructions. In the first example below, the verb *ba* is the short form of *baya* 'dance'.

(30)   Na-mina-miele tisy   ba     tela.
       ART-girl           three  dance  land
       'The three girls dance the traditional dances.'

(31)   A      xa    baya   ba-tela      na-name     tesyi.
       3gen   TMA   dance  dance-land   ART-brother three
       'The traditional dances are danced by three friends.'

(32)   Ba     tela   a     xa    baya  na-name     tesyi.
       dance  land   3gen  TMA   dance ART-brother three
       'The traditional dances are danced by three friends.'

(33)   Ba-tela-sai     sa     baya  na-masyivín   tisy.
       dance-land-DEM   COP    dance ART-youngsters three
       'The traditional dances are danced by three youngsters.'

In (30) we have an unmarked active sentence. (31) shows the same verb-object order but here the passive meaning is maintained through the use of a generic personal pronoun which is placed in subject position, whereas the fully specified subject noun phrase has been moved to a final position in the sentence. Example (32) shows a similar construction but it differs from (31) in that the DO is topicalized. The last example, (33), could be regarded as a real passive: the object of the active sentence has been moved to the subject position and the verb, which is preceded by an auxiliary, is followed by a prepositionless agent.

Examples (30) and (32) represent the normal strategies for passives and example (31) may be regarded as a less frequent alternative to (34). Example (33), though correct, is fairly rare.

### 16.5.5 Fronting

Two types of fronting seem to exist in Fa d'Ambu: topicalization, as in example (34) above and possibly also clefting, which however requires further investigation. A frequent alternative is left dislocation, as in (34). Fronting as well as left dislocation always seem to be used for bringing a constituent into focus.

(34)    Mem-bo      odyai amu  na    be    li    markete-f.
        mother-2SG  today ISG   NEG   see   3SG   market-NEG
        'I did not see your mother at the market today.'

### 16.5.6 Serial verb constructions

Serial verb constructions, or SVCs (see chapter 23), constitute an important part of Fa d'Ambu syntax. They may express location, dative/benefactive, resultative, excessive and complementizer with the modifying verb (Vm) in V2 position. Furthermore, they can mark iteration and inchoativity with the Vm in V1 position, and direction and terminative with the Vm in V1 or in V2 position. An instrumental SVC does not occur. SVCs will be illustrated by means of the verb *da* 'give'. The following example shows a benefactive construction.

(35)    A      ska    fe      wan   xadyi **da**    na-namay.
        3gen   TMA    make    ART   house give   ART-family
        'They were building a house for the family.'

This sentence is nearly identical to (19). They differ in their choice of construction, with the preposition *pa* in (9) and a SVC with the Vm *da* in (35). Although obviously both alternatives are present in the language, Fa d'Ambu speakers show a strong preference for the use of SVCs when dealing with benefactives.

When used in a dative construction, the Vm *da* 'give' is always placed in a position directly after the DO, followed by the IO (the opposite of the unmarked order):

(36)    Amu    da    wan   kuzu  **da**    bo.
        ISG    give  ART   thing give   2SG
        'I gave you something.'

In the following examples the verb *fa* 'say' is used as a di-transitive verb in (37a) which obligatorily calls for the basic IO DO word order, whereas in (37b) the IO-argument has been assigned to the Vm of an SVC.

(37)  a.  Amu  fa        bo   xo-sai.          b.  Amu  fa      **da**   bo.
          ISG  speak 2SG  thing-DEM                ISG  speak   give   2SG
          'I tell you this.'                        'I speak to you.'

In fact serialization of di-transitive verbs (when used with both internal arguments) is nearly impossible. The structure as shown in example (33) is a rare variant of a sentence with a double object construction. In sentences with only one internal argument, (37b), this problem does not exist: both sentence types, with or without SVC, are commonly used.

The serial verb *da* 'give' may appear as part of a more complex SVC which contains various verb markers. Together they constitute a new complex verbal concept. Compare the following examples:

(38)  a.  Malía  **ma**  dyana   **ba da**  pe-d'eli.
          Maria  take   banana  go give   father-3SG
          'María brought a banana to her father.'
      b.  María  **da**  dyana   **ba da**  pe-d'eli.
          Maria  give   banana  go give   father-3SG
          'Maria sent a banana to her father.'

In both examples three verbs are involved, all of which have lost part of their lexical meaning. Furthermore, in both cases the object of the first verb (V1) also functions as the subject of the second (V2), which indicates direction away from the speaker. (V3) marks the recipient. The main verbs of the respective constructions are the V1s *ma* 'take' and *da* 'give'. They don't indicate the first action in the respective events taking place, but they say something about the way these events take place. That is, in sentence (38a) the subject is agent of the whole complex action, but not in (38b) where the same subject is only the causer.

### 16.5.7 Noun phrases
Noun phrases are constructed in such a way that all the attributive elements follow the head, except for the article, which appears to the left. Schematically this would be as follows:

(39)   ART - N - ADJ - NUM -  DEM - RC
       POS

For example:

(40)    mina    kitsyi    tesy-nensay
       child    small    three-DEMpl
       'the/these three small children'

Complex NPs are formed by a head noun followed by a relative clause, which may or may not be introduced by a relativizer. Compare the following examples:

(41)    Xadyi    no       xata-e      sa      xa          tudyia.
       house    IPL      live-ADV    COP     (some)thing  old
       'The house that we live in is very old.'

(42)    Amu    sa-xa    funda     **ku**    sa     xa      me-mu.
       ISG    have     packet    CONJ     COP    thing   mother-ISG
       'I have a packet for my mother.'

(43)    Nova-**syi**    **ku**     a      da     no-e       bi     sa     wa      nova gav.
       news-DEM       CONJ     3GEN    give    IPL-ADV    ANT    COP    ART     news good
       'The news he gave us was fine.'

(44)    Amu    mata    layan-**syi**    bi      sa      xodyian-mu osesyi.
       ISG    kill    spider-DEM      ANT     COP     room-ISG    then
       'I killed the spider that was in my room.'

As is clear from the above examples, relative clauses may be optionally introduced by the relative conjunction *ku*. If the head is definite this may be expressed through adjunction of the demonstrative *-syi*. Notice that *-syi* is the sole demonstrative to appear in this environment. Relative clauses may be followed by what seems to be the adverbial *iai* 'here', which functions as an additional definiteness marker.

## 16.6  Text

The following text is taken from a story told by a 52 year old man living in Malabo who grew up in Annobón.

(a)   Desyi ku   amu bila-oio tela   me-mu     ku    pe-mu
      when CONJ ISG   open-eye land   mother-ISG   CONJ father-ISG
      When I was a child in the village of my mother and my father     [FAI]

(b)   liba    d'alá      d'Ambu,     tela-mu,
      above   of-beach   of-Annobón land-ISG
      in Annobón, my homeland

(c)   amu    fo      namina,..
      ISG     COP    child
      When I was a ...

(d)   se      amu bila-oio    tela-mu Ambu.
      CONJ   ISG   open-eye    land-ISG Annobón
      I was born in my homeland Annobón.

(e)   amu    na     xonse pe-mu-syi       pali      mu-f
      ISG     NEG   know father-ISG-DEM give-birth   ISG-NEG
      I did not know who my father was

(f)   se      amu sxa    ma    mavida ku    me-mu
      CONJ   ISG   TMA   take   suffering with   mother-ISG
      and I suffered with my mother

(g)   se      amu sxa    ma    xa      mavida-syi...
      CONJ   ISG   TMA   take   FOC   suffering-DEM
      And I suffered so much.

(h)   se..     amu tyila poxodulu
      until   ISG   turn   adult
      Until I grew up

(i)   amu   ga    geza     ku    panu amu ga    skuela   ku     panu
      ISG    TMA   church   with   rag   ISG   TMA   school   with    rag
      I went to church in rags, I went to school in rags

(j)   na     sa      mavida-syi-f.
      NEG   COP   suffering-DEM-NEG
      It was a real hard life.

(k)   Amu   na     suku nge-syi      zuda me-mu
      ISG    NEG   have person-DEM help   mother-ISG
      I had nobody to help my mother

(l)   pa da    ma   xa    pa    amu bisyi-f.
      for give   take thing for   ISG   dress-NEG
      to offer me something to wear.

**Further reading**

The main studies on Fa d'Ambu are Barrena (1957), Valkhoff (1966), Ferraz (1976, 1983) and Post (1992, 1993). For more information about the other Gulf of Guinea creoles one can consult works of Ferraz (1974, 1975, 1979, 1983), Ferraz and Traill (1981), Ferraz and Valkhoff (1975), Günther (1973) and Maurer (1992).

# 17 Papiamento

Silvia Kouwenberg & Pieter Muysken

## 17.1 Introduction

Papiamento is spoken on the leeward Netherlands Antilles (Curaçao and Bonaire) and on Aruba, and by migrants from these areas in the Netherlands and elsewhere. The total number of speakers is perhaps 200.000. It is a fairly well established creole, in which a number of newspapers are published, possessing its own literary tradition, an official spelling, and playing some role in the educational system (see chapter 6). In fact, Aruba has one official spelling, more etymological in nature (The sound /k/ for instance, is represented as *k* in words derived from Dutch, and as *c* and *qu* in words derived from Spanish), and Curaçao and Bonaire another one, more phonological in nature (*k* everywhere). Here we use Curaçoan orthography.

Papiamento emerged in the second half of the 17th century, and is primarily based on Portuguese and Spanish. Although a number of theories have been proposed for its origin, we will follow Goodman's (1987) account, who stresses the role of the Sephardic Jews, who were expelled from formerly Dutch northern Brazil, and arrived on Curaçao from 1659. The earliest form of Papiamento is assumed to be largely Portuguese in its lexicon; later extensive contact with Spanish has obscured this early contribution. In addition it has some African and Amerindian vocabulary, as well as words from Dutch and English.

At the end of the 18th century there were 16.000 blacks on the island of Curaçao, both slaves and freedmen, and 5500 whites, including 1500 Sephardic Jews. Of the 2400 slaves in 1683, only 25% worked in the plantations. In the 18th century, the majority of plantations employed 5 slaves or less. The overall impression is that the cradle for Papiamento was far more a *société de habitation* than a *société de plantation*, to use Chaudenson's terminology (1992; see chapter 2). Thus it is more like the creole of Réunion, which is close to French, in this respect, than like the maroon creoles like Saramaccan or the 'deep' plantation creoles like Sranan or Haitian. In fact, its relative typological distance from Ibero-Romance may need to be explained in terms of the fact that Dutch, and not Spanish or Portuguese, was the colonial language from 1634 onward. Papiamento is not directly related to another Portuguese-based or Spanish-based creole, though there may be links to the Portuguese element in Saramaccan (Smith 1987).

A priest, Padre Schabel, mentions a kind of 'broken Spanish' in his diary from 1705. The earliest written attestations in the language date from 1775. Wood (1971) has published a love letter written by a Sephardic Jew from that year, which closely resembles the modern language. There is also a written dialogue between two servants from the same year. In fact, these early written testimonies are the beginning of a long tradition of writing in Papiamento, including quite a bit of poetry, some popular novels, literary narrative prose, school books, catechisms, and in recent years a number of newspapers and magazines, scholarly texts, educational materials, reglements, etc. An example of the way Papiamento serves as a urban vernacular is given in the three advertisements from a popular daily newspaper.

Their translation is as follows:
(a)    You want to sell your Japanese car? You want a good price? Come by today at: Rooi Catootje Auto Park, and we'll buy it for CASH on the spot!
(b)    Caracas, every weekend! 3 days/3 nights. Departure (Thursday night). Return (Sunday morning). 4 days/4 nights. Departure (Wednesday night). Return (Sunday morning). ... Adults (2 or 3 in a bedroom) 248/263 Antillean guilders. Return ticket by plane. Tips for the porter at the airport and the hotel. Transport by bus airport/hotel/airport. Stay in the Plaza Catedral hotel. Call us right now at ...

(c) Have you already heard of the Brand Bonus Polis? Brand Bonus Polis is the new policy introduced by Prome Seguro with wide coverage. Brand Bonus polis gives you a bonus on your insurance premium to compensate all the years you have paid a premium for your fire insurance. So it does not matter with which company you were insured. Remember that only Prome Seguro has got it. Get our information. At Prome Seguro ... (near the Viaduct).

Notice the use of English loans (pronounced as in Dutch), such as *kèsh*, *wikènt*, and *tips*, and the coexistence of the non-adapted Dutch loan *Brand Bonus Polis* and the adapted loan *polisa* '(insurance) policy'. *Pasashi* 'ticket' has the French form (presumably via Dutch) but the meaning of Spanish *pasaje*. Much of the vocabulary is very similar to Spanish, such as *salida* 'departure' and *regreso* 'return' or even a direct loan such as *ida i buelta* 'return, round trip'. In other cases the relation with Spanish and Portuguese is less direct, e.g. *djaweps* for 'Thursday' (<Sp. *(día) jueves*) and *djarason* 'Wednesday', where Spanish has *miércoles*.

## 17.2 Sound system

The best information on the Papiamento sound system can be gathered from the work of Römer (e.g. 1992, which contains a posthumous synthesis of his work).

There are ten vowels in Papiamento, which can be presented as in (1) (spelling given in parentheses):

(1)     i     y(ü)     u

         e     ø(ù)     o

         ɛ(è)     ə       ɔ(ò)

                a

There are 24 consonant phonemes, as in:

(2)     p     t     tç(ch)     k

         b     d     dz(dj)     g

         f     s     š(sh)     x(g)     h

         m     n     ñ

              l, r

         w          j(y,j)

There are two main stress patterns in Papiamento, penultimate and ultimate. Penultimate stress is the regular pattern for words ending in vowels or in *-er, -el, -en* (where *e* represents a schwa rather than a full vowel): *kuminda* 'food', *korda* 'remember', *liber* 'free'. Words ending in any other speech sound generally have stress on the last syllable: *kantor* 'office', *kurason* 'heart', *robes* 'wrong'. The largest group of exceptions consists of verbs of three or four syllables, which are distinguished from other words of the same length by the fact that they are always stressed on the final syllable; this is indicated in Papiamento orthography by means of an acute accent: *kumindá* 'greet', *ekibòká* 'make a mistake'. There is also a sizable number of bisyllabic exceptions, such as *doló* 'pain', *muhé* 'woman', *mashá* 'a lot', *piská* 'fish'.

Römer (1992) describes tonal phenomena in Papiamento. We find level high and low tones, which in many - but by no means all - cases correspond to accented and unaccented syllables, respectively. A major class of exceptions is formed by the bisyllabic verbs. These have a Low High pattern with the Low tone realised on the accented syllable, as in *'pone* 'to put', *'kwèrdè* 'to wind', *'laba* 'wash'. There are minimal pairs such as *papa* 'porridge; the Pope' with a High Low pattern, and *papa* 'dad' with a Low High tonal pattern (Römer 1992). Joubert (1991) lists 251 pairs of bisyllabic words which can be distinguished only by their tone patterns. In the vast majority of these cases (+230), a Low High pattern over a bisyllabic word is a verb, a High Low pattern is a noun: *biaha* [Low High] 'to travel'/[High Low] 'voyage', *warda* [Low High] 'to wait, to keep, to guard'/[High Low] 'guard service, guard post'. However, the tone alternation cannot be purely the result of a derivational rule (e.g. nominalization through tonal shift). For some 85 of these pairs, there is no lexical relationship between the verb and the noun: *sala* [Low High] 'to salt'/[High Low] 'living room', *para* [Low High] 'to stand, to stop'/[High Low] 'bird'.

## 17.3  Morphology and lexicon

The best recent survey of Papiamento morphology is Dijkhoff (1993), a work primarily devoted to nominal compounds and lexicalized syntactic formations. Dijkhoff shows that constructions which at first sight seem syntactic or phrasal in nature, of the type *N di N* 'N of N', in fact have many lexical characteristics. They may undergo reduction processes, as in *lens'i saku* (< kerchief of pocket) 'handkerchief', and often have a specialized or shifted meaning, as in *kabe'i boto* (< head of boat) 'the front part of a boat; lift'.

Among the affixes, there are cases where the element is only borrowed in conjunction with a set of lexical items, with which it is combined already in the donor language. Examples include Spanish suffixes in Papiamento (Dijkhoff 1993) such as *-shon* (< Sp. *-ción*) in *akumula-shon* 'accumulation' and *akusa-shon* 'accusation'. From these cases no evidence for productive morphology can be distilled. Cases in which an affix is borrowed include Papiamento *-dó* (<Sp. *-dor*), cf. (3a). It can be applied freely to recipient language items (3b), and is not restricted in its application (3c):

(3)   a.   pèrdè-dó      'loser'                                          (from Spanish)
           warda-dó      'keeper, guard'
      b.   uza-dó        'user'                                           (newly formed)
           traha-dó      'worker'
           lubida-dó     'absent-minded'
      c.   hür-dó        'tenant'                                  (from a Dutch base)

Like -*dó*, -*mentu*, as in the name of the language itself, is a highly productive affix, and not restricted to Spanish/Portuguese bases.

The particle *nan* is used to pluralize nouns and noun phrases (see also chapter 21). It is used particularly with definite noun phrases, and is a clitic rather than a true affix.

## 17.4 Syntax

### 17.4.1 Basic word order

The basic word order in Papiamento is not unlike that of other creole languages:

(4)    Su - TMA - Verb - IO - DO - PP

The indirect object precedes the direct object both with full noun phrases, as in (5a), and with pronouns, as in (5b,c):

(5)   a.   Maria    a     duna   Wanchu   un     buki.
           Mary     TNS   give   John     a      book
           'Mary gave John a book.'
      b.   Maria    a     dunami    un    buki.
           Mary     TNS   gave-me   a     book
      c.   Maria a dunami e.
           'Mary gave me it.'

Notice that here Papiamento permits the order IO - DO, which is prohibited in Spanish and Portuguese.

The category TMA will be discussed in 17.4.4. There is one deviation here from (4), since the *lo* 'future' precedes rather than follows the subject pronoun. This optional alternate order is possible only with *mi* 'I', *bo* 'you', and *e* 'she/he/it'. The same phenomenon occurs with the future marker *bai* and the personal pronouns *mi* and *yu* in Tok Pisin.

| (6) | Lo | mi | laga | e | buki | pa | bo | den | e | kas. |
|-----|-----|-----|------|-----|------|-----|-----|-----|-----|------|
| | FUT | 1SG | leave | the | book | for | 2SG | in | the | house |

'I will leave the book for you in the house.'

When there is a preposed locative or temporal phrase, it is possible to switch the order of subject and verb. Both (a) and (b) are grammatical:

(7)    a.   Riba e isla aki un mion hende ta biba.
          'On this island a million people live.'
     b.   Riba e isla aki ta biba un mion hende.
          'On this island live a million people.'

There is a verb + particle construction that seems limited to the verbs *bai* 'come' and *bini* 'go' and the particle *bèk* (<Eng. *back*):

(8)    Wanchu a bini kas bèk
        'John has come back home.'

However, sometimes Dutch particle constructions, such as *bel … op* 'telephone', are borrowed:

| (9) | Lo | mi | bèl | bo | òp. |
|-----|-----|-----|-----|-----|-----|
| | FUT | 1SG | call | 2SG | up. |

'I will call you.'

## 17.4.2 The copula

In contrast with other creole languages, Papiamento has a clearly defined set of adjectives, which can occur in attributive, and in predicative position preceded by a copula. The following examples show that the locative, (10), predicative, (11)-(13), and presentational or equative, (14), functions of the copula are all fulfilled by the same explicit copula *ta*, no matter whether the predicate is a noun phrase, prepositional phrase, or adjective:

(10)    Mi ta na kas. 'I am in the house.'
(11)    Mi ta Pedro. 'I am Pedro.'
(12)    Mi ta un yu di Korsow. 'I am a native son / an islander / a Curaçaoer.'
(13)    Mi ta grandi. 'I am big.'
(14)    Esaki ta Maria. 'This is Mary.'

However, we will see below that the existential copula is not *ta* but *tin* (where Portuguese has *tem* and Spanish *hay*).

### 17.4.3 Passive and fronting rules

Papiamento is unique among Caribbean creoles in having a passive construction similar to that found in the European lexifiers, i.e. one in which the agent is optionally realised in a PP (introduced by *dor di* or *pa*, a passive auxiliary appears (*wordu* or *ser*, in free variation), and the verb appears in the passive participle form. The passive with the Dutch-derived auxiliary *wordu* is illustrated in (15), which contains a realisation of the agent in a *dor di*-phrase.

(15)  E    pòtrèt  aki    a      wordu  saká  dor    di e   mucha  hòmber.
      the picture here PAST be     taken through of the child  male
      'This picture was taken by the boy.'

Participle forms are formed in two distinct ways, following a so-called Iberian and a Dutch pattern.

(16)  Iberian pattern: *morde* 'bite'-*mordé* 'bitten', *dividí* 'divide'-*dividí* 'divided', *harka* 'rake'-*harká* 'raked', *pupu* 'relieve oneself / dirty by excrement'-*pupú* 'dirtied by excrement'

(17)  Dutch pattern: *fèrf* 'paint'-*hefèrf* 'painted', *wèlder / wèldro* 'weld'-*hewèlder / hewèldro* 'welded', *tren* 'train'-*hetren* 'trained', *dal* 'hit'-*hedal* 'hit'

Apart from passive, there are three types of fronting in Papiamento (see chapter 24). First, it is possible to focus on noun phrases or prepositional phrases, often but not necessarily preceded by *ta*. An example is (18):

(18)  Ta    e     buki  m'a      dunabu.                                    (Cleft)
      FOC  the   book ISG=PAST give=2SG
      'I gave you the BOOK.'

One of the advertisements has an example of subject focus:

(19)  Korda     sí: ta  Prome  Seguro   so    tin-e.
      remember  if FOC Prome  Seguro  alone have=3SG
      'Remember: only PROME SEGURO has it.'

Frequently, though not obligatorily, and without much of a change in meaning, questioned constituents are focused:

(20)    (*Ta*)   *kiko*   bo    tin    den    bo    man?
        FOC    what   2SG   have   in    2SG   hand
        'What (is it that/do) you have in your hand?'

In a second type of structure, the verb is fronted and repeated:

(21)    Ta    duna m'a    dunabu   e    buki.                    (Predicate cleft)
        FOC   give  1SG=PAST give=2SG the   book
        'I GAVE you the book.'

However, it is possible to include an emphatic adverb with the fronted predicate:

(22)    Ta    **djis**   fia    m'a    fiabo    e    buki.
        FOC    just    lend   1SG-PAST lend=2SG the   book
        'I have just lent you the book (not given it).'

In the third construction a noun phrase or prepositional phrase is fronted without focusing it, and without *ta*:

(23)    Un    dia    mi    tabata    kana    na    Punda.
        One   day   1SG   PAST=PR   walk   LOC   Punda
        'One day I was walking downtown Willemstad.'

Here the fronted element is interpreted as background information or as an already established topic. Construction (23) is distinguished from a focus construction through its intonation.

The focus element *ta* resembles the copula, and it may be negated, but not modified for TMA, and neither can the object pronoun be included:

(24)   a.  No    ta    duna m'a    dunabu   e    buki.
           NEG   FOC   give  1SG=PAST give=2SG the   book.
           'I didn't GIVE you the book.'
       b.  *tabata    e    buki   mi    tabata    dunabu
           PAST=PR   the   book  1SG   PAST=PR   give=2SG
       c.  *ta    *dunabu*   m'a    dunabu   e    buki
           FOC   give=2SG   1SG=PAST give=2SG the   book

### 17.4.4 TMA and gerundive clauses

The Papiamento TMA system is not quite like that of other Caribbean creoles. It has been described in great detail by Maurer (1988) and Andersen (1990). There are basically five TMA markers, with roughly the meanings indicated:

(25)  ta       present, progressive
      tabata   imperfective past (Aruba has *tawata*)
      a        perfective, past
      lo       future, potential
      sa       habitual

While often *a* is interpreted as past (and glossed as such here), its aspectual rather than tense character is clear in examples such as:

(26)  M'a        kasi     kla.
      1SG=PAST   almost   ready
      'I am almost done.'

In addition to the distinction between two kinds of past tense, there is the striking feature of a gerundive system. In (27) this participle is overtly expressed with the marker *-ndo*:

(27)  E    ta    kana bai   bini  [papia**ndo**  den  djé mes].
      'He  walks back  and   forth talking       to   himself.'

This suffix can be attached to many verbs. However, the participle can also be expressed by the combination *ta* + verb in a number of constructions. Consider first perception complements:

(28)  E-l-a      weta  un   homber  yongotá  ei     bou   [ta saka awa ku un makutu].
      3SG=PAST   see   a    man     knelt    there  down  PR take water with a bucket
      'He saw a man kneeling (lit. knelt) down below taking out water with a bucket.'
      (Andersen 1990)

With telic verbs, the absence of *ta* in perception complements implies that the completion of the act is witnessed, according to Maurer (1988: 267), citing unpublished work by Muller. Consider the contrast in (29):

(29)   a.   M'a miré kap e palu.
            'I saw him cut the tree (including the moment the tree fell down).'
       b.   M'a miré ta kap e palu.
            'I saw him cutting the tree (but not necessarily also the final result of the act of cutting).'

Some verbs take a *ta* complement:

(30)   a.   E-l-a bin ta trata nan malu.                              (Andersen 1990)
            'He started treating them badly.'
       b.   E-l-a kumisá ta kome djente.                            (Maurer 1988: 262)
            'He started grinding his teeth.'

A third context is adverbial clauses:

(31)       Kuantu aña nan tin [ta kana tre'i dokter].
           'How many years have they been [running after doctors]?'

Finally, there is a type of relative clause using this form:

(32)       ... e plantashi ta yen di hende [ta kòrta i piki tabaku].
           '... the plantation was full of people [cutting and picking tobacco].'    (Maurer 1988: 264)

The relationship between constructions with *ta* and constructions with *-ndo* requires much further analysis; sometimes they appear to be interchangeable, but not always.

### 17.4.5 Serial verbs
Some kinds of serial verbs are extremely frequent in the language, but the total range is more limited than in some other Caribbean creoles, like those of Surinam, it appears. Particularly frequent are cases where the second verb indicates a direction for the action of the first verb:

(33)   Cha   Tiger   a        **hala**   stul   **pone**   na     mesa.
       Cha   Tiger   PAST     drag      chair  put       LOC    table
       'Cha Tiger dragged a chair to the table.'                       (Baart 1983: 142)

(34)   Mi ta   **lastrabo**  **bai**   fiernu.                            (Baart 1983:78)
       1SG PR  drag=2SG     go      hell
       'I drag you to hell.'

Some combinations, such as *bula bai* 'fly go' are lexicalized to the extent that the two verbs can undergo predicate cleft together, (35):

(35)  Ta   **bula bai**   nos   ta bula bai   Hulanda.
      FOC  fly  go   we   PR fly   go   Holland
      'We really fly to Holland.'

This is not possible generally, e.g. with a combination such as *kore sali* 'run go out of':

(36)  *Ta   **kore sali**   hopi hende   kore sali   for   di   sine.
      FOC  run  go out   many people   run  go out   out   of   cinema
      'Many people really run away from a cinema.'

The aspectual element *kaba* 'already' (< Romance *acabar* 'finish') may have been a serial verb earlier; in present-day Papiamento there is no reason not to treat it as an adverb. An example from the advertisements:

(37)  Bo   a   **tende**   **kaba**   di Brand   Bonus   polis?
      2SG  PAST  hear   already   of Brand   Bonus   policy
      'Have you heard already about the Brand Bonus policy?'

### 17.4.6 Pro-drop, object clitics

In chapter 11 we discussed the matter of pro-drop, i.e. the possibility of pronominal elements to be absent. Unlike Spanish, ordinary pronoun subjects cannot be absent in Papiamento, (38b). Neither is it possible to have a subject to the right of the verb, (38c):

(38)  a.  E   ta kome.                    (compare Spanish **él está comiendo**)
          he   PR eat
          'He is eating.'
      b.  *ta kome                        (compare Spanish **está comiendo**)
          PR eat
      c.  *ta kome Maria                  (compare Spanish **está comiendo Maria**)
          PR eat   Maria

However, with impersonal subjects sometimes there is no subject present:

(39)   a.   Ta    bende    flor.                    b. *Flor ta bende.
            PR    sell     flower
            'Flowers are sold (here).'

With expletive, semantically empty, subjects lexical elements are prohibited:

(40)   a.   Tin        baliamentu.              b. *Nan   tin        baliamentu
            there.is   dance                       3PL    there.is   dance
            'There is a dance.'

The same holds for weather verbs, except when a (restricted) lexical subject is used, as in (41c):

(41)   a.   Tabata    yobe.      b. *E tabata yobe.      c.   Awa   tabata yobe
            PAST-PR   rain                                    water PAST-PR
            'It rained.'                                      'It rained water.'

The different classes of null subjects can occur in subordinate contexts as well, as shown by the grammaticality of (42)-(43):

(42)   Mi ta kere      (ku)    ta bende    sapatu   ei.
       1SG PR believe  (that)  PR sell     shoes    there
       'I believe they sell shoes there.'

(43)   Mi ta hañá (ku)  ta     muchu   lat    pa     nos   bai.
       1SG PR think (that) COP  very    late   for    1PL   go
       'I think it is too late for us to go.'

When its subject is extracted out of an embedded complement clause of a verb such as *kere* 'believe', the trace is null. This is what we mentioned in chapter 11 as a violation of the [that trace] filter:

(44)   Ken bo ta kere (ku) ___ ta parse mi tata?
       'Who do you believe (that) ___ resembles my father?'

A second issue is the status of object pronouns. It is clear that they are phonologically attached to the verb, as we saw already. Further examples are:

(45)  Bo      a      dunami  e      buki.
      2SG    PAST   give=1SG  the    book
      'You have given me the book.'

(46)  Nos    lo     kumpré  kèsh   mesora.
      we     FUT    buy-it  cash   right away
      'We will buy it from you for cash right away.'

Ordinarily, there is no special form for the object pronoun:

(47)          *subject*       *object*       *poss.*
              mi              mi             mi
              bo              bo/bu          bo
              e               e              su
              nos             nos            nos
              bosnan          bosnan         boso(nan)
              nan             nan            nan

The apparent exception is the second person, which in Curaçao Papiamento becomes *bu*:

(48)  Mi ta mira**bu**.
      'I am looking at you.'

In perception complements, where it is really the subject of the complement clause, we have *bu* as well:

(49)  Mi ta mirabu    ta sali.
      1SG PR see=2SG   PR leave
      'I see you leaving.'

This shows that the effect is in part phonological: it has to do with the fact that *bo* is a clitic on the preceding verb. Notice that *bo* does not cliticize onto the verb when it is a possessive pronoun in a noun phrase:

(50)  Mi ta mira [bo    tata].
      1SG PR see    2SG   father
      'I see your father.'

Nor does it cliticize onto the verb when it is the subject of a finite complement clause:

(51)    Mi ta kere    [bo   parse    mi    tata].
        1SG PR believe   2SG   resemble 1SG   father
        'I believe you resemble my father.'

Nonetheless, there is some reason to assume that there are syntactic object clitics in Papiamento, but only with specific reflexive verbs. Consider the following contrast:

(52)    a.    Mi ta sinti mi/mi mes un tiki tristu.
              'I feel a bit sad.'
        b.    Mi ta sinti *mi/mi mes dor di e deken.
              'I feel myself through the blanket.'

When used with an experiencer interpretation as in (52a), meaning 'to have a certain feeling', *sinti* + object pronoun is acceptable. When used with an agent interpretation as in (52b), meaning 'to feel a texture', it is not, presumably because of Principle B of the Binding Theory (Chomsky 1981) which states that pronouns must be referentially free, i.e. not anaphorical, in their domain. Thus ordinarily bare pronouns cannot be used reflexively.

We will assume that the *sinti+mi* version of (52a) has the structure in (53), where *mi* is a clitic and is linked to an empty anaphoric element in the predicate:

(53)    Mi ta sinti+mi [ (null anaphor) un tiki tristu].
        1SG PR feel+1SG [... a bit sad]

### Further reading
Although Papiamento is a well-known and relatively well-described language, there is no standard work in English that deals with the full complexities of the language. Maurer (1988) deals with tense, mood, and aspect in great detail. Dijkhoff (1993) is a detailed study of nominal morphology. Kouwenberg & Murray (1994) is a useful general sketch.

# 18 Sranan

Lilian Adamson and Norval Smith

## 18.1 Introduction and position within lexifier language creole group

Sranan is an English-based creole language spoken in Surinam, South America. It is a member of the Atlantic group of English-based creole languages. This group can be justified in terms of shared histories, lexical items, and other linguistic features.

As far as the shared histories of these languages are concerned, we may point to such aspects as the common supplier of the vast majority of the imported slaves – the Dutch, and the history of colonization, whereby a new colony was founded by groups from one or more existing colonies. Surinam, for instance, was first settled from Barbados, St. Kitts, Nevis and Montserrat. In this way it is linked to the other Caribbean English-based creoles.

The phonological development of English lexical items within the Atlantic group displays various degrees of Standard English influence which complicates the question of the precise interrelationships of these languages. In general, however, it can be said that the Atlantic Anglophone creoles possess a more or less constant cluster of features that together distinguish them from other groups of creole languages: the particular selection of English lexical items that serve as function words; the structure of grammatical subsystems such as the personal pronoun system; shared non-standard phonological developments in their English-derived vocabulary; etc.

Within this group Sranan belongs to a clearly defined Surinam subgroup. This subgroup can be demonstrated in historical linguistic terms (with languages Sranan, Ndjuka-Aluku-Paramaccan-Kwinti, Saramaccan-Matawai). Outside this subgroup Sranan has a particular relationship with Krio, and other similar languages on the West African coast, as well as with the Maroon Spirit Language of Jamaica (Bilby 1983).

## 18.2 History and current status

The origins of Sranan (see also chapters 2 and 10) must be sought in the seventeenth century. Surinam started its post-Amerindian history as an English colony in 1651. The period of English occupation only lasted officially until 1667. English influence can be considered to have become negligible by 1680. So the period in which the direct linguistic influence of English can be assumed to have been operative was less than thirty years.

Research has demonstrated that there are at least two phonological strands of English influence to be found in Sranan. Both an 'r-ful' and 'r-less' dialect of English can be traced in the Sranan vocabulary (Smith 1987), for example *fara* 'far', *fo* 'four' (see also chapter 8).

How precisely English functioned in the development of Sranan is highly controversial. In for instance the bioprogram hypothesis of Bickerton (see chapter 11), English lexical items and language universals combined to produce Sranan. In the substrate approach the African language(s) of the early slaves had a decisive influence (chapter 9). For other approaches see chapters 8 and 10.

Sranan is the national lingua franca of Surinam, a Dutch colony between 1667 and 1775. Sranan is spoken by virtually the whole population of Surinam, either as a first or as a second language, as well as by the considerable emigré population in the Netherlands. The total number of speakers is around 500,000, of whom perhaps 300,000 are first language speakers.

While the official language of Surinam is Dutch, Sranan is utilized in many day-to-day functions. There is a perceptible on-going shift whereby Sranan is taking over certain functions which were performed by Dutch in the past, e.g. the language used to address political rallies. Government and civil service are conducted through the medium of Dutch, as well as education at all levels. However, public information is tending to be disseminated more and more through the medium of Sranan (e.g. on matters of public health).

Sranan is also known as **Sranantongo** (literally 'Surinam-tongue'); **Nengre(tongo)** (another term with colonial connotations, literally 'Negro(-tongue)'); **Surinaams** (literally Dutch: 'Surinam-ish'). The name **Takitaki** often found in older publications (e.g. Hall 1948) is unknown to many Surinamers as the name of their language and has negative connotations (it is literally Sranan for 'chatter').

## 18.3 Phonology and phonetics

The sounds of Sranan fall into the following categories:

(1) | **Consonants** | *labial* | *dental/alveolar* | *palatal* | *velar* |
|---|---|---|---|---|
| stops | p b | t d | ty dy | k g |
| fricatives | | s f | sy | x |
| nasals | m | n | ny | ŋ |
| liquids | | l r | | |
| semivowels | w | | y | |

The 'palatal' consonants /ty, dy, ny/ can be defined as dorso-postalveolar, while /sy/ is rather a dorso-prepalatal sibilant. The vowels /e/ and /o/ have phonetic values of respectively high-mid front centralized, and mid back round centralized. The quality of the vowel /a/ varies according to context: /tyari/ [tɕæ·hi] /kaN/ [kᴀ̃ŋ]. The quantity of vowels is half-long in contact with /r/. We write such vowels with [·]. The vowels we have indicated below as being pronounced as nasal vowels are in fact pronounced as [ṽ, ṽŋ, vŋ]. These we write as /iN, eN, aN, oN, uN/ for convenience.

(2)   **Vowels**         *oral*                          *nasal*

|  | front | back | front | back |
|---|---|---|---|---|
| high | i [i] | u [u] | iN [ĩ] | uN [ũ] |
| mid | e [ɪ] | o [ɔ] | eN [ẽ] | oN [õ] |
| low |  | a |  | aN [ã] |

In contradistinction to the other creole languages of Surinam, Sranan does not make systematic **lexical** use of tone. In general we can characterize Sranan as an accent language, making occasional use of distinctive vowel length. In this respect it is to be compared to English or Dutch. Each non-clitic word has one primary accented syllable. In longer words secondary accents will appear. The basic accent pattern is in terms of bisyllabic feet with a strong-weak pattern. For example /táki/ 'speak', /nófo/ 'enough', /fára/ 'far', /bróko/ 'break'. Bisyllabic words with the accentual pattern weak-strong are rare and recessive: /fadóN/ or /fádoN/ 'fall'.

Words traditionally spelled $C_1V_1C_1V_1$... with the accent on the second syllable are usually pronounced [$C_1C_1V_1$...]. For instance, in unemphatic speech /kaká/ is [kká] 'defecate', and /fufúru/ [ffúru] 'steal'. These double consonants are pronounced with extra length. Examples have been found of:

(3)     /pp bb tt dd kk gg ff ss mm nn nyny ll ww/.

One exception to the above statement regarding tone concerns the so-called double accent phenomenon (see Smith & Adamson, to appear), where a vowel is given **double** length ([:]), and pronounced on a **high** tone. We encounter this feature in certain **intensive** constructions, and with certain **ideophones**. See below for exemplification.

## 18.4 Morphology

It is frequently said of creole languages that they possess no morphology. In fact this is completely untrue for Sranan as we will go on to illustrate. The morphological resources of Sranan can be characterized as follows. Of the three basic types of morphology – derivational morphology, compounding and inflection – all three could with reason be claimed to be present in Sranan.

### 18.4.1  Derivational morphology

Derivational morphology is not present in the sense of a large number of phonologically fully specified affixes, but we can still distinguish various types of formation.

**Suffixation** is used sparingly, e.g. by attaching *-maN* to a verb, adjective, or noun:

(4)   *verb*            *noun*

| | | | |
|---|---|---|---|
| taki | 'speak' | taki-maN | 'speaker' |
| wroko | 'work' | wroko-maN | 'worker' |

    *adjective*

| | | | |
|---|---|---|---|
| siki | 'sick' | siki-maN | 'sick person' |
| blaka | 'black' | blaka-maN | 'black person' |

    *noun*

| | | | |
|---|---|---|---|
| bere | 'belly' | bere-maN | 'pregnant woman' |
| boto | 'boat' | boto-maN | 'boatman' |

It can be observed from the glosses that the meaning of *-maN* in these formations is 'person' or 'doer'. By contrast, the independent lexical item *maN* means 'man'.

Similarly, *-waN* can be attached to verbs, adjectives, or locative nouns:

(5)   *verb*            *noun*

| | | | |
|---|---|---|---|
| lobi | 'love' | lobi-waN | 'loved one' |
| ferfi | 'paint' | ferfi-waN | 'painted one' |

    *adjective*

| | | | |
|---|---|---|---|
| tranga | 'strong' | tranga-waN | 'strong one' |
| siki | 'sick' | siki-waN | 'sick one' |

    *locative noun*

| | | | |
|---|---|---|---|
| baka | 'back' | baka-waN | '(the) one behind' |
| sey | 'side' | sey-waN | '(the) one at the side' |

Here again we observe a difference in the semantic value of the independent word and the suffix. *waN* means 'one (numeral), a, exceptional case (idiomatic)', whereas the suffix *-waN* only functions to provide a referent.

**Zero-derivation** , also known as **multifunctionality** and **morphological conversion**, is used to convert lexical items of one category to another category.

(6)  | **Base category** | | **Derived category i** | | **Derived category ii** | |
|---|---|---|---|---|---|
| *adjective* | | *verb* | | *noun* | |
| siki | 'sick' | siki | 'be sick, sicken' | siki | 'illness' |
| hebi | 'heavy' | hebi | 'make heavy' | hebi | 'burden' |
| *noun* | | *verb* | | | |
| fisi | 'fish' | fisi | 'fish' | | |
| ferfi | 'paint' | ferfi | 'paint' | | |
| *verb* | | *noun* | | | |
| wroko | 'work' | wroko | 'work' | | |
| krey | 'cry' | krey | 'cry' | | |

There are various processes using **reduplication**, a selection of which we will mention here. Some are productive and others not. Productive is for example reduplication resulting in:

(7)  diminutive/pejorative:  VV, AA
augmentative:  VV
iterative:  VV
intensive:  VV, AA

Nonproductive is reduplication resulting in:

(8)  deverbal nominalizations:  VV > N

Voorhoeve 1980 claims that the **diminutive/pejorative**, **iterative** and **augmentative** reduplication types represent the same formation. However, they clearly represent different processes since the accentuation is different. The diminutive/pejorative is equally accented on both elements, the augmentative has an accent on the final member, while the iterative has the accent on the first element.

(9)  **Diminutive-pejorative**
A  fatu 'fat'  fát(u)fátu 'a bit fat, fattish'
V  kaN 'comb'  káNkáN 'to comb a bit'
(10)  **Augmentative**
A  fatu 'fat'  fat(u)fátu 'too fat'
V  ferfi 'paint'  ferfiférfi 'to paint a lot'
(11)  **Iterative**
V  bow 'build'  bówbow 'to build in different places'

Examples of the above include:

(12)    Mi e jérejére deɴ.    'I hear them a bit (diminutive).'
        Mi e jérejere deɴ.    'I hear them at times (iterative).'

Deverbal nominalizations are exemplified in (13):

(13)    ari    'to draw'    arári            'rake'
        kaɴ    'to comb'    kaɴkáɴ/káɴkaɴ    'comb'

**Modification** is used to mark the **intensive**. The modification consists of the lengthening and raising in pitch of the accented vowel.

(14)    A    blaka 'black'    blᴀᴀka    'very black'
        V    seri    'to sell'    sᴇᴇri    'to sell a lot'
        (vv = high-toned long vowel)

## 18.4.2  Compounding

Compounding is used a great deal in Sranan as in most creole languages. It is the favored way of extending the lexicon. In (15) the three frequent types are shown, exemplified in (16):

(15)    [noun-noun]$_{noun}$
        [adjective-noun]$_{noun}$
        [verb-noun]$_{noun}$

(16)    ɴɴ
        mofo-neti      mouth-night    'early evening'
        agu-meti       pig-meat       'pork'
        ᴀɴ
        drey-teɴ       dry-time       'dry season'
        dungru-oso     dark-house     'prison'
        ᴠɴ
        dray-ay        turn-eye       'dizziness'
        kweki-pikiɴ    nurse-child    'foster child'

### 18.4.3 Inflection

Inflection is the morphological phenomenon least in evidence in Sranan. While not everyone would accept their characterization as inflectional elements, the preverbal negative and tense/mood/aspect (TMA) particles can plausibly be regarded as inflectional elements. These elements occupy a fixed position preceding the verb, with no possibility that other elements may intervene. In this they resemble the weak forms of the pronouns to some extent. These exhibit however a less cohesive relationship with the verb, and may occupy a variety of structural positions.

The TMA-particles have been considered to consist maximally of *beN sa e* (e.g. Voorhoeve 1957). This system would then be identical to the classical TMA system assumed to be generally present in the Atlantic creole languages (see chapter 20). In fact we consider this to be erroneous as far as *beN* and *sa* are concerned. The distribution of *beN* and *sa* corresponds rather to that of auxiliary verbs. *e* (and *o*) on the other hand do not behave like verbs. Consider the possibilities of predicate cleft formation, which can be seen as a test for verbhood.

(17)   a.   Na *musu* a musu suku a buku. 'He MUST look for the book.'
         Na *suku* a musu suku a buku. 'He must LOOK FOR the book.'
       b.   Na *kan* a kan taygi en. 'He CAN tell him.'
         na *taygi* a kan taygi en. 'He can TELL him.'
       c.   Na *sa* a sa taygi en. 'He WILL tell him.'
         Na *taygi* a sa taygi en. 'He will TELL him.'
       d.   Na *beN* a beN suku a buku. 'He HAD looked for the book.'
         Na *suku* a beN suku a buku. 'He had LOOKED FOR the book.'
       e.   *Na *o* a o taygi en. 'He IS GOING TO tell him.'
         na *taygi* a o taygi en. 'he is going to TELL him.'
       f.   *Na *e* a e suku a buku. 'He IS looking for the book.'
         na *suku* a e suku a buku. 'He is LOOKING FOR the book.'
       (Note that all of these are pronounceable, e.g.: *na e a e..* > [nay ay..])

The only true TMA-particles – as against auxiliary verbs – appear to be *e* and *o* (*e* = nonpunctual, progressive; *o* = future/irrealis). The question of the possible combinations of auxiliaries and particles will be discussed further in section 18.6.3 below, and in chapter 20.

## 18.5  An 'African' word category: ideophones

An undoubtedly African feature in Sranan – though less pervasive perhaps than in the other Surinam creoles – is the ideophone. This is a basically adverbial category expressive of various degrees of a particular quality, and not standing in any derivational relationship to adjectives, as is normally the case with most adverbs. In Sranan they normally function as intensifiers of the meaning of adjectives or verbs.

(18)    A blaka so *pii*.              'He is so *very* black.'
        A weti so *fAAN*.          'He is so *very* white.'
        A weti *fanfaN*.            'He is *very* white.'
        A supu broN *petepete*.  'The soup is *completely* burnt.'

Note the existence of ideophones with narrow collocational restrictions, such as *fAAN* which is solely an intensifier of 'whiteness'. Note also the long high-toned vowels in some ideophones. Some of these items, such as *pii*, only occur with high tone and lengthened vowel.

## 18.6 Syntax

### 18.6.1 The order of the main constituents of the sentence

The syntactic properties which are typically thought of as distinguishing creoles from other languages can all be found in Sranan. One of these properties which we will address here concerns word order. Sranan has a strict SVO word order due to the lack of morphological material in the sentence capable of marking the syntactic hierarchical relationships. This basic word order can be seen in the following two different sentence types, namely the declarative sentence (1a) and the interrogative sentence (1b).

(19)    a.  I e skrifi waN brifi. [ye skrif waN brifi ↓]
            'You are writing a letter.'
        b.  I e skrifi waN brifi? [ye skrif waN brifi ↑]
            'Are you writing a letter?'

The only distinguishing feature between these two sentences is phonological. The intonation pattern of the interrogative sentence is different from that of the declarative sentence, with a rise at the end, instead of a fall. There is no structural difference between the two sentences.

As has been said the strict word order of Sranan does not allow for other constituents to intervene between the subject and the verb of the sentence, apart from parenthetical structures (e.g. *Jan, i sabi, e sutu waN fowru* 'Jan, you know, is shooting a bird'). The direct object and indirect object are less strictly ordered relative to each other. The basic word order is .. IO DO .. (IO = indirect object/DO = direct object) as in (20).

(20)    I e skrifi i sisa waN brifi.
      'You are writing your sister a letter.'

These two objects of the verb, the IO and the DO, may change places with one another on condition that the IO is introduced by the preposition *na* 'to' (21).

(21)    I e skrifi waN brifi na i sisa.
      'You are writing a letter to your sister.'

We may add other optional adverbial phrases. These can occupy different positions in the sentence with the restriction that they cannot appear directly following the verb. The unmarked order appears to be sentence-final.

(22)    I e skrifi i sisa waN brifi na ini a dyari.                    IO DO ADV
      'You are writing your sister a letter in the garden.'

The adverbial can be either a prepositional phrase or an adverb like *safrisafri* 'slowly' (< softly):

(23)    I e skrifi i sisa waN brifi safrisafri.                        IO DO ADV
      'You are writing your sister a letter slowly.

The unmarked word-order in the sentence is then:

(24)    S V IO DO Adjunct

In this order S, IO and DO appear as NPs. The adjunct is either a PP or an adverb. As we can see from the above sentences moving the IO results in a PP form for this constituent. All constituents which appear as PPs (modifying the verbal action) must follow the DO. Adjuncts can have different semantic functions, such as time, place, benefactive, manner, etc.

### 18.6.2 The structure of adpositional phrases
The question of adpositional structures is a very complex part of the grammar of Sranan. Here we will restrict our attention to three types of structure:

(25)    a.    simple prepositional phrases
      b.    complex prepositional phrases with an extra locative preposition
      c.    complex prepositional phrases with a possessed locative noun

Sranan has simple prepositions such as:

(26) a.  a general locative preposition *na/a* 'at/to/in';
     b.  dative *na/gi* 'to';
     c.  a general associative preposition *fu* 'of', which also functions as:
     d.  an ablative/abessive preposition *fu* 'from';
     e.  a benefactive *fu/gi* 'for', and
     f.  a comitative/instrumental preposition *nanga* 'with';
     g.  and a number of more specific prepositions:

         *te*          'until'
         *sondro*      'without'
         *boiti*       'except'
         *sensi*       'since'.

Complex prepositional phrases with an extra locative preposition would be:

(27)  *na fesi* a skowtu-oso        '(to) in front of the police-station'
      *na tapu* a skowtu-oso        '(to) above the police-station'

Complex prepositional phrases with a postposed locative noun, finally, would be:

(28)  *na* a skowtu-oso *fesi*      'to/at the front of the police-station'
      *na* a skowtu-oso *tapu*      '(to) on top of the police-station'

The translations of these complex phrases are imprecise. What we want to express here is that the phrases in (28) indicate a location closer to or in contact with the reference point.

### 18.6.3  The verbal system

In addition to the negative *no* and TMA-prefixes *o/e* , as discussed above in section 18.5.3, the verbal system of Sranan involves auxiliary verbs – as in many other languages – and serial verbs, which are often regarded as a typical creole feature, although by no means restricted to creole languages. We will however have nothing to say about serial verbs in this chapter – for these see Chapter 23. The auxiliary verbs of Sranan include the following:

(29)  beN   'was'                          maN   'can'
      go    'be going to'                  kaN   'can'
      sa    'will'                         max   'may'

| sabi | 'know how to' | | koN | 'get (...ed)' |
| mu(su) | 'must' | | k(a)ba | 'finish (preverbal usage)' |
| wani | 'want to' | | | |

The negative particle and the TMA-particles may occur before these verbs too. This gives us the following expansion of the (non-serial) verb complex:

(30)    ([<no o e> AUX])ⁿ          [<no o e> v]

These combinations generally exhibit a high degree of vowel elision leading to a very opaque system. Compare:

(31)    A beN o beN e dray.       [a bɔːbɛːdray]
        'He would have been turning.'

We give some examples of the combinations of particles and auxiliaries found with a typical non-stative verb. The translation between two languages with differing tense-aspect systems is always tricky, so that the glosses here are only meant to give a rough idea of the meanings.

(32)  a.  A ferfi a oso.
          'He painted the house.'
      b.  A e ferfi a oso.
          'He **is** paint**ing** the house.'
      c.  a o ferfi a oso.
          'He **is going to** paint the house.'
      d.  a beN ferfi a oso.
          'He **had** painted the house.'
      e.  a beN e ferfi a oso.
          'He was/**had been** paint**ing** the house.'
      f.  a sa ferfi a oso.
          'He **will** paint the house.'
      g.  a sa beN e ferfi a oso.
          'He will have **been** paint**ing** the house.'
      h.  a beN sa ferfi a oso.
          'He **would** paint the house.'
      i.  a beN sa e ferfi a oso.
          'He **would be** paint**ing** the house.'
      j.  a beN sa beN ferfi a oso.
          'He **would have** painted the house.'
      k.  a beN sa ben e ferfi a oso.
          'He **would have been** paint**ing** the house.'
      l.  a beN o beN e ferfi a oso.
          'He **would** have **been** paint**ing** the house.'
      m.  a beN o e beN o ferfi a oso.
          'He **would** have **been going** to paint the house.'

## 18.7 Text

We now provide a short text. This is adapted from a story by Edgar Cairo in Voorhoeve & Lichtveld (1975).

(a)    Te   mi   papa Nelis ben   friyari,
    when  1SG  father Nelis PAST  have.birthday
    furu  sma    no   ben  e    kon.
    many  people  NEG  PAST  CNT  come
    'When my father Nelis had his birthday, not many people were in the habit of turning up.'

(b)    Wanwan kompe  so,   ben  kan  kon  trus'    ede   pikinso.
    few    friend  just  PAST  can  come thrust  head  a-little(-while)
    'Just a friend or two could pop in for a short while.'

(c)    Ma es'esi      den  ben  e    ari   pasi,
    but quick-quick they  PAST  CNT  pull  path
    'But left soon afterwards,'

(d)    bika     mi   papa no   ben  e    taki  tori.
    because  1SG  father NEG  PAST  CNT  tell   story
    'because my father did not like shoptalk.'

(e)    A  ben  e    sidon fow  en   anu  na    ondro   en   kakumbe.
    3SG PAST  CNT  sit    fold  3SG  hand LOC  under  3SG  chin
    'He was sitting as usual with his chin on his hands.'

(f)    Ma yu  si,   te   Basedi      ben  doro,    dan  tori  ben  dray.
    but 2SG  see,  when Master-Eddy  PAST arrive,  then story PAST  change
    'But when Master Eddy arrived, then it was a different story.'

(g)    Now  den  ben  de    fu  lo    pondo.
    now   they  PAST  COP  to row  boat
    'Then they got down to business.'

(h)    Den ben  e    nati den   neki nanga dyindyabiri èn   tesi  wan  mofo   fiadu
    they PAST  CNT wet  3PL    neck with   ginger-beer and  taste  one   mouth   fiadu
    'They would wet their whistle with ginger-beer and take a piece of birthday-cake.'

(i)    Tranga  sopi noyti ben  e    de,
    strong   drink never PAST  CNT  COP
    'There was never any strong drink around,'

(j)    bika     no    dringi,  no smoko,    mi   papa ben  e    du
    because  NEG  drink,   NEG  smoke,  1SG  father PAST  CNT  do
    'because my father didn't drink or smoke.'

(k)  "Mi   moni   na   mi   sopi  èn   mi   wroko   na   mi   smoko."
"1SG  money  COP  1SG  drink and 1SG  work    COP  1SG  smoke"
"My money is my drink, and my work is my smoking."

(l)  Te   den       yonkuman  fu wrokope    yere  na    tori  disi,
when  DET-PL   young-man  of work-place hear  DET   story this
'Whenever the boys at work heard this,'

(m)  dan   den   e     lafu.
then  3PL   CNT   laugh
'they would burst out in laughter.'

(n)  Dati  na    wan   bigiman srefsrefi.
that  COP   a     big-man self-self
'That's one hell of a guy.'

(o)  Basedi       srefi ben   e     lafu   tu    nanga  ala   den    tifi
Master-Eddy even  PAST  CNT   laugh  too   with   all   DET-PL  tooth
'Even Master Eddy would laugh too, baring all his teeth'

(p)  di    blaka fu soso   tabaka.
which black of only   tobacco
'which were black from pure tobacco.'

(q)  Now   a     ben   de    na    en    yuru.
now   3SG   PAST  COP   LOC   3SG   hour
'Now it was his turn.'

(r)  Nanga wan  lekti dyeme  a     ben   e     opo   en    tori
with  a     light groan  3SG   PAST  CNT   open  3SG   story
'With a sigh he would begin to tell his story.'

Notes:

(a) One of the uses of *te* is as a subordinating complementizer with the meaning 'when(ever), until'. *friyari* is a stative verb in Sranan – literally 'to birthday'. *e*, the continuative aspect marker, may be used in habitual, iterative and durative senses. Here, and throughout this text, it is habitual.

(b) *kon trusu* is a serial verb construction. *trus' ede* (lit. 'thrust head') is an idiom – like *pop in* in English.

(c) *ari pasi* (lit. 'pull path') is an idiom – like *make tracks* in English.

(e) *sidon fow* is a manner serial construction. *na ondro en kakumbe* is a prepositional phrase. *na* is general preposition of location or time, while *ondro* has been analysed both as a second preposition, and as a locative noun. *na ondro* might conceivably represent *na a ondro*, in which case only the latter analysis would be possible.

(g) In *de fu* we have an example of the copula selecting a purpose clause complement.

(i) Here the copula has an existential force.

(j) *no dringi, no smoko* represents the topic of the sentence, which appears in a topicalized structure. *du* is a dummy verb. Compare English 'drinking and smoking, I don't do.'

(k) Here we have a copular sentence with a noun phrase complement; the copula is *na*.

(l) *na* is an older form of the article. It would now only be used to indicate emphasis. Here we see the proximate demonstrative/deictic structure: article .... *disi*. There is no tense-aspect marking in this subordinate clause, because this is determined in the main clause.

(p) Once again we have no tense-aspect marking in a subordinate clause.

(q) *na en yuru* is an idiom.

## Further reading

There is no modern grammar of Sranan, although there are a number of course books with grammatical information. One example would be Voorhoeve (1980). A grammatical sketch is contained in a recent word-list (Sordam & Eersel 1985). A preliminary dictionary is Wilner (1992). Charry, Koefoed & Muysken (1983) contains articles on various aspects of the language.

# 19 Berbice Dutch

Silvia Kouwenberg

## 19.1 Dutch-lexicon creole in Guyana

At the time of writing this, early 1993, the last speakers of Berbice Dutch Creole (BD) number only four or five. BD was once the vernacular of the Dutch-owned Berbice colony, which consisted of plantations and small settlements along the Berbice River, Canje River, and Wiruni Creek in Guyana. Its demise started around 1800 when plantations were relocated to the coastal area, while around the same time the colony changed to British ownership, and Guyanese Creole, an English-lexicon creole, developed in the coastal area. Not until the mid seventies, when Ian Robertson discovered that the language was still spoken, was BD studied (Robertson 1976, 1979). Up to this time it was assumed that if a Dutch-lexicon creole had ever existed in Guyana, it would certainly have become extinct. In fact, Robertson found vestiges of another Dutch-lexicon creole, Skepi Dutch (SD), in the Essequibo area of Guyana, also a one-time Dutch colony. The communities in which these languages were spoken were a good distance apart and the character of the natural terrain was such that traveling from one to the other was not easy. This explains why we find two different Dutch-lexicon creoles developing at roughly the same time. A comparison of the basic vocabulary of these two creoles in Robertson (1989) shows that they are dissimilar to the point of being mutually unintelligible. The lexical differences are of three kinds (Dutch etyma are given in their modern orthography; where an Eastern Ịjọ etymon is given, the Kalabạri form has been selected for reasons explained in Smith, Robertson & Wiliamson 1987).

(a) Some words have the same Dutch (DU) etymon, but have different forms in BD and SD. For example, quite a few words end in consonants in SD but in vowels in BD, and some show differences in voicing of consonants: SD *frag* BD *fragi* 'ask' < DU vragen, SD *blut* BD *blutu* 'blood' < DU bloed, SD *slanka* BD *slangi* 'snake' < DU slang, SD *brant* BD *brandi* 'burn' < DU branden.

(b) Some words have different DU etyma: 'under' is SD *bɛnɛr* < DU beneden, BD *ondro* < DU onder, 'roast' is SD *brai* < DU braaien, BD *brandi* < DU branden, 'back' is SD *kɛnt* < DU lende, BD *atrɛ/atri* < DU achter.

(c) A large proportion of BD basic vocabulary is not of DU etymology; many of these words have Eastern Ịjọ (EI), a Nigerian language, as their source (Smith et al. 1987): 'black' is SD *swati* < DU zwart, BD *kurkuru* < EI kúrúkúrú, 'eat' is SD *skaf* < DU schaften, BD *jefi* < EI yé fi, 'woman' is SD *jufrau* < DU juffrouw, BD *jɛrma* < EI éré-me.

Only about 200 basic vocabulary items are known from SD, and the people who remembered them when Ian Robertson interviewed them in the seventies may be referred to as 'terminal' speakers, incapable of conversing, bartering, or any other communicative effort in SD. Their memory did not include sentences other than formulaic expressions such as *hos mɛt ju* 'how are you?'. We may conclude that SD stopped being taught to children before the turn of this century. BD on the other hand, was still used in some families in the Berbice River area early this century; children growing up in and around these families learned both BD and Guyanese Creole. As adults, although Guyanese-dominant, they retain the ability to engage in conversation in BD. Their ability to do so ranges from that of fluent speakers (four or five), to that of semispeakers (about ten). The youngest of the fluent speakers was born in 1923. Modern BD contains many Guyanese Creole elements in vocabulary and grammar, reflecting its history of contact with Guyanese and the speakers' Guyanese dominance.

## 19.2  Berbice Dutch grammar

In the following, we will examine some aspects of BD grammar, organized as follows: 1. word order and other properties of the clause, 2. lexicon and morphology, 3. phonology. Bear in mind that the discussion below is very summary, and that the properties of BD are merely indicated, not described in any detail. Exceptions and constructions of minor importance have been left out of consideration altogether.

### 19.2.1  Word order and other properties of the clause

In general, we can say that word order in BD shows mixed characteristics. Most of the phenomena illustrated below are typically associated with SVO order: complements follow verbs and prepositions, relative clauses follow nouns, auxiliaries and similar elements precede the main verb; in each of these cases, a dependent follows a head. But we will see some divergences from this pattern in the form of postpositions, suffixes on the verb, and clause-final negation.

As in other Caribbean creoles, BD basic word order is strictly SVO in all sentence types: in interrogatives and non-interrogatives, in main and in embedded clauses. Where a verb takes two internal arguments (e.g. *pi* 'give', *tiri* 'send', *twa* 'put'), an indirect object precedes a direct object, a location argument follows a direct object. BD does not employ morphological case marking of subjects and objects or agreement marking on the verb form: word order carries the full functional load of the differentiation of arguments. The foregrounding strategies of focus, passive, and dislocation may produce word orders different from the basic svo order. Each of these is illustrated below. Focus optionally uses the copular form *da* as 'highlighter' (glossed as BE), and/or a focus marker *sa/so* (glossed as FOC) which follows the focused constituent, both of which are present in (1). Passive constructions, as in (2), show no passive morphology. In (3) we have a case of left-dislocation.

(1)  Da  hatbeʃi  bwa  so   o    wa    hangitɛ  fini  ofro.        [HH lukubaɪ:p8]
     BE  deer     foot  FOC  3SG  PAST  hang-PF  fire  over
     '(It) was deer feet he had hung over the fire.'

(2)  O    kor   djas  kɛk  hos  di..  kori.                    [AK 050390:p1]
     3SG  work  just  like  how  this  work
     'It is made just like this one is made.'

(3)  Di  wari  wato       wa    lefa      daŋa, o   kikjo    babaka.  [HH lukubaɪ:p4]
     the  house  what=3SG  PAST  live-IPF  there  3SG  see=3SG  anymore=NEG
     '(As for) the house that he had been living in there, he doesn't see it anymore.'

The formation of question-word questions involves the movement of the questioned constituent to initial position in the clause. The elicited judgements indicate that, if the questioned constituent is the complement of a preposition, the preposition optionally moves too. Below, the questioning of a subject human referent is illustrated in (4), the questioning of the adverbial complement of a preposition, with pied-piping of the preposition in (5). Note the use of the focus marker *sa/so* in both examples; focus is optional, but quite frequent in question-word questions.

(4)  Wisa     das  kom   hir   kom   mja  di   bɛ-rap     di?      [AH 010788:8]
     who=FOC  HAB  come  here  come  do   the  story-PL   this
     'Who comes here to do these things?'

(5)  Fan   waŋsin        kumtɛ?                    [!HA 020490:p21, !AK 0500490:p40]
     from  where=FOC=3PL  come-PF
     'Where have they come from?'

Determiners, numerals, adjectives and genitives precede the noun, relative clauses and demonstratives follow it (* indicates the possibility of recursion):

(6)  ⎰ Determiner ⎱  Adjective* Noun Demonstrative Relative Clause
     ⎱ Possessor  ⎰
     ⎰ Numeral    ⎱

Relative clauses are introduced by the initial element *wati*, which may have human as well as non-human and inanimate reference; human reference is illustrated in (7) below, inanimate reference in (3). *Wati* also occurs as a question word, but can only have non-human and inanimate reference when used that way, whereas human referents are questioned by use of the question word *wi* 'who'. This combined with some other differences between question formation and relative clause formation leads us to suspect that *wati* is a complementizer rather than a relative pronoun when heading relative clauses.

(7)    di jɛrmatoko    wat jɛnda birbiʃi,    ori    da də    laʃtijɛ    [AH 060588:4,38]
       the woman=child    what be=there Berbice    3SG    be the    last-NOM
       'The daughter who lives on the Berbice River, she is the last one (of my children).'

Interestingly, BD has both prepositions and postpositions, most of which have DU prepositions as their etymons. BD prepositions are the following: *mɛtɛ* 'with', *fan* 'from, of', *tutu* 'until', *foro* 'before', *fulfi* 'for', *sondro* 'without', *afta* 'after', *abot* 'about'. Of these, *fulfi*, *afta*, *abot* are Guyanese Creole, while all others have DU prepositions as their etymons. Example (5) above contains *fan* 'from'.

BD also has a class of words which may either refer to a part of an object or body (*atrɛ* 'back', *ben* 'inside', *bofu* 'top', *foro* 'front', *kandi* 'side', *ondro* 'underside') or to the situation of an object or body in relation to another one (behind, inside, on top of, in front of, near, underneath). For instance, ɛkɛ *atrɛ* [1SG back] is ambiguous between possessive 'my back' and spatial 'behind me'. In their former use, these words are clearly nouns, in their latter use they are referred to as postpositions and behave ambiguously: they have some noun-like properties, some preposition-like properties. In addition, three postpositions, viz. *anga* locative marker, *tosn* 'between' and *ofru* 'over' are not used as nouns at all. Example (1) illustrates the use of *ofru*. Of these words, the only ones which do not have DU prepositions as their etyma are *kandi* < DU kant 'side' (n.) and *anga* < EI ángá 'side' (n.).

Markers of tense, mood and aspect either precede the verb, in the form of auxiliary verbs and particles, or are suffixes on the verb (aspectual only). The examples below illustrate a combination of preverbal particles *wa* (tense), *sa* (mood) with the suffix *-tɛ* (aspect) in (8), the use of an auxiliary in (9). The past tense marker *wa* with a perfective verb form creates an anterior reading as in (1), its appearance with an irrealis mood marker creates a future-in-the-past reading. (8) shows that a combination of past, irrealis and perfective is also possible. If a past reading rather than an anterior is intended, only the perfective form of the verb will appear, without the preverbal tense marker. Examples are (5) and (11). Furthermore, overt tense reference is conditioned by principles governing discourse: in a chronologically ordered account of events, past is not marked overtly, while an overt mark appears in utterances that provide background information for such an account. Thus, (10) below is given a past tense translation, while no overt past tense reference appears; it is taken from a chronologically ordered account of events.

(8)  ɛk  wa    sa   kutɛ      en   or twe  fan  eni.                    [AK 250190:17]
     1SG PAST  IRR  catch-PF  one  or two  of   them
     'I would have caught a couple of them.'

(9)  Ju   mu    jefi,  ju   mu    talma      jefi.                      [EK lukuba2:p4]
     2SG  must  eat    2SG  must  dish.out   food
     'You must eat, you must serve yourself.'

The standard negator *kanɛ* or its short form *ka* is clause-final, certain other types of negation employ a preverbal negator in addition to the standard negator. Both are illustrated below.

(10) ɛk  suk   mu  lasan eni  ka.                                       [AK 290488:p4]
     1SG want  go  leave 3PL  NEG
     'I didn't want to leave them.'

(11) Titi  ori  kumtɛ     en   wa    noko    la   noko kanɛ.            [BB 160488:p1]
     time  3SG  come-PF   3PL  PAST  not=RES reach yet  NEG
     'When he came they hadn't arrived yet.'

Although BD does not have the instrumental and benefactive serial verb constructions which are typically quoted in discussions of such constructions in creole languages, it does have a number of other serial verb constructions with a variety of functions such as dative, direct object, location, direction, complementation, and others.

### 19.2.2 Lexicon and morphology

BD major word classes are nouns, adjectives, verbs. Closed classes are pronouns, prepositions, postpositional nouns, conjunctions, auxiliary verbs, and other functional items such as negators and particles. In this section, we will look at BD morphological processes; in general, these affect only words of major class membership, with the exception of the plural pronouns which sometimes appear with the plural suffix.

In the preceding section, we have seen an illustration of the existence of verbal inflection in BD. There are three suffixes which mark aspectual categories: *-tɛ* for perfective aspect, *-arɛ* or the short form *-a* for imperfective aspect, and a reduplicative suffix for iterative aspect. A reduplicated verb form can take one of the other suffixes, as shown in the following example.

(12)    Kaljap,        kɛkɛ  di    wat    mangimangja.                [BC 130688:2]
        small-NOM-PL   like  this  what   run-run-IPF
        'Small ones, like this one that is running up and down.'

BD reduplication is totally productive over the classes of adjectives (where it marks either intensity or distribution) and verbs (where it marks different kinds of iterative aspect), while the reduplication of nouns occurs only ocassionally; the latter marks an individuated plural, and may be contrasted with the normal process of plural formation, which involves the suffixation of -*apu* to the noun, as in (4) above. The use of a normal plural in (13) would have meant that the speaker received several 8 cents pieces every day. The plural suffix -*apu* may also be used to mark an associative plural, as in ɛkɛ *papapu* 'my father and people of his generation'.

(13)    Idri  daka  ɛk   justu      krik  skeliŋskeliŋ            [HA 020490:p16]
        every day   ISG  PAST,HAB   get   8 cent-8 cent
        'Every day I would get an 8 cents piece.'

BD makes fairly extensive use of the process of zero derivation, whereby a word of a different category is derived without a change in phonological form. The following processes of zero derivation can be distinguished:
(a) Zero derivation applies to verbs, also reduplicated forms, and derives deverbal nouns, e.g. *kapu* 'cut (V/N), operation', *kosokoso* 'coughing (V/N)'. This process is not very productive.
(b) Zero derivation applies to adjectives, and derives intransitive and transitive process verbs, e.g. *kurkuru* 'black/become black/blacken'. This process is almost fully productive over the class of adjectives.
(c) Zero derivation applies to intransitive verbs, and derives transitive and causative verbs, e.g. *kori* 'work/construct', *sara* 'fall, drop (INT/TR)'.
Lastly we mention here a derivational process which involves the bound morpheme -*jɛ*, possibly a clitic element, by means of which adjectives, possessive pronouns, and attributive nouns may be nominalized: e.g. *kalijɛ* 'small one', *jujɛ* 'yours', *jɛrmajɛ* 'female kind'. Another example may be found in example sentence (7) above.

    BD compounds are always headed by a nominal element, and rarely consist of more than two members. We find N-N compounds (*jɛrmatoko* woman=child 'girl, daughter', *mingikui*

water=cow 'manatee'), A-N compounds (*bambita* nice=dress 'clothes for special occasions',
*grotala* great=boss 'Governor'), V-N compounds (*branhautu* burn=wood 'firewood', *jagiman*
hunt=man 'hunter'). Temporal and location compounds are formed with nouns: *titi* 'time',
*ʃi* 'side' (combined with *kandi* 'side') as right-most elements (*ɛnɛtiti* rain=time 'rainy season',
*bofuʃi(kandi)* top=side(=side) 'upriver').

The BD pronoun system does not differentiate for features such as gender, animateness,
in/exclusivity, or case, except for a special genitive form of the third person singular. The
variation in the plural forms is dialectal: the forms preceding the slashes are used by a
different set of speakers from those following the slashes. Where the 3SG forms are concerned, the use of *a* is peculiar to the speech of one particular speaker of BD, and only occurs
as a subject.

(14)    *Singular*                    *Plural*

1.  ɛkɛ                              enʃi/iʃi,içi

2.  ju                               jɛndɛ

3.  ori      (all positions)         eni/ini

    o        (subject/object)

    a        (subject)

    ʃi       (genitive)

All personal pronouns except for the short 3SG forms and the special genitive form may
appear in any syntactic position, may be focused/conjoined/modified by the reflexive *selfu*
'self' (the 3SG reflexive forms being either *ori selfu* or *ʃi selfu*), modified by adverbs *oko* 'too'
and *alen* 'only', or modified by the emphatic markers *-jɛ* and *di*. Of the 3SG pronouns, *ori*
only may appear in left-dislocated position, while all forms may be used as resumptive
pronouns; if *ori* is dislocated, the short form is employed as the resumptive pronoun.

### 19.2.3 Sound system

BD has an asymmetrically distributed six vowel system. The mid front vowels /e/ and /ɛ/
are in near-complementary distribution, and may have been allophones of a single vowel
phoneme at an earlier stage.

(15)         *Front*    *Back*

High         i          u

Mid          e          o

             ɛ

Low                 a

Thus, the lower mid front vowel occurs as final vowel, as in *kanɛ* 'NEG', or in mono-morphemic polysyllabic words which contain more than one mid front vowel, as in *kɛnɛ* 'person'. The higher mid front vowel occurs as sole mid front vowel in non-final position, as in *alen* 'alone'. Due to the existence of some exceptions, e.g. *jɛrma* 'woman' (possibly from earlier *\*jɛrɛma*) and *twe* 'two' (a variant of *twɛ*), we need to postulate a marginal phonemic distinction between the two in modern BD.

There is considerable overlap in the allophony of adjacent phonemes. Thus, /i/ and /e/ share [ ] as a possible allophone, /a/ and /o/ share [ʌ] as a possible allophone, and [o] is an allophone of /u/ (but [u] is an allophone of /u/ only). This allophony is not conditioned, i.e. the various allophones are in free variation. Unstressed vowels are frequently reduced by centralization, i.e. [ə] is a possible allophone of all vowel phonemes. Length is not phonemic; long vowels occur phonetically as a result of emphatic stress.

For oral stops, BD distinguishes three points of articulation and exploits voiceless/voiced pairing. Only two points of articulation, labial and alveolar, are contrastive for fricatives and nasals. Voicing is not distinctive for fricatives: voiced fricatives /v,z/ occur only as borrowed phonemes in a few Guyanese Creole loanwords. The palato-alveolar fricative is a predictable realization of /s/ in most of its occurrences, viz. preceding the high front vowel /i/, but there are a few words where its occurrence is not predictable, e.g. *ʃurum* 'dirty', *ʃepu* 'soap'.

(16)

|  | labial | labio-dental | alveolar | velar | glottal |
|---|---|---|---|---|---|
| oral stop | p,b |  | t,d | k,g |  |
| nasal stop | m |  | n |  |  |
| fricative |  | f | s,ʃ |  | h |
| approximant |  |  | l,r |  |  |

A velar nasal occurs as a predictable realisation of /n/, viz. preceding a velar plosive, as in *gungu* 'sift', *pringi* 'jump'. The occurrence of [ŋ] in many of the examples without the accompaniment of a velar plosive results from the application of processes of reduction.

BD does not employ pitch or length distinctively, i.e. independent from stress, except in that rising final intonation over an utterance distinguishes yes/no questions and confirmative questions from the corresponding statements. Regular stress assignment assigns penultimate main stress in monomorphemic words. Irregular stress means, in the majority of cases, initial stress in a trisyllabic word, as for instance in *alala* 'tongue', *stelingi* 'jetty'. Suffixation, including the suffixation of a reduplicative morpheme, does not affect the position of stress (but see below for 'therapeutic' measures connected with suffixation and the position of stress). In compounds, the right-hand member of the compound receives main stress.

Several processes of reduction may apply within and between words. We will briefly discuss the most frequent of these. Unstressed vowels may delete irrespective of their position in the word, e.g. initially in *baba* < *ababa* 'anymore', medially in *korma* < *koroma* 'lay (eggs)', finally in *war* < *wari* 'house'. A favourable environment is that in which deletion results in penultimate stress, for instance in irregularly stressed monomorphemic words such as *'korma* < *'koroma* and in the case of words which have antepenultimate stress due to suffixation, as in *'koptɛ* < *'kopu-tɛ* 'buy-PF'. Deletion also takes place where two syllabic vowels are adjacent, for instance as a result of suffixation or cliticisation. In these cases, the first vowel is suppressed, as in *tokapu* < *toko-apu* 'child-PL'. If the first vowel is a high vowel, it may either be suppressed or changed to the corresponding glide, as in *gutapu/gutwapu* < *gutu-apu* 'thing-PL'.

Syllable suppression takes place in a phonological environment of the form $..c_1v\text{-}c_2..$ in which $c_1$ and $c_2$ share all place and manner features but may differ in voicing. In such an environment, reduction applies optionally but quite frequently, resulting in $..c_2...$ The boundary and vowel between $c_1$ and $c_2$ are ignored; thus, '-' ranges from morpheme-boundaries to word-boundaries across sentences. For instance, the regularly used expression *kɛ.na.pan.tɛ.kɛ* 'people told me../I was told..' (the dots indicate syllable boundaries) derives from *kɛnɛ-apu pama-tɛ ɛkɛ* 'person-PL tell-PF 1SG', which contains the sequence *..pu-p...*

## 19.3 Text

In the following text, Ernest King tells us about the time he worked pulling logs on the timber-grants. He sings a worksong (*timbabos* 'timber song') which bears witness to a limited form of contact that must have existed between workmen of SD, BD and Guyanese Creole linguistic backgrounds in the second half of the 19th century, before SD and BD entered their final stages of decay. Seeking work in logging, these men met on the timber-grants where they were employed to pull logs to the riverside, where the trees were then tied into rafts to be transported to the saw-mill through the river. The men used to form chaingangs, pulling in pairs on a long chain. Worksongs, sung as call-and-answer, served to synchronize their movements. The worksong in this text is meant to be used at the break of day, when work begins. The songs recorded are probably just frozen versions of songs in continuous change. In addition to the transcribed recording, the literal gloss and the free translation, there is also a morpheme by morpheme representation given.

| (a) | titi3 | wa | korja | timbagrant, | i3 | wa | justu | (Ernest King 080688:1-5) |
| | titi=iʃi | wa | kori-a | timba=grant | iʃi | wa | justu | |
| | time=1PL | PAST | work-IPF | timber=grant | 1PL | PAST | PAST,HAB | |

(b)    nunu  timbə,  wat   en    rup   grestik,     ju    nim, ju    nok
       nunu  timba   wati  eni   rupu  gred=stik    ju    nimi ju    no=ko
       pull  timber  what  3PL   call  grade=stick  2SG   know 2SG   not=RES

(c)    horəbə        dida  ka?
       horo=abot     dida  ka
       hear=about    that  NEG

'When we worked on the timber-grants, we used to pull timber, what they call gradesticks. Do you know.. haven't you heard about that?'

(d)    ɛk  mɛten      man  mai,  hab   en..  stoko nangwa  so,   an   di..  tau
       ɛkɛ mɛtɛ=en    man  ma    habu  en    stoko nangwa  so    an   di    tau
       1SG with=one   man  IRR   have  one   stick long    so    and  the   rope

(e)    nangwa  kɛk   fa    hi    tut   so,   somtit        13 gre,   di   gre
       nangwa  kɛkɛ  fan   hiri  tutu  so    somtiti       13 gred   di   gred
       long    like  from  here  until so    sometimes     13 grade  the  grade

(f)    en rup,    ɛk   mɛt   ju    da en     gred.
       eni rupu   ɛkɛ  mɛtɛ  ju    da en     gred
       3PL call   1SG  with  2SG   be one    grade

'Me and another man would have a stick about this long, and the rope is as long as from here to over there. Sometimes (there are) 13 grades. The grades they call.. me and you is one grade.'

(g)    da sosiʃ       das   nun,  en    hondid   salid, fu    di    dak,
       da soso=iʃi    das   nunu  en    hondrid  salid  fu    di    daka
       BE thus=1PL    HAB   pull  one   hundred  solid  for   the   day

(h)    bibiru      iȝ     wa    briŋ   miŋkan         fu    di    dak, wɛl  i
       bibiru      iʃi    wa    bringi mingi=kandi    fu    di    daka wɛl  iʃi
       greenheart  1PL    PAST  bring  water=side     for   the   day  well IPL

(i)    da  ʃiŋi di    timbabos,    ju    suka    hor?
       das ʃingi di    timba=bos    ju    suku-a  horo
       HAB sing  the   timber=song  2SG   want-IPF hear

'This is how we pulled, one hundred solid for the day, greenheart we would bring to the waterside, for the day. Well we would sing the timber song. Do you want to hear it?'

(j)    daka daka, nani brɛku, mi jungu jalu, daka daka, nani skweru

| (k) | [then you go say] | háb | héb | datiʃ | mu | nau, | jɛn | fal |
| | | háb | héb | dat=iʃi | mu | nau | jɛndɛ | fala(?) |
| | then you go say | háb | héb | let=1PL | go | now | 2PL | follow(?) |

| (l) | jɛn | ma | nun, | titimba | tantɛ | wɛr | ju | ma | ʃingi | wɛ |
| | jɛndɛ | ma | nunu | titi=timba | tan-tɛ | wɛrɛ | ju | ma | ʃingi | wɛrɛ |
| | 2PL | IRR | pull | time=timber | stand-PF | again | 2SG | IRR | sing | again |

'Then you say: up! up! let us go now! you... you pull. When the timber stands (i.e. rests) again you sing again.'

Notes:

(a)-(c) The men pulled in pairs; the gradesticks are the sticks that the men on each side of the chain held on to pull.

(g)-(i) Greenheart (Ocotea rodiaei): a hardwood. *hondid* and *salid* are Guyanese Creole loans. The formative *bos* is only used in the combination *timbabos*.

(j) According to EK and other men, *daka daka, nani brɛku* refers to the break of day. *daka* means 'day' in BD, and *brɛku* can be related to BD *brɛkɛ* (the final *u* is a rhyming vowel), but the meaning of *nani* is unknown. Note also that BD uses *bidaka*, not a construction of the type *\*daka brɛkɛ*, for 'daybreak'. Everyone agrees that *mi jungu jalu* means 'my young lady'. *mi* would have to be Guyanese Creole (BD has *ɛkɛ*, SD has *ɛk* for 1SG), *jungu* is BD (compare SD *junk*), while *jalu* probably represents a adaption of Arawak *hiaro* 'woman', not unlikely in view of the instability of /r/ in AR as well as in BD: both have [l] as an allophone of /r/. *skwer* in the next line is Guyanese Creole for squaring timber.

## Further reading

Kouwenberg (1994) contains a comprehensive grammar, a vocabulary and a number of texts. Smith, Robertson and Williamson (1987) and Kouwenberg (1992) discuss the Ịjọ element in the language. Bruyn & Veenstra (1993) compare BD to other Dutch creoles.

# Part IV
# Grammatical features

# 20 TMA particles and auxiliaries

Peter Bakker, Marike Post and Hein van der Voort

## 20.1 Introduction

The categories of tense, mood and aspect are a universal phenomenon in languages, but their role in the grammar and the way they are expressed varies. They may be marked morphologically (e.g. by inflection on the verb) or syntactically, (e.g. by pre- or postverbal markers and/or auxiliaries), but may also be expressed in a purely lexical manner (e.g. by using an adverbial expression). Sometimes they are not expressed at all, and then their interpretation depends on context and situation. What is meant by the terms tense, mood and aspect? Here we give a short explanation of the three terms:

**Tense.** The term tense refers to the indication of the time of an utterance in relation to the time of the event described by this utterance. The action or event may have taken place already (past tense), may take place later (future tense) or may take place at this very moment (present tense). These tense distinctions can be refined, e.g. **remote past** vs. **recent past** etc. Tense may be **absolute** in that it is defined in relation to the time of the moment of speech, or **relative** when the reference of a moment in time is related to some other point in time.

**Mood.** Mood presents a statement about the truth or realization of a state or event. It refers to the attitude of the speaker or of one of the persons involved in the situation described. Examples of moods are: realis, irrealis, possibility, acceptability, necessity, obligation.

**Aspect.** The term aspect refers to the internal temporal constituency of an event or state. An action may take place repeatedly or once, or during a long or short time. Also an action or event may be presented from an external or internal point of view. Examples of some common types of aspect in languages are perfective, durative, habitual, iterative, ingressive, progressive etc.

In creole languages, the categories tense, mood and aspect (henceforth TMA) are generally expressed by preverbal markers and adverbial elements, but as we will see later on, the use of modal auxiliaries, serial verb constructions (see chapter 23), and verb suffixes also represent possible strategies.

In pidgins, which tend to lack a grammaticalized TMA system, adverbial expressions may serve to express these notions. In some expanded pidgins such as Tok Pisin, West African English (Singler 1990b), but not Chinook Jargon (Anthony Grant p.c.), we find preverbal

TMA particles with semantic ranges reminiscent of those of creoles. However, as argued in chapter 3, these expanded pidgins had already acquired some creole-like properties, which makes it reasonable not to regard them as still resembling restricted pidgins, but having properties similar to those of true creoles.

## 20.2  The TMA system in creoles

The TMA systems of creole languages play a central role in creole studies. These languages often show remarkable similarities in their TMA systems, and in such a way that these may be regarded as distinguishing features of creole languages in general. These similarities include semantic and syntactic aspects. For instance: in creole languages there is a limited number of grammaticalized TMA morphemes, which are nearly always preverbal, which always appear in the same order and which apparently have the same semantic values. These similarities call for an explanation, and much research has indeed focused on creole TMA. Another reason for its central role is the fact that the creole TMA system differs from what is typologically common for such systems.

Theoretically it could have been the case that creoles, being natural languages (albeit with a specific history and time of genesis) would have had the same TMA system as found elsewhere in the languages of the world. This appears not to be the case, however. Creole TMA particles typically display the order: Tense-Mood-Aspect-Verb stem. In cross-linguistic research on the morphological expression of TMA markers (Bybee 1985), however, the order is different in one crucial respect: tense morphemes are almost always closer (88% in the relevant subset of Bybee's sample) to the stem than mood morphemes. In other words, whereas creole languages display the order TMA-verb, non-creole languages tend to display the order MTA-verb. Of course there are also many languages where tense, mood and/or aspect are expressed in other ways than through pre-verbal particles.

This typologically uncommon TMA system is found in creole languages which emerged in geographically separate places, under different circumstances, and with completely unrelated input languages. In this chapter we will show that some creoles with different superstrate languages appear to have identical core systems. We will also show that not all creoles share exactly the same system, and that they may also mark distinctions not present in the core system.

## 20.3  Genesis of the TMA system in creoles

Many hypotheses have been put forward to explain why creoles show such strong similarities in spite of their different lexifier languages.

One hypothesis is that the creole TMA system is derived from a putative nautical Portuguese proto-pidgin (e.g. Thompson 1961 and chapter 8). This is difficult to sustain since it is doubtful that such a system actually existed in this pidgin; as mentioned before, only expanded pidgins have grammatical expression of TMA.

Another hypothesis, proposed for French-based creoles e.g. in Kraan (1993) is that the strong lexical and semantic correspondence between Haitian and Seychelles creole TMA are due to the common etymological sources of words or expressions from 16th and 17th century French. Although Kraan found historical evidence for some of the markers, her hypothesis does not explain why the French-based creoles have TMA systems very similar to creoles based on other languages.

Another hypothesis is that TMA systems of the Atlantic creoles would be inherited from the substrate languages involved (Alleyne 1980; see chapter 9). West African languages display similar (though not identical) TMA systems, and this was continued in the Caribbean creoles. However, Alleyne does not deal with the Indian Ocean creoles and Pacific creoles, which have similar systems.

Universalist hypotheses have been put forward as explanations since the 1970s, e.g. Kay & Sankoff (1974). Bickerton (1974) is the most outspoken defender of a universal theory, claiming TMA is biologically encoded in the brain (language bioprogram, see chapter 11). Muysken (1981) suggests the creole system is the universal semantically unmarked way to express TMA. Givón (1982) claims that at least the ordering is semantically determined: aspect has semantic scope only over the verb, mood has scope over the whole proposition (including aspect) and tense puts the proposition in a wider, discourse setting. Notice that this claim contradicts Bybee's findings mentioned above. Labov (1990) [1971] claims that the development of tense markers from temporal adverbs is due to the need for stylistic flexibility, which adverbs lack.

At this point, the origin of creole TMA remains a matter of controversy with a wide variety of current opinions. A more comprehensive approach should not only account for the general core system, but it should also be able to relate this to non-core TMA elements and deal with exceptions.

## 20.4  The creole core TMA system

In this section we will describe the core system of two creoles: Saramaccan (see chapter 14) and Fa d'Ambu (see chapter 16). For this purpose we will use the analysis of the creole core TMA system proposed by Bickerton (1981) as a descriptive framework, because it gives exact definitions of the semantics involved. The term **core TMA system** is to be understood as pertaining only to a system of grammaticalized markers of TMA. Bickerton's description was not based on these languages. However, they both seem to possess a system fitting this description to a certain extent.

As far as tense is concerned, the reference point ('tense locus' in Chung & Timberlake 1985) is not 'point present' as in the European languages like English, French and Portuguese (which distinguish roughly past, present and future), but the time of the event under discussion. This means that in creoles we are dealing almost exclusively with 'relative tense'.

As far as mood is concerned, real events are distinguished from non-real events. Realis events have actually occurred or are occurring at the moment of speaking; irrealis events are imagined, conditional or future events. A special preverbal morpheme marks irrealis events, and realis events are unmarked.

As far as aspect is concerned, nonpunctual events (which occur over a stretch of time or repeatedly) are distinguished from punctual events (which occur at one specific point in time and not over a long time). Nonpunctual events are marked with a preverbal morpheme, while punctual events are left unmarked.

Thus, there are three classes of preverbal morphemes in Bickerton's prototypical system and they mark [+anterior] tense, [+irrealis] mood, [+nonpunctual] aspect. These morphemes may occur in all possible combinations, always in the same order, and yielding predictable semantic distinctions. Bickerton (1981) formulates ten characteristics for these creole TMA markers, which are mentioned below. The accompanying examples are taken from Saramaccan (examples a) and Fa d'Ambu (examples b):

A.  The zero form of verbs marks simple past for non-stative verbs and nonpast for state verbs .

(1)     a.   Mi nján dí físi.
             'I ate the fish.'
        b.   Ineni tabaya.
             'They worked.'


(2)     a.   Mi lóbi dí físi.
             'I love the fish.'
        b.   Bo sa namina kitsyi.
             'You are a little child.'


B.  A marker of anterior tense indicates past for state verbs and past-before-past, or past, for non-stative verbs.

(3)     a.   Mi **bi**-nján dí físi.
             'I had eaten/I ate the fish.'

    b.   Ineni **bi** tabaya.
        'They had worked.'

(4)    a.   Mi **bi**-lóbi dí físi.
        'I loved the fish.'
     b.   Bo **bi** sa namina kitsyi.
        'You were a little child.'

C.   A marker of irrealis mood indicates 'unreal time' (= future, conditional, subjunctives, etc.) for all verbs.

(5)    a.   Mi **o**-nján dí físi.
        'I will/would eat the fish.'
     b.   Ineni **ske** tabaya.
        'They will go to work.'

(6)    a.   Mi **o**-lóbi dí físi.
        'I will/would love the fish.'
     b.   Bo **ske** sa namina kitsyi.
        'You will be a little child.'

D.   A marker of nonpunctual aspect indicates durative, habitual or iterative aspect and is indifferent to the nonpast-past distinction.

(7)    a.   Mi **tá**-nján dí físi.
        'I am eating fish/I eat fish habitually.'
     b.   Ineni **xa** tabaya.
        'They work (habitually).'

(8)    a.   A tá saí dέ.
        'He is there.'
     b.   Se a **xa** sa iai.
        'And one (the people) is there.'

E.   All markers are in preverbal position.

F.   The markers can be combined, but in an invariant ordering, which is 1. anterior TENSE, 2. irrealis MOOD, 3. nonpunctual ASPECT.

G. The meaning of anterior + irrealis is 'an unrealized event in the past'.

(9)  a.  Mi **bi-o-**nján dí físi.
         'I would have eaten the fish.'
     b.  Ineni **bi ske** tabaya.
         'They would have worked. / They would have gone to work.'

(10) a.  Mi **bi-o-**lóbi dí físi.
         'I would have loved the fish.'
     b.  [Not attested]

H. The meaning of anterior + irrealis + nonpunctual is 'an unrealized event in the past, of a nonpunctual nature', something like '[if only] x would have gone on doing y.'

(11) a.  Mi **bi-o-tá-**nján dí físi.
         'I would have been eating the fish.'
     b.  Ineni **bi ske xa** tabaya.
         'They would have been working.'

I. The meaning of anterior + nonpunctual is 'a durative action or a series of nondurative actions taking place either before some other event under discussion, or during a period of time regarded as definitively closed.'

(12) a.  Mi **bi-tá-**nján dí físi.
         'I was/ had been eating the fish.'
     b.  Ineni **bi xa** tabaya.
         'They worked (habitually).'

J. The meaning of irrealis + nonpunctual is future progressive.

(13) a.  Mi **o-tá-**nján dí físi.
         'I will be eating the fish.'
     b.  Ineni **ske xa** tabaya.
         'They will be working.'

The English translations are, of course, approximations. As regards the terms non-punctual and irrealis, they should be interpreted in their most abstract sense.

Apparently, Saramaccan and Fa d'Ambu conform to the creole TMA pattern as given by Bickerton. However, this only covers the core of their TMA systems. In fact, most creoles do not conform to the ideal pattern. In the following section we will present a number of deviations and extensions, on the basis of Negerhollands, Saramaccan, Fa d'Ambu, and Berbice Dutch.

## 20.5 Negerhollands and categorical distinctions

The core system of Negerhollands deviates from those of the other creole languages. First, it does not display the characteristic tense difference in non-stative (a) and state (b) verbs as suggested under (B) in 20.4 above. In both cases, the anterior marker marks past tense. As regards zero marking of non-stative indicative verbs, the Negerhollands material tends to have a past tense interpretation. However, this must be due to the fact that in the narrative type of material recorded by De Josselin de Jong (1926) past is almost always marked proleptically (already earlier on in the discourse), yielding a 'historical present', rather than to an inherent (creole) property of Negerhollands. Present tense interpretation of zero-marked non-stative verbs is encountered in some rare cases in De Josselin de Jong (1926) and often in 18th and 19th century material. Furthermore, overt marking of the category [+non-punctual] implies that the unmarked case is [punctual]. Perfective, as is rightly noticed in Singler (1990c), is equal to the notion 'punctual', which should not require overt marking. However, the absence of perfective *ka* in Negerhollands renders the proposition imperfective.

In contrast to many other markers, *ka* is found in nearly all possible combinations and occurs certainly no less frequently than the others, often being encountered on occasions where other creoles would not use a perfective marker. For example the 'unrealized condition in the past' is not realized by the anterior + irrealis markers, but rather by the irrealis + perfective (with anteriority marked earlier on in the sentence) or anterior + irrealis + perfective (which implies a punctual interpretation, as we have said above) markers:

(14)  Ju    **sa**   **kā**   drā   di    a ju    han.          (Negerhollands: 1926)
      2SG   IRR   PERF  carry  DET   in 2SG  hand
      'You should have carried this in your hands.'

Negerhollands, the creole nature of which is above question, is then in contradiction with several of the markedness properties of Bickerton's creole TMA prototype.

Also, the strict categorial distinction between T, M and A that Bickerton's analysis implies, does not always reflect reality. For instance, Negerhollands *le*, which in a later stage became homophonous with irrealis *lo*, and which is traditionally (including Van Name 1871) regarded as a present tense marker, is nowadays (in its non-modal use) often interpreted as a marker of progressive aspect. Still, it must not be forgotten that there is a logical relationship between present tense, and incompletive aspect. These differences between the analyses of *le/lo* in the various grammatical sketches throughout the centuries are not justified by any attestable historical development of the meaning of these particles (which does not mean that there were no other developments involving *le/lo*). Rather, they may serve to illustrate what Chung & Timberlake (1985) mean by the interaction between tense and aspect, tense and mood, and also aspect and mood, and the impossibility of keeping the categories neatly separated, as Bickerton attempts to do.

## 20.6 Extensions: Modality

Saramaccan has a number of mood-marking and aspect-marking morphemes in addition to the three described for the core system. Some of these have exact equivalents in other creole languages, whereas others seem to occur only in Saramaccan.

Saramaccan has a mood morpheme marking 'obligation' (deontic mood). In Saramaccan this preverbal morpheme is *fu*:

(15)  a.  A **fu** nján dí físi.                                               (Saramaccan)
          'He must/should eat the fish.'
      b.  A **fu** lóbi dí físi.
          'He should love the fish.'

Deontic mood morphemes are common in creoles. In Saramaccan there is another preverbal morpheme marking deontic mood, which is *músu*:

(16)  a.  A **músu** nján dí físi.                                            (Saramaccan)
          'He has to eat the fish.'
      b.  A **músu** lóbi dí físi.
          'He has to love the fish.'

The difference between (15b) and (16b) is that (15b) indicates a (moral) obligation imposed by the speaker and that (16b) is seen as a general obligation or necessity.

In Negerhollands, the auxiliary verb *kan* 'can' has in some usages acquired the sense of a habitual marker, with which it is attested in both Old and New Negerhollands:

(17)  Mi **kan** verloor altit.                                    (Negerhollands: 1770)
      1SG HAB  lose   always
      'I always lose.'


(18)  En   am   a    **kan** dif  də   blaŋku ši   kalkún.    (Negerhollands: 1926)
      and  3SG  ANT  HAB  steal the  White  3PL  turkey
      'And he used to steal the Whites' turkeys'.


## 20.7 Interaction of auxiliary and TMA in Fa d'Ambu

As far as aspect marking is concerned, the preverbal Fa d'Ambu TMA system is a rather complex one, much more than one might conclude on the basis of the examples listed in 20.4. These examples suggest that in Fa d'Ambu there is only one aspect marker, *xa*, which indicates non-punctuality. This conclusion would be too simple. In fact, Fa d'Ambu has two preverbal aspect marking elements: the auxiliary *sa* and the core system marker *xa*, which may appear independently or in combination with another element. When used together, they may appear as *sa xa*, which merges and surfaces as *sxa*, or as *xa sa*.

The difference between the two aspect markers is as follows: the marker *xa* (*ga* in combination with 1SG) forms sentences with a non-punctual or imperfective aspect. The auxiliary *sa* marks the proposition as 'perfective', 'as a whole'. Compare the next examples:


(19)  Ineni  **xa** tabaya.                                        (Fa d'Ambu)
      3PL    XA  work
      'They work (normally).'


(20)  Ineni  **sa** tabaya.
      3PL    SA  work
      'They work.'


When the markers appear combined, the respective orders, *xa sa* and *sa xa*, yield (partly) different interpretations. The most common combination and probably the least marked one is *sa xa* (*sxa*), but the combination *xa sa* is not rare either.

The two combinations have in common that they are used to indicate an event as taking place within a non-punctual, yet delimited span of time, which results in a progressive reading of the sentence. The difference between them lies in the relative time references assigned to the respective expressions. The combination *sa xa* (*sxa*) reflects an 'imperfective' progressive. It has an implicit starting point but no definite end point. It describes the action as seen 'from the inside': *xa* marks the verb for indefinite duration, while *sa* marks the combination of *xa* with the verb as effectively taking place but seen 'from the outside'. The result is that the action is to be seen as having a definite starting point, which may lie in the past (x is already doing it at this moment) or in the present (x is about to do it), and an indefinite end point.

The combination *xa sa* indicates a 'perfective' progressive. It describes the action as 'seen as a whole', without an explicit starting point and again with a durative time span. In this combination *xa* is combined with the auxiliary *sa*, which changes the 'perfective' aspect of *sa* into a 'perfective' carrying a durative time span with it. When this combined aspect is assigned to the verb, it provides the meaning of an action seen as a whole but with an open starting point and an open time span as far as its duration is concerned. Compare the following examples:

(21)    Zwan  **sxa**      kumu   ampan.                              (Fa d'Ambu)
        John  SA=XA    eat     bread
        'John is eating bread.'

(22)    se      na=pe      **xa sa** ma    masyivín, …
        and    PL=adult  XA SA take  child
        'and the adults took the children, …'

The particle *xa* is not restricted to one occurrence in a clause. It may as well occur twice with successive verbs. The meaning of such a construction would be: an action 'seen as a whole' but with an implicit starting point and an implicit ending. Compare the next example:

(23)    Amu   **ga sxa**    zuda   ineni.                             (Fa d'Ambu)
        ISG     XA SA=XA help   3PL
        'I always helped them.'

From the above it can be concluded that the markers *xa* and *sa* are both indispensable to the description of the aspect marking system in Fa d'Ambu. *Xa* can be seen as a fully grammaticalized preverbal marker, and thus as forming part of the core system, whereas *sa* is formally an auxiliary but functions as an integrated part of the system.

## 20.8 Serial completives

Many creoles have an aspectual element marking completion of the action. In contrast to other markers this one is not preverbal, but it occurs at the end of the sentence. In some languages it can be analyzed as a serial verb (see chapter 23), in others as an adverb. In Saramaccan this element is *káá* (etymologically derived from Portuguese *acabar* 'to finish'), as in the following example:

(24)     A nján di físi **káá**.                                                          (Saramaccan)
         'He already ate the fish.'

In other creoles this sentence-final morpheme is also (etymologically) related to a verb meaning 'finish' or 'done'. In Berbice Dutch this morpheme is *fama*, which derives from Eastern Ịjọ (Kouwenberg 1994):

(25)     Tutu   a   was-tɛ        fama,      a   skono.                     (Berbice Dutch)
         when   it   wash-PERF   finish,    it   clean
         'When the washing is done, it is clean.'

Completive aspect can be expressed in Negerhollands by *kaba* (again from the Portuguese verb *acabar* 'to finish'). Although this form is mainly found as a clause final aspect marker, its verbal origin is evident from its appearance as the only predicative element in sentence (27):

(26)     wani  sini   **a**    dig    di    grāf   **kabā**, ...              (Negerhollands: 1926)
         when   3PL    ANT    dig    the    grave  finish
         'when they had dug the grave, ...'

(27)     Die    **ka**    **kabae**.                                          (Negerhollands: 1770)
         DET    PERF    finish
         'It is over/finished.'

It is possible that it developed into an aspect marker from its use as a predicate in serial constructions. It is, in fact, sometimes difficult to judge whether it still is part of such a construction.

(28)     tē   weni  am    **kabā** kap    di    bus                          (Negerhollands: 1926)
         till  when  3SG   finish  cut    DET   wood
         'until when he had cut the wood'

| (29) | en | as Em | **a** | **ka** | wasch | sender | die | Voeten | **kabba,...** |
|---|---|---|---|---|---|---|---|---|---|
| | and | as 3SG | ANT | PERF | wash | 3PL | DET | foot-pl | finish |

'and now as He had washed their feet,...'                    (Negerhollands: c. 1780)

## 20.9  Conclusion

Although there is indeed a core TMA system which is to a large extent shared by unrelated creoles, many creoles in fact deviate from most descriptions of this core. However, one may conclude that all creoles possess a grammaticalized TMA system consisting of at least three markers: one for tense, one for mood and one for aspect (but see chapter 18). Apparently, these markers are always placed in an invariant order immediately preceding the verb stem. In some rare cases they may follow the verb. If negation is involved in the sentence, this element will generally appear immediately before the preverbal TMA markers.

The morpho-syntactic status of these markers is an item of some discussion between linguists. This is partly due to the different behavior of the markers across creoles. In some creoles there are reasons to regard the appearance of preverbal TMA markers as syntactic phenomena and therefore regard the markers as particles or perhaps clitics. In other creoles there are indications that the markers are morphological elements, prefixes.

Apart from the core system, other strategies are also used to indicate TMA. The most common one is the use of an adverbial expression, a modal verb or, in case of the completive, the use of a serial verb. Furthermore, in some cases auxiliaries are combined with TMA markers for the purposes of aspect marking. It is not always easy to decide whether a marker should be regarded as forming part of the grammaticalized core system or as belonging to some other syntactic construction type.

Although much work has been done to clarify the complexities of the creole TMA core system, much more research will be necessary to obtain a deeper insight. In particular, aberrant systems should be taken into serious consideration, as they have mostly been used as arguments against the existence of a creole TMA core system so far.

### Further reading

There is one collection dealing exclusively with pidgin and creole TMA systems: Singler (1990b). There are also comparative discussions of creole TMA, e.g. Muysken (1981a) and Givón (1982), and many descriptive studies. As for TMA in non-creole languages, some influential works are Comrie (1976, 1985). For TMA typology in general, see Chung & Timberlake (1985) and for morphological facets see Bybee (1985). An interesting volume of a general nature is also Hopper (1982). Some recent research dealing with Negerhollands TMA is found in Stolz (1986, 1987a) and Bruyn & Veenstra (1993).

## 21.1 Introduction: the loss of articles and plural morphemes

In earlier chapters the loss of inflectional morphology and other non-salient grammatical elements has been mentioned as one of the processes influencing the shape of pidgin and creole languages. The consequences of such loss can also be observed in the structure of the NP, and the distinctions playing a role in the expression of reference.

The European languages which provided the lexicon for many creoles all have articles conveying information on the grammatical categories of definiteness, number, gender or case. This information is not always coded in a transparent way. For example, French *les* is a portmanteau morpheme indicating [+plural] and [+definite] at the same time. Such complex form-function relationships, together with the fact that articles do not have their own semantic content and are often not very salient perceptually, leads to them frequently getting lost. The English determiner system, on the other hand, is somewhat more transparent. This may explain the fact that in many English-lexifier creole languages there is a determiner *di*, probably a reflex of the emphatic article ([ði]), whereas French *le*, *la*, and *les* are generally lost as articles. Their phonetic form may survive, as in Haitian *lari* 'street' < French *la rue*. Here, however, *la-* is part of the noun, not a separate morpheme expressing definiteness or number. So, *lari* can be preceded by the indefinite article *youn* to refer to 'a street'.

Inflectional plural endings do not survive in creole languages in general, although in some acrolectal varieties the plural morphology of the superstrate language is found. So, in Jamaican English Creole *di gyalz* 'the girls' is possible alongside the regular creole form *di gyal-dem* (Bailey 1966).

Where elements from the lexifier language have been retained, their function may differ from that in the source language. In the following sections we will look at how and to what extent the loss of plural morphology, articles, and possession markers has been compensated for in various creole languages, devoting special attention to the case of Sranan.

## 21.2 Number marking

While a language can easily dispense with a grammatical gender distinction, some mechanism to express number is a feature it would seem more meaningful to have.

In pidgins number is often not marked on the noun, but if needed, it can be expressed by numerals and words denoting 'many/much', 'heaps of', and so forth. In Hausa Pidgin for example, a noun can be followed by *deyawa*, derived from standard Hausa *da yawā* 'many, in large quantity' (Heine 1973). In the Indian Ocean French creoles, *ban*, from *une bande de*, 'a bunch of', has developed into a plural marker (Manessy 1985).

As reduplication, especially the repetition of whole words, is a phenomenon often regarded as typical of pidgins and creoles, it could be expected to signify plurality, as an iconic representation of the numbers of the entity referred to. As remarked upon in chapter 3, reduplication is in fact quite rare in pidgins, and there seems to be no case in which it has evolved into a regular plural-marking mechanism. In those creole languages which use reduplication in this function, it conveys specialized meanings, such as distributive plural. In Berbice Dutch, reduplication exists alongside the general plural suffix *-apu* (< Eastern Ịjọ [+human] pluralizer *-apụ*; see chapters 9 and 19). The use of reduplication emphasizes the individuality of several occurrences of the noun involved, as in *boʃboʃ* [bush-bush] 'separate bundles' (Kouwenberg 1994).

In Ndjuka, reduplication can be used to stress abundancy:

(1)     den    peesipeesi                                    (Huttar & Huttar 1992)
        DEF.PL place-place
        'all those many places'

In (1), there is a plural determiner present as well, *den*, which has the same form as the third person plural pronoun. The use of a plural pronoun to mark plural is a strategy employed in many creoles, and is sometimes attributed to substrate influence (e.g. Boretzky 1983). The pronouns themselves are often reflexes of oblique forms in the lexifier languages. For example, Ndjuka *den* is derived from English *them*, and Haitian *yo* 'they, them' from French *eux* 'them'.

(2)    a.   tab    (la)**yo**                                     (Haitian)
             table  (DEF )-PL
             'the tables'

       b.   e      kas-**nan**                                    (Papiamento)
             DEF    house-PL
             'the houses'

       c.   di     gyal-**dem**      or:   **dem**     gyal         (Jamaican)
             DEF    girl-PL                 DEF.PL    girl
             'the girls'

d. **den**       bon                                                (Sranan)
   DEF.PL    tree
   'the trees'

Nouns with a plural meaning are not always marked as such morphosyntactically. In Papiamento, the use of *-nan* is obligatory when a plural NP is definite, i.e. when it contains a definite article, demonstrative, or possessive pronoun (3a). With indefinite NPs plural is only coded if there is no other indication of plurality in the same clause, as in (3b). In (3c) however, plurality can be inferred from the presence of *hopi* 'many', and *-nan* is not allowed. With generic NPs, plural is never marked (3d).

(3)   a. tur    su       yu-**nan**    (*tur su yu)                     (Dijkhoff 1983b)
         all    3SGPOSS   child-PL
         'all his children'

      b. Kachó-**nan** a    keda  grita  henter  anochi.
         dog-PL        PAST  stay  scream  whole   night
         'Dogs kept barking all night.'

      c. hopi  buki  (*hopi buki-**nan**)
         many  book
         'many books'

      d. Muhé  ta   kompañera       di  homber. (*Muhé-**nan** ... homber-**nan**.)
         women COP  companion=FEM   of  man
         'A woman (women) is (are) the companion(s) of a man (men).'

In Jamaican, as in Papiamento, indefinite NPs cannot contain the plural marker if plural is already indicated. Definite NPs, however, **can** contain a numeral as well as the plural marker: *di tuu hous(-dem)* 'the two houses'.

In several creoles, including Papiamento and Jamaican, the morpheme expressing plural comes after the noun and can be regarded as a clitic-like element. In certain varieties of Jamaican *dem* may precede the noun as a determiner (2c).

Ndjuka and Sranan *den* (1 and 2d) always occurs before the noun. It expresses not only plurality but definiteness as well; here again, definiteness and plural marking are tightly connected.

In 18th-century Sranan plural marking is much less extensive than in the modern language. Since the earliest sources, the use of *den* has been increasing gradually. A similar development, which can be interpreted as grammaticalization (see chapter 10.4), has also taken place in Tok Pisin. Mühlhäusler (1981, 1986) distinguishes various factors favouring the use of the plural marker *ol* (< English *all*) in stabilizing Tok Pisin. In the sources he studied, nouns denoting humans tended to be marked for plural, while nouns occurring after a preposition were marked less often than nouns in subject or object position. According to Mühlhäusler, the route of the extension of plural marking to more and more contexts in Tok Pisin is not influenced by the lexifier or substrate languages but rather reflects universal semantic and pragmatic factors, such as animacy and pragmatic relevance.

The contexts in which plural is marked and the morphosyntactic means of doing this vary across the creole languages. A feature shared by many creoles is that nouns that are not marked for plural may have plural reference nevertheless. In some cases, a numeral or quantifier renders the coding of plurality semantically redundant, and morphosyntactic marking is not necessary or even impossible. In other cases, plurality has to be inferred from the context.

(4)  Mi tin   ku laba  **outo**  ainda.                    (Papiamento. Muller 1989)
     1SG have  to wash car     still
     'I still have to wash the car / cars.'

Although not marked for plural, *outo* may get a plural reading if, for example, the hearer knows that the speaker earns money washing cars. In other cases the choice of either a singular or a plural interpretation is not relevant. For example, *muhé* in (3d) is generic, and can therefore be regarded as neutral with respect to number, or, in the terminology of Mufwene (1981, 1986b), as non-individuated. The notion of (non)individuation is comparable to the more familiar count-mass distinction. Count versus mass can be conceived of as a lexical feature: *table* is [+count], *milk* is [-count]. Individuation, on the other hand, pertains not to a certain noun, but to the usage of a noun in a certain context. In English, a few nouns, such as *cake*, can be either [+count] or [-count], and can occur in an individuated NP - e.g. *How many cakes did he eat?* - or in a non-individuated one - e.g. *How much cake did he eat?* Mufwene argues that in certain languages, including the basilectal varieties of Gullah and Jamaican creole, any noun can be used as individuated or as non-individuated. Articles and plural marking occur only in individuated NPs. With non-individuated nouns, the distinction between singular and plural is irrelevant - just as with mass nouns. While Jamaican *buk* can be regarded as a count noun, it can be used as non-individuated, and as such it is not marked for plural:

(5)  **Buk**  de       aal   uova di   tiebl ina   im   afis.      (Mufwene 1986b)
     book  COP=LOC all   over the  table 3SG  his  office
     'Books were all over the table in his office.'

Individuation may be relevant for plural marking and article usage in other creole languages as well.

## 21.3  Articles

NPS without any determiner occur rather frequently in many creole languages. In the approach proposed by Mufwene the absence of an article (henceforth 'zero-article' for short) corresponds to non-individuation, as referred to in the previous section. Non-individuation is comparable to what is called non-specificity by Bickerton (1981, 1984), who distinguishes generic NPS, NPS within the scope of negation, and cases where the exact identity of an existing referent is either unknown or irrelevant as non-specific. On the basis of Hawaiian Creole English, Bickerton has proposed that in the prototypical creole it is only NPS with specific reference that contain an article, and that the zero-article corresponds to non-specificity. This is not borne out in all creole languages, however. In Haitian and modern Sranan, for example, the use of articles is not restricted to specific NPS.

In 18th-century Sranan, where article usage is rather limited in general, some non-specific NPS contain a determiner as well:

(6)   Wi no   doe   **wan**   ogeri.                          (Sranan. Van Dyk c.1765)
      IPL NEG  do    DET     harm
      'We didn't do anything wrong.'

The NP *wan ogeri* is in the scope of negation, hence non-specific, and it is difficult to see how such an NP can be meant to refer to individual members of a set. The use of *wan* in (6) must rather be attributed to emphasis. In other cases as well, the occurrence of *wan* can be considered as marked in some sense, the unmarked option being no article. This is understandable if we take into account that *wan* is the reflex of English *one*. The development of the lowest numeral in the direction of indefinite article, often attested cross-linguistically, proceeds gradually (Givón 1981). As long as this development was not completed, as in 18th-century Sranan, *wan* was not just a plain article, but may have conveyed a special meaning, such as emphasis. Conversely, it is absent from many indefinite singular NPS.

Zero-articles in 18th-century Sranan are abundant as well with NPS of which the referent can be regarded as known, either because it is mentioned before, or through knowledge of the situation or general knowledge. In such cases, not *wan*, but definite *da* (sg.) or *den* (pl.) would be the alternative.

In early Sranan, as in other creoles, definite NPS inside a PP often lack an article:

(7)    Da koffi no    tan    klari **na**    **tappe**    **tafelen.**                (Van Dyk c1765)
       the coffee NEG    stay    ready LOC    top/on    table
       'The coffee was not standing ready on the table.'

As the specific identity of nouns inside PPs is often not important, Bickerton's non-specificity or Mufwene's non-individuation may explain the frequent occurrence of bare nouns after
a preposition, even if the noun can be assumed to have definite reference, as with *tafelen*
in (7).

   It is not always the case that zero-articles can be explained in terms of individual identity.
In (8), the speaker wants to travel from the town to his plantation:

(8)    Myki    Koridon go hakkesi    na da    misi disi    libi    na zy    kerki
       make    Koridon go ask        to the    miss REL    live    at side    church
       offe    a        plessi    mi    kan    kisi    passi    lange **boote.** (Van Dyk c1765)
       if    3SGNOM    (be-)good    1SG    can    get    journey    with boat
       'Have Koridon go and ask the young lady who lives next to the church, if she would be so
       kind to let me travel with her boat.'
       (Van Dyk: '[...] of ik met haar Boot mag meê gaan.')

Note that the speaker wants to travel with a certain boat, not just 'by boat'. Cases like (8)
show that *da* is not obligatory with definite NPs, even if the individual identity of the
referent is pragmatically relevant.

   Just as in 18th-century Sranan the usage of *wan* is marked in comparison with a bare
noun, so is the use of *da*. In fact, *da* can sometimes be regarded as a demonstrative rather
than a definite article. This is in line with the assumption that *da* is not derived from the
English article *the*, but that it is the reduced form of *dati*, which is, in its turn, derived from
English *that*. Like the development of the numeral 'one' to an indefinite article, the shift
from demonstrative to definite article is a common one, and not restricted to creole languages.

   Both developments can be regarded as instances of grammaticalization, be it without
syntactic reanalysis (see e.g. Heine et al. 1991). The demonstrative and the numeral gradually
lose their deictic and numeral features and evolve into articles. As long as they have not
become plain articles, they alternate with zero. And as long as the overt determiners are not
used categorically they keep a stronger value, such as demonstrative or emphatic. If there
is no reason to use *wan*, *da*, or *den* to give emphasis, to single out a referent, or for other
purposes, the bare noun will suffice.

   Bare nouns occur with a considerable higher frequency in early Sranan than in the present-day language. This indicates that if we are looking for a 'typical creole' system we have to be careful in comparing languages: they might be in different stages of development with regard to articles. Also, one may doubt whether the development proceeds in exactly the same way in different languages. The case of early Sranan illustrates that there is not always a one-to-one correspondence between zero-articles and non-specificity as proposed by Bickerton, nor between bare nouns and non-individuation, as suggested by Mufwene. Although neither of these notions can fully account for the distribution of determiners in early Sranan, both appear to capture a factor influencing the presence or absence of articles, and, especially in combination with a diachronic perspective, provide a useful perspective for investigating article usage in creole languages.

## 21.4 Demonstratives

In section 21.3 it was mentioned that the early Sranan determiner *da* sometimes functions as a demonstrative. Note that the source of the 18th-century plural determiner *den* - them - may serve as a demonstrative in substandard English. In Sranan it is comparable to *da* in so far as it is not obligatory, and that, concomitantly, its presence may convey not only plurality and definiteness but also emphasis, or deixis. Alongside *da* and *den*, there are the demonstratives *disi* (< *this*) and *dati* (< *that*). Whereas *disi* is used both attributively and as an independent pronoun, in 18th-century Sranan *dati* has only the latter function, as in *wi du dati* 'we did that'. Inside NPs, *dati* is not used, but *da* or *den* are; both are sometimes translated as demonstratives. With the extension of the use of *da* and *den* as plain articles in the course of time, the demonstrative force of these forms diminishes. Around 1800, *dati* comes to function as a noun-modifying demonstrative, as the non-proximal counterpart of demonstrative *disi*. What we see here is a development with a cyclic aspect: what was originally derived from a demonstrative becomes, in the reduced form *da*, a definite article, thereby losing its demonstrative value. The resulting gap is filled by the full form *dati*, the use of which is extended from independent pronominal to attributive demonstrative. In this function, it follows the noun. Also *disi*, predominantly preceding the noun in the 18th-century sources, occurs more and more in postnominal position. Besides *disi* and *dati*, the adverbs *dyà* 'here' and *drape* 'there' can be used after a noun to express deixis.

| (9) | a. | den | pikin **disi** / **dyà** | (19/20th-century Sranan) |
|---|---|---|---|---|
| | | DEF.PL | child this / here | |
| | | 'these children' | | |
| | b. | den | pikin **dati** / **drape** | |
| | | DEF.PL | child that / there | |
| | | 'those children' | | |

Not only in Sranan but in many Atlantic creoles the demonstrative element occurs after the noun. However, its position relative to other elements of the NP is not always the same. The postnominal Sranan demonstrative does not interfere with the plural article *den*, which comes before the noun. In Papiamento, the deictic element *aki* (< Portuguese *aqui* 'here') comes after the plural marker *-nan*, whereas in Haitian *sa* (< French *ça* 'that') precedes the phrase-final determiner.

(10)    e    mucha-nan   **aki**                              (Papiamento)
        the child-PL    this/here
        'these children'

(11)    pitit   **sa**-yo                                    (Haitian)
        child   this-PL
        'these children'

The postnominal position of deictic elements such as *aki* can be explained with reference to their adverbial origin or usage and thus regarded as a language-internal matter. On the other hand, the particular ordering of noun *-sa -al yo* in Haitian is strikingly similar to the pattern that occurs in Fon(gbe), suggesting substrate influence in this case.

## 21.5 Complex NPs: the expression of possession

So far we have been looking at simple NPs, consisting of a noun plus contingent plural marker, article, or demonstrative. The head noun of a NP may also be modified by a relative clause, or by a non-sentential constituent, such as a PP.

(12)    [NP    a   [N oso ]  [PP    fu [NP   (a)    datra ] ] ]      (Sranan)
               the   house       of        (the)  doctor
        'the house of the doctor', 'the doctor's house'

The complex NP in (12) contains a PP expressing the possessor of the head noun *oso*. Comparing creole languages, there are quite a wide range of possibilities for expressing possessive relationships inside NPs, and even within one language we sometimes find alternative constructions.

The possessive construction exemplified by (12) can be found in many creole languages:

(13)  a.  ti-moun  a  man  Pòl  yo   (Haitian, northern dialect. Lefebvre & Lumsden 1992)
      children  of  Mrs.  Pòl  PL
      'the children of Mrs. Pòl', 'Mrs. Pòl's children'
   b.  di     horən fa di    kabrita            (Negerhollands. De Josselin de Jong 1926):
      the    horn of the   goat
      'the horn of the goat', 'the goat's horn'

This construction has parallels in the lexifier languages involved. French, for example, has *la maison de/à Pierre* 'Peter's house', and the Haitian construction in (13a) may be modelled on French. Another variety of Haitian, however, does not have *a* in this position:

(14)  tab   Jan   an              (Haitian, Center and South. Lefebvre & Lumsden 1992)
      table  John  the
      'the table of John's', 'John's table'

Such phrases do not have a French equivalent; it is sometimes suggested that they are modelled on certain West African languages (Holm 1988, 1990; Lefebvre & Lumsden 1992).

The construction types illustrated so far, either with or without a preposition, all exhibit the order possessed - possessor. The reverse order occurs as well in several creoles, including Miskito Coast Creole English, Berbice Dutch, and the creole languages spoken in Surinam.

In Sranan, (15) is an alternative for (12), especially when the possessor is a person:

(15)  a  datra    oso
      the  doctor   house
      'the doctor's house'

The juxtaposition of possessor and possessed is an instance of syntactic phrase formation, in contrast with morphological compounds, which constitute one word. Phonologically these differ. For example, Sranan *a anansi titey* 'the spider's thread', 'the thread of the spider' differs in stress pattern from the compound *anansititey* 'spider web'.

If two nouns occur in juxtaposition in Sranan, a preceding adjective can only relate to the first noun, the possessor:

(16)  a   moy      frigi  tere                            (Donicie 1954)
      the [beautiful   kite]  tail
      'the tail of the beautiful kite'   (not: 'the beautiful tail of the kite')

At the same time, it is uncommon to have an adjective intervening between the two nouns to modify the possessed, and if the possessor is not a person or a personification, it is impossible (17a). This is not to say that a possessed noun cannot be modified. One possibility is to use a PP, as in (17b) (cf. (12). The other is a construction that is similar to the juxtaposition type with regard to the ordering possessor - possessed, but contains an intervening pronoun, *en*, the 3rd-person singular non-nominative form (17c).

(17)     'the tail of the kite':          'the beautiful tail of the kite':

a.   a frigi tere                   *a frigi moy tere

b.   a tere fu a frigi              a moy tere fu a frigi

c.   a      frigi  **en**   tere    a      moy      frigi  **en**  tere
     the    kite   3SG    tail      the    beautiful kite   3SG   tail

The occurrence of an intervening pronoun is not restricted to cases where there is a modifying adjective; neither is it restricted to Sranan. In Sranan and Negerhollands it is optional, in other languages, for example in Papiamento, it is obligatory.

(18)   a.   di     mēnši   ši        kop          (Negerhollands. De Josselin de Jong 1926)
            the    girl    3SGPOSS   head
            'the girl's head'

       b.   di     kiniṅ   hus
            the    king    house
            'the king's house'

(19)   a.   Pedro su      kas                     (Papiamento)
            Peter 3SGPOSS house
            'Peter's house'

       b.   *Pedro kas

The Negerhollands form *ši* (and variants) is probably related to the Dutch possessive pronoun *zijn* (or *z'n*) which can occur in a similar position, although *zijn* is used when the possessor is [+masculine] and [+singular], whereas the gender distinction is neutralized in Negerhollands, as shows from (18a). However, the construction possessor - pronoun - possessed occurs in a variety of creole languages, including several that do not have a lexifier language exhibiting this pattern. Even if Dutch had been the source of the construction in Negerhollands and other Dutch-influenced creole languages, the respective superstrate languages could not account for the other cases.

The function of Negerhollands *ši* and Papiamento *su* is restricted to possessive phrases. In other languages, pronominal possessors are expressed by pronouns that are not marked as possessive. The pronoun in Sranan *mi oso* 'my house' is the same as the regular 1st person singular pronoun.

To emphasize a pronominal possessor in Sranan, *di fu* can be used, either before or after the head noun (Donicie 1954):

(20)  di      fu mi    oso      or:   a      oso   di     fu mi
      this    of 1SG   house          the    house this   of 1SG
      'this house of mine', 'MY house'

Like a nominal possessor, a pronominal possessor can be expressed by a PP. This option is likely to be used especially if the possessor is 3rd-person plural, because in Sranan the pronoun *den* is homophonous with the plural article, resulting in potential ambiguity:

(21)  den           oso
      DEF-PL/3PL    house
      1. 'the houses'    2. 'their house(s)'

Explicitness of number marking may also play a role in favoring the prepositional option if the possessed noun is plural. Number is overtly expressed in *a/den oso fu mi* 'the house/s of mine', while it is not in *mi oso* 'my house(s)'. The same goes for *a/den oso fu datra*, 'the house/s of the doctor' and *den datra oso* 'the house(s) of the doctors'.

In Sranan, then, there are various factors that may influence the choice of a certain type of possessive construction: number marking, emphasis, the use of an adjective or other modifier, as well as whether the possessor is a person or not. In Sranan as in other creoles, the use of a particular possessive construction in a certain context is a matter of tendency rather than being categorically determined.

**Further reading**

Holm (1988, 1990) gives an overview of determiners, number, gender, and possession in the Atlantic creoles, with reference to potential substrate languages. Janson (1984) challenges the universality across creole languages of the category non-specific as proposed by Bickerton. Baker (1984a, 1984b, 1993a) discusses agglutinated elements and their origins. Stolz (1986, 1987b) deals with possessive constructions in Negerhollands and other languages related to Dutch. The Sranan NP in a diachronic perspective is the subject of Bruyn (in prep.).

Pieter Muysken and Norval Smith

## 22.1 Introduction

This chapter is concerned with a class of function words in pidgin and creole languages that can contribute both to the on-going debate on the role of universal and substratum features in creole formation, and to the debate on gradual versus abrupt creolization: the reflexives. As we will see below, reflexives tend to be innovative in creoles with respect to their lexifier languages. While content words are often reflexes of the lexemes of the colonial languages, for function words, and particularly for reflexives, there is a much more indirect correspondence.

Reflexives in creole languages raise all the issues that have been under discussion in the field in recent years. How does the **lexical reconstitution** of a grammatical morpheme class proceed: by taking elements from substrate languages; through the gradual transformation of superstrate patterns; through the influence of a linguistic bioprogram; or through processes of grammaticalization of content words? Reconstitution is the process through which a morpho-syntactic category lost in the process of pidginization is reintroduced into the nascent or developing creole. In addition these issues link creole studies to the mainstream of theoretical linguistics, where the distribution and properties of reflexives have been central issues for many years (Chomsky 1981; Reinhart & Reuland 1991).

Creole reflexives are formed with the **analytic** word formation procedures characteristic of creole lexical extension in general. Earlier accounts, typified by such survey studies as Holm (1989), were mostly focused on the forms the reflexives took and on their possible resemblance to the superstrate languages, with some reference to the substrate issue. Reflexives are often found to consist of two parts, as seen in (1):

| (1) | a. | ko li (body 3SG) | (Martinican) |
| | | her/himself  (cf. Fr 'se/soi-même') | |
| | b. | en srefi (3SG self ) | (Sranan) |
| | | her/himself  (cf. Eng 'himself') | |
| | c. | my yet (1SG head) | (Tok Pisin) |
| | | myself    (cf. Eng 'myself') | |

The nature of these complex forms will be discussed in some detail below.

The orientation of the work in this area has changed due to the publication of Carden & Stewart's seminal article of 1988. They argue on the basis of the distribution of the reflexives in Haitian dialects, coupled with some scant diachronic data, that early Haitian had bare pronoun reflexives. This raises the issue of whether the early stages of creoles represent fully natural languages, since this may go against universal grammatical principles (as defined in Chomsky's Binding Theory, 1981), or whether they resemble rather the pidgins from which they are derived. Corne's work on Mauritian reflexives (1988; 1989) has introduced a new dimension into this research: different sets of verbs often select different reflexive forms. Thus there is an intimate link as well with verb semantics and the way it is reflected in the argument structure and subcategorization frame of verbs.

A dimension which needs to be explored further is to what extent principles of discourse organization influence the distribution of reflexive forms in those cases where several different forms are possible with a single verb.

## 22.2  Diversity among the creoles

Creole languages exhibit a fair variety of reflexive structures. This section represents a preliminary attempt to classify the forms found. Due to lack of data, we will restrict ourselves to a small number of creole languages here, so we do not wish to pretend that our conclusions are in any way definitive. In (2) we present an overview of the different types of reflexive forms encountered in the languages of the world.

| (2) | *definition* | *example* |
|---|---|---|
| 1a. | 3rd person pronoun | Haitian *li* |
| 1b. | 1st/2nd person pronoun | French *me/te* |
| 2a. | reflexive pronoun | French *se* |
| 2b. | reflexive + identifier | Du. *zichzelf* |
| 3a. | pronoun + identifier | *himself* |
| 3b. | possessive + identifier | *myself* |
| 4. | body word (body, head, skin) | Fon *wu* |
| 4a. | pronoun + body word | Saram. *en sinkii* |
| 4b. | pronoun + identifier + body word | Saram. *en seei sikin* |
| 4c. | possessive + body word | Papiamento *su kurpa* |
| 5. | a null form | Eng. *bathe* (comp. Sp. *bañar-se* 'bathe oneself') |
| 6. | verb + reflexive affix | Quechua riku-ku-n [see-RE-3SG] |
| 7. | verb + body incorporation | Bini *egbe* |

In table 1 the distribution of these forms over a number of creoles is presented:

Table 1. Distribution of types of reflexives

|      |                  | HT | MA | SR | SA | PA | AN | NH | BE |
|------|------------------|----|----|----|----|----|----|----|----|
| 1a.  | 3pron            | +  | +  | +  |    | +  |    | +  |    |
| 1b.  | 1/2pron          | +  | +  | +  |    | +  |    | +  |    |
| 2.   | refl             |    |    |    |    |    |    | +  |    |
| 3a.  | pron+idnf        | +  | +  | +  | +  | +  |    | +  | +  |
| 3b.  | poss+idnf        |    |    |    |    | +  |    | +  |    |
| 4.   | body             |    |    |    |    | +  | +  |    |    |
| 4a.  | pron+body        | +  |    |    | +  |    |    |    |    |
| 4b.  | pron+idnf+body   |    |    |    | +  |    |    |    |    |
| 4c.  | poss+body        | +  | +  | +  |    | +  |    |    |    |
| 5.   | null             | +  | +  | +  |    | +  |    | +  |    |
| 6.   | verb+refl af     |    |    |    |    |    |    |    |    |
| 7.   | verb+body inc    |    |    |    |    |    |    |    |    |

(HT = Haitian, MA = Mauritian, SR = Sranan, SA = Saramaccan, PA = Papiamento, AN = Fa d'Ambu, NH = Negerhollands, BE = Berbice Dutch Creole)

Most frequent are bare pronouns, pronoun + identifier combinations, and null forms. Only a few of the possibilities attested in the languages of the world are not attested in creoles.

## 22.3 The role of the lexifier languages

For French-lexifier creoles the colonial lexifier can only have played a limited role. The reflexives in the English-based creoles are not directly inherited from the lexifier model, either (cf. Smith 1987). Unlike the question words in the colonial lexifier languages, which tend to be uniformly mono-morphematic in structure (i.e. consist of one meaning-bearing element), as in (3), reflexive pronouns in these languages are different in their morphological structure, as in (4):

(3)  who    what   when       where   etc.            (English)
     wie    wat    wanneer    waar    etc.            (Dutch)
     qui    que    quand      ou      etc.            (French)
     quem   que    quando     onde    etc.            (Portuguese)

(4)    myself    himself    herself    etc.                                    (English)

me(zelf)    zich(zelf)    etc.                                                  (Dutch)

me    se    se    etc.                                                          (French)

me    se    se    etc.                                                          (Portuguese)

Speaking in terms of loss of elements and their reconstitution, the problem raised by reflexives is the following. In Portuguese and in Spanish – the languages that have provided most of the lexicon for Papiamento – we find constructions such as (5):

(5)    a.    Eu me vejo no espelho.                                            (Portuguese)
              'I see myself in the mirror.'
       b.    Maria se corta en la mano.                                        (Spanish)
              'Mary cuts herself in the hand.'

Ibero-Romance reflexive clitic forms are the following:

(6)    me    nos

       te    os    etc.

       se    se

As was the case with the other clitic pronouns, reflexive clitics were lost in the process of genesis of Papiamento, perhaps in a phase when the language existed only as a rudimentary second language pidgin. The question is of course what replaced them.

    Superstrate explanations are inadequate also. If superstrate influence were the proper explanation in most cases, then we would expect the following patterns in French and English-lexifier creoles:

(7)                          1st/2nd          3rd
       French-based    Pronoun          Reflexive Pronoun
       English-based    Possessive +    Pronoun +
                        Identifier       Identifier

Substandard English also has possessive + identifier for the 3rd person: *theirselves, hisself*. In fact we observe the pattern in table 2:

Table 2. Reflexives in various French and English-based Creole languages

| English-based | | | | |
|---|---|---|---|---|
| | Pron | Pron+Idnt | Pron+Body | Pron+Head |
| Sranan | − | + | + (?) | − |
| Saramaccan | − | + | + | − |
| Jamaican (?) | − | + | + | − |
| **French-based** | | | | |
| a. | | | | |
| Louisiana | + | + | + | − |
| Seychelles | + | + | + | + |
| Cayenne | − | + | + | − |
| b. | Pron | Idnt+Pron | Body+Pron | Head+Pron |
| Haiti | + | − | + | − |
| Trinidad | − | − | + | − |
| St. Lucia | − | − | + | + |

(Pron = pronoun; Idnt = identifier)

The most striking fact that springs to the eye here is the uniformity among the various systems. There is quite obviously no question of any major superstrate influence. The analytic constructions Pron+Idnt (*him-self*), and Pron+Body/Body+Pron (*li-ko/ko-li*) are shared between English-based and French-based creoles. Pron+Head/Head+Pron (*li-tet/tet-li*) occurs only in the French-lexifier creoles.

There are two possible cases of superstrate influence to be discerned. The first concerns the use of the bare Oblique pronoun as a reflexive in Seychellois and some other French-based creoles. This differs slightly from the French facts in that the third person form is an Oblique pronoun rather than a true reflexive form as in French, but we could put this down to a regularization of the system, removing what is a minority pattern in French.

(8)     ...i bey li partu                                                                          (Seychellois)
        '...(he) washes himself all over'

More striking is the use of the Pron+Ident pattern in certain English-based creoles. Once again we have a difference in the overall pattern, however, but this time in the majority of cases.

Table 3. Reflexives in English, Saramaccan, and Sranan

| English | Saramaccan | Sranan | |
|---------|------------|--------|---|
| myself | mi-seei | mi-srefi | |
| yourself | ju/i-seei | ju-srefi | |
| himself | en-seei | en-srefi | = |
| ourselves | wi/u-seei | wi-srefi | |
| yourselves | unu-seei | unu-srefi | |
| themselves | den-seei | den-srefi | = |

In fact only the two patterns indicated with an '=' sign are equivalent to the English pattern, and then only if we ignore the fact that plurality is marked in English reflexives. The significant differences in the pattern of Personal Pronouns are as follows:

Table 4: Contrasts between Sranan and English Reflexives

| Pronoun | English | Sranan | *Sranan |
|---------|---------|--------|---------|
| 1s Pron. | I | mi | *ai |
| | me | mi | mi |
| Poss. | my | mi | *mai |
| Ident. | my-self | mi-srefi | *mai-srefi |
| 2s Pron. | you | ju/i | ju |
| Poss. | your | ju/i | *juwa |
| Ident. | your-self | ju-srefi | *juwa-srefi |
| 1p Pron. | we | wi/u | wi |
| | us | wi/u | *osi |
| Poss. | our | wi/u | *owa |
| Ident. | our-selves | wi-srefi | *owa-srefi |

If the Sranan reflexives were cognate with their English congeners we would have expected the non-occurring phonetic forms in the *Sranan column (cf. Smith 1987 for details of phonetic developments in the Surinam creoles). This suggests that superstrate influence in itself cannot provide an acceptable explanation of more than a small part of these phenomena, morphologically speaking.

There were, it should be mentioned, cases of 'body' reflexives in Old French (Einhorn 1974: 69), but there is no reason to assume that there is a historical link between these and the 'body' reflexives in the Caribbean creoles:

(9)     por lor cors deporter                                                      (Old French)
        'to amuse themselves'

Notice finally that the forms in (10) correspond to each other, but not directly to a European model.

(10)  a.  su mes, e mes                                          (Papiamento)
      b.  sie-self, am-self                                  (Negerhollands)

## 22.4  Grammaticalization

One may hypothesize that 'self' forms started as emphatic or delimitative discourse markers and slowly developed into a grammatical formative. This trend is illustrated with an example from Quechua, where *-lla-tak* is used both to delimit reference and mark a pronoun as a reflexive.

(11)  a.  Xwan pay-ta    riku-n.                                   (Quechua)
          Juan  he-AC     see-3
          'Juan sees him/*himself.'
      b.  Xwan pay-lla-ta-tak    riku-n.
          Juan  he-DEL-AC-EMP  see-3
          'Juan sees himself/just him especially.'

The evidence for grammaticalization so far is limited, however. We will consider two cases here.

### 22.4.1  Negerhollands

Did Negerhollands *self* evolve from an emphatic highlighter to a non-discourse-oriented anaphoric marker? Consider first the data in Table 5. Here two periods in the early history of Negerhollands are contrasted, 1780 and 1800 (Van der Voort & Muysken 1995).

The percentage of *self* forms (marked with s) increases in this period, as we would expect from the perspective of a shift from discourse marker to grammatical formative, in conformity with a gradualist hypothesis. It does so more for 1st and 2nd persons, however, where grammatical disambiguation is not needed, than for 3rd persons, where it is.

Table 5. The relation between the person of the pronoun
and the presence of *self* in Negerhollands.

|        | I          | II         |
|--------|------------|------------|
| 1/2    | 99         | 22         |
| 1/2 S  | 48 = 33%   | 19 = 46%   |
| 3      | 250        | 59         |
| 3 S    | 107 = 30%  | 34 = 36%   |

I = period around and before 1780; II = period around
and shortly after 1800. 1/2 = first/second person; 3 = third
person; *self* forms are marked with S

## 22.4.2 Papiamento

A similar question can be posed for Papiamento. Did Papiamento *kurpa* evolve from an inalienably possessed body noun to a freely occurring anaphor? The form *kurpa* is mostly used with physical action verbs, taken in the widest sense of the word:

(12)     E ta kana bai bini sin duna su kurpa sosiego.                    (Papiamento)
         'He walks back and forth without giving himself rest.'

(13)     E ta kita nan for di su kurpa.
         'He takes them off himself/his body.'

(14)     ??M'a siña mi kurpa ingles.
         'I taught myself English.'

Notice, however, that it cannot be used together with another inalienably possessed noun:

(15)    a.   M'a korta mi mes/*mi kurpa na mi man.
             'I cut myself in the hand.'
        b.   Mi ta dal mi mes/*mi kurpa na mi kabes.
             'I hit myself on the head.'

Here *man* 'hand' is inalienably possessed by the subject. Even though the action is quite physical, kurpa is impossible. We can interpret this contrast by assuming that *kurpa* itself is an inalienably possessed element, and hence blocked in (15a). When the anaphor and the antecedent are not co-arguments of the same predicate, *kurpa* cannot be used either:

(16) Mi a mira un kulebra serka di mi/*mi mes/(*)mi kurpa.
'I saw a snake near me (near my body (as in a dream))'

(17) Mi a mira mi mes/(*)mi kurpa kai.
'I saw myself fall.'
('I saw my body fall (as in a dream)')

Thus *kurpa* is not fully grammaticalized yet(?) as a reflexive element.

## 22.5 Substrate

There is also quite a variety of forms to be found in the various (potential) substrate languages (see also Carden 1993):

| (18) | wu | 'body' | (Fon/Gbe) |
|---|---|---|---|
| | egbe | 'body' | (Bini) |
| | me ho etc. | 'my body' | (Twi) |
| | ara mi etc. | 'body my' | (Yoruba) |

If the form of the reflexives in the creole languages was purely a question of substrate or superstrate influence, we would expect clear evidence one way or the other, considering the great variety of morphological structures into account.

Let us now consider substrate influence. We will only analyse those cases where we appear to have some evidence for particular West African languages having played a major role in the formation of particular creoles. Can we observe direct substrate influence in the reflexive formation in such languages? The following languages have been argued to be substrate languages:

| (19) | *Creole Language* | *Substrate Language* | *Source* |
|---|---|---|---|
| | Berbice Dutch | E. Ịjọ (Kalabạrị) | (Smith et al. 1987) |
| | Saramaccan/Sranan | Gbe (Fon) | (Smith 1987; Bakker 1987) |
| | Haitian | Gbe (Fon) | (Lefebvre 1986) |
| | Annobonese | Bini | (Ferraz 1970) |

Let us consider these cases one by one.

| (20) | Pron + selfu | (Berbice Dutch) |
|---|---|---|
| | bu 'body' | (Kalabạrị) |

Here there is no correspondence whatsoever.

(21)    Pron + seei       'self'                          (Saramaccan)
        Pron + sinkii     'body' <skin
        wu                'body'                          (Fon)

(22)    kadav + Pron      'corpse'                        (Haitian)
        kor + Pron        'body'
        wu                'body'                          (Fon)

Here there is a partial semantic correspondence between Haitian and Saramaccan on the one hand, and Fon on the other.

(23)    ogue              'body'                          (Annobonese)
        egbe              'body'                          (Bini)

The only case involving a complete equivalence (i.e. morphological, etymological-phonological and semantic) of these four is the last, that of Annobonese/Bini. The cases of Haitian and Saramaccan are semantically equivalent, but not equivalent either phonologically or morphologically. Overall the claim for substrate influence is not particularly strong for reflexives.

     The evidence for an African basis for the body reflexives is not very strong at present, but cannot be plausibly denied. To summarize:
a.   There is no Ibero-Romance reflex for Papiamento *kurpa*, as there is for French creole *kor*.
b.   No body-part reflexives in Berbice Dutch.
c.   Some West-African languages (e.g. Ewe) do not have body-part reflexives; this needs to be studied in much more detail.
d.   The absence of grammaticalization of Papiamento *kurpa* (and a similar analysis could be given for Saramaccan *sinkii*) pleads against direct calquing, since in the West-African languages the body reflexives are often fully grammaticalized.

     Note that in cases where we can identify both substrate and superstrate the N is lexically supplied in one of three ways:

(24)    a.   the superstrate form
        b.   the substrate form
        c.   the substrate form reinterpreted or relexified in the superstrate language

In Saramaccan we have examples of options (a.) and (c.). Note that where we have the actual substrate form, as in the case of Annobonese, this is associated with the morphological pattern of the substrate language - in this case the form 'body' alone - as forecast by recent versions of the Language Bioprogram Hypothesis, incorporating the Lexical Learning Hypothesis (see chapter 11).

We can summarize the alleged substratum cases as in Table 6:

Table 6. Reconsideration of substratum cases

| *mi-seei* | Morphosyntax | | (Saramaccan) |
|---|---|---|---|
| | Constituency: | Universal | |
| | Order: | Sup. (English) | |
| | Phon.Etym.: | Sup. (English) | |
| | Semantics: | Sup. (English) | |
| *mi-sinkii* | Morphosyntax | | |
| | Constituency: | Universal | |
| | Order: | Sup. (English) | |
| | Phon.Etym.: | Sup. (English) | |
| | Semantics: | Sub. (Fon)? | |
| *kadav-mwe* | Morphosyntax | | (Haitian) |
| | Constituency: | Universal | |
| | Order: | Sub. (Fon) | |
| | Phon.Etym.: | Sup. (French) | |
| | Semantics: | Sub. (Fon)? | |
| *ogue* | Morphosyntax | | (Annobonese) |
| | Constituency: | Sub. (Bini) | |
| | Order: | irrel. | |
| | Phon.Etym.: | Sub. (Bini) | |
| | Semantics: | Sub. (Bini) | |

Note that it is conceivably a frequent historical semantic process that reflexives develop from inalienable possessives through the use of words with the meanings 'head' or 'body'. This does not necessarily imply that it is the default case that reflexives should be expressed by such words. So, all in all, the explanation of the causation of creole reflexive forms is much more complex than might have been expected. Different factors require to be taken into consideration when these are being analysed.

The influence of universals in reflexives seems to be restricted to one aspect of morpho-syntax. For this influence to even be present it is necessary for the substrate item not to have been inherited. It also appears that we have to reckon with the effects of relexification. However, extrapolating once again here from the very small number of clear cases at our disposal we appear to have a situation where relexification does not involve maintaining a lexical morphosyntactic pattern. This does not augur well for much of the more grammatical interpretation of substratist claims.

We suggest, in line with the ideas of Bickerton (1981), and to a lesser extent, those of Wekker & Seuren (1986), that the unexplained morphosyntactic patterns derive from universal aspects of the internalized grammar of the early speakers of the relevant creole languages.

It might be remarked that while the analytic type of reflexive appears to be dominant in creole languages, the order of the two constituents is not invariable. However, recent versions of Bickerton's Language Bioprogram Hypothesis regard syntactic constituency as universal, but the order of constituents as language-specific. Note that the universal structure of reflexives would then be: [Pronoun, N]. The problem remains of how the lexical filling of the N is to be defined.

The Papiamento case suggests that there are complex semantic motivations for the choice of either the identifier or inalienable possessive reflexive. If the use of *kurpa* derives from some African pattern, it was not simply a case of relexifying an African form, but a complex process of reinterpretation of African pattern to fit the [Pronoun, N] mould.

## 22.6 Bare pronoun forms

Is there evidence for a pidgin or early creole generalized bare pronoun reflexive (as argued Carden & Stewart 1988) or are the bare pronouns a late development under the influence of superstrate reflexive clitic systems (Corne 1988)? Again, several languages provide relevant evidence on this point.

### 22.6.1 Papiamento
The following data show that in present-day Papiamento bare pronoun reflexives are clitics occurring with lexicallly specified verbs, but even then only with specific meanings:

(25)    a.    Mi ta sinti mi/mi mes/*mi kurpa un tiki tristo.
              'I feel a bit sad.'
        b.    Mi ta sinti *mi/mi mes/mi kurpa dor di e deklo.
              'I feel myself through the blanket.'

The two following structures correspond with the two possibilities in (25a):

(26)     a.   Mi ta sinti+mi [**pro**(**anaphoric**) un tiki tristo].

       b.   Mi ta sinti [mi mes un tiki tristo].

In (26a) the *mi* element is an object clitic (see chapter 17), linked to an anaphoric null pronoun in the bracketed small clause structure, and in (26b) *mi+mes* is a reflexive noun phrase.

    Some of the verbs taking bare pronoun reflexives are listed below; the verbs are generally inherently reflexive verbs denoting an abstract action:

(27)     sinti e x          'feel x'

       haña e            'find oneself'

       gana e            'reach, find oneself'

       okupá e           'occupy oneself'

       imagina e         'imagine oneself'

       komportá e        'behave oneself'

Notice also that these verbs are often part of the more 'educated' vocabulary, almost certainly not dating from the early stages of the creole. Another factor worth taking into consideration is the fact that many of these verbs contain more than two syllables: perhaps their phonological weight favors a light reflexive object pronoun.

### 22.6.2 Negerhollands

A similar situation holds in 18th century Negerhollands, where the bare pronoun reflexives are all inherent reflexives. Compare *bedink* 'think, (re)consider (lit. think by oneself)', *erger* 'get annoyed at (lit: to irritate oneself)'. Some verbs taking an inherent reflexive have also been attested as zero-reflexive in Negerhollands: *bekeer* 'convert oneself', *boek* 'stoop, lean down (lit: to lean oneself down)'.

### 22.6.3 Sranan

The data from 18th century Sranan (Bruyn, in prep.) merit much closer investigation. On preliminary inspection, a similar picture emerges:

(28)     Da zo mi za beri dem zomma di kili **den srefi**.          (Sranan, c. 1765)

       'It is thus I will bury the people who kill themselves.'

This example indicates that reflexives based on English 'self' were present in the oldest known substantial body of textual material in Sranan. There are also bare pronoun reflexives, but often with verbs that take an inherently reflexive direct object in the meaning intended:

(29)  a.  Mi gi **mi** abra na hem.                                    (Sranan, 1783)
          'I give myself (over) to him.'
      b.  Bunne jorka kibri **hem**.
          'The good ghost hides himself.'

However, in this context 'self' reflexives are not excluded:

(30)  Wan libisomma membre, takki, hem kann helpi **hem srefi**, a kori **hem srefi**.(Sranan, 1783)
      'Someone who thinks he can help himself is deceiving himself.'

As for 20th century Sranan, Adamson (1993) has argued that with a certain class of verbs bare pronouns can function as reflexive objects. Thus *en* in (31a) can be interpreted both as a reflexive and as a referential pronoun, non-coreferential with the subject:

(31)  a.  John$_i$ syi en$_i$/$_j$ ini a spikri.                        (Sranan, 20th century)
          'John saw him/himself in the mirror.'
      b.  John$_i$ syi ensrefi$_i$/-$_j$ ini a spikri (non-emph. reading).

The reflexive *ensrefi* in (31b) can only be interpreted as coreferential with the subject. Adamson (1993) argues that reflexive *en* in (31a) is in fact an object clitic on the verb.

## 22.7  Overlap in use

In several creoles a number of competing forms exist, partially overlapping in use. We will illustrate this with three examples. The first concerns contemporary Papiamento (Muysken 1993). In Papiamento no less than seven different forms have replaced the Ibero-Romance clitics:

(32)  a.  null reflexive                                               (Papiamento)
      b.  *paña* ← Port. pano, Sp. paño 'cloth'
      c.  *kurpa* ← Port. corpo, Sp. cuerpo 'body'
      d.  possessive + *kurpa*
      e.  pronoun + *mes* ← Port. mesmo 'self, precisely'
      f.  possessive pronoun + *mes*
      g.  pronoun

Examples for the principal reflexive forms are given in (33):

(33)    a.    peña                comb oneself                                 =(32a)

                feita                 shave (oneself )

           b.    sofoká kurpa      exert oneself                                   =(32c)

                (sofoká 'stifle')

           c.    yuda su kurpa     help oneself                                    =(32d)

                sisti su kurpa      serve/stuff oneself

           d.    weta su mes        look at oneself                                 =(32f )

                yuda su mes        help oneself

           e.    sinti e tristo       feel sad                                          =(32g)

                haña e                 find oneself

In (33a) we find the null reflexive, in (33b) the bare body word. The latter is limited to a specific set of, often idiomatic, expressions. (33c) illustrates the possessive + body word construction, and (33d) the possessive + identifier construction. In (33e), finally, there is a bare pronoun.

     Of course, these forms are not all usable interchangeably. In table 7 a rough outline of their distribution is given, along the dimensions [±physical action] ((non-)phys.) and [inherent (inher.) versus transitive (trans.)]. Inherent reflexives are those where the action of the verb is typically directed at the agent itself (*shave*), while transitive reflexives are those where it is directed to another being or object (*kiss*).

Table 7. The rough distribution of Papiamento reflexives

|  | ø | kurpa | pro+kurpa | pro+mes | pro |
|---|---|---|---|---|---|
| phys.inher. | some | some |  |  |  |
| phys.trans. |  | idiom | many | many |  |
| non-phys.inher. | some |  |  | many | many |
| non-phys.trans. |  |  | many |  |  |

In Papiamento, *mes* can be used as an identifier, in addition to being a reflexive, but *kurpa* cannot:

(34)    a.    Mi mes ta hunga.

                'I myself am playing.'

           b.    *mi kurpa ta hunga

The main factor in the choice between *mes* and *kurpa* as reflexives seems to be whether the verb expresses a physical action or not. With some verbs both forms are possible, although one may be preferred (as with *bo mes* in (36)):

(35)    El a hoga su mes/su kurpa na lama.
        'He has drowned himself in the sea.'

(36)    Bo a yuda bo mes/bo kurpa.
        'You have helped yourself.'

In other constructions, only *mes* is possible. These are principally cases where the 'self' is purely mental or figurative:

(37)    M'a ekiboka mi mes/*mi kurpa.
        'I made a mistake.'

(38)    El a hasi su mes/*su kurpa sokete.
        'He made himself out to be stupid.'

(39)    El a lolea/hode su mes/*su kurpa.
        'He made an asshole of himself.'

In cases such as (11), which is purely corporeal, *kurpa* but not *mes* is possible:

(40)    El a dal su kurpa/*su mes na un palo.
        'He walked into a pole.'
        (lit. 'he walked himself into a pole')

We will discuss the use of bare pronoun forms below.

The distribution in Papiamento is not dissimilar to that in Mauritian, as described by Corne (1988; 1989). The following four categories and distributions are distinguished by Corne:

(41)    null            inherent reflexives
        pronoun         inherent reflexives / transitive verbs / preferred with datives
        pro + *mem*     transitive verbs; preferred with prepositional phrases
        pro + *lekor*   physical action verbs

Mauritian *lekor* has a distribution very much like Papiamento *kurpa*. We will see below that the same holds for bare pronoun and null forms.

A partially different picture is suggested by 18th century Negerhollands (Muysken and van der Voort 1991), which lack body part reflexives altogether. Some examples are given in (42) of different forms occurring in different contexts:

(42)  a.  wies ju selv na die Priester (Mat 8, 4)                             Object (DO)
              'show 2SG self to the priest'
      b.  ha openbaar sie selv (Mat 2, 19)                        (Object 3SG)
              'TNS reveal REFL self'
      c.  Partie van die Skriftgeleerden ha seg bie sender selv    Adv. Prep. Phrase (ADVPP)
              part of the Pharisees PAST say with 3PL self (Mat 9, 3)
      d.  en Jesus ha ruep sie twaelf Disciplen na sie (Mat 10, 1)
              and Jesus TNS call his twelve disciples to REFL    Small Clause Prep. Phrase (SCPP)
      e.  maer die Volk ha verwonder sender (Mat 8, 27)                   Inherent (INH)
              but the people TNS marvel [themselves]

In Table 8 it is made clear that there are considerable differences amongst the different contexts where the *selv* forms occur most frequently.

Table 8. Distribution of *selv* over different contexts in Negerhollands (van der Voort & Muysken to appear)

|  | DO | IO | ADVPP | SCPP | INH |
|---|---|---|---|---|---|
| pronoun | 49 | 12 | 25 | 103 | 222 |
| pronoun + *selv* | 64 | 6 | 97 | 23 | 18 |

Forms with *selv* are very common in direct object position and particularly in adverbial phrases, but much less so elsewhere.

## 22.8 Conclusion

The above survey of creole reflexive systems has of necessity been incomplete. It has yielded some preliminary answers, but it has led to further questions as well. Before we can state a more definite set of conclusions, more representative data from a wider variety of creoles are needed, embedded in an explicit diachronic perspective.

**Further readings**

The key reference to the study of reflexives in creoles is Carden and Stewart (1988). Later articles by Carden, Corne, Muysken and Muysken & van der Voort deal with specific aspects. Déchaine & Manfredi (1994) provides a new and original perspective on reflexives in Haitian.

# 23 Serial verbs

Pieter Muysken and Tonjes Veenstra

## 23.1 Introduction

Since the work of Hugo Schuchardt (1914), who noted the resemblance between Ewe serial verbs and Surinam creole constructions, there has been a continuous discussion of serial verbs in the literature on creoles. The main issue is to what extent these serial verbs can be traced back to West African or other specific substrate sources, and to what extent they are autonomous developments. Serial verb constructions occur in the Kwa-languages of West Africa, in the Sino-Tibetan language family, in the languages of Cambodia, in the Austronesian languages of New Guinea, in Malagasy, and in the creole languages of the Atlantic and Pacific areas among others.

In 23.2 we present a general description, a preliminary definition, and an enumeration of frequently occurring types of serial verb constructions. Section 23.3 is aimed at the problem of typology and parametrization: what makes serial verb constructions possible in a language? In 23.4 we discuss the different possible structures proposed for the serial verb construction: coordination, complementation, adjunction, and in 23.5 the problem of 'shared arguments': one noun phrase sometimes appears to belong to different verbs. Section 23.6 treats some of the temporal and aspectual dimensions of the serial verb constructions: do the different verbs in serial verb constructions mark different events or a single event?

## 23.2 Overview and definition

It is time for some illustrative examples. Sentence (1) contains a frequently occurring type in which a verb of movement, *bula* 'fly', is modified by a directional verb, *bay* 'go':

(1)  E-l a    **bula  bay.**                                        (Papiamento)
     3SG ASP  fly   go
     'He flew away.'

In (2) a benefactive adjunct is made possible by using the verb *bay* 'give':

(2)  Li **pote** sa   **bay**  mo.                                  (Guyanais)
     3SG bring that  give   1SG
     'He brought that for me.'

Finally, sentence (3) illustrates the case of *tɛk* 'take', that introduces a comitative adjunct:

(3)    Dɛm    go in    tɛk    im        **go** bak.                                    (Gullah)
       3PL     go and   take   3SG.ACC   go back
       'They are going back with him.'

In (1) to (3) only some of the possible functions of serial verb constructions are illustrated. Below, a somewhat more extensive overview of the functions of serial verb constructions in the creole languages is given, partly based on the overview in Jansen et al. (1978). In the study of serial verb constructions several criteria are implicitly assumed in respect of serial verb constructions. Generally, they amount to something like the following. A serial verb construction contains two verbs which have:

(4)    a. only one expressed subject
       b. at most one expressed direct object
       c. one specification for tense/aspect
          – often only on the first verb
          – sometimes on both verbs, but semantically one specification
          – sometimes only on the second verb
       d. only one possible negator
       e. no intervening coordinating conjunction
       f. no intervening subordinating conjunction
       g. no intervening pause possible

Generally one verb is fixed, the other one drawn from a certain semantic or aspectual class. In the overview in (5) only the fixed verb in the serial verb constructions is mentioned. It is always the second verb of two, except with *take*:

(5)    *Functions*
       locational    *go*          direction away
                     *come*        direction towards
                     *surround*    around
                     *be*          locative
       argument      *give*        benefactive, dative
                     *take*        instrumental, comitative, object
                     *say*         finite complementizer

| aspectual | *finish* | perfective |
|-----------|----------|------------|
|  | *return* | iterative |
|  | *be* | continuative |
| degree | *pass* (NP) | comparative, excessive |
|  | *suffice* | enough |

Four major groups of meanings are distinguished: directional, argument introducing, aspectual serial verbs, and degree marking. These four are arranged very roughly in the order of frequency in which these semantic categories are marked by serial verbs in different groups of creole languages. Then, within each semantic category, typical verbs are listed, again in rough order of frequency, which encode a specific type of meaning.

The distribution of the serial verb constructions in the creole languages is roughly as follows:

(a) creoles with serial constructions, including *take*, are Saramaccan, Sranan, Krio, Gullah, Jamaican, Guyanais, Haitian, (Seselwa, Negerhollands);

(b) creoles with serial constructions, but excluding *take* are São Tomense, Principense, Tok Pisin, Negerhollands, Papiamento, Berbice;

(c) creoles with no serial verbs: Philippine Creole Spanish, Hawaiian Creole English, Senegal Crioulo, Mauritian Creole, Réunionais.

Next to the specific verbs in (5), in various languages other verbs may sometimes occur in serial verb constructions. It is a matter of debate as to what extent serial verb constructions are limited to specific lexical items.

## 23.3 Parametrization and typological correlates

If there were something like a **serializing language-type**, we would expect a number of typological correlates (co-occurring linguistic features) of serial constructions. In some theories, these typological correlates are accounted for by parameters (see chapter 11). Often the idea in the background is that serial verbs are there to express certain notions that could not otherwise be expressed. We will briefly discuss some of the possible correlates:

**Word order** is not promising. The Caribbean creole languages are all svo-languages, but some West African serializing languages are underlyingly sov (as suggested in work inspired by Koopman 1984), and some are sov on the surface as well, like Ijọ. Malagasy is verb-initial, and in the Pacific and Sino-Tibetan cases we find both sov and svo-languages.

**Verbal derivational morphology** is absent. This is surely the case for verbs in the Caribbean creole languages, which are mostly monomorphemic, and seems to be true to a certain extent, for West African cases. Exceptions are reduplication and e.g. obsolete causative formation in Berbice Dutch. Many serializing languages have null case marking and case assignment under strict adjacency.

P and V are non-distinct in serializing languages. Problems with this approach are that, first, serial verbs allow **stranding**, as verbs usually do, Ps (in Sranan and Haitian) generally do not:

(6)   a.  San   Edgar   **koti** ___?                     (Sranan)
          what   Edgar   cut
          'What did Edgar cut?'

       b.  San   Edgar   **teki** ___  koti  a      brede?
          what   Edgar   take    cut   the   bread
          'What did Edgar cut the bread with?'

       c.  *a   nefi  san  a    e    koti  a      brede **nanga** ___
          the  knife  that  3SG  ASP  cut  the   bread  with
          'the knife that he cuts the bread with'

Second, (some) serial verbs allow **predicate cleft** (see chapter 24) just like verbs, and Ps do not (but see chapter 24 for a discussion of particles):

(7)   a.  Na  **koti**  Edgar  **koti**  a    brede.             (Sranan)
          FOC  cut    Edgar   cut   the   bread
          'Edgar really cut the bread.'

       b.  Na  **teki**  Edgar  **teki**  a    nefi  koti  a    brede.
          FOC  take  Edgar  take  the   knife  cut   the   bread
          'Really with the knife Edgar cut the bread.'

       c.  *Na  **nanga**  Edgar  koti  a    brede **nanga**  a    nefi.
          FOC  with   Edgar  cut  the   bread with  the   knife
          'With the knife (really) Edgar cut the bread.'

Third, some creole languages (e.g. Principense) distinguish oblique (assigned by P) from accusative case (assigned by V). Fourth, all creole languages have a number of prepositions lacking verbal properties. Serial verbs are also used non-prepositionally, as shown in (5).

A further parameter or typological correlate might be that serial verbs are additional **case markers**, because the other verbs only assign case on a limited basis. Problems with this approach are that all creole languages have double object-constructions, and that there are a great many intransitive verbs that are used serially. Compare for the first point (8) and (9) from Principense (Günther 1973):

(8)  PwE  sa  **da**  minu dyo    /   **da**  dyo    **da**  minu.    (Principense)
     father ASP  give  child money  /...  give  money  give  child

     'Father gives the child money. / ... gives money for the child.'

(9)  N  ka  **futa**  mwi   m   dyo    /...  **futa**  dyo    **da**  mwi   m.
     1SG ASP  steal  mother  my   money  /...  steal  money  give  mother  my

     'I stole money from my mother. /... stole money for my mother.'

Here it is clear that in each case there is also a double object construction, with a specific meaning.

Serial verbs are additional **markers of thematic roles**. Problems with this approach are first that it presupposes that languages are serializing because in one way or the other verbs cannot assign more than one internal and one external theta-role. This goes against the idea that verbs tend to have the same arguments cross-linguistically, cf. the UTAH principle (Baker 1988). Second, serial verbs can have a whole range of interpretations. Finally, serial verbs can occur together with prepositions. This last property would be unexpected if the serial verb construction was there to assign a thematic role.

There are two possible typological features that can only be stated in highly theory-specific terms, and within those theories, may indeed be the defining feature of a serializing language. First, it may be that in serializing languages the verb is **separate from** INFL, the markers for tense and aspect, and VP can function as a secondary predicate, since there is no direct link to a tense anchor for a proposition. Normally a predication is the core of a proposition, as in *Mary walks*, where *walks* is predicated of *Mary*. Here *walks* is the primary predicate of the clause, and is anchored by the finiteness of the verb (in this case present tense). Suppose there were a secondary, non-finite, predicate *go*, indicating the direction in which Mary's walking takes place: we then have a serial construction. Second, it could be that in serializing languages it is possible to have VP-**complements** instead of full clausal (CP) complements. In any case this is an area for further exploration.

## 23.4  Structure and order

If serial verb constructions form chains, what are the concatenation principles, and what is the structural configuration? In the literature three possibilities are suggested: coordination, subordination, and adjunction. The argument is for an analysis in terms of coordination that in some cases there is a temporal order between the actions expressed in the serial verb constructions. Compare the following example from Saramaccan:

(10)    Mi bi    kisi    wan    pingo kii    boi    nyan.    (Saramaccan)
        1SG ANT  catch   a      boar   kill  boil   eat
        'I had caught a boar, killed, boiled, and eaten it.'

While here one can doubt the serial (versus coordinated) status of the construction, we also find sequential effects with classic contrasts such as that between (11a) and (11b) (cf. Sebba 1987):

(11)    a.    Mi    teki    fisi    seri.    (Sranan)
              1SG   take    fish    sell
              'I sold the fish.'
        b.    *Mi   teki    fisi    bai
              1SG   take    fish    buy
              'I bought the fish.'

Nonetheless Jansen et al. (1978) and Sebba (1987) show that serial verb constructions never show the island effects that have been associated with coordinated structures since Ross (1967; see chapter 24).

A second possibility is suggested in Schachter (1975), and adopted in Jansen et al. (1978), Sebba (1987), and in a modified form in Baker (1989), namely that serialization involves a form of subordination. Arguments for this supposition are in particular the extractability of elements from serial verb constructions, which we have already seen in (6), and the close semantic relationship between the verbs in most serial verb constructions, often comparable to that between a v and a p in a [v pp]-construction.

An argument against subordination – an otherwise highly plausible analysis – is constituted by the arrangement of the verbs in a serial verb construction. How are the verbs in the chain placed in a specific order? In the case of subordination an arrangement determined by verb-complement order, that is, by the directionality of government, would be a plausible answer. The comparison of serial verb constructions in Sranan (Sebba 1987) and Ijọ (Wiliamson 1965) suggests that the matter must be more complicated. (12) shows that Ijọ governs to the left:

(12)    a.    keni    bila        eri-mi    (NP V. Ijọ)
              an      elephant    see-PAST
              'saw an elephant'
        b.    bele-bi-o nama tua    (NP P NP V)
              pot-T-in  meat  put
              'put meat in the pot'

    c.  Ari   u-di   yo-koo       bo-mi.                 (Compl v)

        3SG   see   in.order.to  come-PAST

        'I came in order to see him.'

The same direction holds for [NP v] in (12a), for [[PP NP] v] in (12b), for [s v] in (12c). Note also that tense marking is completely to the right in all cases, thus [vp Infl].

    In Sranan the directionality of government is rightward:

(13)   a.  koti a brede                               (v NP. **Sranan**)

        'cut the bread'

     b.  poti  a      brede a     tafra  tapu          (v NP PP)

        put  the    bread LOC  table  top

        'put the bread on the table'

     c.  Eddy e    koti  a     brede fu nyan en.       (v Compl)

        Eddy ASP  cut   the    bread to eat   it

        'Eddy cuts the bread to eat it.'

Nonetheless it turns out that the order of the verbs in serial verb constructions in both languages is the same in a number of constructions. We give two examples. Consider first the *take* serial verb constructions in (14) and (15):

(14)   ... aki ... v                                       (Ijǫ)

     a.  ye    aki-ni u-bee

        thing take  3SGM-say

        'say something to him'

     b.  aru-bi  aki   tin    kaka-mo

        canoe-T take  tree   tie-D

        'tie the canoe to a tree'

(15)   teki ... v ...                                     (Sranan)

     a.  no   teki  baskita  tyari watra

        no   take  basket   carry water

        'don't carry water with a basket'

     b.  teki  Dia  poti  na    brakoto

        take  Deer  put   LOC  barbecue

        'put Deer on the grill'

The same holds for the *give* serial verb constructions in (16) and (17):

(16)     ... v... piri                                                                                          (Ịjọ)
   a.  duma tun-ni  a-piri
     song sing   3SGF-give
     'sing a song for her'
   b.  egberi  gba-ni  u-piri
     story   say   3SGM-give
     'tell him a story'

(17)     v... gi...                                                                                          (Sranan)
   a.  seni  wan  boskopu gi   tigri
     send  a   message give  tiger
     'send a message to Tiger / send Tiger a message'
   b.  prani a   karu gi   yu
     plant the   corn give  2SG
     'plant the corn for you'

The fact that the arrangement of the elements in the serial construction is independent of the directionality of government suggests that there can be no government relation, which would be typical of subordination.

  The third possibility to concatenate the vps is by way of adjunction. For this conclusion recent work by Law & Veenstra (1992) provides us with additional arguments. There are two options: either $vP_1$ is an adjunct to $vP_2$, or $vP_2$ is an adjunct to $vP_1$. We will give two arguments suggesting that the latter approach is more fruitful.

  First, as Déchaine (1988) points out for Haitian, the object of the first verb is referentially more prominent than (in structural terms: asymmetrically c-commands) the object of the second verb:

(18)     a.  M  pran manch panyen$_i$ an   mete bo   kote l$_i$.   (Haitian)
     1SG  take handle basket  the  put LOC  near 3SG
     'I put the basket$_i$'s handle near to it$_i$.'
   b.  *M  pran manch li$_i$   mete bo   kote panyen$_i$ an.
     1SG  take handle 3SG  put LOC  near basket  the
     'I put it$_i$'s handle near to the basket$_i$.'

Sentence (18b) is ungrammatical under the intended coreferentiality. For an NP to bind a pronoun, it must c-command the pronoun. The explanation for the difference in grammaticality is that the NP in (18b) fails to c-command the pronoun and, hence, coreferentiality is barred. The conclusion is that there is an asymmetrical c-command relation between the two NPs. This observation is easily accommodated if the VP *mete bo kote l* is an adjunct of the VP *pran manch panyen*.

The second argument concerns adjunct extraction. If the first VP were adjoined to the second VP, we would expect that an adjunct WH-phrase could only be construed with the second VP, since adjunct extraction out of an adjoined maximal projection is not possible. The reverse is true, however. As shown in Veenstra (1993) for Saramaccan and Sranan Tongo it is only possible to construe an adjunct WH-phrase with the first VP and not with the second VP:

(19)  Ufa  m    faa   di   pau   tue?                            (Saramaccan)
      how  1SG  fell  the  tree  throw
      'How did I fell the tree?'

The answer to the question in (19) can only refer to the way the cutting of the tree was done, and not to the way the tree fell down.

In conclusion, a good case can be made for adjunction as the guiding principle for the stacking of VPs in serial verb constructions. See for a similar conclusion Law & Veenstra (1992).

## 23.5  Shared arguments

An observation which goes back to Stewart (1963) is that overt subjects and overt objects in serial verb constructions are semantically related to both verbs, i.e. the verbs share their arguments. Thus, in (20) the object *liv la* is an object of *pran* as well as of *montre*. Similarly, *men* is the subject of both predicates:

(20)  Men  pran  liv   la    montre  Jan.                        (Haitian)
      1SG  take  book  the   show    John
      'I showed the book to John.'

The question is whether the (semantic or syntactic) sharing of arguments, both subject and object, is obligatory in verb serialization. The most explicit answer to this question has been formulated in the work of M. Baker (1989). The sharing of arguments is seen there as one of the defining properties of the construction. Moreover, this sharing is not random, but is thematically restricted. In constructions with more than one internal argument, as in (20), the order in which arguments appear obeys the following thematic hierarchy:

(21)    Agent < Instrument < ... < Theme < Goal < Location

We will see that neither subject- nor object-sharing is obligatory and that there is cross-linguistic variation with respect to the thematic restriction on argument sharing. We proceed in the following way: first, we discuss data in which there is no subject sharing. Part of the evidence is based on the behavior of reflexives and pronouns. Second, we present cases where there is no overt object to be shared or where the second verb (v2) does not have a covert object. Third, we turn to cases that violate the thematic restriction on object sharing.

In example (22) it is evident that the different verbs do not share the same subject. In (22) it is John who gives the book to Paul, who gives the book to Mary. Note that although the verbs do not share subjects, they share the object *liv la*:

(22)    Jan    bay    Pol    liv    la    bay    Mari.                    (Haitian)
        John   give   Paul   book   the   give   Mary
        'John gave the book to Paul to give to Mary'

That the different verbs do not necessarily share the same subject is also shown by the behavior of reflexives and pronouns (cf. Veenstra 1989 on Sranan):

(23)    a.  Mi$_i$    kai    di    mujɛɛ$_i$    (ko)    luku   enseei$_i$/en$\cdot_{i/k}$.        (Saramaccan)
            1SG     call   the    woman       (come)   look   3SG-self/3SG
            'I called the woman (to come and) look at herself.'
        b.  Mi      kai    di    mujee    (ko)    luku   mi/*miseei.
            1SG     call   the    woman   (come)   look   1SG/1SG-self
            'I called the woman (to come and) look at me.'

The facts in (23) can be accounted for in a straightforward manner. Reflexives have to be bound in their governing category and pronouns must be free in their governing category. Therefore, there has to be a covert subject in front of v2 that is coreferent with the matrix object *di mujee* in order to account for the pattern in (23). Note that the two verbs do not share an object either.

The last set of data we discuss also comes from Saramaccan (Bickerton & Iatridou 1987). In these cases, both verbs appear to share an object and the behavior of reflexives and pronouns clearly shows that the two verbs have different subjects:

(24)    Di mujee$_i$   da   di    pikin$_j$ di   sopi wasi enseei$_{i/j}$.        (Saramaccan)
        the woman   give   the    child the    soap wash 3SG-self
        'The woman gave the child the soap to wash himself with it.'

(25)    Di mujee$_i$   da   di    pikin$_j$ di   sopi wasi en$_{i/j}$.
        the woman   give   the    child the    soap wash 3SG
        'The woman gave the child the soap to wash her with it.'

In (24) it is the woman who gives the soap, but it is the boy who washes with it. Note that, as in (22), v1 selects two internal arguments, of which one acts as the subject of v2, while the other can be regarded as an argument of v2. In all cases in which v1 introduces two internal arguments, there is no subject sharing and, moreover, the Goal argument of v1 is interpreted as the subject of v2.

As far as the obligatory sharing of objects is concerned, we have evidence that this is not necessarily the case. In the examples in (26) and (27) there is no object sharing:

(26)    A   de wan   bunu mujee   d'en.                    (Saramaccan)
        3SG be a     good   woman   give=3SG
        'She is a good woman for him.'

(27)    Mi kai   di    daata    (ko)    kii   di    sindeki.
        1SG call   the    doctor   (come)   kill   the   snake
        'I called for the doctor (to come and) kill the snake.'

There is no sharing either because v1 does not have an object, as in (26), or because v2 does not have a covert object coreferent with the object of v1, as in (27).

The last issue we discuss concerns the thematic restriction on object sharing as proposed by Baker (1989). It implies that if v2 selects a Theme and an Instrument, it is only the Instrument that can be shared with v1. Similarly, if v2 is a regular three-place verb (like *give*), it is the Theme that is shared with v1 rather than the Goal. This restriction may cover the observed facts for some serializing languages. Nonetheless, it is too restrictive for other languages, such as Haitian, Sranan and Saramaccan (Law & Veenstra 1992; Veenstra 1993):

(28)    a.   Jan    pran pen   an    koupe   ak   kouto a.         (Haitian)
           John take bread the    cut    with knife the
           'John cut the bread with the knife.'

b. Jan   pran  Mari  montre  liv    la.
   John  take  Mary  show    book   the
   'John showed the book to Mary.'

It appears that the cross-linguistic variation with respect to the ordering of arguments in SVCs is rather due to language-specific constraints than universal ones on the process of serialization.

In conclusion, we have seen that in verb serialization it is not obligatory for the different verbs in the construction to have the same subject or object. Although argument-sharing is not obligatory, we still find many cases in which one would like to say that arguments, both external and internal, are being 'shared' by the verbs. For different proposals to account for this phenomenon, we refer to Collins (1993), Déchaine (1993) and Law & Veenstra (1992).

## 23.6 Lexical and semantic aspects

A problem that serial verb constructions pose for grammatical theory is how their lexical and their syntactic properties interact. On the one hand, they are clearly lexically determined: the verbs in a serial chain are in part lexically restricted, they sometimes form idioms (though this appears to be the case more often in the Kwa-languages than in the Caribbean, where true serial idioms are rare: Saramaccan v *lúku* 'try to v' may be the exception), they often appear to undergo thematic restructuring to form complex predicates. On the other hand, the individual verbs in the chain are clearly separate verbs assigning cases and thematic roles to intervening objects. Also, the different verbs may denote different sub-events.

What are the semantic relations between the verbs? How do the different verbs in the chain interact? Two possibilities come to mind:
a.  all the verbs in the chain are separate predicates and the relation between them is one of adverbial modification.
b.  the verbs undergo thematic restructuring and become one predicate semantically;
There are several ways in which to approach this issue. One is to set up a division between languages of type (a) with clausal serial constructions, relatively more independence between the different sub-events denoted by the separate verbs, and free lexical selection; and type (b) with phrasal serial constructions, relatively less independence, thematic restructuring, and a limited set of participating verbs.

(29)    a. clause-serializing: Saramaccan, Berbice
        b. vp-serializing: Haitian, Papiamento, etc.

A second possibility is to construct a scale which runs from coordination to subordination (Fugier 1987):

| (30) | coordination | enumeration of two distinct events |
| --- | --- | --- |
| | I | two distinct events in tight juxtaposition |
| | II | one event and its consequence |
| | III | one event and the aim towards which it tends |
| | IV | two concomitant events |
| | V | one event and its reformulation |
| | VI | one event and the way it is realized |
| | subordination | one event, and a second one on the occasion of the first one |

A major drawback for the lexicalist approach is that it assumes there has to be a tight relation between the two verbs in the construction. As we have already seen in 23.4, it cannot be a relation in terms of government, given the similarity of typologically different languages (VO versus OV) with respect to the arrangement of the different elements in the construction. If, on the other hand, the relation between the verbs rather resembles adverbial modification, it is not evident how to account for the certain restrictions that hold between the two verbs.

A possible synthesis of the two approaches would be to say that although the different verbs head their own predicate, the relationship is one in terms of predication and, as such, they resemble secondary predication constructions in non-serializing languages. The main difference would be that in serializing languages verbs can head a secondary predicate (cf. Muysken 1987). It is possible to state lexical restrictions, the fact that particular verbs select only certain classes of verbs, on such structures. See Larson (1991) and Law & Veenstra (1992) for suggestions and analyses along these lines.

## Further reading

An early overview of serial verbs in the creoles is given in Jansen, Koopman & Muysken (1978). Serial verb constructions in Papiamento are analysed in Bendix (1972). Sebba (1987) has given the most complete description of serial verb constructions in Sranan. Byrne (1987) deals with Saramaccan, and Veenstra (1990) is dedicated to Jamaican. In Wingerd (1977) and Déchaine and Lefebvre (1988) Haitian is studied.

# 24 Fronting

Tonjes Veenstra and Hans den Besten

## 24.1 Introduction

The term **fronting** derives from the observation that certain phrases appear in sentence-initial position, although one might expect them to be realized elsewhere. For instance, in (1) the verb *meet* does not have an object to its right (the position indicated by *ec*), which instead is realized in the first position of the sentence:

(1)     **Which man** don't you want to meet *ec*?

In this example we say that the NP *which man* has been fronted to a sentence-initial position.

Movement processes have been well-studied in creoles (e.g. Muysken 1977, Lefebvre et al. 1982; the various contributions in Byrne & Winford 1993). Before we start our exposition, we must first distinguish between movement and non-movement of an element that appears at the left. In the latter case the element only **seems** to have been moved to the front, while in fact it is base-generated in that position. This is called Left Dislocation, a typical main clause (also called **root**) phenomenon:

(2)     John, I don't like him.

In what follows we are mainly concerned with constructions where **real** movement can be argued to have taken place.

The movement constructions can be divided into three classes, depending on the context in which they appear: (1) Fronting in a **declarative** context; (2) Fronting in an **interrogative** context; (3) Fronting in **relative clauses**. Not all creole languages necessarily have each variant.

Fronting in a declarative context involves the information structure of the sentence, and notions like **topicality** of constituents or **focalization**. It subsumes the following constructions: a. Topicalization: movement of a non-verbal expression to clause-initial position, without additional marking. b. Cleft: movement whereby the fronted element is accompanied by a marker corresponding to the equative copula in form. c. Movement to clause-initial position of an XP accompanied by a focus particle. Another fronting process is the

**predicate cleft** or **predicate doubling** construction: movement of a verb to clause-initial position, leaving a copy behind. The fronted element can be accompanied by a marker.

Fronting in an interrogative context involves **wh-movement**: movement of a WH-word to clause-initial position, thereby turning the sentence into a question. Relative clause formation involves movement of a relative element to clause-initial position, thereby turning the clause into a predicate of the head noun or antecedent.

One of the central questions in creole studies is whether creoles pattern with their superstrates or with their substrates. Now two features of fronting phenomena in (the Atlantic) creoles seem to reflect an African substrate:the predicate cleft construction and the presence of a highlighter in clefts and questions. Beyond this, diversity seems to be the rule, i.e. we find the same variation among creoles as we do among other languages. This questions the uniformity of creoles.

## 24.2  Declarative context

### 24.2.1  Topicalization

Topicalization involves fronting of a non-verbal expression to clause-initial position. All major categories can be topicalized. Generally, the fronted element is an already known discourse topic or refers to background information (see chapter 17). In languages lacking the cleft construction (see below), like Saramaccan, fronting without an overt marker can also be interpreted as foregrounding or focalizing an element. Unless otherwise mentioned the Saramaccan data in this chapter are based upon research by the first author.

(3)     a.   Feledi    mi    si    a    di    djai.           NP            (Saramaccan)
              Freddy   1SG   see   Loc   the   garden
              'Freddy, I saw in the garden.'

        b.   A    di    djai    mi    si    en.              PP
              Loc   the   garden   1SG   see   3SG
              'In the garden, I saw him.'

        c.   Libilibi   de    feni   en.                     AP
              alive     3PL   find   3SG
              'Alive, they found him.' (Alleyne 1987)

Saramaccan topicalization does not exhibit a root/non-root asymmetry, i.e. it is possible in main clauses as well as in embedded clauses. Compare the following case of PP topicalization:

(4)   Mi meni [taa   a     di    djai     mi   bi    si    en].          (Saramaccan)
      1SG think that  Loc   the   garden   1SG  PAST  see   3SG
      'I think it is in the garden that I had seen him.'

Furthermore, topicalization is unbounded. This means that a topic originating in the
embedded clause may end up in main clause-initial position:

(5)   a.   Di    gwamba Kofi   sabi   taa    mi    njan.              (Saramaccan)
           the   meat   Kofi   know   that   1SG   eat
           'The meat, Kofi knows that I eat.'
      b.   Di    wagi  u     bi    ke    fu    de    wasi.
           the   car   1PL   PAST  want  for   3PL   wash
           'The car, we wanted them to wash.'

It also obeys the island constraints of Ross (1967). In (6a) an example is given of a wh-island.
You cannot move a topic out of a clause starting with a question word. In (6b) it is shown
that topicalization out of an NP is unacceptable:

(6)   a.   *Di   hogima  a     konda  da    di    sikoutu
           the   thief   3SG   tell   give  the   police
           [ka    dee    sodati  hondi].                             (Saramaccan)
           where  the    soldiers hunt
           'The thief told the police where the soldiers hunted.' (Byrne 1987)
      b.   *Di   womi  mi   si    [wan peentju di    fefi].
           the   man   1SG  see   a   painting that  paint
           'The man I see a painting that (he) painted.'

The constraints that hold for topicalization, also hold for cleft constructions (next section),
wh-movement (section 24.3) and relative clause formation (section 24.4).

### 24.2.2 Cleft

The main difference between topicalization and cleft constructions is the presence of a so-
called 'highlighter' accompanying the fronted phrase. In most cases this marker resembles
the equative copula. An example from Krio is given below:

(7)   Na    snek  kil   am.                                          (Krio)
      COP   snake kill  3SG
      'It is the snake that killed him.'

Not all creole languages employ this option. Saramaccan, for instance, does not have such clefts. For other languages a highlighter seems to be obligatory (Krio, Haitian).

Since the same constraints on possible dependencies are at work here as in topicalization structures, we might be inclined to say that the two constructions should receive a similar analysis. Two possibilities come to mind: (1) the clefted phrase has undergone actual movement; (2) the clefted phrase is base-generated and is related to the gap via an empty operator. The latter option treats the cleft construction as a kind of left dislocation.

An argument against such an analysis for Haitian would be the fact that there is no root/non-root asymmetry, i.e. clefts can also occur in embedded contexts (Hall 1953):

| (8) | Li | we | ke | se | manman pa | li | li | te | manje. | (Haitian) |
|-----|-----|-----|-----|-----|-----|-----|-----|-----|-----|-----|
| | 3SG see | | that | COP | mother own | 3SG | 3SG | PAST | eat | |

'He saw that it was his own mother he had eaten.'

This might be construed as an argument for an analysis on a par with clefts in English and French. Recall that left dislocation occurs only in root clauses.

### 24.2.3 Focus

Focus constructions are quite similar to clefts, the main difference being that the focused element contains (new) information that is 'foregrounded' in the information structure of the sentence. Saramaccan has a separate focus marker (FOC), an element that accompanies the focused element:

| (9) | Di buku we | mi | bi | lesi. | (Saramaccan) |
|-----|-----|-----|-----|-----|-----|
| | the book FOC | ISG | PAST | read | |

'I read THE BOOK.'

Byrne & Caskey (1993) argue that Saramaccan *de* 'there' also is a focus marker. There are reasons for not accepting this analysis. One reason is that if *de* was a focus marker, Saramaccan would have three focus markers specified according to the distance with respect to the speaker, as the following examples indicate.

| (10) | a. | Di | buku aki | mi | bi | ta lesi. | (Saramaccan) |
|-----|-----|-----|-----|-----|-----|-----|-----|
| | | the | book here | ISG | PAST | PR read | |

'This book here I have been reading.'

| | b. | Di | buku de | | mi | bi | ta lesi. |
|-----|-----|-----|-----|-----|-----|-----|-----|
| | | the | book there (nearby) | | ISG | PAST | PR read |

'That book (there) I have been reading.'

    c.  Di   buku ala          mi   bi   ta lesi.

        the   book  there (far away) 1SG   PAST  PR read

        'That book (there) I have been reading.'

Therefore *de* must be an NP-final deictic element.

### 24.2.4 Predicate cleft

Predicate cleft constructions are constructions in which a copy of a verb appears in sentence-initial position optionally accompanied by a highlighter. The main function is to focus on the verbal action. Although in most cases it will be a verb that is repeated, in principle other predicative elements can be repeated as well.

    The basic characteristics of the construction are (following Koopman 1984:161): (1) predicate clefting of the matrix verb is always possible, provided the verb has a base form and no WH-phrase occurs in sentence-initial position; (2) the clause must contain a copy of the focused verb; (3) a focused verb may not be related to an identical verb inside a WH-island or a complex NP; (4) long predicate clefting is possible when the matrix verb is a bridge verb. Syntactically, this movement process shows the same dependency effects as WH-movement.

    There are four types of predicate cleft (Lefebvre 1994): (1) predicate cleft proper; (2) temporal adverbial clauses; (3) causal adverbial clauses; (4) factive clauses. Examples are given below. Note the presence of a highlighter in (11a) versus its absence in (11b-d):

(11)    a.  Se   rive  Jan   rive.                              (Haitian)

           FOC  arrive John arrive

           'Arrive John did (not e.g. leave).'

    b.  Rive  Jan   rive   Mari  pati.

          arrive John  arrive Mary  leave

          'As soon as John arrived, Mary left'

    c.  Rive  Jan   rive   Mari  pati.

          arrive John  arrive Mary  leave

          'Because John arrived, Mary left'

    d.  Rive  Jan   rive   a     fe    li      kontan.

          arrive John  arrive DET   make 3SG   happy

          'The fact that John arrived made her happy.'

With respect to predicate cleft proper the main issue in the literature is the status of the focused verb. There are four possibilities: (1) the verb has moved leaving a copy in the base position (Piou 1982; Koopman 1984); (2) a copy has been moved and the actual verb stays behind (Byrne 1987); (3) a nominalized verb moves to clause-initial position originating from 'an abstract object clitic position', as posited by Roeper & Keyser (1992) (cf. Manfredi 1993); (4) the cognate object (in the sense of Hale & Keyser 1993) of the verb moves to clause-initial position (Lefebvre 1994). The first two options treat predicate cleft as head movement, the latter two as XP-movement. From the latter two options it follows that predicate cleft equals WH-movement and topicalization. A question that remains, however, is whether predicate cleft mimics the behavior of adjuncts or arguments with respect to extractability (see chapter 23 and section 24.3.1).

Above we have noted the constraints on the movement of the clefted verb. This conclusion was based mainly on data from Haitian where the verb can undergo long movement. In Saramaccan, on the other hand, long movement of the verb is not possible. The process is clause bound (van den Berg 1987). This constitutes another domain of variation in the group of creole languages.

There also exists variation as regards the presence of a highlighter introducing the clefted verb. Haitian, Jamaican Creole and Sranan Tongo have such a particle, Saramaccan does not. Not surprisingly this particle resembles the equative copula in the relevant languages.

Larson and Lefebvre (1991) show that not just any verb can undergo predicate cleft. The distinction 'stage-level predicate' versus 'individual-level predicate' of Carlson (1977) is relevant here. Only stage-level predicates, predicates denoting actions or temporary properties, can undergo predicate cleft:

(12)   a.   Se      mache   Jan     mache   al lekol.                                    (Haitian)
            FOC     walk    John    walk    go school
            'John WALKED to school (i.e. did not run).'

       b.   *se     konnen  Jan     konnen  Franse.
            FOC     know    John    know    French
            'John really knows French.'

Thus, it is usually assumed that only (a class of) verbs can undergo Predicate Cleft. Grosso modo this might be the correct generalization (predicate cleft is used as a test for verbhood in many studies, e.g. Sebba 1987), but in Jamaican Creole particles can also undergo predicate cleft, unless we analyse *wind ... bak* as a serial verb construction.

(13)   A       bak     mi      wind bak  di      kasset.                          (Jamaican Creole)
       COP     back    1SG     wind back the     cassette
       'I am REwinding the cassette (i.e. not idling)'

This observation can be used as an argument for analyzing particles as small clause predicates, in accordance with Den Dikken (1992), and could lead to the generalization that all predicative categories can undergo predicate cleft.

Lefebvre & Ritter (1993) argue that despite their surface similarities the two adverbial clauses exemplified in (11b-c) should be distinguished syntactically as well as semantically. Arguments involve the categorial status of the doubled element: only a verb in the case of temporal adverbial clauses, but in the other case it can be any major (lexical) category. This is shown below for nominal predicates:

(14)  a.  Avoka    Jan    avoka    a,    li    kwe      li                          (Haitian)
          lawyer   John   lawyer   the,  3SG   believe  3SG
          kapab    joure  tout    moun.
          able     insult every   one
          'Since John is a lawyer, he thinks he can insult everyone.'
      b.  *Avoka   Jan    avoka    a,    li    ap kapab  jwenn   travay   fasil.
          lawyer   John   lawyer   the   3SG   PR able    find    work     easy
          'As soon as John becomes a lawyer, he will be able to find work easily.'

Other arguments concern the presence of INFL particles, which is possible in causal adverbial clauses but not in temporal ones, and the fact that causal adverbial clauses permit clefting of individual-level predicates, whereas temporal ones do not. Finally, note that predicate cleft in these adverbial clauses is clause bound, unlike predicate cleft proper.

Consider finally the factive clause exemplified by (11d). Here, a clearly nominal element that is identical to the verb appears in clause-initial position. Here too predicate cleft is clause bound. It has more similarities with causal adverbial clauses than with temporal ones (see Lefebvre & Ritter 1993 for more details).

## 24.3 Interrogative contexts

### 24.3.1 WH-movement

WH-movement is the fronting of a WH-phrase to clause-initial position in interrogatives. The constraints on possible wh-dependencies are identical to those on topicalization. One cannot extract WH-phrases out of WH-islands or complex NPs (see section 24.2.1). This seems to be true for most creole languages. As far as we know, only Haitian and Papiamento are exceptions to the island constraints. In those cases a resumptive pronoun is needed in the extraction site.

There is an interesting difference in extraction possibilities between arguments and adjuncts. Domains that block extraction of arguments and adjuncts, are called 'strong islands' and domains which allow argument extraction, but not adjunct extraction are called 'weak islands'. In chapter 23 we have already seen how patterns of extractability of both arguments and adjuncts can be used to determine the basic configuration of serial verb constructions.

In some languages, e.g. Krio, a highlighter is present in wʜ-questions:

(15)    Na     udat  bin   kam?                                          (Krio)
        FOC    who   PAST  come
        'Who came?'

The same observation can be made for Jamaican Creole: the highlighter *a* is optionally used with wʜ-words, but due to decreolization it is disappearing. Holm's suggestion that there is a highlighter in Saramaccan wʜ-questions (Holm 1988:180) can be dismissed, since *na* in the pertinent wʜ-phrase (*na unse* 'where') is not the equative copula (*da*), but an allomorph of the locative preposition.

Muysken & Smith (1990) discuss the internal make-up of wʜ-words and try to answer the question of how these function words are reconstituted in creole genesis. There happens to be quite a bit of variation in the way creole languages go about the formation of these elements (see chapter 11).

### 24.3.2 The extractability of constituents

*Subject extraction.* In addition to the argument-adjunct distinction, the distinction between subject and object extraction has attracted much attention in current linguistic theorizing. Important in this respect is the so-called 'that-trace effect', which refers to an asymmetry with respect to the extractability of subjects and objects out of embedded clauses. In certain languages (e.g. English) subject extraction is forbidden, while object extraction is acceptable. Most analyses look for the main reason for this asymmetry in the difference in status of these arguments (the object being an internal argument and the subject being an external argument of the verb) combined with their structural positions in the sentence.

There is quite a bit of variation among creole languages with respect to this asymmetry. In Jamaican Creole extraction of an embedded subject across an overt complementizer leads to ungrammaticality, whereas extraction of an embedded object does not (Veenstra 1990):

(16)    a. *Wu   yu    tink    se    gowe?                               (Jamaican)
           who   2SG   think   that  leave
           'Who do you think had left?'

b.  Wu   yu   tink  se     im    lik?
    who  2SG  think that   3SG   hit
    'Who do you think that he had hit?'

In Saramaccan there is variation among speakers as regards extraction of an embedded subject. Some accept it, others do not:

(17)  (*)Ambe mi   si     taa    naki  en?                                (Saramaccan)
      who    1SG  see    that   hit   3SG
      'Who did I see that had hit her?'

Papiamento, on the other hand, does not display such an asymmetry at all, as can be seen from the following example:

(18)  Ken   bo    ta bisa  ku    a  bai?                                  (Papiamento)
      who   2SG   PR say   that  PR leave
      'Who did you say that had left?'

A related asymmetry in Haitian is the following: displacement of a subject within its own clause (be it an embedded subject or a main clause subject) requires the presence of the morpheme *ki* in preverbal position, whereas this morpheme does not surface when the object is fronted (see Koopman 1982; Law 1993):

(19)  a.  Kimoun *(ki)   vini?                                           (Haitian)
          who     KI     come
          'Who came?'
      b.  Kimoun (*ki)   li    bat?
          who     KI     3SG   beat
          'Who did he beat?'

This morpheme may be in the complementizer position in order to govern the subject position (Koopman's position) or in the subject position (thereby acting as a resumptive element) (Law's position).

DeGraff (1994) notes that for some speakers there is a root/non-root asymmetry with respect to *ki*: while for them *ki* is obligatorily present in root environments, it is optional in non-root (i.e. embedded) contexts:

(20)  a.  Kimoun *(ki)   di     Jan    pral  vini?
          who     KI    say    John   will  come
          'Who said that John will come?'

      b.  Kimoun ou    di     (ki)   pral  vini?
          who     2SG   say    KI     will  come
          'Who do you say will come?'

In conclusion we can say that there is not much uniformity among creoles with respect to extraction asymmetries.

*Island Violations.* As noted in the beginning of this section, Haitian and Papiamento can violate the island constraints which most creole languages obey. This also holds of relativization, which will be dealt with in section 24.4. In all cases that can be characterized as violations, a resumptive pronoun surfaces in the extraction site. Below examples are given of extraction out of a complex NP (21a) in a relative clause and out of a WH-island (21b) in an interrogative. Both examples are taken from DeGraff (1994):

(21)  a.  Men  eleman  mwen   te    we    makout ki  te    bat    *(li)   an.
          here fellow   1SG    PAST  see   thug    KI  ANT   beat   RP     the
          'Here is the fellow who I saw the thug who beat him.'
      b.  Kimoun ou    pral   mande  lapres si  *(li)  te     mouri?
          who     2SG   will   ask           press  if  3SG   ANT    die
          'Who will you ask the press whether he died?'

In both cases, the resumptive pronoun *li* is obligatorily present and rescues the sentence from ungrammaticality. Law (1993) observes that the resumptive pronoun agrees in number with its antecedent, as in the next example:

(22)  Ki     etidyan  sa    yo Jan  mande  Mari si yo/*li achete  liv    la?
      which  student  that  PL John ask     Mary if RP    buy     book   DET
      'Which students (among those) did John ask Mary whether they bought the book?'

Here, the antecedent *ki etidyan sa yo* is plural, and the resumptive pronoun is also plural (*yo*) and not singular (*li*).

Papiamento also allows for apparent violations of the island constraints. As in Haitian, the repair strategy involves resumptive pronouns. These also agree in number with their antecedents:

(23)  **Kwa**  **homber-nan**   Wancho a konta bo   e    kwenta
      which  man-PL            Wancho PR tell  you  the  story

 

ku    ela      laga  **nan**  drenta?
that  he-PAST  let   RP    enter
'Which men has Wancho told you the story that he has let them enter?'

More resumptive strategies will be discussed immediately below and in section 24.4 (on relative clauses).

*P-stranding.* WH-movement out of PPs plays a role in the discussion on the supposedly unmarked character of creole languages (Muysken 1988a). The absence of preposition-stranding is usually assumed to be the unmarked option (van Riemsdijk 1978). Yet, within the group of creole languages we find the following variation (Muysken 1994):

(24)  a.  stranding allowed:              Jamaican Creole
                                          Krio
                                          Berbice Dutch
                                          Negerhollands

 

     b.  stranding not allowed:          Saramaccan
                                          Sranan Tongo
                                          Haitian

 

     c.  stranding with trace spell-out:  Papiamento
                                          Capeverdean

Examples from each group for Negerhollands, Saramaccan and Papiamento, respectively, are given below:

(25)  a.  Am   ne   kan  fin   it   widi di   skun hotu   **fa.**   (Negerhollands)
          3SG  NEG  can  find  out  who  the  shoe belong of
          'He couldn't find out who the shoe belonged to.'
          (Bruyn & Veenstra 1993)
      b.  **Kuambe**   mi   ta wooko?                          (Saramaccan)
          with-who  1SG  PR work
          'With whom am I working together?'

   c. **Ken** nan  a    papia kune?                         (Papiamento)
      who  3PL  PAST  speak with-3SG
      'Who did they speak with?'

Extraction out of PPs has been given detailed treatment in Papiamento (Muysken 1977; Dijkhoff 1983a). Movement out of manner PPs, temporal PPs and certain locative PPs is not possible. To be more specific, only 'locative' PPs that are arguments of a verb permit extraction of their complements. For this contrast compare the following examples from Dijkhoff (1983a):

(26)  a.  Nan  a   konta riba  e      boto.
          3PL  PR count  on   the  boat
          'They counted while on the boat' OR
          'They relied on the boat.'
    b.  **Kiko** nan  a   konta riba  **dje?**
          what  3PL  PR count on     RP
          'What did they rely on?'
          NOT 'What did they count while being on?'

In principle, the form *dje* (actually, a contraction of inserted *di* 'of' and *e* '3SG') could be either analyzed as a resumptive pronoun or as a spelled-out trace. An argument for the latter analysis is the fact that those forms are always non-agreeing, in contradistinction to resumptive pronouns, which do agree with their antecedents in number, as was shown for Papiamento and Haitian above.

## 24.4 Relative clauses

Relative clauses share certain properties with WH-questions. They come in two sorts: restrictive and non-restrictive. Restrictive relative clauses identify the head they modify, while non-restrictive ones prototypically contain new information. The two types display similar syntactic behavior.

    There are no restrictions on the relativizability of NPs (see Keenan & Comrie 1977). All NPs in a sentence can undergo relativization. Only when the NP is a possessor or an object of a preposition (without the PP undergoing pied-piping), a resumptive pronoun is needed in the extraction site (see below).

    Creoles vary as to whether they have a relative marker or not. Saramaccan, Sranan Tongo and other creoles do, while Haitian does not: only in subject relatives does an obligatory *ki* surface (see the discussion on subject extraction above). However, French-influenced varieties of Haitian use *ke* as a relative marker (Dreyfuss 1977).

Apart from the usual repair strategies, resumptive pronouns occur in two environments: (1) as objects of prepositions; (2) as possessor NPs. Examples are from Saramaccan:

(27)  a.  di    womi di    mi    wooko   ku    **en**
          the   man  REL   ISG   work    with  RP-3SG
          'the man I worked with'
      b.  di    womi di    mi    booko   **en**     futu
          the   man  REL   ISG   break   RP-3SG    leg
          'the man whose leg I broke'

They agree in number with their antecedent:

(28)  dee      womi di    mi    wooko   ku    de
      the-PL   man  REL   ISG   work    with  RP-3PL
      'the men I worked with'

This shows that languages that do not allow for P-stranding at all, can have a resumptive pronoun strategy for extraction out of a PP in relative clauses. It is not clear from the literature what the cause of this rather unexpected difference is.

**Further reading**
The major works on fronting are Muysken (1977), Lefebvre et al. (1982) and Byrne & Winford (1993). The last work contains a useful bibliography.

Part v.
**Conclusions and annotated language list**

# 25 Conclusions

Jacques Arends, Pieter Muysken and Norval Smith

## 25.1 Introduction

In this book we have considered a number of aspects of pidgins and creoles, and competing theories accounting for their origin. Now we are in a position to better evaluate the different theories in terms of their explanatory potential, and this will be done in the first section of this chapter. We then presented a number of case studies of individual pidgins and creoles of the Atlantic area (in a broad sense), and lastly analyzed specific syntactic phenomena in a comparative perspective. We find quite a bit of variation, as well as uncanny resemblances between the different creoles. Furthermore, a number of the phenomena under discussion have turned out to be quite complex. Both the variation in the creoles and their complexity will be further illustrated in this chapter in a discussion of the copula, and creole phonology and morphology. We conclude with a number of issues for further research.

## 25.2 Scenarios for creole genesis

In the second part of this book (chapters 8 through 11) various theories, hypotheses and models were discussed that have been put forward to explain the origin and genesis of creole and - to a lesser extent - pidgin languages. In this section each of these theories will be briefly evaluated.

### 25.2.1 Theories focusing on the European input

*Foreigner Talk/Baby Talk.* While there are not many recent theories of creole genesis that explicitly refer to Foreigner Talk as an explanatory concept, the one that has done so most explicitly, Naro's (1978) Reconnaissance Language Theory, has been severely criticized in recent years (Clancy Clements 1992; Goodman 1987; but see also Naro 1988, 1993). The role of Foreigner Talk itself is not questioned as a factor in creole genesis. Seuren & Wekker (1986) incorporated Naro's Factorization Principle, which is an operationalization of the role of Foreigner Talk in creole genesis, into their Semantic Transparency Theory. Foreigner Talk as a general concept and the Factorization Principle still occupies an important place in at least some theories of creole genesis. In order to maintain this position, more attention should be paid to recent results from the study of Foreigner Talk as such.

*Imperfect Second Language Learning.* Earlier ideas regarding possible parallels between creolization and pidginization on the one hand and natural second language acquisition on the other, as expressed in Andersen (1983) and Schumann (1978), have not been followed up by many creolists. Nonetheless, the role of second language learning in creole genesis has received a new impetus in the gradualist model of creolization. In a community where the rate of nativization of the creole speaking population is low, the process of creolization must be partly a matter of second language acquisition by adults. Up to now parallels between both processes have largely been hinted at rather than investigated in any detail. A notable exception, however, is the work by Wekker (1982, 1989, 1996). Further research along these lines will be required in the future.

*Monogenesis.* After a period of popularity in the 1960s and early 1970s, the Monogenesis-Relexification Theory, which claims that many or all creoles go back to a Portuguese Pidgin once spoken along the West African Coast (and perhaps ultimately to the Mediterranean Lingua Franca), does not seem to have any supporters anymore. A weaker version of it was proposed by Hancock (1986) under the name of Domestic Hypothesis. It claims that the English-lexifier Atlantic creoles go back to a Guinea Coast Creole English once spoken in mixed African-European households along the West African Coast, and it has been adopted by a number of creolists, such as Smith (1987) for the Surinam creoles. In order to develop this hypothesis in the future, not only linguistic but also historical evidence will have to be adduced concerning the actual links between the Atlantic English-lexifier creoles. Similarly, the relation between the French-lexifier pidgins and creoles is still an open issue. Hull (1979) assumes a source in Guinea Coast Pidgin French.

*European Dialects.* For some time theories referring to regional European varieties of the lexifier language were more or less in disrepute, especially when related to African-American language varieties (either for methodological or ideological reasons). In recent years there has been a renewed interest in this type of explanation (e.g. Lalla & D'Costa 1990). As far as the French-lexifier creoles are concerned, the European Dialect Hypothesis has been forcefully defended by Chaudenson (e.g. 1974, 1992) for Réunionais. Chaudenson's earlier views have been severely criticized by Baker (1982), both on internal-linguistic and on external, especially demographic, grounds. Whatever the merits of this hypothesis, in order to survive it will have to rid itself of its methodological flaws (i.e. its use of the Cafeteria Principle).

### 25.2.2 Theories focusing on the non-European input
*Substrate and relexification.* Apart from the methodological problems involved in assessing

the role of substrate influence, at least some of the disagreement about that role has to do with theoretical conceptions about language structure, i.e. the question whether surface structures or more abstract structures are the point of departure for the analysis. At the moment two strands of substrate research can be distinguished: the more descriptive, surface-oriented approach of Alleyne, Boretzky and others, and the more theory-driven, abstract approach of Lefebvre, Lumsden and their associates. Both approaches could benefit more than they have done up to now from the results of historical investigations into the demographics of slave populations. This may serve to reduce the set of substrate languages to those that were actually spoken at the right moment, and at the right place.

### 25.2.3 Gradualist and developmental hypotheses

*Gradual creolization.* The principal weakness of the gradualist model is that up to now it has not been articulated with enough precision to allow falsification. On the other hand, it has given rise to a number of historical studies, both linguistic and extra-linguistic, that provide evidence against some of the other theories, especially the Bioprogram Hypothesis. Also, now that more and more earlier texts are being discovered it becomes feasible to include other creoles in research carried out in this framework. As indicated above, a serious effort should be made by proponents of this view to explore the parallels between creolization and second language acquisition. In order to approach the historical situation as closely as possible, an experimental design could be developed whereby the acquisition of e.g. English as a second language by speakers of West African languages is compared with the structural features of English-lexifier creoles.

*Grammaticalization.* While the concept of grammaticalization itself is not entirely new, it has only recently begun to be more widely used in linguistics in general. One of the first scholars to introduce it in the study of pidgins and creoles was Gillian Sankoff, who explained the origin of the Tok Pisin future marker *be* and the relative marker *ia* from this perspective (Sankoff & Laberge 1974; Sankoff & Brown 1978). More recently, grammaticalization was invoked by Plag (1993) in an attempt to explain the diachronic development of Sranan *taki* from a main verb into a complementizer. Although until now this approach has not been used often enough to allow of any definitive assessment, it seems that the concept of grammaticalization can be most fruitfully employed in the study of creoles, especially in diachronic investigations. This is so because in their earlier stages these languages abound with cases crying out for an explanation in terms of grammaticalization processes. The question is, of course, whether grammaticalization in creoles occurs in the same way, and at the same rate, as it does in non-creole languages. The application of the concept of grammaticalization to the development of creole languages could thus contribute both to an elucidation of creolization processes, and to a further elaboration of the concept of grammaticalization itself.

### 25.2.4 Universalist approaches

*Bioprogram Theory.* Twenty years after its inception, Bickerton's Language Bioprogram Hypothesis still occupies an important place in creole studies. In these two decades two major innovations have been incorporated. First, the concept of parameter setting was adopted from GB theory in Bickerton (1984), where the bioprogram is defined as the set of unmarked parameter settings. Second, in Bickerton (1988) orthodox GB theory was replaced by Wexler & Borer's Lexical Learning Hypothesis, which considers that all languages have basically the same syntax, surface variations being lexically determined. In evaluating Bickerton's theory a striking paradox appears: while there is no question that Bickerton's views are still quite influential among creolists, they are not shared by many of them in their most complete version (although they seem more in favor among scholars from other disciplines, such as the cognitive sciences; cf. the peer commentary in Bickerton 1984). This indicates that Bickerton's influence is primarily an indirect one: rather than his views being adopted by other creolists, they have generated an enormous amount of activity, either aimed at accumulating evidence against his views, or at improving the methodological validity of the argumentation used. Since it leads to many new insights and much specific new research, the bioprogram hypothesis has proved a very successful theory.

*Generative Theory.* The fact that during the last two decades generative linguists have actively begun to include creole languages in their databases has had the effect of bringing linguistic theory into a discipline that was up to then largely descriptive. In addition to this, it has shown the relevance of creole studies for linguistic theory. On the other hand, the amount of theoretical sophistication coupled with the ever-continuing adjustments in the theory may cause communication problems between generative and non-generative creolists. In order to benefit optimally from each others' activities, the two parties will have to make sure that no knowledge gap prevents communication.

*Semantic Transparency.* Unfortunately, this hypothesis (like some of the others discussed earlier) has never been elaborated into a full-blown theory of creole genesis. Rather it has the status of a single explanatory principle among others. One particularly profitable way of exploring it further might be its incorporation in the comparative study of creolization and second language acquisition that was referred to above (cf. Wekker 1982, 1989). In addition, the availability of older creole texts now makes it possible to apply the concept of semantic transparency not only to present-day varieties but also to diachronic developments.

*Common Social Context Theory.* This approach has been used primarily by Gillian Sankoff (1980) with regard to the grammaticalization phenomena in Tok Pisin referred to above. In this, largely functionalist, framework these phenomena are analyzed as the result of a process whereby discourse markers change into structural syntactic elements. To the extent that discourse in different pidgins and creoles functions in a more or less similar context certain similarities may occur. Taking into account the fact that pidgins and creoles, perhaps more than any other type of language, are so intimately linked with the social context in which they have arisen, it is somewhat surprising that the functionalist approach has not gained a wider following. The fact that more and more information is being made available about the sociohistorical circumstances of pidginization and creolization may provide it with a new impetus in the future. Whether this will confirm the idea of a common social context for all or most pidgins and creoles is an open question.

### 25.2.5 Conclusion

During the last decade, several proposals have been made that try to reach some sort of compromise by incorporating several of the ideas expressed in the theories discussed above. The motive for devising a theoretical compromise is not so much the desire among creolists to reach a consensus, but rather the awareness that each of the above theories by themselves is incapable of explaining the phenomenon of creole genesis by itself. One of these 'compromise theories' is Mufwene's Complementary Hypothesis, which allows both for substrate and superstrate influence in creole genesis with Universal Grammar operating as a regulating mechanism determining the selection of particular substrate and superstrate features (Mufwene 1986a, 1990). Whatever the precise make-up of such a theory, it will always have to be more than simply the sum of any number of contributing hypotheses, since otherwise it will not be falsifiable. In other words, it will have to state as precisely as possible the division of labor among the several sub-theories as well as any interactions between them.

### 25.3 Unity and diversity

Something that every creolist has to come to grips with is the tension between the diversity between the structures of the different creoles around, and the fact that they present striking similarities. Both aspects are a challenge. Can we set up scenarios specific enough to come to grips with this apparent contradiction?

We will exemplify this issue with the copula. The original assumption in many studies was that creoles have a null copula. This was the background assumption in Labov's (1990) [1971] work on copula deletion in the Black English Vernacular, and Ferguson's (1971) pioneering study of simplified registers and foreigner talk. However, the actual patterns of copula usage in creoles are much more complex. In Papiamento we have *ta* in all contexts, locative, predicative, identificational:

(1)     a.     Mi ta na kas.
               'I am in the house.'
        b.     Mi ta di Korsow.
               'I am from Curacao.'
        c.     Mi ta Pedro.
               'I am Pedro.'

In Guyanais (Saint-Jacques Fauqenoy 1972) we find a null copula. The form *ès* in (2a) is not a copula but a question particle.

(2)     a.     Ès tó la?
               'Are you there?'
        b.     Wòm masō.
               'The man is a bricklayer.'

The impersonal subject is either *a* or emphatic *sa*. The latter is restricted in its use:

(3)     a.     A / sa bō.
               'It's good.'
        b.     A / ?*sa mó.
               'It's me.'

In Principense (Günther 1973) the copula *sa* is optional:

(4)     Ína (sa) mígu mútu.
        'They are good friends.'

When *sa* is present, the weak clitic form of the subject pronoun must be used:

(5)     a.     Amí unú.
        b.     *Amí sa unú.
        c.     N sa unú.
        d.     *N unú.
               'I am naked.'

In Jamaican (Bailey 1966), a distinction is made between locative and non-locative use:

(6)    a.    Di tob de ina kichin.
                'The tub is in the kitchen.'
         b.    Disya buk a fi-Mieri
                'This book is Mary's.'

With adjectives, there is no copula, a common pattern in the Caribbean creoles (see below):

(7)    di kaafi kuol
         'The coffee is cold.'

## 25.4  The lexicon and multifunctionality

In all creoles we find that lexical items are multifunctional in that they can belong to several word classes at a time. Assuming there to be a base category for each item, we can assume a morphological process of conversion or zero-derivation (different theoretical claims are embodied in these terms, but this need not concern us here).

Voorhoeve (1981) has studied this problem in some detail for Sranan. He posits rules of conversion, on the basis of regular patterns of correspondence (see chapter 18). Thus the word *siki* can be the adjective 'ill', the noun 'illness', the transitive verb 'make (someone) ill' and the intransitive verb 'be ill'.

A complex case of multifunctionality, where the category of the element involved appears to be determined by the syntactic context, involves adjectives/stative verbs in Sranan. These elements function as stative verbs when used predicatively and cannot have a preceding copula (*de* in Sranan):

(8)    a.    A liba bradi.
                'The river is wide.'
         b.    *A liba de bradi.

*bradi* is a verb here, and a copula is not allowed. Consider now a case where *bradi* is preceded by the adjectival modifier *so*:

(9)    a.    *A liba so bradi.
         b.    A liba de so bradi.
                'The river is so wide.'

Here the copula is suddenly obligatory. The same holds when *bradi* is questioned with the particle *o* 'how':

(10)    a.  *O bradi a liba?
        b.  O bradi a liba de?
            'How wide is the river?'

When *bradi* is modified, it behaves as an adjective. Similarly, it must be viewed as an adjective in attributive position:

(11)    a bradi liba
        'the wide river'

## 25.5  Phrasal compounding

The primary means of lexical expansion in almost all, if not all, creoles is compounding, which tends to be highly productive. Compounding is used in all categories. Sranan has *mofoneti* [mouth night] 'midnight' and *bobimofo* [breast mouth] 'nipple', Haitian has *bouch kabrit* [mouth goat] 'Cassandra' (Hall 1953: 41). Where Papiamento has *bula bay* [fly go] 'fly away', a compound derived from a serial construction, Haitian has *magne māje* [touch eat] 'just eat a little' (Hall 1953: 42).

Very common in some creole languages is phrasal compounding. It involves (a) cases where one of the members of the compound is a phrase rather than a word, and (b) cases where the structure of the compound itself reflects a syntactic rather than a morphological pattern.

An example of the first type is Saramaccan agentive formation, historically derived from the 18th century form *man*, and now a suffix *ma* (see chapter 14), which is attached to verbs or verbal complexes:

(12)    pai ma [bear man] 'pregnant woman'
        tja buka ma [carry mouth man] 'messenger'
        pai ku mujee ma [bear with woman man] 'midwife'

Notice first of all that the meaning of *ma* is no longer exclusively masculine but rather 'person that ...', i.e. the form is somewhat grammaticalized. Second, the lefthand member can contain noun phrases (*buka* 'mouth'), prepositional phrases (*ku mujee* 'with woman' above), and even clauses and serial constructions.

Similar perhaps are cases in Haitian where verbal complexes function as nouns (Hall 1953: 41):

(13)    pase raj [pass rage] 'exotic dance'
        lanvi mouri [want die] 'imprudent person'
        pote mak [bear mark] 'he who is scarred'

An example of the second type is Papiamento, where most compounds include a linking morpheme *di/i* 'of') (Dijkhoff 1993):

(14)    palu di garganta [stick of neck] 'neck bone'
        kabes di boto [head of boat] 'lift'
        barba di yònkuman [beard of young man] 'herb'

It can be shown that these forms, in spite of their syntactic appearance, behave as lexical islands for pluralization, adjectival modification, extraction, etc. (Dijkhoff 1987).

## 25.6  Phonology

What continues to be striking is that so little is published on pidgin/creole phonology. For morphology there is always the weak excuse that pidgins and creoles have little morphology, although the areas of compounding, reduplication, nominalization, and conversion tend to be quite complex, and result in interestingly different patterns among the languages involved. For phonology a comparison with 'non-creole linguistics', exemplified e.g. in a journal such as *Natural Language and Linguistic Theory*, is sobering, and we feel this is an unfortunate historical accident. The areas of tone, vowel epenthesis or epithesis, and syllable structure, to name but a few areas, all demand the same kind of scrutiny that serial verbs and the copula have been subjected to.

### 25.6.1  Segmental phonology

Few synchronic studies of pidgin or creole phonologies go beyond the stage of a simple phonemic description. Clearly a great deal of work remains to be done in this field. In a sense, the Saussurean principle that synchronic work must precede diachronic work has been largely ignored in the creole field.

   The diachronic work done in the creole field has largely been haphazard and methodologically poor. Researchers have been generally too keen to do large-scale comparisons across groups of creoles with a common lexifier language. Since it is not a priori obvious that such comparisons are legitimate, i.e. that having a common lexifier language necessarily implies any **direct** historical (linguistic) connection, this is equivalent to putting the cart before the horse. By proceeding from small-scale comparisons first, it should be possible to find evidence of linguistic relationships, enabling us to sort creoles into groups. Smith (1987) provides ample evidence that the Surinam creoles form one such group; that this group includes the Jamaican Maroon Spirit Possession Language; and that the next closest relationships are with the West African creoles/pidgins of which Krio is the best-described representative.

Another type of historical research which has been carried out in a very unsound fashion is the important task of tracing African lexical items in European language-lexifier pidgins and creoles. The wildest etymologies have sometimes been proposed. Bickerton (1981) has criticized the use of the **Cafeteria principle**, by which he means the practice of going through randomly selected dictionaries of African languages in an attempt to trace possible African lexical items that might be present in some creole language, without any attempt to establish the historical relevance of a particular African language.

If the selection of dictionaries is made on an arbitrary basis, such as those that just happen to be in one's library at a certain moment, it is not likely to lead to anything significant. If the exercise leads to the apparent conclusion that creole x has two words from African language A, one word from B, one word from C, two words from D, etc. we should at least ask ourselves the tricky question of how such a strange result could come about, since it is inherently unlikely that many languages could have **equal** influence on the development of a creole. Rather than enhancing the general level of intercomprehension, such a process would appear to inhibit it.

If the phonological relationships between the creole lexical item and its supposed African cognate are extremely complex, or even worse if no consistent **sound-laws** in the neogrammarian sense may be established, then we should once again ask ourselves if we are on the right track. The clear cases of established African etyma in creole lexicons demonstrate that, given the small time-intervals involved – usually not more than a few hundred years –, we should beware of any claims involving other than the most obvious relationships.

### 25.6.2 Prosodic systems

One area which promises to be rewarding when sufficient work is done is that of the tone and accent systems of creole languages. For some creoles no indication has been provided that they involve anything other than the types of system familiar from most Western European languages, that is, some kind of word-**stress** system, combined with an **intonation** system. In both cases the primary mechanism utilized has been claimed to be relative-pitch, with amplitude and duration playing a subsidiary role. It must be pointed out however that

Beckman (1986) has claimed that a combination of amplitude and duration is the main indicator of English stress. Van der Hulst & Smith (1988) claim that stress is best not defined in terms of any physical property at all, although it must of course be ultimately realised in terms of some physical property, but that 'stressed syllables are designated syllables in terms of prosodic constituent structure, which by themselves do not convey any tonal information' (Van der Hulst & Smith 1988:xi).

For a number of Atlantic creoles it has been claimed that a third suprasegmental system is involved, which is not utilized in most West European languages, i.e. *tone*. This has been investigated to varying degrees for different creoles, but much work still remains to be done, both on the tone-systems or claimed tone-systems of the individual languages, and as regards the consequences for previous historical stages in the development of the various languages. The claims that have been made so far can be conveniently categorized into four groups.

(a) The **Surinam Maroon** languages Saramaccan and Ndjuka (and the other dialects associated with it) have been convincingly demonstrated to be true tone-languages.

(b) A number of languages in the **Caribbean** and **West Africa** have been claimed to exhibit tonal phenomena in their phonology. These include Jamaican (Alleyne 1980), Krio (Carter 1987), British Jamaican English (Sutcliffe 1992), Guyanese (Devonish 1989, Carter 1987), and Cameroonian Pidgin (Dwyer 1967). Carter claims that the Guyanese, Krio and Cameroonian Pidgin systems are related, despite her description of the first as pitch-accent, and the latter two as tonal. Smith & Adamson (in prep.) suggest that Sranan possesses a somewhat similar tonal behavior.

(c) **Papiamento** has been analysed as a tone language (Römer 1992).

(d) The Portuguese-lexifier creoles of the **Gulf of Guinea** have been claimed to be tone-languages (e.g. Principense by Günther 1973). Traill & Ferraz (1981) disagree, preferring to characterize Principense as possessing free pitch accent.

It is clear that what we find in these languages cannot be described in all cases as involving true lexical tone oppositions. Of course the distinctive use of tone in the languages of the world is not restricted to the marking of lexical distinctions. A second very important use of tone is to mark morphosyntactic distinctions, and this function is employed in a number of the above-mentioned languages. Furthermore, even a cursory examination of a number of languages will reveal that it does not make sense to speak about an opposition between two types of language – stress-languages and tone-languages. Tone and stress are in fact two separate phonological dimensions - tone being basically a property of segments, and stress not – which may well occur combined in the same language in quite a variety of ways. The fact that stress may be primarily articulated by pitch may also confuse the issue.

## 25.7 Language change and language contact

Another area of future concern is the relation between creole studies and language contact studies. Apart from the attempt at a synthesis in Thomason & Kaufman's (1988) book, few recent studies have linked creoles and language contact explicitly. This is unfortunate, we feel, because much of the time creolists are drawing up scenarios about what happened in some fort, slave market or plantation as much as several hundred years ago. These scenarios are subject to two potentially fatal flaws: first, often the historical knowledge about who, when, where, and how is scanty, although the study of demographic and social history is continually providing us with new results. Second, assumptions are often made about second language learning, interference, relexification, etc. which are not based on what has come to be known about these processes. In the areas of acquisition, code-switching and mixing, borrowing, and bilingual processing tremendous progress has been made, which has not had sufficient effect on the scenarios around, it seems.

Again, this criticism is sometimes countered with the objection that contemporary research in these fields is irrelevant because the process of enslavement and subsequently the situation of slavery, were so extreme and so different from what is ordinary in contemporary societies that the uniformitarian principle does not apply. All the processes mentioned have been shown to be strongly determined by the social context in which they occur. Learning German in a classroom in a French 'lycée' is very different from learning it in the streets of Kreuzberg, the Turkish quarter in Berlin. The type of code-switching and lexical interference from a national language that we find in minority language radio broadcasts is again quite different from what we find when bilingual adolescents joke in conversations involving those same minority and national languages. Language contact research is at the stage, however, where variability and social embedding are usually taken into account, in terms of typologies of bilingual speech behavior. These typologies, in turn, could be the basis for more realistic pidgin and creole scenarios. The field would profit greatly from closer links with neighboring subdisciplines.

The same holds for language change. For an essentially historical discipline, pidgin and creole studies has more often than not had a *persona* steeped in synchrony, not diachrony. Again, this ahistorical perspective is rather beside the point. The dynamic nature of pidgins and creoles is often ignored, whereby, say 20th century Papiamento is taken as representative for a putative early stage, and this without further comment. In addition, the recent methodological innovations and theoretical insights of historical linguistics have not had much impact yet in the creole field.

# 26 An annotated list of creoles, pidgins, and mixed languages

Norval Smith

## 26.1 Introduction

This list is not to be taken as in any way complete. It has only the modest aim to attempt to give a very tentative idea of the distribution of the known creoles, pidgins, and mixed languages of the world. All three categories are without doubt underrepresented, although the categories of pidgins, and what we have termed symbiotic mixed languages, are probably the most incomplete.

The recently published *Atlas of the world's languages* (Moseley & Asher 1994) virtually ignores most of the more than 500 languages and dialects included here, one notable exception being the section on Oceania edited by Wurm. This must surely demonstrate to some extent a continuing prejudice against these languages. In any case this list then has the added function of a supplement to the Atlas.

The idea for such a list, and the basis for it, came from Ian Hancock's (1971, 1977, 1981) lists of pidgin and creole languages. We have attempted to extend his lists in certain new directions, and provide a classification in terms that might be relevant for various kinds of research. The present state of our knowledge about creoles and pidgins in particular is of course much advanced as compared to twenty years ago, in the sense that we know much more about a large number of these languages and their development than we did then. However, precisely because of the expanding interest in such matters, many new examples of lesser-known languages have emerged to keep a list like this fuzzy at the edges.

As it is not our intention to provide a bibliography of creoles, pidgins and mixed languages, we will not supply bibliographical references for each language or dialect mentioned. Such a bibliography would in any case go far beyond the scope of this book. We do however list a number of works which we have found it profitable to consult, as well as a small number of interesting references outside the normal creolist literature. References for most languages should be fairly easy to trace. For a detailed survey covering large parts of the same ground as this list, the interested reader should examine Holm (1988, 1989).

The known **creoles** (c) are clearly clustered in locations that were the scene of the European colonial expansion between about 1500 and 1900. In particular this involves the Caribbean, coastal areas of West Africa, India, and large parts of the Pacific. That this should be so is related to the general problem of identifying creoles. Unless both the linguistic history and social history of a particular group are known – and we have relatively little detailed knowledge about either kind of history for most of the world – we cannot identify languages as creoles with any certainty. Thus the clustering of creoles in the above-mentioned locations is certainly an artefact deriving from the lack of historical knowledge on the part of creolists concerning other parts of the world where creolization might have taken place in different places and times. One may wonder for instance whether some of the perplexing problems of classification of certain South American Indian languages are not due to their origin as creoles or mixed languages.

**Pidgins** (P) on the other hand are geographically of much more widespread occurrence. Despite this there are also areas where pidgins could be expected to be more frequently encountered than elsewhere. Areas with numerous smaller tribal societies – and hence languages – are prime candidates for pidgin-rich territory. New Guinea is obviously such an area, with its roughly 1000 tribal languages and relatively small population. The need for many trading pidgins is of course now passing, with the spread in Papua New Guinea this century of Tok Pisin, but it would be reasonable to expect that many pidgins remain to be discovered. As was stated in chapter 1, Pidgins are divided into **jargons** (PJ), **stabilized pidgins** (PS), and **expanded pidgins** (PE) according to the classification of Mühlhäusler (1986) (see chapter 3). Where possible, we will attempt to classify pidgins in these terms, although in the present state of our knowledge some classifications must be regarded as provisional.

**Mixed languages** arise under conditions of bilingualism, when groups attempt to define, redefine, retain or even regain their ethnic status. This often results in a degree of language mixture. The most frequent type encountered is that where the grammar of one of the languages originally spoken in the group in question is combined with the content-words of another language known to the group (see chapter 4). The resultant language replaces the original ethnic language(s), and is in general the only language spoken. This type we will refer to as (plain) mixed languages (M). The number of these in the list is certainly much too low, as mixed languages frequently suffer from the same prejudice as was previously often directed at creoles – that they are either not regarded as proper languages, or else are treated as dialects of one or other contributory language. Obviously pidgins and creoles may also be mixed (MP/MC).

A category resembling mixed languages in a number of ways, but which we have deliberately excluded from this list is the **interlanguage** or intermediate stage in second language-learning. Where whole language communities are becoming bilingual these may be quite widely used for community-internal communication, like Taglish – the Tagalog-English of bilinguals in the Manilla area. The only cases of interlanguage that have been included are some of the cases where the interlanguage has been institutionalized, and therefore itself becomes a target in language-learning, whether as a 1st language or a 2nd language, in any case no longer an interlanguage. The precise form the result of this institutionalization takes – mixed language, or pidgin – depends on the particular circumstances of the case.

Also excluded are the final stages of **language death**, where semi-speakers' renditions of their ethnic languages are frequently reminiscent of the kind of things that appear in mixed languages, with drastic grammatical and lexical interference from the replacing language.

An important subtype of mixed language is what we term the **symbiotic mixed language** (MS). This type combines the grammatical structure of one language, and a varying number of lexical items – from hundreds to thousands in number – either from another language (often the original language of the group), or else from a variety of different sources, some words possibly being constructed or deformed deliberately. These languages exist in a symbiotic and dependent relationship with (dominant) unmixed languages with (virtually) the same grammar, and a lexicon from the same source as that grammar. This type of situation must presumably have pertained originally in the case of all mixed languages.

An MS is by definition never the only language of its speakers. Often an MS will have the function of a **secret language**. There is variation within this class as to the age at which the MS is acquired. In some cases, like those of Inner Mbugu and (English) Shelta, the MS is acquired more or less simultaneously with the other language used by the group – Pare Mbugu and English respectively in the examples given. In other cases this takes place at a later age – during childhood, at puberty or initiation, or later. In general it can be observed that the earlier the age at which the MS is acquired the larger the size of the vocabulary. It may be the case that an MS is used in the same range of domains as the first language of the speakers. Depending on the size of the lexicon, a greater or lesser use may have to be made of compounds and circumlocutions to be able to talk about the same topics the dominant language is capable of dealing with. In other cases, more or less free use is made of the lexical resources of the dominant language. Often, however, a more restricted range of topics will be addressed with an MS. Secret languages formed solely by phonological 'transformations' applied to the dominant language are not included in this list.

Because a potentially restricted replacive lexical component may be involved in the MS, it is difficult to draw the line between some such languages and the systematic use, for example, of a rich body of **slang**. One criterion we have adopted here is to require that the replacive component not be unduly semantically restricted, for example to terms with sexual connotations, or to the technical vocabulary related to a particular trade such as horse-dealing. One example often listed as an example of a contact language – Pachuco of the American South-West – seems basically to consist of a rich sexual slang element. Still there will remain doubtful cases where the question of classification as an MS or just as slang will be problematic. This problem is compounded by the frequent tendency of young people to adopt words taken from MS languages employed by marginal(ized) social groups as slang terms in the dominant language.

The criteria of non-restrictive lexical scope also rules out many **ritual languages** of a secret nature, with vocabularies solely connected with the worship of certain deities. One criterion we have adopted is to restrict the category of MSS to those lects where a certain (quasi-)ethnic distinction is relevant. So such languages used by separate ethnic groups such as Romani have been included. We have also included trade or caste MSS when closed groups seem to be involved. These groups do not require to be strictly ethnically distinct in their place of origin, but by their distinctive lifestyle – often nomadic or semi-nomadic – they have created a separate social identity.

**Taboo languages** are ruled out, like the **mother-in-law languages** (Dyalŋuy, etc.) of Dyirbal and other Australian languages, which are only used in the presence of certain groups of relatives. These Australian examples do conform to the general linguistic character-istics of MSS, although not to the social criteria described above. Taboo languages are also frequently used by hunters and fishermen in many cultures. These would normally also be excluded on the above-mentioned grounds of restriction to a narrow semantic domain. Typical of such languages too is a large use of paraphrases and periphrases (circumlocutions).

The various **sign(ed) languages** used around the world, both by the deaf and by the hearing, have been claimed to be creoles or pidgins – depending on the nature of the individual sign language. We have however not generally included sign languages in this list since this book does not, nor is it meant to, deal with the specific concerns of these languages. We have included a very few such languages however, which by nature of their function seemed to resemble typical spoken pidgins in that they are used for inter-ethnic communication.

## 26.2 The list and the classification

The classification we have given here of these languages is largely one of convenience. It conceals the fact that it has been made with regard to many different criteria: historical linguistic, lexifier language-related, (quasi-)ethnic, geographical, and others.

It must therefore not be assumed that where creoles and pidgins involving the same lexifier language are grouped together there is necessarily any direct historical or linguistic connection between the different cases. This is, however, in some cases true, as for example in the case of Krio and the various West African forms of pidgin English. And it may well be the case that a particular non-linguistic criterium for a classification coincides wholly or partially with a classification involving a shared linguistic origin, or at least a shared linguistic component, usually lexical.

It must also not be assumed to be the case that each entry corresponds to a distinct **language**. What we have attempted to do is to list each case separately 'identified' in the literature, whatever this implies. So it is of course not our intention to suggest that the English-lexifier creole lects spoken on Montserrat and Nevis are different languages, or that this is the case with the French-lexifier creole lects spoken on St. Lucia and Guadeloupe. Both cases represent similar dialects of a single language.

The linguistic 'density' of the entries themselves is very variable. For instance, the double entry for Cape Verde Portuguese – corresponding to the two main dialects – might suggest that the various subdialects spoken on the separate islands are less distinctive than the above-mentioned dialects of the Leewards Islands French and English-lexifier creoles. This is in fact not always the case. We have in general chosen to represent dialects in separate entries where either they are spoken in politically distinct entities, or else separated by large areas where other languages are spoken, or by large stretches of ocean. A case illustrating the second condition is that of Indo-Portuguese, where we have dialect-islet-clusters scattered across a huge area of land occupied by speakers of Dravidian or Indic languages.

There are also many cases where not too much is known about a particular lect – we may only have short word-lists or the odd sentence. In general the reader may conclude however that in most cases at least some material is available. In two or three cases we have included apparently logically necessary 'hypothetical' languages, where the existence of other lects could not reasonably be explained if they had not existed. This is of course a subjective matter. We have restricted the inclusion of 'reported' languages to cases we felt to be fairly reliable.

In general we have put mixed languages in a separate section, so as to avoid problems of dual or even multiple classification. We have deviated from this practice in the case of mixed creoles and pidgins, where we have put the main entry in the section concerned with what we regarded as the dominant or most relevant component. We have however also listed these cases in a section at the end of the list with cross-references to the main entries.

## 26.3 The annotations

We have attempted to provide certain basic information in the entries. However, the amount of detail given is extremely variable. Partly, this is due at least to our sources, which are themselves very variable in this regard. The information we aim to provide comprises:

1) alternative names;
2) precise geographical locations;
3) whether a lect is extinct or not;

4) numbers of speakers;

5) information on dialects;

6) linguistic resemblances to other lects;

7) historical origin;

8) whether the creole status of a lect is dubious;

9) whether we are dealing with a (claimed) creoloid or decreolized language;

10) whether we are dealing with a post-pidgin (depidginized) language;

11) whether the locus of the language has any unusual political status or history.

Of course the detail or degree of accuracy in the various entries depends on the interpretation we have put on the information contained in the various sources we have used. In cases of conflicting information we have attempted to give what seemed to us to be the most reasonable interpretation of the facts. The figures for numbers of speakers will often be out of date, which sometimes will mean that they are too high, in other cases that they are too low.

We have attempted to provide the name(s) for a language that is most frequently used. If the name of a language is unknown, or it does not have one, or an obvious designation did not present itself, we have referred to it as 'Unnamed'.

Following the name, one of the codes given below indicates the linguistic status of the language as a pidgin, creole, etc. This indication of status will sometimes be of a provisional nature.

C = creole; CD = creoloid/semi-creole; CP = post-creole/mesolect;
  (see Chapter 10 for the precise meanings of these terms);
P = pidgin; PJ = jargon; PS = stabilized pidgin; PE = extended pidgin; PP = post-pidgin;
SP = signed pidgin;
M = mixed language;
MS = symbiotic mixed language;
MC = mixed creole.
MP = mixed pidgin; MPJ = mixed jargon; MPS = mixed stabilized pidgin;
* = extinct; r = only survives as a ritual language; ? = doubtful case.

## 26.4  Index

## 26.5  The list

A. English-lexifier Creoles and Pidgins
  1. Atlantic Area
    a. Northern
      i. Newfoundland
        1 Newfoundland Pidgin English (Canada) * P
      ii. Gullah
        2 Sea Island Creole English/Gullah/Geechee (USA) C

        *Gullah is spoken on the coast and islands between Jacksonville, North Carolina and Jacksonville, Florida by around 250,000 speakers concentrated in Georgia and South Carolina. There are under 10,000 monolinguals. The area corresponds in large part to the English Carolina colony, founded in 1670 (including Georgia, part of Florida, and the Bahamas). Gullah probably dates from before 1700.*

        3 Geechee (USA) CD?

        *A semi-creole spoken mostly by black sharecroppers in Louisiana and Eastern Texas.*

        4 Afro-Seminole (USA/Mexico) C

        *Afro-Seminole is spoken by several hundred people in Bracketsville, Texas, and Naciamento de los Negros, Mexico. It is also dying out on the Canadian River and Salt Creek, Oklahoma. The speakers descend from maroons who fled the Carolina colony between 1690 and 1760 to Spanish St. Augustine in Florida.*

        5 Bahamian Creole English (Bahamas) C

        *Bahamian Creole is spoken in the Bahamas by around 225,000 people. Settled originally by the English in the 1640's to 1660's from Bermuda, the Bahamas formed part of the Carolina colony from 1670.*

      iii. Indian
        6 American Indian Pidgin English (USA) P
        7 Lumbee Creole English (USA) C?

        *Spoken in a group made up of the remnants of various Indian tribes in North Carolina.*

    b. Black English
      8 American Black English/African-American Vernacular English/Black Vernacular English (USA) CD?

      *It is sometimes claimed that American Black English is a post-creole. This is however controversial. Several million speakers.*

      9 Nova Scotian Black English (Canada) CD?
      10 Liberian Settler English/Merico (Liberia) CD?

      *Spoken by the 60,000 descendants of freed American slaves who came here starting in 1787.*

      11 Cape Palmas English/Kepama (Liberia) CD?

      *Spoken by the descendants of freed American slaves from Maryland. Displays phonological and lexical influence from Grebo.*

      12 Samaná English (Dominican Republic) CD?

      *Spoken by the 8000 descendants of freed American slaves who arrived in the early 19th century.*

A.I.    c. Eastern Caribbean

 i. Lesser Antilles

  *More or less closely related varieties of English Creole are spoken on the various islands of the Lesser Antilles. These display a fair degree of similarity to Jamaican. On Saba an English dialect is spoken.*

  13 Virgin Islands Creole English (British/US Territory) C
   *70,000 speakers.*

  14 Anguillan Creole English (British Territory) C
   *6500 speakers.*

  15 St. Maarten Creole English (Dutch/French Territory) C

  16 St. Barts Creole English (French Territory) C
   *Spoken in Gustavia, the capital of St. Barthélemy.*

  17 Statian Creole English (Dutch Territory) C
   *Spoken on St. Eustatius.*

  18 Antiguan Creole English (Antigua) C
   *75,000 speakers.*

  19 Barbudan Creole English (Antigua) C
   *1100 speakers.*

  20 St.Kitts-Nevis Creole English (St. Christopher) C
   *60,000 speakers. English colonies from 1624 (St. Kitts) and 1627 (Nevis).*

  21 Monserrat Creole English (British Territory) C
   *12,000 speakers. An English colony from 1633.*

  22 Bajan/Barbadian Creole English (Barbados) C
   *250,000 speakers. An English colony from 1625.*

  23 Vincentian Creole English (St. Vincent) C
   *138,000 speakers.*

  24 Carriacou Creole English (St. Vincent) C
   *Spoken on one of the Grenadines.*

  25 Grenadan Creole English (Grenada) C
   *110,000 speakers.*

  26 Tobagonian Creole English (Trinidad and Tobago) C
   *50,000 speakers.*

  27 Trinidadian Creole English/Trini Talk (Trinidad and Tobago) C
   *Spoken by the majority of the 1,100,000 population of Trinidad, either as a 1st or 2nd language. Displays Bajan influence.*

 ii. Guyanan

  28 Creolese/Guyanese Creole English (Guyana) C
   *Similar in some aspects to Jamaican, this creole underwent some 19th century Krio influence. It has around 650,000 speakers. Also 50,000 speakers in Surinam. The components of present Guyana came under effective British control in 1796, but British settlement had started in Demerara from 1745 under the Dutch, mostly from Barbados.*

  29 Rupununi Creole English (Guyana) C
   *Possibly a separate creole language from Creolese.*

A.1.c.ii.       30 El Callao Creole English (Venezuela) C

*The speakers of this creole are traditionally assumed to have migrated from Guyana.*

d. Western Caribbean

*Some islands do not possess creole forms of English, but rather 'ordinary' dialects of English. Among these would appear to be the Cayman Islands, and the Bay Islands of Honduras.*

i. Jamaican-type

31 Jamaican Creole English/Patwa (Jamaica) C

*This creole is estimated to have about 2,250,000 speakers. Numerous emigré Patwa speakers in New York and Toronto. An English colony from 1655.*

32 British Jamaican Creole/Patwa (Britain) C

*This creole is spoken by many 2nd and 3rd generation West Indians (not just Jamaicans) living in Britain - several hundred thousand speakers in all. It is less basilectal than Jamaican Creole.*

33 Limon Creole English/Mek-ay-tel-yu (Costa Rica) C

*55,000 speakers. The descendants of immigrant labourers, who arrived from 1870 onwards, mainly from Jamaica.*

34 Panamanian Creole English/Wari-wari (Panama) C

*100,000 speakers in Bocas del Toro, Colón, and Rio Abajo. The descendants of immigrant labourers, who arrived from 1850 onwards.*

ii. Central American

35 Miskito Coast Creole English (Nicaragua) C

*Has about 40,000 L1 speakers on the Atlantic coast of Nicaragua. Plantations and African slaves appear first at the beginning of the 18th century. The Amerindian Miskito, mixed with escaped African slaves since the 17th century, have had close contacts with the English since the 1630's, and speak Miskito Coast Creole English as a 2nd language.*

36 Rama Cay Creole English (Nicaragua) C

*Rama Cay Creole has virtually replaced the native Amerindian language of the 500 Rama living on Rama Cay in Bluefields Lagoon. Introduced by German missionaries in the mid-19th century.*

37 Belizean Creole English (Belize) C

*115,000 speakers in coastal areas. African slaves were in Belize by the beginning of the 18th century.*

38 San Andres-Providencia Creole English (Colombia) C

*About 15,000 speakers on San Andres and Providencia Islands. San Andres was settled by the English in the late 17th century, Providencia, not for the first time, in the 18th century.*

39 Corn Island Creole English (Nicaragua) C

*On Corn Island a dialect similar to that of San Andres and Providencia is reportedly spoken.*

e. Surinam

*Surinam was an English colony from 1651-1667. It was settled principally from Barbados.*

40 Sranan (Tongo) ('Surinam (Language)')/Negerengels (Surinam) C

*Spoken by the population of the coastal area in Surinam, as well as the considerable emigré population in the Netherlands. The total number of 1st and 2nd language speakers is around 500,000.*

41 Ndjuka-Paramaccan-Aluku-Kwinti (Surinam/French Guiana) C

*A Maroon language, spoken mainly in Eastern Surinam, by the Ndjuka (Upriver Marowijne, Downriver Marowijne, Cottica River, and Sara Creek dialects), Paramaccan, and Aluku tribes,*

A.1.e.    *as well as by the small Kwinti tribe in Central Surinam. The creation of the Ndjuka tribe has been dated to 1712. Most Aluku and some Ndjuka are in French Guiana. The total number of speakers is around 30,000.*

42 Jamaican Maroon Spirit Possession Language/MSL. (Jamaica) r
*This ritual language's sole present use is for addressing the spirits of Jamaican-born Maroons. It is assumed to derive from a former creole spoken by the Eastern Maroons. It is not close to Jamaican creole phonologically, however, but rather resembles the Surinam creoles.*

43 Saramaccan-Matawai (see also section z.4) (Surinam) MC
*A mixed English-based/Portuguese-based creole language spoken by the Saramaccan (Upper Suriname River and Lower Suriname River dialects) and Matawai tribes in Surinam. The creation of the Saramaccan tribe has been dated to 1690. The number of speakers is about 25,000.*

44 Dju-tongo ('Jew-language') (see section z.4) (Surinam) * MC?
*This very poorly recorded mixed English/Portuguese-based pidgin or creole was used on the largely Jewish-owned plantations of the middle Surinam River from the late 17th century for an unknown period. It is not the same as Saramaccan-Matawai, as is sometimes assumed, but is its precursor.*

f. Guinea Coast

i. Krio

45 Aku/Krio (Gambia) C
*A dialect of Krio spoken at the mouth of the Gambia River by 3500.*

46 Krio (Sierra Leone) C
*A long-established Creole language spoken by 500,000 1st language speakers, and 3½ million 2nd language speakers. Krio was probably creolized around 1600.*

47 Porto Talk/Fernandino/Fernando Poo Krio (Equatorial Guinea) C
*A dialect of Krio spoken at Santa Isabel and San Carlos on Fernando Poo (Bioko) by about 4000.*

48 Cameroonian Krio (Cameroon) C
*A dialect of Krio spoken in Victoria on the Gulf of Guinea, since 1858.*

ii. Liberia

49 Kru Pidgin English (Liberia) PE
*The second language of the Klao, Grebo, and Bassa tribes. Kru Pidgin English is close to West African Pidgin English. The 'Krumen' have worked widely on boats along the whole of the Guinea coast since at least the 17th century. Hence the name 'Kru' for Pidgin English in Ghana.*

50 Liberian Interior Pidgin English (Liberia) PE
*A Mande-influenced pidgin.*

iii. Lower Guinea

51 Cameroonian Pidgin English/West African Pidgin English PE
Bush English/Broken English/Weskos/Kamtok (Cameroon, Fernando Poo)
*A second language for more than 2 million people, Cameroonian Pidgin English is also spoken on Fernando Poo by two-thirds of the population.*

52 Creolized Cameroonian Pidgin English P
*For a growing number of people Cameroonian Pidgin English is a first language.*

53 Fulani Pidgin English (Cameroon) C
*Different from Cameroonian Pidgin English.*

A.1.f.iii.      54 Nigerian Pidgin English/West African Pidgin English (Nigeria) PE
                *The de facto national language, with more than 30 million speakers.*
                55 Creolized Nigerian Pidgin English (Nigeria) C
                *More than 1 million speakers for whom Nigerian Pidgin English is the first language, in the tribally mixed cities of Southern Nigeria.*
                56 Ghanaian Pidgin English/Kru (Ghana) P
                57 Togolese Pidgin English (Togo) P

2. India
                58 Butler English/Madras Pidgin English (India) P?
                *Spoken by domestic staff, guides, and market traders. Still spoken in Hyderabad, Bangalore and Madras. Possibly just an interlanguage.*

3. Pacific Area
    a. Northern Pacific
                59 Chukotka Pidgin English * PJ
                *Used in the 19th century by and with whalers. Contained Hawaiian and Portuguese words.*
    b. Japanese Pidgin English
                60 Japanese Pidgin English (Japan) P
                *Used in the 19th century in some Japanese ports such as Yokohama.*
                61 Hawaiian Japanese Pidgin English (Hawaii) PJ
                *Used by immigrant plantation workers.*
                62 Cape York Japanese Pidgin English (Queensland, Australia) P
                *Used in the pearling area at Thursday Island.*
    c. Chinese Pidgin English
                63 Chinese Pidgin English/China Coast Pidgin (China) * PS
                *Formerly a trading pidgin in use along the China Coast as far north as Shanghai between Chinese and Europeans. It derived originally from Canton.*
                64 Taiwan Pidgin English (Taiwan) P
                *A Chinese Pidgin English is reported to be in use in Taiwan, between Chinese maids and taxi-drivers, and Europeans.*
                65 Nauru Chinese Pidgin English/Ham Soi ('Seawater Language') P
                *A mixed dialect used for communication between Cantonese shop and restaurant personnel and other Nauruans. Combines features of Chinese Pidgin English and Mid-Pacific Pidgin English.*
    d. Military Pidgins (Bamboo English)
                *In particular employed in bars and brothels frequented by military personnel.*
                66 Japanese Bamboo English (Japan) PJ
                *Used on American military installations in Japan, especially in the Hamamatsu area. Recently most widely used in Okinawa.*
                67 Korean Bamboo English (South Korea) PJ
                *Used in the 50s, especially during the Korean War.*
                68 Vietnamese Pidgin English/Námglish (Vietnam) PJ
                *Used during the Vietnam War in American-Vietnamese interactions.*
                69 Thai Pidgin English (Thailand) PJ

A.3.    e. Singapore

70 Singlish (Singapore) PE

*The L-variety (i.e. basilect) of Singapore English. Influenced by Hokkien Chinese. Originally an interlanguage.*

f. Hawaii

71 Hawaiian Creole English (Hawaii) C

*Spoken by nearly half of the inhabitants of Hawaii - around 500,000 speakers.*

72 Hawaiian Pidgin English (Hawaii) PJ

*Only used by some elderly former plantation workers.*

g. Mid-Pacific

73 Tok Pisin/New Guinea Pidgin English/Neo-Melanesian (Papua New Guinea) PE

*Up to 2 million speakers. The two dialects - Rural and Urban Tok Pisin - are very divergent. Stabilized 1880 from a jargon deriving from Samoan Plantation Pidgin English.*

74 (Creole) Tok Pisin (Papua New Guinea) C

*For around 50,000 speakers Tok Pisin is a 1st language. In 1980 this was particularly the case in the Admiralty Islands.*

75 Bush Pidgin (Papua New Guinea) PJ

*Many 'Bush' (Jargon Pidgin) varieties of Tok Pisin are spoken in New Guinea.*

76 Tok Masta (Papua New Guinea) PJ

*The vestigial Tok Pisin-based pidgin used by Europeans with the locals. This may be just an interlanguage.*

77 Papuan Pidgin English (Papua New Guinea) * P

*Used from 1880 to 1925 in the Samarai, Kiwai and Daru areas. Also in a less stable form in the Port Moresby area.*

78 Pijin/Solomon Is. Pidgin English/Neo-Solomonic (Solomon Is.) PE

*175,000 speakers.*

79 (Creole) Pijin/Solomon Islands Pidgin English (Solomon Is.) C

*In 1976 there were 1300 1st language speakers.*

80 Bichelamar/Bislama (Vanuatu) PE

*90,000 speakers of a pidgin stabilized around 1900. Existed as a jargon pidgin from the 1830's.*

81 (Creole) Bislama (Vanuatu) C

*Creolization has started on a small scale in urban areas.*

82 Loyalty Islands Pidgin English (French Territory) P

83 New Caledonian Pidgin English (French Territory) * P

*Used until the second half of the 19th century.*

84 Micronesian Pidgin English (American Territory) * P

*Used up till the early 20th century.*

85 Queensland Kanaka English/Queensland Canefields English  (Australia) PS

*Spoken by about 10 Melanesians in Central and Northern Queensland. Falling into disuse.*

86 Maori Pidgin English (New Zealand) * P

*Used in the inital phase of colonization.*

87 Samoan Plantation Pidgin (Samoa) * P

*Used from about 1860. Effectively extinct.*

A.3.     h. Southern Pacific

88 Pitcairnese (British Territory) C

*The 100 speakers on Pitcairn Island are descendants of the mutineers of the Bounty, who colonized the island in 1790.*

89 Norfolk Island Creole English (Australian Territory) C

*500 speakers. An offshoot of Pitcairnese.*

i. Australia

90 S.E. Australian Pidgin English/Port Jackson Pidgin English (N.S.W.) * P

*Used at Port Jackson (= Sydney) in the early days of the British colony.*

91 Port Augusta Pidgin English (South Australia) P

92 Cape Barren English (Tasmania) PP

*100 mixed race speakers.*

93 Eastern Queensland Aboriginal English (Queensland) PP

*Spoken at Yarrabah (1300 speakers), Palm Island (1250 speakers), Woorabinda (500 speakers), Cherbourg (1500 speakers), and Armidale (N.S.W.) (300 speakers). Coexists with Pidgin.*

94 Northern Territory Pidgin English P

*Used by 10,000 2nd language Kriyol speakers.*

95 (Northern Territory) Kriyol C

*10,000 1st language speakers in N.W. Queensland, Northern Northern Territory, and the Kimberleys area of W. Australia. First creolized around 1908 in the Roper River area from Northern Territory Pidgin English.*

96 Torres Strait Pidgin English (Queensland) P

*Used by 15,000 2nd language Broken speakers.*

97 Broken/Torres Strait Creole English (Queensland) C

*Spoken since the end of the 19th century. 3000 speakers as a 1st language on the Torres Strait islands, and more in N. Queensland. Creolized from Torres Strait Pidgin English.*

98 Queensland Urban Creole English C

*Mergers of Queensland Kanaka English, Kriyol, and Broken.*

99 Alice Springs Aboriginal English (Northern Territory) PP

*About 2000 speakers.*

100 Wangkayi English (Western Australia) PP

*Spoken around Kalgoorlie by detribalized aborigines.*

101 Lingua Franca English (Western Australia) PP

*Spoken in N. Western Australia in a multilingual context.*

102 Broome Pidgin English (Western Australia) P

*Used by the mixed Asian and Aboriginal community in Broome. Some influence from Broome Pearling Lugger Pidgin.*

103 Neo-Nyungar/Nyungar (Western Australia) PP

*8000 speakers in S. Western Australia. Neo-Nyungar has many Nyungar words.*

B. French-lexifier Creoles and Pidgins

  1. Atlantic Area

    a. Louisiana

        104 Louisiana Creole French (USA) C

*Spoken in Louisiana and Eastern Texas, mainly at Lake Charles, Lafayette, New Roads, and Vacherie. Formerly also spoken in Western Mississippi. The 80,000 speakers include both blacks and whites. In some areas decreolization in the direction of Cajun French, particularly around St. Martin among the 10,000 white speakers.*

        105 Alabama Creole French (USA) * C

*Formerly spoken in Mobile and the surrounding area. The last speakers died at Mon Louis Island in about 1990.*

        106 Missouri Creole French (USA) * C

*Has influenced Missouri (non-creole) French (Ste Genevieve/Old Mines region). Now extinct.*

    b. Haiti

        107 Haitian Creole French (Haiti) C

*Haitian Creole is spoken by the more than 5,750,000 inhabitants of Haiti, for most of whom it is the only language. There are three dialects: Northern, Western, and Southern.*

    c. Lesser Antilles

*The various dialects of Lesser Antilles Creole French are basically very similar.*

      i. Guadeloupean

        108 Guadeloupean Creole French (French Territory) C

*335,000 speakers.*

        109 Marie Galante Creole French (French Territory) C

*15,000 speakers.*

        110 Ile des Saintes Creole French (French Territory) C

*2500 mainly white speakers.*

        111 St. Barthélemy Creole French/St. Bartian (French Territory) C

*The mainly white creole speakers share the island with speakers of a regional French dialect.*

        112 St. Thomas Creole French (US Territory) C

*St. Bartian French creole spoken at Northside on St. Thomas in the US Virgin Islands by a few hundred.*

        113 Old St. Thomas Creole French (Virgin Is.) (US Territory) * C

*A different form of Creole French from that now spoken on St. Thomas, incorporating Haitian features. Now replaced on St. Thomas by St. Bartian.*

      ii. Martiniquais

        114 Martiniquais Creole French (French Territory) C

*325,000 speakers.*

        115 Dominican Creole French (Dominica) C

*83,000 speakers.*

        116 St. Lucian Creole French (St. Lucia) C

*120,000 speakers, excluding those in Great Britain, and Guyana (1930's on).*

        117 Vincentian Creole French (St. Vincent) * C

        118 Carriacou Creole French (St. Vincent) C

*Spoken on one of the Grenadines.*

B.1.c.ii.    119 Grenadan Creole French (Grenada) C

*Extinct except for a few speakers in North Grenada.*

120 Tobagonian Creole French  (Trinidad & Tobago) * C

121 Trinidadian Creole French (Trinidad & Tobago)  C

*Spoken mostly by the older generation in the Northern Range and in coastal areas. In the Dragon's Mouth area still spoken by children.*

122 Güiria Creole French (Venezuela) C

*This is spoken on the coast of Venezuela in the town of Güiria by a shrinking number of elderly speakers. Güiria is geographically very close to Trinidad.*

123 El Callao Creole French (Venezuela) C

*Traditionally speakers associate their community with immigration from Guadeloupe, Martinique, and Trinidad. The town of El Callao is trilingual between French and English Creole, and Spanish.*

124 San Miguel Creole French (Panama) C

*The speakers emigrated from St. Lucia in the mid 19th century.*

iii. Assorted

125 Dominican Carib Pidgin French (Dominica) * PJ

d. S. America

126 Guyanais Creole French (French Guiana) C

*Spoken by around 50,000 speakers. There are three dialects: Cayenne, St.-Laurent-de-Moroni, and Oyapock River.*

127 Karipuna Creole French/Crioulo (Brazil) C

*Spoken by 500 Amerindians on the Curipi River in Brazil. Basically a sub-variety of the Oyapock River dialect of Guyanais.*

2. Indian Ocean Area

a. Mauritian

128 Mauritian Creole French/Morisyen (Mauritius) C

*This language is spoken by about 700,000 people as a 1st language in Mauritius, and 300,000 as a 2nd language.*

129 Rodriguais Creole French C

*34,000 speakers on Rodrigues.*

130 Seychellois Creole French/Seselwa (Seychelles/Ghana) C

*Spoken by about 66,000 inhabitants of the Seychelles. Also spoken by a small number in Ghana since the 19th century.*

131 Ilois Creole French/Ilwa (British Territory) C

*Spoken by the 1800 Ilois formerly inhabiting the Chagos Archipelago, including Diego Garcia, but now forcibly moved to Mauritius. Linguistically very close to Seychellois. Now obsolescent.*

132 Agalega Creole French (Mauritius) C

b. Réunionnais

133 Réunionnais Creole French (French Territory) C

*This is frequently claimed not to be a creole language, but a dialect of French. It is spoken by about 550,000. It is probably a creole continuum.*

B.   3. Africa

    134 Petit Nègre (Ivory Coast, etc.) P

    *A name referring to pidgin French reported to be spoken in the Ivory Coast and other West African countries by a few elderly people, mostly retired soldiers.*

    135 Burundi Pidgin French (Burundi) P

    *Spoken by around 200,000 in Burundi.*

  4. Vietnam

    136 Tây Bôy (Vietnam) PJ

    *Used in various cities in Vietnam from 1860 to 1960.*

  5. Pacific

    137 New Caledonian Pidgin French (French Territory) * P

    *Used from about 1855. Now virtually extinct.*

    138 Tayo/St.Louis-Creole/Kaldosh (French Territory) C

    *Spoken by the St. Louis tribe on New Caledonia since about 1920. The number of speakers is about 4000.*

    139 New Hebrides Pidgin French (Vanuatu) * P

    *Imported from New Caledonia. Recently extinct.*

C. Portuguese-lexifier Creoles and Pidgins

  1. Atlantic area

    a. Northern

      140 Unnamed (Canada) * PJ

      *Supposedly used by Portuguese cod-fishers with the Indians of the Gulf of St.Lawrence area around 1500. The evidence for this is mostly in the form of individual words, with the odd sentence.*

    b. West Africa

      i. General

        141 West African Pidgin Portuguese * P

        *Formerly widely used in Western Africa. In Upper Guinea the Portuguese presence dates from the mid-15th century, in Lower Guinea from the late 15th century. On the Gold and Slave Coasts it was the dominant trade language from the 16th to the 18th centuries. On the Gold Coast it was replaced by English during the 18th century. Assumed to be ancestral to all the lects in section C.1.b.*

      ii. Cape Verde

        *300,000 speakers of all dialects of Cape Verde Crioulo. The Sotavento and Barlavento dialects are fairly divergent.*

        142 Sotavento Crioulo (Cape Verde) C

        *Island dialects of Santiago, Fogo, Maio, and Brava. Also spoken in Massachusetts by the descendants of 19th century emigrants - the Bravas.*

        143 Barlavento Crioulo (Cape Verde) C

        *Island dialects of Santo Antão, São Vicente, Santa Luiza, São Nicolau, Boa Vista, and Sal.*

      iii. Guinea Coast

        144 Gambia River Creole Portuguese (Gambia) * C

        *Formerly spoken by a mixed Portuguese-Mandinka population in the 17th and 18th centuries.*

C.1.b.iii.    145 Ziguinchor Kriul (Senegal) C

*This dialect of Guiné Kriyol is spoken by about 40,000 1st language speakers and 15,000 2nd language speakers in Ziguinchor in the Casamance region, and in Dakar.*

146 Guiné Kriyol (Guiné-Bissau) C

*Kriyol, the national languages, is the 1st language of 100,000 people, and the 2nd language of 600,000. Three dialects: Cacheu, Bafatá, and Bissau-Bolama. Portuguese from the mid 15th century until 1974.*

147 Whydah Portuguese (Benin) C?

*In 1874 it was reported that the numerous mulattoes occupied a separate quarter of Whydah, and spoke a kind of 'Portuguese jargon'. Freed Brazilian slaves were common here. Part of Whydah was a Portuguese possession until 1962.*

iv. Gulf of Guinea Islands

148 São Tomense Creole Portuguese (São Tomé en Principe) C

*This language is spoken on the island of São Tomé by about 85,000 speakers. São Tomé was a Portuguese possession from 1493 to 1975.*

149 Angolar (São Tomé en Principe) C

*Spoken by a 9000-strong Maroon group on São Tomé, this language has considerable KiMbundu influence.*

150 Principense Creole Portuguese (São Tomé en Principe) C

*Spoken on the island of Principe (Portuguese from 1503 till 1975) by about 4000 speakers, this language is being replaced by Portuguese.*

151 Fa d'Ambu (Equatorial Guinea) C

*This language is spoken on the island of Annobón by most of the inhabitants, as well as emigrés in Malabo, the capital of former Spanish Equatorial Guinea, for a total of about 4500 speakers. Annobón was Portuguese until 1778.*

152 Tonga Portuguese (São Tomé en Principe) P?

*Simplified Portuguese spoken by the Tonga on São Tomé, the descendants of 19th century contract labourers from Angola, Mozambique and Cape Verde. The Tonga live on the 'Roças', where São Tomense Creole was not generally spoken. The 1st languages of the various Roças were African languages, sometimes simplified.*

153 Lingua Uba Budo (see section Z.4)(São Tomé and Principe) MC?

*A reported mixture of KiMbundu and São Tomense spoken on the 'Roça' Uba Budo on São Tomé by the Tonga - descendants of 19th century contract labourers.*

c. Brazil

154 Brazilian Creole Portuguese (Brazil) * C

*That this language once existed is widely assumed, but not directly proven. Helvécia Creole Portuguese, Surinam Creole Portuguese, and the Portuguese elements in Papiamento (see section D.1), Dju-Tongo and Saramaccan (see section A.1.e) would derive from it.*

155 Brazilian Portuguese dialects (Brazil) CD/CP?

*Some dialects are claimed to display creoloid or post-creole traits.*

156 Helvécia Creole Portuguese (Brazil) * CP

*A post-creole spoken in Helvécia, Bahia state, in an area where the economically dominant groups did not speak Portuguese. In 1961 only the oldest generation were still familiar with it.*

C.1.c.

157 Surinam Creole Portuguese (Surinam) * C

*This is only preserved in a couple of 19th century proverbs. These presumably date to the late 17th or early 18th centuries. There is evidence for a Brazilian origin.*

158 Nikarikaru Creole Portuguese (Guyana) C

*Reportedly spoken in 1880 as an L1 by the Nikarikaru, a mixed Brazilian-Wapishana group.*

d. Southern Africa

159 Linguajem do Muçeque (Angola) P

*A pidgin used in the slums of Luanda.*

160 South African Creole Portuguese (South Africa) * C

*Spoken in the Cape Colony until the 19th century. It was imported there in the 1700s with slaves from Batavia (Djakarta).*

e. Eastern Africa

161 Madagascar Pidgin Portuguese (Madagascar) * P

*Used in the 16th and 17th centuries on Vinany-Bè Island.*

162 Kenya Coast Pidgin Portuguese (Kenya) * P

*Formerly used in Mombasa and Malindi.*

2. Asian Area

a. China

163 Macanese Creole Portuguese (Macao/Hongkong) C

*Now nearly disappeared in Macao due to decreolization. Obsolescent in Hongkong, due to the dispersal of the community. From the mid-19th century to the mid-20th century also widely spoken in Chinese ports, especially Shanghai. To a lesser extent in Japan, Vietnam and Thailand. Macao has been Portuguese since 1557.*

b. South East Asia

i. Continental

164 Burma-Siam Creole Portuguese C

*Portuguese creole(s) were formerly spoken at various locations in present Burma (Arakan, Syriam, Pegu, Tenasserim) and Thailand. A few speakers from Phuket in Thailand live at Pulau Tikus, Penang.*

165 Papia Kristang (Malaysia/Singapore) C

*This language is spoken in Hilir and Trankera, Malacca by about 1500 persons, as well as by a few hundred in Singapore and Kuala Lumpur. A Portuguese creole was also formerly spoken in Kedah. Some migrants from Malacca also live at Pulau Tikus, Penang. The Portuguese presence in Malacca dates from 1511.*

ii. Indonesia

166 Sumatra Creole Portuguese * C

*Formerly spoken at Banda Aceh, Padang, Telanaipura (Djambi), Bengkulu, and Palembang.*

167 Java Creole Portuguese * C

*Spoken at Tugu near Djakarta until 1978. The language was formerly also spoken in Djakarta itself (Dutch from 1619). The original speakers were brought to Java in the 17th century by the Dutch from former Portuguese colonies.*

168 Borneo Creole Portuguese * C

*Formerly spoken at Martapura.*

C.2.b.ii.     169 Celebes Creole Portuguese * C

*Formerly spoken at Ujung Pandang (Makassar).*

170 Flores-Solor Creole Portuguese * C

*Formerly spoken at Adonara, Solor and Larantuka, Flores. Larantuka was a Portuguese possession till 1859.*

171 Central Moluccas Creole Portuguese * C

*Formerly spoken in Ambon and on the Banda Islands.*

172 Northern Moluccas Creole Portuguese * C

*Formerly spoken at Ternate and Tidore.*

173 Timor Creole Portuguese * C

*Formerly spoken in Bidau (near Dili) till about 1950 and Lifau. East Timor was a Portuguese possession until 1976.*

c. Indian subcontinent

*In additional to the general geographical factors, a division of these scattered Indo-Portuguese dialects in terms of the local adstrate languages seems to be relevant. We give only dates for the first colonial presence in each place. Many places changed hands several times during the 17th and 18th centuries.*

  i. Norteiro

    *a.* Gujurati Adstrate (Indo-European language)

174 Diu Creole Portuguese (Daman, Diu & Goa, India) * C

*Still spoken in 1900. Diu was a Portuguese possession from 1536 till 1961.*

175 Khambat (Cambay) Creole Portuguese (Gujarat, India) * C

176 Surat Creole Portuguese (Gujarat, India) * C

177 Daman Creole Portuguese (Daman, Diu & Goa, India) C

*Several thousand speakers. Daman creole is decreolizing towards Standard Portuguese. Daman was Portuguese from 1559 till 1961.*

    *b.1.* Marathi Adstrate (Dravidian-influenced Indo-European language)

178 Bombay Creole Portuguese (Maharashtra, India) C

*Indo-Portuguese was spoken by around 4000 speakers in 1905 in Vasai (= Bassein), various places in Thane (= Thana) district, various places around Bombay (Portuguese from 1530), Chaul (Portuguese from 1509), and Korlai. Now there are 700 speakers in Korlai, while Vasai had 1 semi-speaker in 1972.*

179 Dapoli (Dabhol) Creole Portuguese (Maharashtra, India) * C

    *b.2.* Konkani Adstrate (Dravidian-influenced Indo-European language)

180 Southern Maharashtra Creole Portuguese (Maharashtra, India) * C

*Indo-Portuguese was spoken in Rajapur and Malvan. Konkani is the main local language.*

181 Goanese Creole Portuguese (Daman, Diu & Goa, India) * CP?

*Goanese creole is being replaced by Standard Portuguese. Goa was a Portuguese possession from 1510 till 1961. Indo-Portuguese was also spoken on Anjadip Island to the south in Karnataka State.*

182 Mangalore Creole Portuguese (Karnataka, India) * C

*Mangalore is a Konkani dialect island.*

  ii. Malabar Coast

    *a.* Kannada Adstrate (Dravidian language)

C.2.c.iv.      183 Honavar-Bhatkal Creole Portuguese (Karnataka, India) * C

*b.* Malayalam Adstrate (Dravidian language)

184 Northern Kerala Creole Portuguese (Kerala, India) * C

*Indo-Portuguese is recently dead in Cannanore (350 speakers in 1884) and Tellicherry. It was also spoken in Mahé (a French possession until 1954) and Calicut, the first Portuguese possession in India (1498-).*

185 Central Kerala Creole Portuguese (Kerala, India) C

*Indo-Portuguese is dead in Cranganur and Cochin city (Portuguese from 1502) (a Konkani dialect is spoken by Hindus in Cochin), and still just spoken on Vypeen Island (near Cochin) by about 30 elderly people.*

186 Southern Kerala Creole Portuguese (Kerala, India) * C

*Indo-Portuguese was spoken in Quilon and Anjengo.*

iii. Ceylon

187 Sri Lanka Creole Portuguese (Sri Lanka) C

*Formerly spoken in various locations including Jaffna, Trincomalee, Batticaloa, Galle, Kalatura, Colombo, Negombo, Chilaw, Puttalam, and Mannar Island. Probably still spoken in the Batticaloa area. The total number of speakers for Sri Lanka was 2250 in 1971. The Portuguese presence lasted from the early 16th to the early 17th centuries, when the Dutch replaced them. Heavy Tamil influence.*

188 Portuguese-Dutch Creole (see also section Z.4) (Sri Lanka) MC?

*Possibly spoken by a few people in Wattala, near Colombo.*

iv. Coromandel Coast

*a.* Tamil Adstrate (Dravidian language)

189 Tuticorin Creole Portuguese (Tamil Nadu, India) * C

190 Kilakkarai Creole Portuguese (Tamil Nadu, India) * C

191 Nagappattinam Creole Portuguese (Tamil Nadu, India) * C

*Indo-Portuguese was spoken in Nagappattinam (Portuguese from 1519) (20 families in 1883; still spoken in 1915), Tarangambadi (= Tranquebar) (a Danish possession in 1620; still spoken in 1884), and Karikal (a French possession till 1954).*

192 Puduchcheri Creole Portuguese (Tamil Nadu, India) * C

*Indo-Portuguese was spoken in Puduchcheri (still spoken in 1884) (= Pondicherry; a French possession from c.1674 till 1954), Devanapattinam, Cuddalore (still spoken in 1884), and Parangipatti (= Porto Novo).*

193 Madras Creole Portuguese (Tamil Nadu, India) * C

*Indo-Portuguese was spoken in Sadras, Covelong, various places in the Madras area (still spoken in 1884), and Pulicat.*

*b.* Telugu Adstrate (Dravidian language)

194 Machilipatnam Creole Portuguese (Andhra Pradesh, India) * C

*The Portuguese post here dated from 1570.*

195 Vishakhapatnam Creole Portuguese (Andhra Pradesh, India) * C

*Indo-Portuguese was spoken in Vishakhapatnam and Bhimunipatnam (Bimlipatnam).*

v. Orissa/Bengal

*a.* Oriya Adstrate (Indo-European language)

*Indo-Portuguese died out in the mid-19th century in Orissa.*

C.2.c.ix.          196 Pipli Creole Portuguese (Orissa, India) * C

197 Balashwar (Balasore) Creole Portuguese (Orissa, India) * C

*b.* Bengali Adstrate (Indo-European language)

198 Calcutta Creole Portuguese (West Bengal, India) * C

> *Indo-Portuguese was still spoken by a few people in 1919. It was spoken in Calcutta, Chandan-*
> *nagar (= Chandernagore - a French possession from c.1674 till 1950), and Bandel (Hugli district).*

199 Dacca Creole Portuguese (Bangla Desh) * C

200 Chittagong Creole Portuguese (Bangla Desh) * C

d. Middle East

201 Gammeron Pidgin Portuguese (Iran) * P

> *Reported to be in general use in the mid 17th century.*

202 Basra Pidgin Portuguese (Iraq) * P

203 Mecca Pidgin Portuguese (Saudi Arabia) * P

D. Spanish-lexifier Creoles and Pidgins

1. Atlantic America

204 Palenquero (Colombia) C

> *This language is spoken by about 3000 inhabitants of San Basilio de Palenque in Colombia.*

205 Bobures Creole Spanish (Venezuela) C

> *A Spanish-lexifier creole is reported at Bobures on Lake Maracaibo.*

206 Papiamentu/Papiamento (see section Z.4) (Dutch Territory) MC

> *This mixed Spanish/Portuguese creole is spoken by around 250,000 speakers on the Caribbean*
> *islands of Curaçao, Aruba, and Bonaire – with corresponding dialects, as well as by emigrés in*
> *the Netherlands. It shows extensive Dutch and English lexicon. The former Spanish islands were*
> *taken over by the Dutch in 1634.*

207 Piñaguero Panare Pidgin Spanish (Venezuela) PJ

> *A pidgin used by Indians and traders in Bolivar state.*

208 Pinal Pidgin Spanish (Venezuela) PJ

> *A trading pidgin reportedly used with the Pinal tribe in Bolivar state.*

209 Cuban Bozal Spanish (Cuba) * P?

> *Sometimes claimed to have been a creole. Perhaps just an interlanguage. Used till c.1950.*

210 Puerto Rican Bozal Spanish (US Territory) * P?

> *Possibly just an interlanguage. Used up till c.1900.*

2. Pacific America

> *Apart from those mentioned below there are unconfirmed reports of further Spanish-lexifier*
> *pidgins in the Amazon region of Ecuador.*

211 Chileno (California) * P

> *A pidgin recorded in 1960 among the Bodega Miwok.*

212 Piojé Pidgin Spanish (Ecuador) PJ

> *Recorded in 1886 among the Piojé Indians in Oriente province.*

213 Jívaro Pidgin Spanish (Ecuador) PJ

> *Used in the Amazonian province of Oriente by the Jívaro (Shuar) Indians.*

D.  3. Philippines

> *The total number of Creole Spanish speakers is now around 280,000.*

214 Chavacano/Caviteño (Philippines) c

> *Many of the 28,000 inhabitants of the town of Cavite on Manilla Bay speak this language. Has existed since the 18th century. An offshoot of Ternateño.*

215 Chavacano/Ternateño (Philippines) c

> *In the town of Ternate, Ternateño is spoken by about 4000 speakers. Ternate was settled in 1660 by emigrés from, and named for, the island of Ternate in the Moluccas. It is assumed to have developed from the Portuguese-lexifier creole formerly spoken in Ternate.*

216 Chavacano/Ermiteño (Philippines) * c

> *In the Ermita district of Manilla, this dialect has now virtually died out. In 1942 there were still 12,000 speakers. An offshoot of Ternateño.*

217 Chavacano/Zamboangueño (see Z.4) (Philippines/Malaysia) MC

> *More than 200,000 speakers of this partly Caviteño-lexifier mixed creole live mostly in or near Zamboanga City in S.W. Mindanao, and on Basulan Island. The grammar is much influenced by Hiligaynon Visayan. Possibly did not exist before the mid-19th century. Also spoken in one village in Semporna, Sabah, Malaysia.*

218 Chavacano/Cotabateño (see also section Z.4) (Philippines) MC

> *A dialect of Zamboangueño, spoken by about 7000 speakers in Cotabato City.*

219 Chavacano/Davaoeño (see also section Z.4) (Philippines) * MC

> *A dialect of Zamboangueño, formerly spoken by a few thousand in Davao City from 1900 on. Not functional any more, replaced by the mixed Tagalog-Visayan Davaoeño language (see section Z.3.d.iii).*

220 Bamboo Spanish (Philippines) PJ

> *A pidgin used by older Chinese shopkeepers in Davao. It was previously used by the former numerous Japanese settlers.*

221 Kitchen Spanish/Español de Cocina (Philippines) PJ

> *Used by and with Chinese shopkeepers in Manilla.*

E. Dutch-lexifier Creoles and Pidgins

   1. Caribbean

222 Negerhollands (Virgin Islands) (British/US Territory) * c

> *The last speaker of Negerhollands died in 1987 on St. Thomas. It had died out earlier on St. Croix and St. John. It was the language of both blacks and whites in the former Danish colony of the Virgin Islands.*

223 Skepi Dutch (Guyana) * c

> *This Dutch Creole language was spoken in Essequibo County, Guyana up till about 1950. Essequibo, a former Dutch colony founded in 1613, was taken over by the British in 1796.*

224 Berbice Dutch (Guyana) (see also section Z.4) MC

> *This mixed Dutch-Eastern Ijǫ creole is known by about 3 speakers in Berbice County, Guyana. Berbice, originally a private Dutch colony founded in 1627, was taken over by the British in 1796.*

   2. South Africa

225 Slave Pidgin Dutch (South Africa) * PS

> *Used in the 17th and 18th centuries.*

E.2.

226 Hottentot Dutch (South Africa) * PS

*A 17th century contact pidgin formerly spoken between Khoekhoe (Hottentots) and Dutch colonists.*

227 Afrikaans (South Africa/Namibia/Zimbabwe) CD

*A creoloid spoken by about 3½ million speakers.*

228 Orange River Afrikaans (South Africa/Namibia) CP

*This post-creole is spoken by many descendants of the former Khoekhoe-speaking population in/ from the Orange River area, and derives from a late 18th century creole. A couple of hundred thousand speakers in the Northern Cape, Southern Namibia, and also in Griqualand East in Natal.*

229 'Deep' Cape Afrikaans (South Africa) CP

*A post-creole spoken in Cape Province deriving from an 18th century creole. Roughly 1½ million speakers.*

230 Flaai-Taal/Fly-Taal/Tsotsi Taal (South Africa) P

*A pidginized Afrikaans spoken as a 2nd language by hundreds of thousands.*

3. Indonesia

231 Unnamed (Indonesia) C?

*A possible Dutch-lexifier creole spoken in Depok south of Djakarta.*

F. German-lexifier Creoles and Pidgins

232 Kiautschou Pidgin German (China) * P

*Used in Tsingtao up till the beginning of the 20th century. Tsingtao was a German concession from 1897.*

233 Unserdeutsch/Rabaul Creole German (P.N.G./Australia) C

*The only German-lexifier creole - originally developed at Vunapope near Rabaul, New Britain, in a children's home. Spoken by 15 speakers in New Britain, and 85 in S.E. Queensland. A Boarding School Creole.*

234 Pidgin German (Papua New Guinea) * P

*Formerly spoken on Tumleo Island, and at Alexishafen, and Herbertshohe.*

235 Gastarbeiderdeutsch (Germany) P?

*It is still controversial whether this is just an interlanguage or has developed to being a pidgin.*

236 Estonian 'Halbdeutsch' (Estonia) * P

*With Yiddish and Low German influence, and Estonian-influenced phonology.*

237 Latvian 'Halbdeutsch' (Latvia) * P

238 Bosnian Pidgin German (Bosnia) * P

G. Other Romance-lexifier Pidgins

239 Lingua Franca/Sabir * PS

*Used extensively in the Mediterranean by traders and sailors from around 1000 A.D. up till the beginning of the 20th century. Mainly based on Italian. French and Spanish also contributed to the vocabulary in the Western Mediterranean forms of the pidgin.*

240 Todesche/Lanzi (Italy) * P

*A pidgin Italian used by German mercenaries in Italy during the 16th century.*

241 Asmara Pidgin Italian (Eritrea/Ethiopia) P

*Used in Eritrea and parts of Ethiopia.*

H. Russian-lexifier Pidgins

242 Taymir Pidgin Russian (Russia) P

*Used by the Nganasan (Samoyed) for inter-ethnic contacts with the neighbouring Dolgan, Evenki and Even. Certain Nganasan grammatical features.*

I. Other Indo-European-lexifier Pidgins

1. European

243 Fáskrú sfjardarfranska (Iceland) * PJ

*Literally 'Fáskrú sfjord French', this pidgin from Iceland has basically a Scandinavian lexicon.*

244 Rinkeby Svenska (Sweden) P

*An institutionalized interlanguage. The L2 Swedish of early 20th century Finnish immigrants to Stockholm has become a 2nd language for younger generations beside Standard Swedish.*

245 Bosnian Pidgin Slavic (Bosnia) * P

2. Indic

246 Fiji Pidgin Hindustani P

*Used in Indian-Indian and Indian-Fijian interaction. 50,000 speakers.*

247 Calcutta Pidgin Hindustani P

248 Naga Pidgin/Pidgin Assamese/Nagamese (India) PE

*The lingua franca of the Indian state of Nagaland (population 600,000). Based on Assamese.*

249 Jharwa (India) P

*A pidgin Assamese used in the Garo Hills district of Assam.*

J. Basque-lexifier Pidgins

250 Icelandic Pidgin Basque (Iceland) * P

*Used in contacts between Basque fishermen and Icelanders in Iceland.*

K. Arabic-lexifier Creoles and Pidgins

251 Maridi Pidgin Arabic (Mauretania) * P

*Recorded in a Spanish Arabic text from 1086 A.D. and used in Central Mauretania.*

252 Galgaliya (Nigeria) P

*Used by the Kalamáfi tribe of N.E. Nigeria*

253 Shuwa Arabic/Turku Arabic (Chad/Nigeria) PE

*Spoken by 1,500,000 in Chad, and 200,000 in Nigeria and other countries.*

254 Juba Arabic (Sudan) PE

*Spoken by about 20,000 1st language speakers, and 44,000 2nd language speakers in the town of Juba alone. Many more speakers.*

255 (Ki)Nubi (Kenya/Uganda) C

*A creolized Arabic spoken by around 40,000 descendants of former soldiers of the Egyptian Army in Sudan, who were incorporated into the King's African Rifles under the British.*

256 Ethiopian Pidgin Arabic JP

*A frequently rudimentary trade jargon used with the Arab traders and shopkeepers in many parts of Ethiopa.*

257 Gulf Pidgin Arabic P

*Used between Arabs and foreign workers in the Persian Gulf states and Saudi Arabia, at least since since the 60's.*

L. Bantu-lexifier Creoles and Pidgins

   1. Western and Southern

       258 Ewondo Populaire/Pidgin A70 (based on Ewondo) (Cameroon) PE

          *Spoken around Yaoundé, the capital of Cameroon.*

       259 LiNgala (based on BoBangi) (Zaire/Congo) PE

          *An important lingua franca in Zaire and Congo with about 8,500,000 speakers.*

       260 KiTuba (based on KiKoongo) (Zaire) PE

          *An important lingua franca in Zaire spoken by about 4,200,000 people.*

       261 Kasai Pidgin ChiLuba (based on ChiLuba) (Zaire) P

          *Spoken in Zaire.*

       262 Town Bemba/ChiKopabeluti (based on ChiBemba) (Zambia) P

          *Widespread in the Zambian Copperbelt.*

       263 Fanagaló (based on Zulu) (South Africa/Zimbabwe/Zambia) P

          *Widespread in Southern Africa, especially in mining areas. Used by more than 100,000 speakers.*

       264 Lingua Monte-Café (based on UMbundu)(São Tomé and Principe) C?

          *Reduced variant with many Portuguese loanwords in a continuum relationship with an unre-*
          *duced UMbundu-like Lingua Monte-Café. Spoken on the 'Roça' Monte-Café on São Tomé*
          *by the Tonga - descendants of 19th century contract labourers from Angola, etc.*

   2. KiSwahili-lexifier

       265 Zanzibar Pidgin Swahili (Tanzania) PJ?

          *Used by Europeans and Asians. KiSwahili is native to Zanzibar. Possibly an interlanguage.*

       266 Kenya Coastal Pidgin Swahili (Kenya) PE

          *Used between coastal native speakers of KiSwahili and immigrants from the interior of Kenya.*

       267 Up-country Pidgin Swahili (Kenya/Uganda) P

          *This is the variety spoken in Nairobi and Kampala. Some variation according to the native*
          *language of the speaker.*

       268 KiSetla (Kenya) P?

          *Formerly spoken by white colonists with Africans in Kenya. Now falling into disuse. Possibly*
          *an interlanguage.*

       269 KiVita (Kenya) * P

          *First developed in the 1940's in the British East African Army.*

       270 KiHindi (Kenya) P

          *Formerly used between Asian shopkeepers and their customers in Kenya.*

       271 KiNgwana (Zaire) C

          *A Zairean creole spoken by about 7 million people in Kivu province, Eastern Zaire.*

       272 Shaba Swahili (Zaire) C

          *A creole spoken by about 2 million people in Shaba province, S.E. Zaire.*

       273 (Ki)Settla (Zambia) P?

          *Used by white colonists in Zambia. Possibly an interlanguage.*

       274 Barracoon (Mozambique) * P

          *A trade language used in the Mozambican ports in the 19th century. With Arabic, Portuguese,*
          *Malagasy, Makua and Hinzua elements.*

M. Other African-lexifier Creoles and Pidgins

    275 Pidgin Wolof (Gambia) P

    276 Kangbe (based on Mandinka) P

        *Used among Mandinka, Dyula and Bambara speakers as a lingua franca.*

    277 Barikanči/Pidgin Hausa (Nigeria) P

        *Developed in and around the British army barracks in Northern Nigeria.*

    278 Bilkiire/Kambariire/Pidgin Fula (Nigeria/Cameroon) PE

        *Different subvarieties according to the mother tongue of speakers. Spoken in Adamawa and throughout Northern Cameroon.*

    279 Sango (based on Yakoma) (Central African Republic/Chad/Cameroon/Congo) PE

        *The national language of the Central African Republic, spoken by 5 million as a 2nd language.*

    280 (Creole) Sango (based on (Pidgin) Sango) (C. African Rep.) C

        *Spoken by 200,000 as a 1st language. Distinct from Pidgin Sango.*

N. Japanese-lexifier Creoles and Pidgins

    281 Manchurian Pidgin Japanese (China) P

        *Used during the 30's in Manchukuo.*

    282 Taiwan Pidgin Japanese (Taiwan) P

        *Used in Taiwan among the members of Austronesian tribes under the Japanese occupation during the first half of the 20th century.*

    283 Yokohama Pidgin Japanese/Yokohamese (Japan) * P

        *Used up till the end of the 19th century in Yokohama, the only port where trading with foreigners was allowed.*

    284 Solomon Islands Pidgin Japanese (Solomon Islands) P

        *Used by Japanese fishermen.*

O. Chinese-lexifier Pidgins

    285 Korean Pidgin Chinese (China/North Korea) P

        *Used in Chinese-Korean contacts.*

    286 Malayan Pidgin Chinese (Malaysia) P

        *A market pidgin.*

P. Other Asian Language-lexifier Pidgins

    287 Malayan Pidgin Tamil (Malaysia) P

        *A market pidgin.*

Q. Austronesian-lexifier Creoles and Pidgins

  1. Malay-lexifier Creoles and Pidgins.

    a. Western

    288 Sri Lankan Creole Malay (Sri Lanka) C

        *50,000 speakers.*

    289 Bazaar Malay of Malacca (Malaysia) P

        *A market pidgin.*

    290 Baba Malay (Malaysia) C

        *A Malay-lexifier creole used by 5000 Hokkien Chinese-Malay mixed race people in Malacca, and 10,000 in Singapore.*

    291 Chittie Malay (Malaysia) C

        *A Malay-lexifier creole used by Tamils in Malaya.*

Q.1.a.
    292 Sabah Malay (Malaysia) P

      *A limited contact variety.*

    293 Cocos Islands Malay (Australian Territory/Malaysia) C

      *495 speakers on the Cocos Islands, 558 on Christmas Island, both Australian possessions, and 3000 in Sabah, Malaysia.*

b. Eastern

  i. Eastern Indonesia

    294 Makassarese Malay (Indonesia) C?

      *Spoken in Western Sulawesi (Celebes). Makassar (now Ujung Pandang) was a Portuguese settlement.*

    295 Menado Malay/Minahassa Malay (Indonesia) C

      *Spoken in Northern Sulawesi (Celebes).*

    296 Larantuka Malay (Indonesia) C

      *Spoken in Larantuka, Flores - a Portuguese possession till 1859.*

    297 Kupang Malay (Indonesia) C

      *Spoken in Kupang, Timor by several thousand people. A former Portuguese settlement from the early 16th to the late 17th century. Much influenced by Rotinese.*

    298 Melayu Ambon/Ambonese Malay (Indonesia/Netherlands) C

      *235,000 speakers on Ambon and surrounding islands in the Central Moluccas, and in the Netherlands. Ambon was formerly Portuguese.*

    299 Malaju Sini/Dutch Moluccan Malay (Netherlands) PS

      *Used by younger Moluccans in the Netherlands.*

    300 Banda Malay (Indonesia) C

      *Spoken on the Banda Islands in the Central Moluccas. A former Portuguese settlement.*

    301 Ternate Malay/North Moluccan Malay (Indonesia) C

      *Spoken as a 1st language by a few hundred Christians in Labuhan, Bacan Island, also by speakers on Ternate, Sula, Obi and coastal Halmahera. It is a regional lingua franca, e.g. in many multilingual villages on the Halmahera coast. Many Ternate, Dutch and Portuguese loans. Ternate was a former Portuguese settlement.*

    302 Bacanese Malay (Indonesia) C?

      *2000 speakers on Bacan Island, North Moluccas.*

  ii. New Guinea/Australia

    303 Mbrariri/Mariri (Irian Jaya, Indonesia) P

      *Used on the coast of the Vogelkop Penninsula, this differs from Irian Jaya Pidgin Malay by reason of the numerous Portuguese and Dutch words. The area was long under the control of the Sultan of Ternate.*

    304 Irian Jaya Pidgin Malay (Indonesia/Papua New Guinea) P

      *A 20th century pidgin with c.100,000 speakers in Irian Jaya, and c.2000 in Papua New Guinea. An offshoot of Ambonese Malay.*

    305 Yuan Pidgin Malay (Papua New Guinea) * P

      *Used by the Yuan as a trade language with the surrounding tribes in the Yellow River area from the late 19th century until the 1930's.*

    306 Macassarese Pidgin Malay/Macassan (N. Territory, Australia) P

      *A pidgin used in the Northern Territory between Aboriginals and trepang fishers during the*

Q.1.b.    *19th century, based on Makassarese Malay. Influenced Northern Territory Pidgin English.*
307 Thursday Island Pidgin Malay (Queensland, Australia) P
    *A reduced form of Malay used in the pearling area at Thurday Island.*

2. New Guinea Area Austronesian-lexifier Creoles and Pidgins
    308 Tetun-Praça (based on Tetum) (Indonesia) P
        *A lingua franca (2nd language) variety of Tetum, a major language of Timor*
    309 Police Motu/(New) Hiri Motu (based on Motu) (P.N.G.) PE
        *Used around Port Moresby, the capital of Papua New Guinea, since the 19th century. Now 200,000 speakers.*
    310 (Old) Hiri Motu (based on Motu) (Papua New Guinea) * PJ
        *A trade jargon used between the Motu and the Papuan-speaking tribes of the Papuan Gulf.*
    311 Pidgin Dobu/Gosinga Talk (based on Dobu)(Papua New Guinea) P
        *Several thousand speakers in Milne Bay province.*
    312 Pidgin Nakanai-Tolai (based on Tolai) (Papua New Guinea) * PJ
        *Formerly used among the Nakanai.*
    313 Pidgin Siassi/Tok Siassi Haphap (Huon Penninsula) (P.N.G.) PJ
        *A trade language.*

3. Eastern Pacific Creoles and Pidgins
    314 Current Pidgin Fijian (Fiji) P
        *Used in Indian-Fijian interactions. 50,000 speakers. Is descended from Plantation Pidgin Fijian.*
    315 Plantation Pidgin Fijian (Fiji/Solomons) * P
        *Formerly spoken on Fiji. Also taken back to the Solomons by ex-plantation workers.*
    316 Pidgin Tahitian/Parau Tinito (French Territory) P
        *Used in Chinese-Tahitian interactions. Has about 5000 speakers.*
    317 Pidgin Hawaiian (Hawaii) * P
        *Used until the beginning of the 20th century.*
    318 Pidgin Maori (New Zealand) * P
    319 Beach Kusaien (Micronesia) * P
        *Used on Kusaie in mid-19th century. Words from Kusaien, Hawaiian, Spanish and English.*

R. Papuan-lexifier Creoles and Pidgins
    320 Toaripi Hiri Trading Pidgin (based on Eleman languages) * PJ
        *Formerly used between Motu traders and speakers of Eleman languages, and based on several of the Eleman languages.*
    321 Koriki Hiri Trading Pidgin (based on Koriki) (Papua New Guinea) * PJ
        *Formerly used between Motu traders and the Koriki.*
    322 Manam Trading Pidgin (based on Manam) (Papua New Guinea) PJ
    323 Yimas-Arafundi Trading Pidgin (based on Arafundi) (Papua New Guinea) PJ
        *Used by a few Yimas traders (belonging to one family) with the Arafundi.*
    324 Yimas-Alamblak Trading Pidgin (Papua New Guinea) PJ
        *Used by a few Yimas traders with the Alamblak.*
    325 Yimas-Karawari Trading Pidgin (Papua New Guinea) PJ
        *Used by a few Yimas traders with the Karawari.*
    326 Iatmul Jargon (Papua New Guinea) P
        *Simplified Iatmul widely used in the Middle Sepik area of the Eastern Sepik province.*

R.            327 Dani Police Talk (Irian Jaya, Indonesia) PJ
*Used mostly by the police force in the Central Highlands of Irian Jaya.*

S. Australian-lexifier Creoles and pidgins

           328 Modern Langus (based on Kala Lagau Ya) (Torres Strait) C
*Used on the western Torres Strait islands by about 1000 younger people. A simplified version of the Kala Lagau Ya used by the older generation.*

           329 Ap-ne-ap (see also section Z.4) (Torres Strait) MC
*Ap-ne-ap (lit. half-and-half) is a mixed creole based on Torres Strait Pidgin English and Kala Lagau Ya spoken on the central Torres Strait islands. by more than 600 speakers. Only the elderly still speak pure Kala Lagau Ya.*

T. Amerindian-lexifier Creoles and Pidgins

   1. Palaeosiberian-lexifier

           330 Chukotka Pidgin Chukchee (Russia) * PJ
*Used between Chukchee and outsiders in the 19th century.*

   2. North American

     a. Eskimo-lexifier

           331 Chukotka Pidgin Eskimo (Russia) * PJ
*Used in the 19th century for communication between Central Siberian Yupik speakers, and the Chukchee and other Eskimo groups.*

           332 Alaskan Inuit Trading Jargon (Alaska/Canada) PJ
*Used in communication between American whalers and Inuit at Herschel Island, Point Barrow, Point Hope, Kotzebue, Marble Island and other places on the Alaskan and North Canadian coasts.*

           333 Mackenzie River Eskimo Trade Jargon (N.W. Territories) PJ
*Used for trading between Eskimos and the Loucheux Indian tribe.*

           334 Hudson Strait Pidgin Eskimo (Canada) PJ

           335 Greenlandic Pidgin Eskimo (Greenland) * PJ

     b. Northwest

           336 Jargon Loucheux (based on Gwich'in) (Canada) * P
*Used on the Mackenzie River, in N.W. Canada in the 19th century for trade between whites and Loucheux.*

           337 Broken Slavey (based on Slave) (Canada) * P
*Used on the Yukon and Peel Rivers, in N.W. Canada in the 19th century.*

           338 Haida Jargon (based on Haida) (Canada) * PJ
*Used in the Queen Charlotte Islands between English speakers and Haida, Coast Tsimshian and Heiltsuk in the 1830's.*

           339 Chinook Jargon/Wawa (based on Chinook) (USA/Canada) PS
*Used in the northwestern USA (also northern California) and western Canada in the 19th and early 20th centuries. Still spoken by a few people in British Columbia. Latterly a much greater English element in the lexicon, so that it could be described as an Mixed Stable Pidgin (MPS) (English-Wawa).*

           340 Nootka Jargon (based on Nootka) (Canada) * P
*Used in the 18th and early 19th centuries. Was absorbed into Chinook Jargon, where it was responsible for the Nootka element in Chinook Jargon.*

T.2.b.          341 Kutenai Jargon (based on Kutenai) (Canada) * PJ
                    *A 19th century pidgin used by Europeans for communication with the Kutenai.*
        c. Others
                342 Trader Navaho (based on Navaho) (USA) P?
                    *A simplified form of Navaho used by white American traders. Possibly only an interlanguage.*
                343 Broken Ojibway (based on Ojibway) (USA) * P
                    *Used in the early 19th century in the Western Great Lakes area.*
                344 Delaware Jargon (based on Unami Delaware) (USA) * P
                    *Used in the 17th century for trade between Europeans and the Algonquian tribes of the North-*
                    *East of the American colony.*
                345 Mobilian Jargon/Yamá (based on Chickasaw) (USA) * PS
                    *Used from the 17th till the 20th century. The 20th century variants have many Alabama elements.*
                    *This possibly represents a regional dialect of Mobilian (p.c. Anthony Grant).*
    3. South American
                346 Kariña Pidgin (based on Carib) (N.E. South America) P
                    *A pidgin recorded from the seventeenth century, and possibly still used. In 1937 used between*
                    *the Wayana (Carib) of southern Surinam and the Aluku of Cayenne. Also reportedly used by*
                    *the Palikur in Brazil in 1925.*
                347 Lingua Geral Amazonica/Nheengatu (based on Tupinamba) (Brazil) C
                    *A creole based on the now extinct Tupinamba. Spoken in the Rio Negro valley by more than*
                    *3000 bilingual speakers.*
                348 Lingua Geral Paulista/Tupi Paulista (Brazil/Paraguay) * P
                    *A Tupi-lexifier pidgin or creole of the São Paulo region. The last speakers died at the beginning*
                    *of the 20th century.*
U. Signed Pidgins
    1. Inter-ethnic Pidgin Sign Languages of the Hearing
                349 Plains Sign Language (North America) * SP
                    *Used for intertribal communication from at least the late 18th century. In the 19th century it*
                    *was known to 100,000 Indians. Now its use is largely ceremonial or recreational.*
                350 Plateau Sign Language (North America) * SP
                    *Used among the Colville and neighbouring Salish tribes until the late 18th century, when it was*
                    *replaced in the east by Plains Sign Language, and in the west by Chinook Jargon.*
    2. Inter-ethnic Pidgin Sign Languages of the Deaf
                351 Scandinavian Pidgin Sign Language (Scandinavia) SP
                    *Used among the deaf in Norway, Sweden, Denmark, and Finland.*

Z. Mixed languages
  1. Mixed jargons/pidgins
         *For mixed jargon pidgins (MPJ) the mixture is primarily lexical.*
    a. European North Atlantic Pidgins
        352 Estonian-Finnish Pidgin MPJ        Estonian-Finnish
           *A maritime pidgin.*
        353 Low German-Norwegian Pidgin MPJ      Low German-Norwegian
           *A maritime pidgin.*
        354 Breton-English Pidgin MPJ        English-Breton
           *Used by Cornish and Breton fishermen.*
        355 Icelandic-Breton Pidgin MPJ       Icelandic-Breton
        356 Russe-Norsk * MPJ          Russian-Norwegian
           *Used between Russian and Norwegian fishermen.*
        357 Solombala English-Russian Pidgin (Russia) * MPJ
                           English-Russian
           *Used in the late 18th century in the port of Solombala (Archangelsk).*
    b. American North Atlantic Pidgins
        358 Labrador Inuit Pidgin French (Canada) * MPJ
                           French-Inuit/other elements
           *Used in contacts between Basque and Breton fishermen and the Inuit in the Straits of Belle Isle*
           *until about 1760.*
        359 Montagnais Pidgin Basque (Canada) * MPJ
                           Basque-Montagnais
           *This pidgin was used from 1550 to 1650 by Basque fishermen in the area of Newfoundland and*
           *the Gulf of St. Lawrence to communicate with the Montagnais.*
        360 Souriquois (Canada) * MPJ       Basque-Micmac
           *A largely Micmac and Basque lexicon pidgin used in communication between the Micmac, the*
           *Basques and the French in the late 16th and early 17th centuries in South-east Canada.*
    c. Middle Eastern Pidgins
        361 Amarna Akkadian-Hurrian Pidgin (Syria) * MP
                           Akkadian-Hurrian
           *Recorded in 14th century B.C. letters in the Tell-el-Amarna state archives.*
        362 Amarna-Akkadian (Syria) * MPS     **Canaanite**-Akkadian
           *Recorded in 14th century B.C. letters in the Tell-el-Amarna state archives. Possibly only a written*
           *form of language.*
    d. Siberian Pidgins
      i. Kamchatka
        363 Kamchadal-Russian Pidgin (Russia) MPS  Russian-Kamchadal
        364 Koryak-Russian Pidgin (Russia) MP    Russian-Koryak
      ii. Sino-Russian Pidgins
        365 Kjachta Sino-Russian Pidgin (Russia/Mongolia) * MPJ
                             Russian-Chinese
           *This trading pidgin was spoken on the Russian-Mongolian (then Russian-Chinese) border south*
           *of Lake Baikal from the early 18th to the mid-19th centuries in the trading towns of Kyakhta*

Z.1.d.ii.          *(Russia) and Maimachin (then China, now Altinbulag, Mongolia).*

366 Ussuri Sino-Russian Pidgin (Russia) MP    Russian-Chinese

*This pidgin is a 20th century pidgin used between Russians and members of Tungusic groups, especially Udege and Nanai, in the Ussuri River border region between Russia and China.*

367 Manchurian Sino-Russian Pidgin (China) MPJ

Russian-Chinese

*This contact jargon was used between Russians and Poles, and Chinese in Manchuria, notably in the city of Harbin, with its population of 100,000 Russians. With the departure of nearly all the Russian population of Harbin in the fifties to Australia etc., the raison d'être for this pidgin has disappeared. Two different styles existed - one for Russians, and one for Chinese.*

368 Primor'a Sino-Russian Pidgin (Russia) MPJ

Russian-Chinese

*Used in communication between Russians and Japanese in Primor'a (Russia).*

e. South American Pidgins

369 Ndjuka Amerindian Trading Pidgin (Surinam) MPJ

Ndjuka-Trio (see also section Z.4)

*Used for purposes of trade between the Ndjuka maroons and the Cariban Trio tribe.*

370 Catalangu (see also section Z.4) (Ecuador) MPS?

**Quechua**-Spanish

*Used by Amerindians in Cañar province living close to the provincial urban centres.*

371 Nambikwara-Portugees Telegraaflijn

*Rondônia/Mato Grosso. First decennium 20th century*

f. Australia

372 Broome Pearling Lugger Pidgin/Malay Talk/Broken Malay MPS

**Japanese**-Malay-Aboriginal English

*Used by the mixed Asian (Koepangers, Malays, Chinese, Japanese, Filipinos, Koreans) and Aboriginal (esp. Bardi) crews of the pearling luggers around Broome (1890's-1960's). Apparently relexification from Kupang Malay to Penninsular Malay in the postwar period.*

g. Africa

373 KiSwahili-Malagasy Contact Language * MPJ?

KiSwahili-Malagasy

*Formerly used along the north-west coast of Madagascar.*

2. Symbiotic mixed languages

*The language providing the grammatical framework and sometimes also some lexical items is put in bold letters. The replacive lexical source is given second.*

a. Romany Para-languages

374 Angloromani/Poggedi Jib (England/S. Wales/S. Scotland/USA) MS

**English**-N.Romani

*Used by 75,000 Romanichals in the USA, and 80,000 in England as a 2nd language. The Romani element is 300-800 words in size.*

375 Norwegian Romani MS                    **Norwegian**-N.Romani (Norway)

376 Rommani MS                              **Swedish**-N.Romani (Sweden)

*Used as a secret language by the Tattare.*

Z.2.a.     377 Romish * MS                      **German**-N.Romani (Denmark)

*Virtually extinct. Used by Danish Gypsies (Sindi/Tatere).*

378 Caló/Romano/Calão/Rumanho (Spain/Portugal/S.America) MS

**Andalusian Spanish**-Romani

*Nearly extinct. In Portugal it was slightly Lusitanized.*

379 Errumantxela MS                **Basque**-Romani (Spain)

*A few speakers still in Guipuzcoa.*

380 Catalonian Romani MS           **Catalan**-Romani (Spain)

381 Brazilian Romani MS            **Portuguese**-Romani (Brazil)

382 Provençal Romani MS           **Occitan**-Romani (France)

*Spoken by a few families in the south of France.*

383 French-Sinti/Manouche MS      **French**-Manouche (France)

*Not the same as the unmixed Romani Manouche.*

384 Dortika * MS                     **Greek**-Romani (Greece)

*Formerly spoken by assimilated Gypsies in the Karpenisi area.*

385 Cergar/Bosnian Tent Gypsy MS    **Serbo-Croatian**-Romani (Bosnia)

386 Lomavren/Bosha MS             **W.Armenian**-Romani (Armenia)

*Reportedly some speakers in Azerbaijan, and possibly Armenia.*

387 Qirishmal MS                   **Persian (dialect)**-Romani (Iran)

388 Mughat MS                    **Tadjik**-Lugha Jargon/Romani (Tajikistan)

b. Irish Secret Languages

389 Bearlagar na Saer * MS         **Irish Gaelic**-altered Irish (Eire, USA)

*A professional jargon of stonemasons used in Munster. Also reported in New England in 1909.*

390 (Original) Sheldru/Shelta * MS     **Irish Gaelic**-altered Irish (Ireland)

*The original 'Shelta'. Recorded loans in English date from the 16th century (which form the only evidence for this variety) when of course Gaelic was the virtually universal language in Ireland.*

391 (Scottish Gaelic) Sheldru/Shelta MS    **Scottish Gaelic**-Shelta (Scotland)

*Spoken by the descendants of Irish travellers in the Scottish Highlands and Islands. Possibly extinct.*

392 (Gaelic) Sheldru/Shelta/Gammon * MS   **English**-Shelta (England, Ireland)

*Recorded in the late 19th century.*

393 (English) Sheldru/Shelta/Gammon/Irish Traveller Cant MS

**English**-Shelta (Eire, England)

*Similar to the aforementioned, but with a smaller Shelta component. Spoken by 15,000 Irish Travellers in England and 6000 in Ireland. Learnt from early childhood together with English.*

394 (American) Irish Travellers' Cant MS    **English**-English/Shelta (USA)

*Similar to the aforementioned, but with only 150 Shelta words.*

c. British Itinerants' Languages

395 Scottish Travellers' Cant/Cant/The Crack MS   (Scotland)

**Scots**-English Cant/Shelta/Angloromani

*The secret language of Scottish Tink(l)ers or Travellers.*

396 American Scottish Travellers' Cant MS (USA)

**English**-Cant/Shelta/Angloromani/Scots

397 (The) Cant MS                   **English**-various elements (England)

Z.2.c.            *Former secret language of English thieves and itinerants.*

    398 Polari * MS                                **English**-Italian/Lingua Franca (England)
    *Former secret language of sailors, showmen, and itinerant actors. Now survives in the form of*
    *a slang element used in English by people in show business, the circus, and by homosexuals.*

  d. Dutch/German Travellers' and Chapmen's Languages

    i. Bargoens

      399 (N.W.) Bargoens MS (Netherlands)     **Hollandish Dutch**-various elements/Yiddish
      *Formerly used by travellers etc. in the Western Netherlands.*

      400 Bargoens/Boeventaal MS (Netherlands)     **Hollandish Dutch**-various elements/Yiddish
      *Used in the Western Netherlands. Shares the N.W. Bargoens lexicons, but has a large additional*
      *vocabulary concerning criminal matters: stealing, prostitution, the police, etc.*

      401 (N.E.) Bargoens MS (Netherlands)     **Low German**-various elements/Yiddish
      *Formerly used by dealers, travellers, tramps, etc. in East Groningen, Twente and the Achterhoek.*

      402 (S.W.) Bargoens MS (Belgium/Netherland)

                                  **Brabantish or Flemish Dutch**-various elements
      *Formerly used by chapmen, dealers and many others, both nomadic and settled, in many places*
      *in Northern Belgium. Also in Dutch Brabant. In Roeselare, about 1000 of the 21,000 inhabitants*
      *reportedly knew Bargoens in the 1930's.*

      403 (S.E.) Bargoens MS (Netherland/Belgium)

                                  **Limburgish Dutch**-various elements
      *Formerly used by chapmen, dealers, travellers, tramps, etc.*

    ii. Dutch/Belgian/North German Chapmen's languages

      404 Kramertaal of the Kempen (Belgium) * MS„**Limburgish Dutch**-various elements
      *Used by the Teuten - itinerant chapmen in Belgian and Dutch North Limburg. Spoken between*
      *the 17th and 19th centuries.*

      405 Humpisch/Bargunsch/Tüöttensprache (Germany) * MS

                                    **Low German**-various elements
      *Used by the Tüötten - itinerant chapmen from Mettingen in Westphalia. They also operated*
      *in the Northern Netherlands. Died out around 1930. 260 words recorded.*

      406 Henese Fleck (Germany) * MS     **Limburgish Dutch**-various elements
      *Used by itinerant chapmen from Breyell. Died out around 1940. 400 words recorded.*

      407 Groenstraat-Bargoens/Henese Flik (Netherlands) * MS

                              **Limburgish Dutch**-various elements/Bargoens
      *Formerly used by itinerant chapmen from the Groenstraat, in Ubach-over-Worms in South*
      *Limburg. Extinct c. 1985. Traded from the Kempen to beyond the Eifel.*

      408 Potteferstaal (Belgium) * MS     **Brabantish Dutch**-various elements
      *Used by pot and kettle repairers operating from Tienen in Brabant, until c.1925.*

    iii. Middle German Chapmen's Languages

      409 Eifler Jenisch MS     **German**-various elements
      *Used by peddlars in the Eifel region.*

      410 Frickhöfer Sprache MS     **German**-various elements
      *Used by Hessian peddlars in places near Hadamar and Limburg.*

      411 Sprache Winterfelder Hausirer/Schlausmen MS**German**-various elements

Z.2.d.iii.    iv. South German Chapmen's Languages

      412 Sprache Schwäbischer Händler/Jenisch MS

                            **German**-various elements

      *Used in various villages in Swabia.*

      413 Killenthäler Pleisslen MS       **German**-various elements

      *Used in the district to the east of Hechingen in Baden-Württemberg.*

      414 Sprache Pfälzer Hausirer/Lôchne-Kôdesch MS

                            **German**-various elements

      *Used by peddlars from near Dürkheim in Bavaria.*

      415 Unnamed MS (France)        **German**-various elements

      *Used in Metz.*

    v. Assorted

      416 Rotwelsch MS             **German**-various elements (Germany/Austria)

      *Referred to first in the 13th century, and recorded from the 14th century, this is the former secret language of German criminal groups. Recorded in this century from Hamburg, Dresden, Vienna.*

         417 Kundensprache (Germany) MS  **German**-various elements

      *A secret language of chapmen.*

      418 Masematte (Germany) MS      **Low German**-Hebrew/Yiddish/Romani

      *Spoken around Munster by a few elderly dealers.*

      419 Lekoudesch MS           **German**-Yiddish/Hebrew

      *A secret language of German cattle-dealers.*

      420 Kochemer-Loschen MS      **German**-various/Hebrew

      *A secret language of Jewish traders in Württemberg.*

  e. Assorted Western European Caste Languages

      421 Vasconço/Giria/Calão MS     **Portuguese**-various elements

      *The secret language of the marginal groups in Portugal.*

      422 Germania/Teriganza/Caló MS   **Spanish**-various elements

      *The secret language of the marginal groups in Spain.*

      423 Argot MS                **French**-various elements (France)

      *The secret language of the marginal groups in France.*

      424 Gergo MS               **Italian**-various elements (Italy)

      *The secret language of the marginal groups in Italy.*

  f. Northern European Caste Languages

      425 Keltringe MS             **Danish**-various elements/Romani (Denmark)

      426 Tyvesprog MS           **Danish**-various elements/Romani (Denmark)

      427 Rodi MS                 **Norwegian**-various elements/Romani (Norway)

      428 Månsing MS            **Norwegian**-various elements/Romani (Norway

  g. Central European Caste Languages

      429 Hantýrka MS            **Czech**-various elements/Hebrew (Czechia)

      *Used by traders and petty thieves in Bohemia.*

  h. Balkan Trade Languages

    i. Albania

      430 Dogan (Albania) MS        **Albanian**-various elements

      *Spoken by coppersmiths in Peshtani, Tepelena district.*

Z.2.h.   431 Prur (Albania) MS?

*Spoken by masons in Opar, Korça region.*

432 Çortar (Albania) MS?

*Spoken by masons in Panarit, Korça region.*

433 Delibep (Albania) MS?

434 Jevg MS   **Albanian**-various elements (Albania)

*Reportedly the descendants of Egyptian slaves brought to Albania by the Turks. The lexicon is partly distorted Albanian, partly of unknown origin.*

ii. Bosnia

435 Šatrovački MS   **Serbo-Croatian**-Romani/various elements (Bosnia)

*The Gaunersprache of Bosnia-Herzegovina. The name of this language should not be confused with the same term Šatrovački used to refer to Croatian slang.*

436 Banalački MS   **Serbo-Croatian**-Albanian (Bosnia)

*A secret language of bricklayers in Osaćanima near Srebrenica, Bosnia.*

iii. Greece

437 Krekonika MS   **Greek**-Albanian (Greece)

*A secret language.*

i. Turkish Caste Languages

438 Geygel MS   **Turkish**-various els./Romani (Turkey)

*The language of the Geygel itinerant smiths in the Çivril region of Denizli.*

439 Abdal MS   **Turkish**-Persian/Romani (Turkey)

*Up to 50,000 Abdal living in a symbiotic relationship to the surrounding peoples. Musicians, traditional healers, basketweavers, pedlars, etc.*

440 Elekçi MS   **Turkish**-Armenian (Turkey)

*The Elekçis of Bolu - an Abdal group - use a largely Armenian vocabulary in a Turkish grammatical framework.*

j. Central Asian Caste Languages

441 Lugha MS   **Uzbek**-various elements

*Spoken by the circus folk of the (former) Central Asian USSR.*

k. African City Languages

442 KiNgwana Indoubil MS   **KiNgwana**-various elements (Zaire)

*The in-group language of the young in Bukavu, Kisangani, etc. Around 150,000 speakers in Bukavu.*

443 Shaba Indoubil MS   **Shaba Swahili**-various elements (Zaire)

*The in-group language of the young in Lubumbashi etc.*

444 LiNgala Indoubil MS   **LiNgala**-various elements (Zaire)

*The in-group language of the young in Kinshasa etc.*

445 Sheng MS   **Pidgin Swahili**-English/various elements (Kenya)

*A language of young people particularly in the informal economy in Nairobi: shoe-shine boys, curio-sellers, hawkers, parking boys, etc.*

l. African Guild Languages

446 Ivié MS   **Bini**-Portuguese (Nigeria)

*A secret language of the members of a guild of cloth-dealers to the court of Benin. Has a large Portuguese lexicon.*

Z.2.     m. African Secret Languages

      447 Awo/Hunting Talk MS        **Krio**-Yoruba (Sierra Leone)

*Several hundred Yoruba words used in a Krio grammatical framework by hunters.*

      448 Agbuí-gbe **r** MS        **Gbe**-? (Togo/Benin)

*A dialect of the secret Yeừe-gbe ritual language used by those adherents of the Yeừe or Vodú religion who worship the Sea God Agbuí or Aừleketi.*

      449 So-gbe **r** MS        **Gbe**-? (Togo/Benin)

*A dialect of the secret Yeừe-gbe ritual language used by those adherents of the Yeừe or Vodú religion who worship the Weather God So.*

      450 Ananá-gbe **r** MS        **Gbe**-? (Togo/Benin)

*A dialect of the secret Yeừe-gbe ritual language used by those adherents of the Yeừe or Vodú religion who worship the Female God Ananá.*

      451 Vodú-gbe **r** MS        **Gbe**-? (Togo/Benin)

*A dialect of the secret Yeừe-gbe ritual language used by those adherents of the Yeừe or Vodú religion who worship the Snake God Da or Vodúda.*

    n. Other African

      452 Unnamed MS        **Khoekhoe**-Afrikaans (S. Africa/Namibia)

*A mixed language spoken by Oorlamse (Hottentots who have adopted European culture) since the 17th century in the Orange River area. It is not a 1st language, and is used under specific circumstances only.*

    o. Indian Caste Languages

      453 Rodiya/Gadiya MS?        Telugu-Sinhalese (Sri Lanka)

*Used by a caste of snake-charmers.*

    p. America

      454 Lucumí **r** MS?        Yoruba-? (Cuba)

*A ritual language used by devotees of the Afro-Cuban Santería religion.*

      455 Carabalí/Efí **r** MS?        Efik-? (Cuba)

*A ritual language used by devotees of the Afro-Cuban Santería religion.*

      456 Callahuaya MS        **Quechua**-Puquina (Bolivia)

*50 speakers in N.W. Bolivia, centred on Charazani. A secret language of a caste of 2000 traditional healers of Puquina ethnicity, operating even outside Bolivia. Puquina has been extinct since c.1900.*

      457 Cafundó MS        **Portuguese**-Bantu (Brazil)

*Spoken by 40 speakers 150 km from São Paolo. Used as a secret language.*

    q. Men's Languages

      458 Island Carib Men's Language * MP

                                **Iñeri Arawak**-Kariña Pidgin (Lesser Antilles)

*The Carib conquerors of the Lesser Antilles intermarried with Iñeri (Arawak) women losing their Kariña language. The Kariña pidgin they employed to communicate with the mainland Caribs was embedded in a matrix of Arawak grammar and lexicon to provide an in-group code.*

      459 Ngatik Men's Language MP        **Ponapean**-English (Micronesia)

*Spoken by the offspring of European sailors and Ponapean women.*

      460 Damin MS        **Lardil**-various elements (Australia)

*A secret language of initiated men.*

Z.2.q.       461 Senkyoshigo MS                    **English**-Japanese (Japan)
             *The in-group language of American Mormon missionaries in Japan.*

3. Mixed Languages Proper
             *In the cases where one language is known to provide most of the content-words, and the other*
             *most of the function-words, this is indicated by putting the name of the latter language in bold*
             *letters.*

   a. Americas
      i. North America
         462 Michif M                              **Cree**-French (Canada/USA)
         *Spoken by less than 1000 Métis in Saskatchewan, Manitoba, N. Dakota, and Montana. The*
         *language has existed from before 1840, and is now only spoken by people older than 60. The*
         *ethnic group, which emerged in the 1800's, is descended from European males and Amerindian*
         *women.*

      ii. Central America
         463 Unnamed * M?                          Nahuatl-Spanish (Nicaragua)
         *Recorded in the 16th century.*

      iii. South America
         464 Media Lengua of Salcedo M             **Quechua**-Spanish (Ecuador)
         *Spoken in several communities around Salcedo, Cotopaxi province. It has been in existence since*
         *at least 1920.*

         465 Media Lengua of Saraguro M            **Quechua**-Spanish (Ecuador)
         *Spoken in at least one community near Saraguro, Loja province.*

         466 Unnamed M                             Guajiro-Spanish (Colombia/Venezuela)
         *A mixed language replacing Amerindian (Arawakan) Guajiro.*

   b. Africa
      i. Eastern
         467 Ma'a/Inner Mbugu/KiMbugu cha ndani (Tanzania) M

                                                   **Pare**-Southern Cushitic/various elements
         *The Mbugu speak two languages; one a Bantu language - a dialect of Pare (Normal Mbugu/*
         *Pare-Mbugu) - and the other the mixed language. Roughly 40,000 speakers in the Usumbara*
         *Mountains. One Mbugu clan - the VaGonje - uses only the unmixed Bantu language.*

         468 Ilwana (Kenya) M                      Ilwana (Bantu)-Oromo (E. Cushitic)
         *15,000 speakers in N.E. Kenya. The mixed language came into existence during the last 350 years.*

         469 Unnamed (Somalia) M                   Italian-Somali
         *Spoken in the mixed community of Missioné on the Somali coast.*

      ii. Southern
         470 Unnamed M                             Kutchi-KiSwahili (Kenya)
         *A first language spoken by Gujaratis from Zanzibar.*

         471 KiMwani M?                            ChiMakonde-KiSwahili (Mozambique)
         *Spoken in various coastal towns, and on the islands of the Querimba archipelago, Cabo Delgado*
         *province, by up to 50,000 speakers. The language owes its presence here to the first Swahili*
         *expansion, about 1000 years ago.*

Z.3.b.11.    472 ChiMakwe M?    ChiMakonde-KiSwahili (Mozambique)

*Spoken on the northernmost part of the coast of Cabo Delgado province, to the north of KiMwani.*

473 Ekoti M?    Emakhua-KiSwahili (Mozambique)

*Spoken in the Emakhua-speaking area in Nampula province.*

474 Olumbali M?    KiMbundu-UMbundu (Angola)

*Spoken in Moçamedes.*

c. Oceania

i. Reefs-Santa Cruz Family

*The languages in this family are the result of the mixture of unknown Austronesian and Papuan languages.*

475 Äiwo M    Austronesian-Papuan (Solomon Is.)

476 Nanggu M    Austronesian-Papuan (Solomon Is.)

477 Santa Cruz M    Austronesian-Papuan (Solomon Is.)

d. Northern Asia

i. Siberia

478 Copper Island Aleut/Mednij Aleut M    Aleut-Russian (Russia)

*Less than 10 speakers remain on Bering Island.*

479 Transtundra Christian Russian * M (Russia)

**Dolgan**-Russian/Dolgan

*No longer used. Replaced by Dolgan.*

480 Kamchadal/Itelmen M    **Chukchi/Koryak**-? (473)

*The morphology of this language is identical to Chukchi/Koryak but the lexicon is completely different.*

ii. Xinjiang Province, China

481 Qoqmončaq M    Kazakh-Mongol-Solon (China)

*Spoken in the Altai region of the Xinjiang-Uygur Autonomous Region in China by 200 people.*

482 Aynu M    **Uygur**-Persian (China)

*Spoken in the Xinjiang-Uygur Autonomous Region in China by an Abdal group.*

iii. Qinghai/Kansu Province, China

483 Wutun (China) M    **Amdo Tibetan/Kansu Mongol**-Chinese

*Spoken in Huángnán Tibetan Autonomous Region, Qinghai province by the 2500 descendants of a Chinese military garrison. The Wutun are mostly trilingual, speaking also Tibetan (the lingua franca) and Chinese.*

484 Linxia Chinese M    **Kansu Mongol**-Chinese (China)

*Spoken in Linxia, Kansu province.*

485 (New) Linxia Baonan M?    **Baonan**-Baonan/Linxia Chinese (China)

*Spoken in Linxia, Kansu province by the younger speakers of Baonan (one of the Kansu Mongol languages). Older speakers use less Chinese-influenced Baonan. About 2000 speakers in Linxia.*

486 Tángwàng M    **Santa**-Chinese (China)

*Spoken in Qinghai province by 20,000 people calling themselves 'Santa'. This language requires to be distinguished from the (Kansu Mongol) Santa language.*

Z.3.d.       iv. Other China

          487 Za M?                                Deng-Tibetan (China)
          *Spoken in Tibet by an ethnically Deng population.*

    e. Southern Asia

      i. India

          *This part of the list is a speculative combination of Hancock (1977) and Masica (1991).*

        *a.* Mixed IndoEuropean

          488 Khetran M?                          Lahnda-Dardic
          *Spoken in the Marri hills in Baluchistan.*

          489 Halbi/Bastari M?                     Marathi-Oriya-Chhattisgarhi
          *Spoken by 600,000 semi-Aryanized Gonds of Bastar district, Madhya Pradesh.*

          490 Pendhari M                           Hindi-Marathi-Rajasthani
          *Spoken in Dharwar and Belgaum districts.*

          491 Lodhi **M**                          Bundeli-Marathi
          *Spoken by immigrants in Balaghat district, Madhya Pradesh.*

          492 Bhatneri M?                          Punjabi-Rajasthani
          *185 speakers.*

          493 Rathi/Pacchadi M?                    Punjabi-Haryani
          *Spoken in Ghaggar valley.*

        *b.* IndoEuropean-TibetoBurman

          494 Koch M                              Bodo-Assamese
          *Spoken in the northern part of Mymensingh.*

          495 Haijong M                            Bengali-TibetoBurman
          *Spoken by 23,978 originally TibetoBurman speaking tribesmen in N.E. Bangla Desh and Cachar*
          *district, Assam.*

          496 Chakma M?                           Bengali-Chin
          *Spoken in Bangla Desh and Tripura. 69,000 speakers in India alone.*

        *c.* IndoEuropean-Dravidian

          497 Desiya M                             Oriya-Kui
          *Spoken in Orissa by non-Aryan tribesmen of the Koraput district.*

          498 Malpaharia M?                        Bengali-Malto
          *Spoken in Santal Parganas, Bihar by 100,000.*

        *d.* Dravidian-AustroAsiatic

          499 Horolia Jhagar M                     Mundari-Gond
          *Spoken in Ranchi.*

        *e.* Unknown

          500 Nahali M                             ?-Kurukh
          *A mixture of some unknown language and Dravidian Kurukh, as well as other languages.*
          *Spoken by 2000 speakers. A third of the lexicon is of recent Kurku (Munda) origin.*

          501 Vedda M                              ?-Sinhalese (Sri Lanka)
          *A mixture of some unknown language with Sinhalese spoken by a few hundred.*

      ii. Indonesia

          502 Javindo M                            **Javanese**-Dutch (Indonesia)
          *The language was spoken in Semarang by the Javanese wives of Dutch husbands, and their*
          *offspring.*

Z.3.e.ii.   503 Petjo * **M**                                    **Djakarta Malay**-Dutch (Indonesia)
            *This language was spoken by the descendants of Dutch fathers and Indonesian mothers, from*
            *about 1800 till the 1950s.*
            504 Unnamed **M**                           Sundanese-Dutch (Indonesia)
            *Spoken in Bandung.*
            505 Peranakan Chinese Javanese/Chindo/Baba Indonesian **M**
                                                **Javanese**-Malay (Indonesia)
            *Used in East Central Java by the descendants of Fukienese traders and Indonesian women since*
            *the 17th century. Many thousands of speakers are reported.*

   iii. Philippines
            506 Davaoeño **M**                          Tagalog-Visayan
            *Formed in the early 20th century as the result of immigration to the Davao area from the north.*
            *125,000 speakers.*

  f. Europe
            507 Stadsfries/Stedsk **M**               **West Frisian**-Dutch (Netherlands)
            *This is spoken in the larger urban communities in the Dutch province of Friesland -Leeuwarden*
            *(the capital) and six other towns. In Leeuwarden it is spoken by 16,000 people.*
            508 Pomak **M**?                          **Bulgarian**-Turkish/Bulgarian
            *Spoken by a Bulgarian Moslem group.*

4. Special cases are mixed languages involving one or more creoles or pidgins, already listed.
            – Saramaccan **MC**                         English Pidgin-Surinam Creole Portuguese
            *[see section A.1.c above]*
            – Dju-tongo * **MC**?                       English Pidgin-Surinam Creole Portuguese
            *[see section A.1.c above]*
            – Lingua Uba Budo **MC**?                   KiMbundu-São Tomense Creole Portuguese
            *[see section C.1.b.iv above]*
            – Portuguese-Dutch Creole **MC**?           Ceylon Creole Portuguese-Dutch
            *[see section C.2.c.iii above]*
            – Papiamento **MC**                         Portuguese Creole-Spanish
            *[see section D.1 above]*
            – Chavacano/Zamboangueño **MC**             Hiligaynon-Caviteño Creole Spanish
            *[see section D.3 above]*
            – Chavacano/Cotobateño **MC**              Hiligaynon-Caviteño Creole Spanish
            *[see section D.3 above]*
            – Chavacano/Davaoeño **MC**                 Hiligaynon-Caviteño Creole Spanish
            *[see section D.3 above]*
            – Berbice Dutch **MC**                      Eastern Ịjọ-Dutch Pidgin
            *[see section E above]*
            – Ap-ne-ap **MC**                           Torres Strait Pidgin English-Kala Lagau Ya
            *[see section s above]*
            – Ndjuka Amerindian Pidgin **MPJ**          Ndjuka-Trio
            *[see section Z.1.e above]*
            – Island Carib Mens' Language * **MP**      Iñeri (Arawakan)-Iñeri/Kariña Pidgin
            *[see section Z.2.q above]*

## 26.6 Postscript

Some idea of the importance of these languages might be got when we realise that the total number of speakers given here (for those languages where numbers are provided) is 93,348,410. Taking the languages for which no figures are given into consideration would easily bring the figure above 100 million - still only 2% of the world's population, of course. In fact the numbers of speakers of languages which are effectively unknown creoles must be much greater.

### Further reading

For a general survey of pidgin and creole languages see Holm (1988, 1989). Hancock (1981) is a recent list of pidgin and creoles. For older materials the reader is advised to consult Reinecke et al. (1975). A collection of articles on mixed languages is to be found in Bakker & Mous (1994). Some sources for specific groups of languages are as follows:
- Irish mixed languages: Grant (1994), Macalister (1937)
- Dutch and German chapmen's and criminals' languages: Hinskens (1983-1984), Kluge (1901), Moorman (1932, 1934), Wolf (1956)
- Turkish caste languages: Andrews (1989)
- Siberian pidgins and creoles: Wurm (1992)
- Chinese mixed languages: Sun (1992)
- Swahili-lexifier pidgins and creoles: Angogo (1980)
- Bantu-lexifier pidgins and creoles: Heine (1973)
- Indian creoles and mixed languages: Masica (1991)
- Eastern Malay: Collins (1983)
- Oceanic pidgins and creoles: Wurm & Hattori (1981)
- Australian pidgin and creole English: Sandefur (1979)

# Bibliography

**Abbreviations**

ACS  = *Amsterdam Creole Studies*
AL  = *Anthropological Linguistics*
CLS  = *Papers from the Regional Meeting of the Chicago Linguistic Society*
IJAL  = *International Journal of American Linguistics*
IJSL  = *International Journal for the Sociology of Language*
JPCL  = *Journal of Pidgin and Creole Languages*
SAL  = *Studies in African Linguistics*
SIL  = *Summer Institute of Linguistics*
SPCL  = *Society for Pidgin and Creole Linguistics*

Acton, T. & D. Kenrick (eds.) (1984). *Romani rokkeripen to-divvus. The English Romani dialect and its contemporary social, educational and linguistic standing.* London: Romanestan Publications.

Adamson, L. 1993. The binding of anaphors in Sranan. Paper read at the 5th SPCL Conference, Amsterdam, June 1993.

Adamson, L. & N. Smith (In prep.). Aspects of the verbal system of Sranan.

Adone, D. (1994). *The acquisition of Mauritian Creole.* Amsterdam: Benjamins.

Akinnaso, F.N. (1991). The development of a multilingual policy in Nigeria. *Applied Linguistics 12,* 29-61.

Alleyne, M.C. (1971). Acculturation and the cultural matrix of creolization. In Hymes (ed.), 169-86. (1980). *Comparative Afro-American.* Ann Arbor: Karoma.

Alleyne, M.C. (ed.) (1987). *Studies in Saramaccan language structure.* Caribbean Culture studies 2. University of Amsterdam/University of the West Indies.

Alleyne, M.C. (1993). Continuity versus creativity in Afro-American language varieties. In Mufwene (ed.), 167-81.

Ammon, U., N. Dittmar & K.J. Mattheier (eds.), (1988). *Sociolinguistics. An international handbook of the science of language and society.* Berlin: De Gruyter.

Andersen, R.W. (ed.) (1983). *Pidginization and creolization as language acquisition.* Rowley MA: Newbury House.

Andersen, R.W. (1990). Papiamentu tense-aspect, with special attention to discourse. In Singler (ed.), 59-96. Amsterdam: Benjamins.

Anderson, R. & P. Freebody (1981). Vocabulary knowledge. In J. Guthrie (ed.), *Comprehension and teaching. Research reviews.* Newark DE: Intern. Reading Association. 77-117.

Andrews, P.A. (1989). *Ethnic groups in the Republic of Turkey.* Wiesbaden: Ludwig Reichert.

Angogo, R. (1980). An inventory of KiSwahili-related pidgins and creoles. *Bashira 10,* 22-28.

Anon. (1829). *Da njoe testament va wi masra en helpiman Jesus Christus.* London: British and Foreign Bible Society (Partly reprinted in Anon. (1966), *Den toe boekoe di Lukas skrifi.* Haarlem: Bijbelgenootschap).

Appel, R. & P. Muysken (1987). *Language contact and bilingualism.* London: Edward Arnold.

Arends, J. (1986). Genesis and development of the equative copula in Sranan. In Muysken & Smith (eds.), 103-27.

(1989). *Syntactic developments in Sranan.* Doct. Diss. University of Nijmegen.

(1993). Towards a gradualist model of creolization. In Byrne & Holm (eds.), 371-80.

Arends, J. (ed.) (To appear a). *The early stages of creolization.* Amsterdam: Benjamins.

Arends, J. (To appear b). Demographic factors in the formation of Sranan. In Arends (ed.).

Arends, J. (To appear c). De Afrikaanse wortels van de creooltalen van Suriname. In *Van frictie tot wetenschap. Jaarboek 1993-1994 van de Vereniging van Akademie-onderzoekers.* Amsterdam: KNAW.

Baart, W.J.H. (1983). *Cuentanan di Nanzi.* Amsterdam: Rodopi.

Bailey, B. (1966). *Jamaican Creole syntax.* Cambridge: Cambridge University Press.

Bailey, C.N. (1973). *Variation and linguistic theory.* Arlington: Center for Applied Linguistics.

Baker, M. (1988). *Incorporation.* Chicago: University of Chicago Press.

(1989) Object sharing and projection in serial verb constructions. *Linguistic Inquiry 20,* 513-53.

Baker, P. (1982). On the origins of the first Mauritians and of the creole language of their descendants. A refutation of Chaudenson's 'Bourbonnais' theory. In P. Baker & C. Corne, *Isle de France Creole. Affinities and origins.* Ann Arbor: Karoma. 131-259.

(1984a). Agglutinated French articles in Creole French: Their evolutionary significance. *Te Reo 27,* 89-129.

(1984b). The significance of the French articles in the creole languages of the Indian Ocean and elsewhere. *York Papers in Linguistics 11,* 18-29.

(1993a). Australian influence on Melanesian Pidgin English. *Te Reo 36,* 3-67.

(1993b). Directionality in pidginization and creolization. Paper read at the 5th SPCL Conference, Amsterdam, June 1993.

Baker, P. & P. Mühlhäusler (1990). From business to pidgin. *Journal of Asian Pacific Communication 1,* 87-115.

Bakker, P. (1987). Reduplications in Saramaccan. In Alleyne (ed.), 17-40.

(1989). 'The language of the coast tribes is half Basque.' A Basque-Amerindian pidgin in use between Europeans and Native Americans in North America, ca. 1540 - ca. 1640. AL *31,* 117-47.

(1990). The genesis of Michif: A first hypothesis. In W. Cowan (ed.), *Papers of the Twentyfirst Algonquian Conference.* Ottawa: Carleton University. 11-35.

(1991a). Taalcontact in Noord-Amerika: Hoe sociale omstandigheden de vorm van de handelstaal bepalen. In R. van Hout & E. Huls (eds.), *Artikelen van de eerste sociolinguistische conferentie.* Delft: Eburon. 19-31

(1991b). Trade languages in the Strait of Belle Isle. *Journal of the Atlantic Provinces Linguistic Association 13,* 1-19.

(1992). 'A language of our own'. *The genesis of Michif, the mixed Cree-French language of the Canadian Métis.* Doct. Diss. University of Amsterdam (To be published by Oxford University Press, 1995).

(1993). European-Amerindian language contact in North America: Pidgins, creoles and mixed languages. *European Review of Native American Studies 7,* 17-22.

Bakker, Peter (To appear). Language contact and pidginization in Davis Strait, Hudson Strait and the Gulf of Saint Lawrence (North East Canada). In Broch & Jahr (eds.)

Bakker, P. & M. Mous (eds.) (1994). *Materials on mixed languages.* Amsterdam: IFOTT.

Barbag-Stoll, A. (1983). *Social and linguistic history of Nigerian Pidgin English.* Tübingen: Stauffenberg.

Barbot, J. (1732). *A description of the coasts of North and South Guinea; and of Ethiopia Inferior, vulgarly Angola.* London: A. & J. Churchill.

Barrena, N. (1957). *Grammatica annobonesa.* Madrid: Consejo Superior de Investigaciones Científicas.

Bartelt, G. (1992). Chileno: A maritime pidgin among California Indians. *California Linguistic Notes 23,* 25-28.

Baud, M. & M.C. Ketting (eds.) (1989). *Cultuur in beweging. Creolisering en Afro-Caraïbische cultuur.* Rotterdam: Erasmus University.

Beckman, M.E. (1986). *Stress and non-stress accent.* Dordrecht: Foris.

Bendix, E. (1972). Serial verbs in the Caribbean and West Africa: Their semantic analysis in Papiamentu. MS Hunter College CUNY.

Bennett, L. (1972). *Jamaica Labrish.* Kingston: Sangster.

Bergsland, K. (1986). De Norrøne låneord i Grønlandsk. *Maal og Minne 1-2,* 55-66.

Bergsland, K. & J. Rischel (eds.) (1986). *Pioneers of Eskimo grammar. Hans Egede's and Albert Top's early manuscripts on Greenlandic.* Copenhagen: Reitzel.

Bickerton, D. (1971). Inherent variability and variable rules. *Foundations of Language 7,* 457-92.

(1973). On the nature of a creole continuum. *Language 49,* 641-69.

(1974). Creolization, linguistic universals, natural semantax, and the brain. *University of Hawaii Working Papers in Linguistics 6,* 124-41 (Repr. in R. Day (ed.), *Issues in English creoles.* Heidelberg: Julius Groos, 1980. 1-18).

(1975). *Dynamics of a creole system.* London: Cambridge University Press.

(1977). Putting back the clock in variation studies. *Language 53,* 353-60.

(1980). Decreolisation and the creole continuum. In Valdman & Highfield (eds.), 109-27.

(1981). *Roots of language.* Ann Arbor: Karoma.

(1984). The language bioprogram hypothesis. *The Behavioral and Brain Sciences 7,* 173-188.

(1988). Creole languages and the bioprogram. In Newmeyer (ed.), 268-84.

(1989). The Lexical Learning Hypothesis and the pidgin-creole cycle. In M. Pütz & R. Dirven (eds.), *Wheels within wheels.* Frankfurt: Peter Lang. 11-31.

(1991). On the supposed 'gradualness' of creole development. JPCL 6, 25-58.

(1992). The sociohistorical matrix of creolization. JPCL 7, 307-18.

Bickerton, D. & S. Iatridou (1987). *Empty categories and verb serialization.* MS University of Amsterdam.

Bickerton, D. & W.W. Wilson (1987). Pidgin Hawaiian. In Gilbert (ed.), 61-76.

Bilby, K. (1983). How the 'older heads' talk. A Jamaican Maroon spirit possession language and its relationship to the creoles of Suriname and Sierra Leone. *New West Indian Guide 57,* 37-88.

Bisang, W. (1985). *Das Chinesische Pidgin Englisch.* University of Amsterdam: Dept. of South and Southeast Asian Studies.

Bloomfield, L. (1933). *Language.* London: Allen & Unwin.

Bobé, L. (1917). Hollænderne paa Grønland. *Atlanten 4,* 257-84.

Bolle, J. & E. de Ruiter (1993). Reflexives in Saramaccan. Paper read at the 5th SPCL Conference, Amsterdam, June 1993.

Bollée, A. (1993). Language policy in the Seychelles and its consequences. IJSL 102, 85-99.

Borer, H. (1984). *Parametric variation in syntax.* Dordrecht: Foris.

Boretzky, N. (1983). *Kreolsprachen, Substrate und Sprachwandel.* Wiesbaden: Otto Harrassowitz.

(1985). Sind Zigeunersprachen Kreols? In N. Boretzky, W. Enninger & T. Stolz (eds.), *Akten des 1. Essener Kolloquiums über Kreolsprachen und Sprachkontakte.* Bochum: N. Brockmeyer. 43-70.

Boretzky, N. & B. Igla (1994). Romani mixed dialects. In Bakker & Mous (eds.) (in press).

Brathwaite, E.K. (1974). The African presence in Caribbean literature. *Daedalus 103,* 73-109.

(1984). *History of the voice.* London: New Beacon Books.

Broch, I. & E.H. Jahr. (1984). Russenorsk: A new look at the Russo-Norwegian pidgin in Northern Norway. In P.S. Ureland & I. Clarkson (eds.), *Scandinavian language contacts*. Cambridge: Cambridge University Press. 21-65.

Broch, I. & E.H. Jahr (eds.) (To appear). *Language contact in the Arctic. Northern pidgins and contact languages*. Berlin: Mouton de Gruyter.

Broek, A.G. (1988). *Het zilt van de passaten. Caraïbische letteren van verzet*. Haarlem: In de Knipscheer.

Brown, R. (1868). Notes on the history and geographical relations of the Cetacea frequenting Davis Strait and Baffin's Bay. *Proceedings of the scientific meetings of the Zoological Society of London for the year 1868*. London: Longmans, Green, Reader and Dyer. 533-56.

Bruyn, A. (1993a). Question words in 18th-century and 20th-century Sranan. In J. van Marle (ed.), *Historical linguistics 1991*. Amsterdam: Benjamins. 31-47.

Bruyn, A. (1993b). Prepositional phrases in early Sranan. Paper read at the 5th SPCL Conference, Amsterdam, June 1993.

Bruyn, A. (In prep.). *The development of the nominal constituent in Sranan* (provisional title). Doct. Diss. University of Amsterdam.

Bruyn, A. & T. Veenstra (1993). The creolization of Dutch. JPCL 8, 29-80.

Burssens, A. (1939). *Tonologische schets van het Tshiluba*. Antwerp: De Sikkel.

Bybee, J. (1985). *Morphology. A study of the relation between meaning and form*. Amsterdam: Benjamins.

Byrne, F. (1987). *Grammatical relations in a radical creole*. Amsterdam: Benjamins.

(1988). Deixis as a noncomplementizer strategy for creole subordination marking. *Linguistics 26*, 335-64.

Byrne, F. & A. Caskey (1993). Focus, emphasis and pronominals in Saramaccan. In Byrne & Winford (eds.), 213-32.

Byrne, F. & J. Holm (eds.) (1993). *Atlantic meets Pacific*. Amsterdam: Benjamins.

Byrne, F. & D. Winford (1993). *Focus and grammatical relations in creole languages*. Amsterdam: Benjamins.

Carden, G. (1993). The Mauritian Creole *lekor* reflexive: Substrate influence on the target-location parameter. In Byrne & Holm (eds.), 105-18.

Carden, G. & W.A. Stewart (1988). Binding theory, bioprogram, and creolization: Evidence from Haitian Creole. JPCL 3, 1-67.

(1989). Mauritian Creole reflexives: A reply to Corne. JPCL 4, 65-102.

Carlson, G. (1977). Reference kinds in English. Doct. Diss. University of Massachusetts.

Carrington, L.D. (ed.) (1983), *Studies in Caribbean language*. St. Augustine (Trinidad): University of the West Indies.

Carrington, L.D. (1992). Images of creole space. JPCL 7, 93-99.

Carter, H. (1987). Suprasegmentals in Guyanese: Some African comparisons. In Gilbert (ed.), 213-63.

Cassidy, F.G. & R.B. Le Page. (1980). *Dictionary of Jamaican Creole English* (2nd. ed.). Cambridge: Cambridge University Press.

Charry, E., G. Koefoed & P. Muysken (eds.) (1983). *De talen van Suriname*. Muiderberg: Coutinho.

Chaudenson, R. (1974). *Le lexique du parler créole de la Réunion*. 2 vols. Paris: Champion.

(1977). Toward the reconstruction of the social matrix of creole language. In Valdman (ed.), 259-76.

(1979). *Les créoles français*. Evreux: Nathan.

(1992). *Des îles, des hommes, des langues*. Paris: L'Harmattan.

Chen, N.X. (1982). A preliminary study of Wutun dialects. *Minzu Yuweng (Feb. 1982)*, 10-18.

Chomsky, N. (1981). *Lectures on government and binding*. Dordrecht: Foris.

(1982). *Some concepts and consequences of the theory of government and binding*. Cambridge MA: MIT Press.

Chung, S. & A. Timberlake (1985). Tense, aspect and mood. In T. Shopen (ed.), *Language typology and syntactic description*, Vol. 3. Cambridge: Cambridge University Press. 202-58.

Churchill, S. (1986). *The education of linguistic and cultural minorities in the* OECD *countries*. Clevedon: Multilingual Matters.

Clancy Clements, J. (1992). Foreigner Talk and the origins of Pidgin Portuguese. JPCL 7, 75-92.

Clark, R. (1979). In search of Beach-La-Mar. *Te Reo 22*, 3-64.

Coelho, A. (1880-86). Os dialectos românicos ou neolatinos na África, Ásia e América. *Boletim da Sociedade de Geografia de Lisboa 2*, 129-96; *3*, 451-78; *6*, 705-55 (Repr. in J. Morais-Barbosa (ed.) (1967), *Estudios linguísticos crioulos*. Lisbon: Academia Internacional de Cultura Portuguesa).

Collins, C. (1993). *Topics in Ewe syntax*. Doct. Diss. MIT.

Collins, J.T. (ed.) (1983). *Studies in Malay dialects*, Part II. Jakarta: Nusa.

Comrie, B. (1976). *Aspect*. Cambridge: Cambridge University Press.

(1985). *Tense*. Cambridge: Cambridge University Press.

Corne, C. (1988). Mauritian Creole reflexives. JPCL 3, 69-94.

Corne, C. (1989). On French influence in the development of creole reflexive patterns. JPCL 4, 103-14.

Crawford, J. (1978). *The Mobilian trade language*. Knoxville: University of Tennessee Press.

Cummins, J. (1984). Wanted: A theoretical framework for relating language proficiency to academic achievement. In C. Rivera (ed.), *Language proficiency and academic achievement*. Clevedon: Multilingual Matters. 2-19.

Curtin, P.D. (1969). *The Atlantic slave trade. A census*. Madison: University of Wisconsin Press.

Daeleman, J. (1972). Kongo elements in Saramacca Tongo. *Journal of African languages 11*, 1-44.

Dahl, Ö. (1985). *Tense and aspect systems*. Oxford: Blackwell.

Dalphinis, M. (1985). *Caribbean and African languages. Social history, language and education*. London: Karia Press.

Damoiseau, R. (1988). Élements pour une classification des verbaux en créole haïtien. *Études Créoles 11*.

Damas, D. (ed.). (1984). *Arctic. Handbook of North American Indians*, Vol. 5. Washington: Smithsonian Institution.

d'Andrade, E. & A. Kihm (eds.) (1992). *Actas do colóquio sobre crioulos de base lexical Portuguesa*. Lisbon: Colibri.

Das Gupta, J. (1968). Language diversity and national development. In J.A. Fishman, C.A. Ferguson & J. Das Gupta (eds.), *Language problems of developing nations*. New York: John Wiley. 17-26.

Debrot, N. (1977). Verworvenheden en leemten van de Antilliaanse literatuur. In R.A. Römer (ed.), *Cultureel mozaïek van de Nederlandse Antillen*. Zutphen (Neth.): Walburg Pers. 96-133.

DeCamp, D. (1971a). The study of pidgin and creole languages. In Hymes (ed.), 13-39.

(1971b). Toward a generative analysis of a post-creole speech continuum. In Hymes (ed.), 349-70.

DeCamp, D. & I.F. Hancock (eds.) (1974). *Pidgins and creoles. Current trends and prospects*. Washington, DC: Georgetown University Press.

Déchaine, R. (1988). Towards a typology of serial constructions in Haitian. In K. Demuth & V. Manfredi (eds.), *Niger-Congo syntax and semantics 1*. Bloomington: Indiana University Linguistics Club.

(1993). *Predicates across categories. Towards a category-neutral syntax*. Doct. Diss. University of Massachusetts, Amherst.

Déchaine, R. & V. Manfredi. (1994). Binding domains in Haitian. *Natural Language and Linguistic Theory 12*, 203-58.

De Drie, A. (1984). *Wan tori fu mi eygi srefi*. (T. Guda, ed.) Paramaribo (Surinam): Ministerie van Onderwijs, Wetenschappen en Cultuur.

(1985). *Sye! Arki tori*. (T. Guda, ed.) Paramaribo (Surinam): Ministerie van Onderwijs, Wetenschappen en Cultuur.

De Goeje, C.H. (1908). De 'handelstaal' der Joeka's met de Trio's en Ojana's. In C.H. de Goeje, *Verslag der Toemoekhoemak-expeditie*. Leiden: Brill. 204-19.

DeGraff, M. (1992). *Creole grammar and the acquisition of syntax*. Doct. Diss. University of Pennsylvania.

(1993). Is Haitian Creole a *pro*-drop language? In Byrne & Holm (eds.), 71-90.

(1994). The syntax of predication in Haitian. ACS XI, 1-15.

DeGraff, M. & Y. Dejean (1994). On Haitian Creole's 'very strict' adjacency principle. Paper read at the 6th SPCL Conference, Boston, January 1994.

De Groot, A. (1977). *Woordregister Nederlands-Saramakaans*. Paramaribo (Surinam): VACO.

De Gruiter, V. (1990). *Het Javindo*. The Hague: Moesson.

Dejean, Y. (1993). An overview of the language situation in Haiti. IJSL 102, 73-83.

De Josselin de Jong, J.P.B. (1926). *Het huidige Negerhollandsch (teksten en woordenlijst)*. Verhandelingen der Koninklijke Akademie van Wetenschappen te Amsterdam, Afdeeling Letterkunde, Nieuwe reeks, 26 (1).

Dekker, P. (1979). De vroege Nederlandse vaart op Straat Davis. *Mededelingen van de Nederlandse Vereniging voor Zeegeschiedenis no. 39*, 15-55.

De Luna, J. (1951). *Gitanos de la Bética*. Madrid. (Repr. 1989, Cadiz: Servicio de Publicaciones, Universidad de Cadiz).

Den Besten, H. (1987). Die Niederländischen Pidgins der Alten Kapkolonie. In N. Boretzky, W. Enninger & T. Stolz (eds.), *Beiträge zum 3. Essener Kolloquium über Sprachwandel und seine Bestimmenden Faktoren*. Bochum: N. Brockmeyer. 9-40.

Den Dikken, M. (1992). *Particles*. (Doct. Diss. University of Leiden) Leiden: HIL.

De Reuse, W.J. (1994). *Siberian Yupik Eskimo. The language and its contacts with Chukchi*. (Doct. Diss. University of Austin, Texas). Salt Lake City: University of Utah Press.

De Reuse, W.J. (To appear). Chukchi, English and Eskimo: A survey of jargons in the Chukotka Peninsula area (Soviet Far East). In Broch & Jahr (eds).

De Rooij, V.A. (To appear). Genesis and development of Shaba Swahili: A case of partial creolization resulting from second learning strategies and substrate pressure. In A.K. Spears & D. Winford (eds.)

De Rooij, V.A. (In prep.). *Codeswitching and style shifting as discourse strategies in Shaba Swahili*. Doct. Diss. University of Amsterdam.

Devonish, H. (1986). *Language and liberation. Creole language politics in the Carribean*. London: Karia Press.

Devonish, H. (1989). *Talking in tones*. London: Karia Press.

Dijkhoff, M.B. (1983a). The resumptive pronoun strategy in Papiamentu. Master's Thesis University of Groningen.

— (1983b). The process of pluralization in Papiamentu. In Carrington (ed.), 217-29. (Also published in ACS IV, 48-61).

— (1990). *Gramátika Modèrno di Papiamentu, Artíkulo i Sustantivo*. Willemstad (Curaçao): ILA/Komapa.

— (1993). *Papiamentu word formation*. Doct. Diss. University of Amsterdam.

Dillard, J.L. (1970). Principles in the history of American English: Paradox, virginity, and cafeteria. *Florida Foreign Language Reporter 8*, 32-33.

— (1973). *Black English. Its history and usage in the United States*. New York: Vintage Books.

— (1992). *A history of American English*. London: Longman.

Dittmar, N. & P. Schlobinski. (1988). Implikations-analyse. In Ammon *et al.* (eds.), 1014-26.

Donicie, A. (1954). *De creolentaal van Suriname*. Paramaribo (Surinam): Radhakishun.

Dorais, L. (1979). The influence of English and French on Northern Quebec vocabulary and semantics. In B. Basse & K. Jensen (eds.), *Eskimo languages. Their present-day conditions*. Aarhus: Arkona Publishers. 77-81.

— (1980). *The Inuit language in Southern Labrador from 1694-1785*. Ottawa: National Museums of Canada.

— (1993). *From magic words to word processing. A history of the Inuit language*. Iqaluit: Arctic College - Nunatta Campus.

Drechsel, E.J. (1981). A preliminary sociolinguistic comparison of four indigenous pidgin languages of North America. AL 23, 93-112.

Drechsel, E.J. (To appear). Native American contact languages of the contiguous United States. In S. Wurm (ed.), *Atlas of languages of intercultural communication in the Pacific hemisphere*. Berlin: Mouton de Gruyter.

Drechsel, E.J. & T.H. Makuakāne (1982). Hawaiian loanwords in two native American pidgins. IJAL 48, 460-67.

Dreyfuss, G.R. (1977). *Relative clause formation in four creole languages*. Doct. Diss. University of Michigan.

Du Plessis Scholtz, J. (1963). Oor die herkoms van Afrikaans. In J. du Plessis Scholtz, *Taalhistoriese opstelle*. Pretoria: J.L. van Schaik. 232-56.

Dwyer, D. (1967). *An introduction to West African Pidgin English*. East Lansing, Michigan State University.

Eastman, C. (1983). *Language planning. An introduction*. San Francisco: Chandler & Sharp Publ.

Eersel, C.H. (1971). Prestige in choice of language and linguistic form. In Hymes (ed.), 317-23.

Egede, H.P. (1722). *Nogle Grønlandske Vocabula*. In Bergsland & Rischel (eds.) (1986), 49-52.

Egede, H.P. (1725). *Dictionarium* and *Formula Conjugandi etc.* In Bergsland & Rischel (eds.) (1986), 53-76.

Egede, H.P. (1750). *Dictionarium Grönlandico-Danico-Latinum*. Copenhagen: Kisel.

Einhorn, E. (1974). *Old French. A concise handbook*. Cambridge: Cambridge University Press.

Escure, G. (1981). Decreolization in a creole continuum: Belize. In Highfield & Valdman (eds.), 27-39.

Fabian, J. (1982). Scratching the surface. Observations on the poetics of lexical borrowing in Shaba Swahili. AL 24, 14-50.

(1986). *Language and colonial power.* Cambridge: Cambridge University Press.

(1990a). *Power and performance.* Madison: University of Wisconsin Press.

(1990b). *History from Below.* Amsterdam: Benjamins.

Faine, J. (1937). *Philologie créole.* Port-au-Prince: Impr. de l'État.

Fauqenoy, M. (1972). *Analyse structurale du créole guyanais.* Paris: Klincksieck.

Ferguson, C.A. (1971). Absence of copula and the notion of simplicity: A study of normal speech, baby talk, foreigner talk and pidgins. In Hymes (ed.), 141-50.

Ferraz, L. (1970). The substratum of Annobonese Creole. *Linguistics 173*, 37-49.

(1974). A linguistic appraisal of Angolar. In *In Memoriam António Jorge Días, 2.* Lisboa: Inst. de Alta Cultura/Junta de Investigações do Ultramar. 177-86.

(1975). African influences on Principense creole. In Valkhoff (ed.), 153-64.

(1976). The substratum of Annobonese Creole. IJSL 7, 37-47.

(1979). *The Creole of São Tomé.* Johannesburg: Witwatersrand University Press.

(1983). The origin and development of four creoles in the Gulf of Guinea. In Woolford & Washabaugh (eds.), 120-25.

Ferraz, L. & M.F. Valkhoff (1975). A comparative study of São-tomense and Cabo-verdiano Creole. In Valkhoff (ed.), 15-40.

Fishman, J.A. (ed.) (1974). *Advances in language planning.* The Hague: Mouton.

Fishman, J.A. & J. Cobarrubias (1983). *Progress in language planning.* Berlin: Mouton.

Focke, H.C. (1855). *Neger-Engelsch woordenboek.* Leiden: Van den Heuvell.

Foley, W.A. (1988). Language birth. The processes of pidginization and creolization. In Newmeyer (ed.), 162-83.

Fortescue, M.D. (1984). *West Greenlandic.* London: Croom Helm.

Fortescue, M.D. (1994). Eskimo word order variation and its contact-induced perturbation. *Journal of Linguistics.*

Fugier, H. (1987). Les verbes sériels en Malgache. *Bulletin de la Société de Linguistique de Paris.*

Gad, F. (1970). *The history of Greenland I, Earliest times to 1700.* London: C. Hurst & Company.

(1973). *The history of Greenland II, 1700-1782.* London: C. Hurst & Company.

Gilbert, G.G. (ed.) (1980). *Pidgin and creole languages. Selected essays by Hugo Schuchardt.* Cambridge: Cambridge University Press.

(1987). *Pidgin and creole languages. Essays in memory of John E. Reinecke.* Honolulu: University of Hawaii Press.

Givón, T. (1972). *Studies in ChiBemba and Bantu Grammar.* (=SAL *3, Supplement 3*).

(1979). *On understanding grammar.* New York: Academic Press.

(1981). On the development of the numeral 'one' as an indefinite marker. MIT *Working Papers in Linguistics 3*, 233-55 (Also published in *Folia Linguistica Historica* II, 35-53).

(1982). Tense-Aspect-Modality: The creole prototype and beyond. In Hopper (ed.), 115-63.

Goddard, I. (1990). Primary and secondary stem derivation in Algonquian. IJAL 56, 449-83.

Golovko, E.V. (To appear). The contribution of Aleut and Russian to the formation of Copper Island Aleut. In Broch & Jahr (eds.)

Golovko, E.V. & N.B. Vakhtin (1990). Aleut in contact: The CIA enigma. *Acta Linguistica Hafniensia* 22, 97-125.

Goodman, M. (1964). *A comparative study of French creole dialects.* The Hague: Mouton.

(1971). The strange case of Mbugu (Tanzania). In Hymes (ed.), 243-54.

(1987). The Portuguese element in the American creoles. In Gilbert (ed.), 361-405.

Grant, A. (1994). Shelta: The secret language of Irish travellers viewed as a mixed language. In Bakker & Mous (eds.) (in press).

Grimes, B.F. (ed.) (1988). *Ethnologue. Languages of the world.* Dallas: SIL.

Gulløv, H.C. (1987). Dutch whaling and its influence on Eskimo culture in Greenland. In Hacquebord & Vaughan (eds.), 75-93.

Günther, W. (1973). *Das Portugiesische Kreolisch der Ilha do Príncipe.* Marburg: Marburger Studien zur Afrika- und Asienkunde.

Guttman, L. (1944). A basis for scaling qualitative data. *American Sociological Review 9*, 139-50.

Gysels, M. (1992). French in urban Lubumbashi Swahili: Codeswitching, borrowing, or both? *Journal of Multilingual and Multicultural Development 13*, 41-55.

Hacquebord, L. & R. Vaughan (eds.) (1987). *Between Greenland and America. Cross-cultural contacts and the environment in the Baffin Bay area.* University of Groningen.

Hale, K. & S.J. Keyser (1993). On the complex nature of simple predicators. MS MIT.

Hall, R.A. (1948). The linguistic structure of Taki-Taki. *Language 24*, 92-116.

(1953). *Haitian Creole. Grammar - texts - vocabulary.* Philadelphia: American Folklore Society.

(1966). *Pidgin and creole languages.* Ithaca: Cornell University Press.

Hanbury, D.T. (1904). *Sport and travel in the northland of Canada.* New York: MacMillan.

Hancock, I.F. (1969). A provisional comparison of the English-derived Atlantic creoles. *African Language Review 8*, 7-72.

(1970). Is Anglo-Romanes a creole? *Journal of the Gypsy Lore Society 44*, 41-44.

(1971). A map and list of pidgin and creole languages. In Hymes (ed.), 509-23.

(1976). Nautical sources of Krio vocabulary. IJSL 7, 23-36.

(1977). Repertory of pidgin and creole languages. In Valdman (ed.), 362-91.

(1979). On the origins of the term pidgin. In Hancock *et al.* (eds.), 81-86.

(1980). Lexical expansion in creole languages. In Valdman & Highfield (eds.), 63-88.

(1981). Répertoire des langues pidgins et créoles. In J. Perrot (ed.), *Les langues dans le monde ancien et moderne.* Paris: Klincksieck. 630-47.

(1984a). Romani and Angloromani. In Trudgill (ed.), 367-83.

(1984b). Shelta and Polari. In Trudgill (ed.), 384-403.

(1984c). Romani. In Acton & Kenrick (eds.)

(1986). The domestic hypothesis, diffusion and componentiality: An account of Atlantic Anglophone creole origins. In Muysken & Smith (eds.), 71-102.

(1987). A preliminary classification of the Anglophone Atlantic creoles, with syntactic data from thirty-three representative dialects. In Gilbert (ed.), 264-334.

Hancock, I.F. (To appear). The special case of Arctic pidgins. In Broch & Jahr (eds).

Hancock, I.F., E. Polomé, M. Goodman & B. Heine (eds.) (1979). *Readings in creole studies.* Ghent: Story-Scientia.

Heine, B. (1973). *Pidgin-Sprachen im Bantu-Bereich.* Berlin: Dietrich Riemer.

(1982). *The Nubi language of Kibera. An Arabic creole.* Berlin: Dietrich Riemer.

Heine, B., U. Claudi & F. Hünnemeyer. (1991). *Grammaticalization. A conceptual framework.* Chicago: University of Chicago Press.

Helman, A. [ps. L. Lichtveld] (1977). Volkswijsheid en orale literatuur van Suriname. In A. Helman (ed.), *Cultureel mozaïek van Suriname.* Zutphen: Walburg Pers. 82-115.

Herlein, J.D. (1718). *Beschrijvinge van de volksplantinge Zuriname.* Leeuwarden : Injema (Partly repr. in Voorhoeve & Lichtveld 1975, 280-82).

Hesseling, D.C. (1905). *Het Negerhollands der Deense Antillen. Bijdrage tot de geschiedenis der Nederlandse taal in Amerika,* Leiden: A.W. Sijthoff.

Hewes, G.W. (1974). Gesture language in language contact. *Sign Language Studies 4,* 1-34.

Highfield, A. & A. Valdman (eds.) (1981). *Historicity and variation in creole studies.* Ann Arbor: Karoma.

Hinskens, F. (1983-1984). 'Versjtrunkelt diene tuuën wat e keeäneske oop e huuëvelke drait?' Enkele structurele en functionele aspecten van het 'Groenstraat-Bargoens'. *Mededelingen van de Nijmeegse Centrale voor Dialect- en Naamkunde* XIX, 17-56.

Holloway, J.E. & W.K. Vass. (1993). *The African heritage of American English.* Bloomington: Indiana University Press.

Holm, J. (1987). Creole influence on popular Brazilian Portuguese. In Gilbert (ed.), 406-29.

(1988). *Pidgins and creoles.* Vol. I. Cambridge: Cambridge University Press.

(1989). *Pidgins and creoles.* Vol. II. Cambridge: Cambridge University Press.

(1990). Features in the noun phrase common to the Atlantic creoles. *Linguistics 28,* 867-81.

(1992). Popular Brazilian Portuguese: A semi-creole. In d'Andrade & Kihm (eds.), 37-66.

Holm, J. (with A. Shilling) (1982). *Dictionary of Bahamian English.* Cold Spring NY: Lexik House.

Hopper, P.J. (ed.) (1982). *Tense-Aspect. Between semantics and pragmatics.* Amsterdam: Benjamins.

Hopper, P.J. & E. Closs Traugott. (1993). *Grammaticalization.* Cambridge: Cambridge University Press.

Hornberger, N. (1990). Bilingual education and English-only: A language-planning framework. *Annals of the American Academy of Political and Social Science 508,* 12-26.

Hosali, P. & J. Aitchison (1985). Butler English: A minimal pidgin? JPCL 1, 51-79.

Hull, A. (1979). On the origin and chronology of the French-based creoles. In Hancock *et al.* (eds.), 210-16.

Huttar, G.L. (1975). Sources of creole semantic structures. *Language 51,* 684-95.

(1982). A creole Amerindian pidgin of Suriname. *Society for Caribbean Linguistics, Occasional Paper 15.*

Huttar, M.L. & G.L. Huttar (1992). Reduplication in Ndjuka: Phonology, syntax and semantics. Paper read at the 3rd SPCL Conference, Philadelphia, January 1992.

Hymes, D. (ed.) (1971). *Pidginization and creolization of languages.* Cambridge: Cambridge University Press.

Ibarguti, F. (1989). 'hamabost egun ijitoen atzetik' (fifteen days after the Gypsies). *El Diario Vasco* Dec. 6 1989.

Jansen, B., H. Koopman & P. Muysken (1978). Serial verbs in the creole languages. ACS 11, 125-59.

Janson, T. (1984). Articles and plural formation in creoles: Change and universals. *Lingua 64,* 291-323.

Jenewari, Ch.E. (1977). *Studies in Kalabari syntax.* Doct. Diss. University of Ibadan.

Jenness, D. (1928). *Comparative vocabulary of the Western Eskimo dialects.* Report of the Canadian Arctic Expedition 1913-18, vol. XV: Eskimo language and technology, part A. Ottawa: F.A. Ackland.

Jennings, W. (To appear). The demographics of creole genesis: Implications of sociohistoric and population studies for the origins of Cayenne creole. In Spears & Winford (eds.)

Joubert, S.M. (1991). *Dikshonario Papiamentu-Hulandes. Handwoordenboek Papiamentu-Nederlands.* Willemstad (Curaçao): Fundashon di Leksikografia.

Jourdan, C. (1991). Pidgins and creoles: The blurring of categories. *Annual Review of Anthropology* 20, 187-209.

Kabamba, M. (1979). Stratigraphie des langues et communications à Lubumbashi. *Problèmes Sociaux Zaïrois 124-125*, 47-74.

Kalunga, M. (1979). Le lexique du swahili standard face au lexique du swahili de Lubumbashi. *Africa (Rome) 34*, 424-42.

Kapanga, A. (1993). Shaba Swahili and the processes of linguistic contact. In Byrne & Holm (eds.), 441-58.

Kashoki, M.E. (1968). A phonemic analysis of Bemba: A presentation of Bemba syllable structure, phonemic contrasts and their distribution. *Zambian Papers 3*.

Kay, P. & G. Sankoff (1974). A language-universals approach to pidgins and creoles. In DeCamp & Hancock (eds.), 61-72.

Kayne, R. (1975). *French syntax*. Cambridge MA: MIT Press.

Keenan, E.L. & B. Comrie (1977). Noun phrase accessibility and universal grammar. *Linguistic Inquiry 8*, 63-99.

Keesing, R.M. (1988). *Melanesian Pidgin and the Oceanic substrate*. Stanford: Stanford University Press.
 (1991). Substrates, calquing and grammaticalization in Melanesian Pidgin. In E. Closs Traugott & B. Heine (eds.), *Approaches to grammaticalization*, Vol. I. Amsterdam: Benjamins. 315-42.

Kisbye Møller, J. (1987). *Peder Hansen Resen, Groenlandia*. Copenhagen: Det Grønlandske Selskab.

Kleivan, I. (1984). History of Norse Greenland. In Damas (ed.), 549-55.

Kloeke, G.G. (1950). *Herkomst en groei van het Afrikaans*. Leiden: Universitaire Pers.

Kluge, F. (1901). *Rotwelsch*. Strassburg: Karl J. Trübner.

Kook, H. & P. Vedder (1989). *Antiano i Arubano den Skol. De onderwijssituatie van Antilliaanse en Arubaanse kinderen en hun klasgenoten*, Vol. II. Utrecht: POA.

Koopman, H. (1982). Les questions. In Lefebvre *et al.* (eds.), 204-41.
 (1984). *The syntax of verbs*. Dordrecht: Foris.

Koopman, H. & C. Lefebvre (1981). Haitian Creole *pu*. In Muysken (ed.), 201-21.

Kotsinas, U. (1988a). Immigrant children's Swedish: A new variety? *Journal of Multilingual and Multicultural Development 9*, 129-49.
 (1988b). Come, stay, finish: On the development of aspect markers in interlanguage and pid-gin/creole languages. In C.G. Larson (ed.), *Proceedings from the second Scandinavian symposium on aspectology*. Uppsala: Almqvist & Wiksell.

Kouwenberg, S. (1992). From OV to VO. Linguistic negotiation in the development of Berbice Dutch Creole. *Lingua 88*, 263-99.
 (1994). *A grammar of Berbice Dutch Creole*. Berlin: Mouton de Gruyter.

Kouwenberg, S. & E. Murray. (In press). *Papiamentu. Languages of the world/Materials 83*. München: Lincom Europa.

Kraan, M. (1993). *De Franse oorsprong van de* TMA *partikels in het Haïtiaans en het Seychellois*. Master's Thesis University of Amsterdam.

Krauss, M.E. (1973). Eskimo-Aleut. In T.A. Sebeok (ed.), *Linguistics in North America. Current Trends in Linguistics*, Vol. 10. The Hague: Mouton. 796-902.

Labov, W. (1971). The notion of 'system' in creole languages. In Hymes (ed.), 447-72.
 (1990) [1971]. On the adequacy of natural languages: I. The development of tense. In Singler (ed.), 1-58.

Lalla, B. & J. D'Costa. (1990). *Language in exile. Three hundred years of Jamaican Creole.* Tuscaloosa: University of Alabama Press.

Larson, R. (1991). Some issues in verb serialization. In Lefebvre (ed.), 185-210.

Larson, R. & C. Lefebvre (1991). Predicate clefting in Haitian Creole. *Proceedings of* NELS *21*, 247-62.

Law, P. (1993). Creole genesis and the ECP. Paper read at the 5th SPCL Conference, Amsterdam, June 1993.

(1994). On the contribution of linguistic theory to creole studies. Paper presented at the 6th SPCL Conference, Boston, January 1994.

Law, P. & T. Veenstra (1992). On the structure of serial verb constructions. *Linguistic Analysis 22*, 185-217.

LeBlanc, M. (1955). Evolution linguistique et relations humaines. *Zaïre 9*, 787-99.

Lefebvre, C. (1974). Discreteness and the linguistic continuum in Martinique. AL 16, 47-78.

Lefebvre, C. (1986). Relexification in creole genesis revisited: The case of Haitian Creole. In Muysken & Smith (eds.), 279-300.

Lefebvre, C. (1988). *Take* serial verb constructions: Please. In C. Tenny (ed.), *Lexicon Project Working Papers 30*. Cambridge MA: MIT Press. 1-33.

Lefebvre, C. (ed.) (1991a). *Serial verbs. Grammatical, comparative and cognitive approaches.* Amsterdam: Benjamins.

Lefebvre, C. (1991b). *Take* serial verb constructions in Fon. In Lefebvre (ed.), 37-78.

(1994). Towards a unified analysis of predicate doubling phenomena in Haitian Creole and in Fongbe. Paper read at the 6th SPCL Conference, Boston, January 1994.

Lefebvre, C. & J. Lumsden (1992). On word order in relexification. *Travaux de recherche sur le créole haïtien 10*, 1-21.

Lefebvre, C., H. Magloire-Holly & N. Piou (1982). *Syntaxe de l'haïtien.* Ann Arbor: Karoma.

Lefebvre, C. & E. Ritter (1993). Two types of predicate doubling adverbs in Haitian Creole. In Byrne & Winford (eds.), 65-94.

Le Page, R.B. & A. Tabouret-Keller. (1985). *Acts of identity. Creole-based approaches to language and ethnicity.* Cambridge: Cambridge University Press.

Lichtveld, L. (1930-31). Op zoek naar de Spin. *De West-Indische Gids 12*, 209-30.

Lichtveld, U.M. & J. Voorhoeve (1980). *Suriname. Spiegel der vaderlandse kooplieden.* (2nd ed.) The Hague: Martinus Nijhoff.

Lightfoot, D. (1982). *The language lottery.* Cambridge MA: MIT Press.

Lumsden, J. (1989). On the distribution of determiners in Haitian Creole. *Revue Québecquoise de Linguistique 18*, 65-94.

(1993). Aspect and lexical semantic representations in Haitian Creole. *Travaux de recherche sur le créole haïtien 13*, 1-20.

Macalister, R.A.S. (1937). *The secret languages of Ireland.* Cambridge: Cambridge University Press.

Magens, J.M. (1770). *Grammatica over det Creolske sprog, som bruges paa de trende Danske Eilande, St. Croix, St. Thomas og St. Jans i Amerika.* Copenhagen: Gerhard Giese Salikath.

Manessy, G. (1985). Remarques sur la pluralisation du nom en créole et dans les langues africaines. *Études Créoles 8*, 129-43.

Manfredi, V. (1993). Verb focus in the typology of Kwa/Kru and Haitian. In Byrne & Winford (eds.), 3-52.

Masica, C.P. (1991). *The Indo-Aryan languages*. Cambridge: Cambridge University Press.

Maurer, P. (1988). *Les modifications temporelles et modales du verbe dans le papiamento de Curaçao (Antilles Néerlandaises)*. Hamburg: Buske.

(1992). L'apport lexical bantou en angolar. *Afrikanistische Arbeitspapiere 29*, 163-74.

(1993). TAM in Principense. Paper read at the 5th SPCL Conference, Amsterdam, June 1993.

McGhee, R. (1987). The relationship between the mediaeval Norse and Eskimos. In Hacquebord & Vaughan (eds.), 51-59.

McWhorter, J. (1992). Substratal influence in Saramaccan serial verb constructions. JPCL 7, 1-53.

Mesthrie, R. (1989). The origins of Fanagalo. JPCL 4, 211-40.

Meyer, J.M. (1767). *J.M. Meyers eines deutschen Chirurgi Beschreibung seiner auf den Wallfischfang nach Spitzbergen gethanen Reise*. Straßburg: Johann Heinrich Heitz.

Mintz, S.W. & R. Price (1992). *The birth of African-American culture. An anthropological perspective*. Boston: Beacon Press.

Moormann, J.G.M. (1932/1934). *De geheimtalen. Een studie over de geheimtalen in Nederland, Vlaamsch-België, Breyell en Mettingen*. 2 vols. Zutphen: Thieme.

Morris-Brown, V. (1993). *The Jamaica handbook of proverbs*. Mandeville (Jamaica): Island Heart Publishers.

Moseley, C. & R.E. Asher (eds.) (1994). *Atlas of the world's languages*. London: Routledge.

Mous, M. (1994a). Ma'a or Mbugu. In Bakker & Mous (eds.).

(1994b). Ma'a as an ethno-register of Mbugu. *Sprache und Geschichte in Afrika* (in press).

Mous, M. (In prep.). *A description of Ma'a*. University of Leiden.

Mowat, F. (1976) [1965]. *Westviking, the ancient Norse in West Greenland and North America*, Toronto: McClelland & Stewart.

Mufwene, S.S. (1981). Non-individuation and the count/mass distinction. CLS 17, 221-38.

(1986a). The universalist and substrate hypotheses complement one another. In Muysken & Smith (eds.), 129-62.

(1986b). Number delimitation in Gullah. *American Speech 61*, 33-60.

(1989). La créolisation en bantou: Les cas du kituba, du lingala urbain, et du swahili du Shaba. *Études Créoles 12*, 74-106.

(1990). Creoles and universal grammar. In Seuren & Mufwene (eds.), 783-808.

(1991). Is Gullah decreolizing? A comparison of a speech sample of the 1930s with a sample of the 1980s. In G. Bailey, N. Maynor & P. Cukor-Avila (eds.), *The emergence of Black English. Text and commentary*. Amsterdam: Benjamins. 213-30.

Mufwene, S.S. (ed.) (1993a). *Africanisms in Afro-American language varieties*. Athens: University of Georgia Press.

Mufwene, S.S. (1993b). Creole genesis: A population genetics perspective. Paper read at the 5th SPCL Conference, Amsterdam, June 1993.

Mühlhäusler, P. (1979). *Growth and structure of the lexicon of New Guinea Pidgin*. Canberra: Research School of Pacific Studies.

(1980). Structural expansion and the process of creolization. In Valdman & Highfield (eds.), 19-55.

(1981). The development of the category of number in Tok Pisin. In Muysken (ed.), 35-84.

(1986). *Pidgin & creole linguistics*. Oxford: Blackwell.

Muller, E. (1989). *Inleiding tot de syntaxis van het Papiamentu*. Doct. Diss. University of Amsterdam.

Muyrers, S. (1993). *Het netwerk van de slaaf. Een onderzoek naar de contacten van Surinaamse plantage-*

*slaven in de achttiende en negentiende eeuw*. Master's Thesis Erasmus University Rotterdam.

Muysken, P. (1977). Movement rules in Papiamentu. ACS I, 80-102.

(1980). Three kinds of movement in Papiamentu. In F. Jansen (ed.), *Studies on fronting*. Lisse: Peter de Ridder. 65-80.

(1981a). Creole tense/mood/aspect systems: The unmarked case?. In Muysken (ed.), 181-99.

(1981b). Halfway between Spanish and Quechua: The case for relexification. In Highfield & Valdman (eds.), 52-78.

Muysken, P. (ed.) (1981c). *Generative studies on creole languages*. Dordrecht: Foris.

Muysken, P. (1987). Prepositions and postpositions in Saramaccan. In Alleyne (ed.), 89-101.

(1988a). Are creoles a special type of language? In Newmeyer (ed.), 285-301.

(1988b). Lexical restructuring in creole genesis. In N. Boretzky, W. Enninger & T. Stolz (eds.), *Beiträge zum 4. Essener Kolloquium über Sprachkontakte, Sprachwandel, Sprachwechsel, Sprachtod*. Bochum: N. Brockmeyer. 193-209.

(1993). Reflexes of Ibero-Romance reflexive clitic + verb combinations in Papiamentu: Thematic grids and grammatical relations. In Byrne & Winford (eds.), 285-301.

(1994). The search for universals in language genesis: État de la question and research program. ACS XI, 16-28.

Muysken, P. & N. Smith (eds.) (1986a). *Substrata versus universals in creole genesis*. Amsterdam: Benjamins.

Muysken, P. & N. Smith (1986b). Introduction: Problems in the identification of substratum features. In Muysken & Smith (eds.), 1-13.

(1990). Question words in pidgin and creole languages. In Seuren & Mufwene (eds.), 883-903.

Muysken, P. & H. van der Voort (1991). The binding theory and creolization: Evidence from 18th century Negerhollands reflexives. In Byrne & Huebner (eds.), *Development and structures of creole languages. Essays in honor of Derek Bickerton*. Amsterdam: Benjamins. 145-58.

Narain, G. & L. Verhoeven (1994). Development of Papiamentu in a first and second language environment. AILA *Bulletin 10* (in press).

Naro, A.J. (1973). The origin of West African Pidgin. CLS 9, 442-49.

(1978). A study on the origins of pidginization. *Language 54*, 314-49.

(1988). A reply to 'Pidgin origins reconsidered' by Morris Goodman. JPCL 3, 95-102.

(1993). Arguing about Arguin. JPCL 8, 109-18.

Nettleford, R. (1989). Creolisation in the Caribbean arts. In Baud & Ketting (eds.), 53-74.

Newmeyer, F.J. (ed.), *Linguistics: The Cambridge survey*, Vol. II. Cambridge: Cambridge University Press.

Nichols, J. (1980). Pidginization and foreigner talk: Chinese Pidgin Russian. In E. Closs Traugott, R. Labrum & S. Shepherd (eds.), *Papers from the 4th International Conference on Historical Linguistics*. Amsterdam: Benjamins. 397-407.

Nichols, J.D. (1993). 'Broken Oghibbeway': An Algonquian trade language. Paper read at the 24th Algonquian Conference, Ottawa, October 1993.

Nkulu, K. (1986). French loans and innovative items in the kinship field of Zaïrean Copperbelt Swahili. AL 28, 169-84.

O'Donnell, W.R. & L. Todd. (1980). *Variety in contemporary English*. London: Allen & Unwin.

Oldendorp C.G.A. (1777). *C.G.A. Oldendorps Geschichte der Mission der evangelischen Brueder auf den Caraibischen Inseln S. Thomas, S. Croix und S. Jan*. Herausgegeben durch J.J. Bossart. Barby:

Christian Friedrich Laur.

O'Reilly, B. (1818). *Greenland, the adjacent seas, and the North-West passage to the Pacific Ocean.* London: Baldwin, Cradock, and Joy.

Oswalt, W.H. (1979). *Eskimos and explorers.* Novato CA: Chandler & Sherp.

Owije (1986/1987). *Kalabari dictionary.* MS University of Port Harcourt.

Pabanó, R.M. (1915). *Historia y Costumbres de los Gitanos.* Barcelona: Muntaner y Simón (Originally published in 1915).

Pakosi, A. (1989). Orale traditie bij de Bosneger. OSO 8, 159-65.

Petersen, J. (1951). *Ordbogêraĸ, tássa kalâtdlit oĸ ausîsa agdlangnerinik najorĸ utagssiaĸ.* Nûngme: ilíniarfigssûp naĸ itertitai.

Petersen, R. (1976). Nogle træk i udviklingen af det grønlandske sprog efter kontakten med den danske kultur og det danske sprog. *Tidsskriftet Grønland 24,* 165-208.

(1982). Oĸ autsit oĸ alugtuagssartagdlit ilait. *Kalâleĸ'* 4, 6-8.

Petersen, R. & J. Rischel (1987). Sproglig indledning og kommentar til Resens tysk-grønlandske ordliste. In Kisbye Møller, 79-121.

Phillip, H.C. (1988). *Description du Créole de la Grenade.* Thèse Doctorat 3ième cycle, University of Grenoble.

Phillipson, R. (1990). *English teaching and imperialism.* Doct. Diss. University of Amsterdam.

Piou, N. (1982). Le clivage du prédicat. In Lefebvre *et al.* (eds.), 122-51.

Plag, I. (1993). *Sentential complementation in Sranan.* Tübingen: Max Niemeyer.

Polomé, E.C. (1968). Lubumbashi Swahili. *Journal of African Languages 7,* 14-25.

(1969). The position of Swahili and other Bantu languages in Katanga. *Texas Studies in Language and Literature 11,* 905-13.

(1971a). The Katanga (Lubumbashi) Swahili Creole. In Hymes (ed.), 57-59.

(1971b). Multilingualism in an African urban centre: The Lubumbashi case. In W.H. Whiteley (ed.), *Language use and social change.* Oxford: Oxford University Press. 364-75.

(1972). Sociolinguistic problems in Tanzania and Zaire. *The Conch 4,* 64-83.

(1983). Creolization and language change. In Woolford & Washabaugh (eds.), 126-36.

(1985). Swahili in the Shaba Region of Zaire. In J. Maw & D. Parkin (eds.), *Swahili language and society.* Vienna: Afro-Pub. 47-65.

(1986). Aspects of language contact in Africa. In J.A. Fishman, A. Tabouret-Keller, M. Clyne, Bh. Krishnamurti & M. Abdulaziz, *The Fergusonian Impact,* Vol. I. Berlin: Mouton de Gruyter. 387-98.

Pontoppidan, E. (1891). Einige Notizen über die Kreolensprache der dänisch-westindischen Inseln. *Zeitschrift für Ethnologie 13,* 130-38.

Post, M. (1992). The serial verb constructions in Fa d'Ambu. In d'Andrade & Kihm (eds.), 153-71.

Post, M. (1993). Relativsätze und einige Relativelemente im Fa d'Ambu. In M. Perl, A. Schönberger & P. Thiele (eds.), *Portugiesisch-basierte Kreolsprachen,* Band 6. Frankfurt: TFM. 167-87.

Postma, J.M. (1990). *The Dutch in the Atlantic slave trade, 1600-1815.* Cambridge: Cambridge University Press.

Price, R. (1975). Kikoongo and Saramaccan. A reappraisal. *Bijdragen to de Taal-, Land- en Volkenkunde 131,* 461-78.

Price, R. (1976). *The Guiana maroons. A historical and bibliographical introduction.* Baltimore: Johns Hopkins University Press.

(1983). *First-Time. The historical vision of an Afro-American people.* Baltimore: Johns Hopkins University Press.

Rafferty, E. (1982). *Discourse structures of the Chinese Indonesian of Malang.* Jakarta: Nusa.

Ray, P.H. (1885). Ethnographic sketch of the natives of Point Barrow. In *Report of the International Polar Expedition to Point Barrow, Alaska, in response to the Resolution of the House of Representatives of December 11, 1884.* Washington: Government Printing Office. 37-60, 87.

Reinecke, J.E. (1971). Tây Bôi: Notes on the Pidgin French of Vietnam. In Hymes (ed.), 47-56.

Reinecke, J.E., S.M. Tsuzaki, D. DeCamp, I.F. Hancock & R.E. Wood (1975). *A bibliography of pidgin and creole languages.* Honolulu: University Press of Hawaii.

Reinhart, T. & E. Reuland. (1991). Anaphors and logophors: An argument structure perspective. In J. Koster & E. Reuland (eds.), *Long-distance anaphora.* Cambridge: Cambridge University Press. 283-321.

Rens, L.L.E. (1953). *The historical and social background of Surinam's Negro-English.* Amsterdam: North-Holland.

Resen, P.H. (1687). *Groenlandia.* MS, partly published in Petersen and Rischel (1987).

Rhodes, R. (1977). French Cree: A case of borrowing. In W. Cowan (ed.), *Actes du huitième congrès des algonquinistes.* Ottawa: Carleton University. 6-25.

Rickford, J. (1987). *Dimensions of a creole continuum. History, texts, & linguistic analysis of Guyanese Creole.* Stanford: Stanford University Press.

Rizzi, L. (1982). *Issues in Italian syntax.* Dordrecht: Foris.

Robbe, P. & L. Dorais (1986). *Tunumiit Oraasiat. La langue inuit du Groenland de l'Est.* Québec: Centre d'études nordiques, Université Laval.

Roberts, P. (1993). Affective factors in the use of creole in the classroom: The resolution of a paradox. Paper read at the 5th SPCL Conference, Amsterdam, June 1993.

Robertson, I.E. (1976). Dutch creole speakers and their locations in Guyana in the nineteenth and early twentieth centuries. *Society for Caribbean Linguistics Occasional Paper 4.*

(1979). *Berbice Dutch. A description.* Doct. Diss. University of the West Indies.

(1982). Redefining the post-creole continuum: Evidence from Berbice Dutch. ACS IV, 62-78.

(1989). Berbice and Skepi Dutch: A lexical comparison. *Tijdschrift voor Nederlandse Taal- en Letterkunde 105,* 3-21.

Roeper, T. & S.J. Keyser (1992). Re: The Abstract Clitic Hypothesis. *Linguistic Inquiry 23,* 89-125.

Romaine, S. (1982). *Socio-historical linguistics. Its status and methodology.* Cambridge: Cambridge University Press.

(1988). *Pidgin and creole languages.* London: Longman.

Römer, R. (1977). Polarization phenomena in Papiamentu. ACS I, 69-79.

(1992). *Studies in Papiamentu tonology.* Caribbean Culture Studies 5. University of Amsterdam/University of the West Indies.

Ross, J.R. (1967). *Constraints on variables in syntax.* Doct. Diss. MIT (Repr. as *Infinite syntax!,* Norwood NJ: Ablex, 1983).

Rountree, S.C. & N. Glock. (1977). *Saramaccan for beginners.* Paramaribo (Surinam): SIL.

Rowlands, E.C. (1979). *Teach yourself Yoruba.* London: Hodder & Stoughton.

Samarin, W.J. (1982). Colonization and pidginization on the Ubangi River. *Journal of African Languages and Linguistics 4,* 1-42.

(1987a). Demythologizing Plains Indian Sign Language history. IJAL 5, 23-34.

(1987b). Lingua Franca. In Ammon *et al.* (eds.), 371-74.

(1988). Creating language and community in pidginization. *Canadian Journal of Linguistics/Revue Canadienne de Linguistique 33,* 155-65.

Sandefur, J.R. (1979). *An Australian creole in the Northern Territory. A description of Ngukurr-Bamyili dialects (part 1).* Darwin: SIL.

Sankoff, D. (1988). Variable rules. In Ammon *et al.* (eds.), 984-97.

Sankoff, G. (1980). *The social life of language.* Philadelphia: University of Pennsylvania Press.

(1990). The grammaticalization of tense and aspect in Tok Pisin and Sranan. *Language Variation and Change 2,* 295-312.

Sankoff, G. & S. Laberge. (1974). On the acquisition of native speakers by a language. In DeCamp & Hancock (eds.), 73-84 (Repr. in Sankoff 1980).

Sankoff, G. & P. Brown (1978). The origins of syntax in discourse. *Language 52,* 631-66 (Repr. in Sankoff 1980).

Schachter, P. (1974). A non-transformational account of serial verbs. SAL, *Suppl. 5,* 253-70.

Schicho, W. (1982). *Syntax des Swahili von Lubumbashi.* Vienna: Afro-Pub.

(1988). Tense vs. aspect in Sango and Swahili of Lubumbashi. In M.A. Jazayery & W. Winter (eds.), *Languages and cultures. Studies in honor of Edgar C. Polomé.* Berlin: Mouton de Gruyter. 565-79.

(1990). AUX, Creole und Swahili von Lubumbashi. *Zeitschrift für Phonetik und Sprachwissenschaftliche Kommunikationsforschung 43,* 476-83.

(1992). Non-acceptance and negation in the Swahili of Lubumbashi. *African Languages and Cultures 5,* 75-89.

Schuchardt, H. (1883). Review of L. Adam, Les parlers negro-aryen et malayo-aryen. *Literaturblatt für Germanische und Romanische Philologie 4,* 236-40.

Schuchardt, H. (1909). Die Lingua Franca. *Zeitschrift für Romanische Philologie 33,* 441-61 (English translation in Gilbert (ed.) 1980, 65-88).

Schuchardt, H. (1914). *Die Sprache der Saramakkaneger in Surinam.* Amsterdam: Johannes Müller (English translation in Gilbert (ed.) 1980, 89-126).

Schumacher, W.W. (1977). Eskimo trade jargon: Of Danish or German origin? IJAL 43, 226-27.

Schumann, C.L. (1778). *Saramaccanisch Deutsches Wörter-Buch.* MS Paramaribo (Surinam). In Schuchardt (1914), 44-120.

Schumann, C.L. (1781). *Die Geschichte unsers Herrn und Heilandes Jesu Christi, aus den vier Evangelisten zusammengezogen, durch Samuel Lieberkühn; in Neger-Englische Sprache übersezt, zum Gebrauch bey der Neger-Gemeine.* MS Paramaribo (Surinam).

Schumann, C.L. (1783). *Neger-Englisches Wörter-Buch.* MS Paramaribo (Surinam). In A.A. Kramp, *Early creole lexicography. A study of C.L. Schumann's manuscript dictionary of Sranan.* Doct. Diss. University of Leiden, 1983. 44-305.

Schumann, J. (1978). *The pidginization process.* Rowley MA: Newbury House.

Sebba, M. (1987). *The syntax of serial verbs.* Amsterdam: Benjamins.

(1993). *London Jamaican. Language systems in interaction.* London: Longman.

Segurola, R.P.B. (1963). *Dictionnaire Fon-Francais.* Cotonou: Procure de l'Archidiocese.

Seuren, P.A.M. & H.C. Wekker. (1986). Semantic transparency as a factor in creole genesis. In Muysken & Smith (eds.), 57-70.

Seuren, P.A.M. & S.S. Mufwene (eds.) (1990). *Issues in creole linguistics* (=*Linguistics 28.4*).

Severing, R. & L. Verhoeven (1994). Tweetaligheid en schoolsucces van kinderen op Curaçao. *Pedagogische Studiën 71* (in press).

Shi, D. (1992). On the etymology of *pidgin*. JPCL 7, 343-47.

Siegel, J. (1987). *Language contact in a plantation environment*. Cambridge: Cambridge University Press.

(1990). Pidgin English in Nauru. JPCL 5, 157-86.

Singler, J.V. (1986). Short note. JPCL 1, 141-45.

(1988). The homogeneity of the substrate as a factor in pidgin/creole genesis. *Language 64*, 27-51.

(1990a). On the use of sociohistorical criteria in the comparison of creoles. In Seuren & Mufwene (eds.), 645-59.

Singler, J.V. (ed.) (1990b). *Pidgin and creole tense-mood-aspect systems*. Amsterdam: Benjamins.

Singler, J.V. (1990c). Introduction. In Singler (ed.), vii-xvi.

(1990d). The impact of decreolization upon T-M-A: Tenselessness, mood, and aspect in Kru Pidgin English. In Singler (ed.), 203-30.

(1992a). Nativization and pidgin/creole genesis: A reply to Bickerton. JPCL 7, 319-33.

(1992b). Looking early, looking late: Sociohistorical factors in the development of French-lexifier creoles in the Caribbean. Paper read at the 4th Amsterdam Creole Workshop, September 1992.

(1993). African influence upon Afro-American language varieties: A consideration of sociohistorical factors. In Mufwene (ed.), 235-53.

Slobin, D. (1978). Universal and particular in the acquisition of language. In E. Wanner & L. Gleitman (eds.), *Language acquisition. The state of the art*. Cambridge: Cambridge University Press. 128-70.

Smith, N. (1983). Review of J. Holm (with A. Shilling), Dictionary of Bahamian English. ACS V, 113-16.

(1987). *The genesis of the creole languages of Surinam*. Doct. Diss. University of Amsterdam.

Smith, N., I. Robertson & K. Williamson. (1987). The Ijo element in Berbice Dutch. *Language in Society 16*, 49-90.

Smith, N. & L. Adamson (In prep.). Tone in Sranan.

Smout, K.D. (1988). A missionary English from Japan. *American Speech 63*, 137-49.

Sordam, M. & C.H. Eersel. (1985). *Sranan Tongo/Surinaamse taal* (Repr. as *Surinaams woordenboek/Sranantongo*, 1989). Baarn: Bosch & Keuning.

Spears, A.K. (1990). Tense, mood, and aspect in the Haitian creole preverbal marker system. In Singler (ed.), 119-42.

Spears, A.K. & D. Winford (eds.) (To appear). *Pidgins and creoles. Structure and status*. Amsterdam: Benjamins.

Spolsky, B. (1978). *Educational Linguistics*. Rowley MA: Newbury House.

Sreedhar, M.V. (1974). *Naga Pidgin: A sociolinguistic study on interlingual communication pattern in Nagaland*. Mysore: Central Institute of Indian Languages.

Stefánsson, V. (1909). The Eskimo Trade Jargon of Herschel Island. *American Anthropologist 11*, 217-32.

Stein, P. (1987). Les premiers créolistes: Les Frères Moraves à St. Thomas au XVIIIe siècle. ACS IX, 3-17.

Stewart, J.M. (1963). Some restrictions on objects in Twi. *Journal of African Languages 2*, 145-49.

Stolz, T. (1986). *Gibt es das kreolische Sprachwandelmodell? Vergleichende Grammatik des Negerhollän-dischen.* Frankfurt: Peter Lang.

    (1987a). Verbale Morphosyntax im Berbice und Negerhollands: Ein Beitrag zur vergleichenden Grammatik der niederländisch-basierten Überseesprachen. In P. Maurer & T. Stolz (eds.), *Varia Creolica.* Bochum: N. Brockmeyer. 167-204.

    (1987b). Kreolistik und Germanistik: Niederländisch-basierte Sprachformen in Übersee. *Linguistische Berichte 110,* 283-318.

Stowell, T. (1981). *The origin of phrase structure.* Doct. Diss. MIT.

Sun Hongkai (1992). Language recognition and nationality. IJSL 97, 9-22.

Sutcliffe, D. (with J. Figueroa) (1992). *System in black language.* Clevedon: Multilingual Matters.

Sylvain, S. (1936). *Le créole haïtien. Morphologie et syntaxe.* Wetteren: Impr. De Meester.

Taylor, D.R. (1961). New languages for old in the West Indies. *Comparative Studies in Society and History 3,* 277-88.

Thalbitzer, W. (1932). *Fra Grønlandsforskningens første Dage.* Copenhagen: Bianco Lunos.

    (1952). Possible early contacts between Eskimo and Old World languages. *Proceedings of the 29th International Congress of Americanists,* Vol.III. Chicago: University of Chicago Press. 50-54.

Thevet, A. (1558). *Les singularitez de la France antarctique, avtrement nommée Amérique,* Paris: Maurice de la Porte (New translation, ed. by R. Schlesinger & A.P. Stabler, 1986. Toronto: University of Toronto Press).

Thomason, S. (1980). On interpreting 'The Indian Interpreter'. *Language in Society 9,* 167-93.

Thomason, S. (1983). Genetic relationship and the case of Maʾa (Mbugu). SAL 14, 195-231.

Thomason, S. (In prep.). *Non-Indo-European pidgins and creoles.* Amsterdam: Benjamins.

Thomason, S. & T. Kaufman. (1988). *Language contact, creolization, and genetic linguistics.* Berkeley: University of California Press.

Thompson, R.W. (1961). A note on some possible affinities between the creole dialects of the Old World and those of the New. In R.B. Le Page (ed.), *Proceedings of the 1959 conference on creole language studies. Creole language studies 2.* London: MacMillan. 107-13.

Tinelli, H. (1981). *Creole phonology.* The Hague: Mouton.

Todd, L. (1982). *Cameroon.* Varieties of English around the world, Text series 1. Heidelberg: Julius Groos.

    (1990). *Pidgins and creoles* (2nd ed.; 1st ed. 1974). London: Routledge.

Traill, A. & L. Ferraz (1981). The interpretation of tone in Principense Creole. SAL 12, 205-15.

Trudgill, P. (ed.) (1984). *Language in the British Isles.* Cambridge: Cambridge University Press.

Turner, L.D. (1949). *Africanisms in the Gullah dialect.* Ann Arbor: The University of Michigan Press. (Repr. 1974, Chicago: University of Chicago Press).

Valdman, A. (1968). Language standardization in a diglossia situation. In J.A. Fishman, C.A. Ferguson & J. Das Gupta (eds.), *Language problems of developing nations.* New York: John Wiley. 313-26.

Valdman, A. (ed.) (1977). *Pidgin and creole linguistics.* Bloomington: Indiana University Press.

Valdman, A. (1978). *Le créole. Structure, statut et origine.* Paris: Klincksieck.

    (1981). Sociolinguistic aspects of Foreigner Talk. In M. Clyne (ed.), *Foreigner Talk* (=IJSL 28), 41-52.

Valdman, A. & A. Highfield (eds.) (1980). *Theoretical orientations in creole studies.* New York: Academic Press.

Valkhoff, M.F. (1966). *Studies in Portuguese and Creole.* Johannesburg: Witwatersrand University

Press.

Valkhoff, M.F. (ed.) (1975). *Miscelânea Luso-Africana*. Lisbon: Junta de Investigações Cientificas do Ultramar.

Van den Berg, H. (1987). A note on predicate cleft in Saramaccan. In Alleyne (ed.), 103-12.

Van der Hulst, H. & N. Smith (1988). The variety of pitch accent systems: Introduction. In H. van der Hulst & N. Smith (eds.), *Autosegmental studies on pitch accent*. Dordrecht: Foris. ix-xxiv.

Van der Voort, H. (1996). Eskimo Pidgin in West Greenland. In Broch & Jahr (eds).

Van der Voort, H. (1997). New light on Eskimo pidgins. In Spears & Winford (eds.)

Van der Voort, H. & P. Muysken (1995). Negerhollands reflexives revisited. In Arends (ed.).

Van Dyk, P. (n.d.) [c1765]. *Nieuwe en nooit bevoorens geziene onderwyzinge in het Bastert Engels, of Neeger Engels, zoo als het zelve in de Hollandsze Colonien gebruikt word*. Amsterdam: Jacobus van Egmont.

Van Name, A. (1871). Contributions to creole grammar. *Transactions of the American Philological Association 1869-70, 1*, 123-67.

Van Riemsdijk, H. (1978). *A case study in syntactic markedness*. Lisse: Peter de Ridder.

Van Stipriaan, A. (1993). *Surinaams contrast. Roofbouw en overleven in een Caraïbische plantagekolonie, 1750-1863*. Leiden: KITLV Uitgeverij.

Veenstra, T. (1989). *Coordinate versus subordinate serial verb constructions*. Review article of M. Sebba, The syntax of serial verbs. ACS X, 49-66.

(1990). *Serial verb constructions in Jamaican Creole and grammatical theory*. Master's Thesis University of Amsterdam.

(1993). Serial verb constructions, parameter settings and thematic restrictions on argument sharing. In F. Drijkoningen & K. Hengeveld (eds.), *Linguistics in the Netherlands 1993*. Amsterdam: Benjamins. 153-64.

(1994). The acquisition of functional categories: The creole way. In D. Adone & I. Plag, *Creolization and language change*. Tübingen: Niemeyer. 99-117.

Veenstra, T. & N. Smith (In prep.). Affixation in a radical creole: The morphology-syntax interface.

Vitale, A.J. (1981). *Swahili syntax*. Dordrecht: Foris.

Voegelin, C.F., F.M. Voegelin & N.W. Schutz Jr. (1967). The language situation in Arizona as part of the Southwest Culture Area. In D. Hymes & W. Bittle (eds.), *Studies in southwestern ethnolinguistics*. The Hague: Mouton. 403-51.

Voorhoeve, J. (1957). The verbal system of Sranan. *Lingua 6*, 374-96.

(1971). The art of reading creole poetry. In Hymes (ed.), 323-26.

(1980). *Tinadri. Een praktische cursus om Surinaams te leren in 13 lessen*. Amsterdam: Centrum Anton de Kom.

(1981). Multifunctionality as a derivational problem. In Muysken (ed.), 25-34.

Voorhoeve, J. & U.M. Lichtveld (1975). *Creole Drum. An anthology of creole literature in Suriname*. New Haven: Yale University Press.

Washabaugh, W. (1975). On the development of complementizers in creolization. *Working Papers on Language Universals 17*, 109-40.

(1977). Constraining variation in decreolization. *Language 53*, 329-52.

Webster, H. (1894). Introduction. In S.T. Rand, *Legends of the Micmac*. New York: Longmans, Green and Co.

Weinstein, B. (1983). *The civic tongue. Political consequences of language choices*. New York: Longman.

Wekker, H.C. (1982). The transparency principle in second language acquisition and creolization. Paper read at the 4th Biennial Conference of the Society for Caribbean Linguistics, Paramaribo (Surinam), September 1982.

(1989). *Over de analogie tussen creolisering en vreemde-taalverwerving.* (Inaugural lecture). Groningen: Wolters-Noordhoff.

Weygandt, G.C. (1798). *Gemeenzame leerwijze, om het basterd of Neger-Engelsch op een gemakkelyke wyze te leeren verstaan en spreeken.* Paramaribo (Surinam): W.W. Beeldsnyder.

Whinnom, K. (1971). Linguistic hybridization and the 'special case' of pidgins and creoles. In Hymes (ed.), 91-115.

Williamson, K. (1965). *A grammar of the Kolokuma dialect of Ijo.* Cambridge: Cambridge University Press.

Wilner, J. (ed.) (1992). *Wortubuku ini Sranan Tongo (Sranan Tongo-English dictionary)* (2nd ed.). Paramaribo (Surinam): SIL.

Winer, L. (1990). Orthographic standardization for Trinidad and Tobago: Linguistic and sociopolitical considerations in an English creole community. *Language Problems and Language Planning 14,* 237-68.

Winford, D. (1993). *Predication in Caribbean English creoles.* Amsterdam: Benjamins.

Wingerd, J. (1977). Serial verbs in Haitian creole. In P. Kotey & H. Der-Housikian (eds.), *Language and linguistic problems in Africa.* Hornbeam Press.

Wolf, S.A. (1956). *Wörterbuch des Rotwelsch.* Mannheim: Bibliographisches Institut.

Wood, R. (1971). New light on the origins of Papiamentu: An eighteenth-century letter. *Neophilologus 56,* 18-30.

Woodbury, A.C. (1984). Eskimo and Aleut languages. In Damas (ed.), 49-63.

Woolford, E. & W. Washabaugh (eds.) (1982). *The social context of creolization.* Ann Arbor: Karoma.

Wullschlägel, H.R. (1856). *Deutsch-Negerenglisches Wörterbuch.* Löbau: T.U. Duroldt. (Repr. 1965, Amsterdam: Emmering).

Wurm, S.A. (1992). Some contact languages and pidgins and creoles in the Siberian region. *Language Sciences 14,* 249-85.

Wurm, S.A. & S. Hattori (1981). *Language atlas of the Pacific area.* Canberra: Australian Academy of the Humanities.

# Index of languages

## Index of place names

## Author index

In the series *Creole Language Library* the following titles have been published thus far or are scheduled for publication:

3  **BYRNE, Francis:** Grammatical Relations in a Radical Creole. Verb Complementation in Saramaccan. With a foreword by Derek Bickerton. 1987. xiv, 293 pp.

2  **SEBBA, Mark:** The Syntax of Serial Verbs. An investigation into serialisation in Sranan and other languages. 1987. xv, 218 pp.

1  **MUYSKEN, Pieter and Norval SMITH (eds.):** Substrata versus Universals in Creole Genesis. Papers from the Amsterdam Creole Workshop, April 1985. 1986. vii, 311 pp.